Exploring the
OLD TESTAMENT

Exploring the
OLD TESTAMENT

W. T. Purkiser, Ph.D., Editor

C. E. Demaray, Ph.D.

Donald S. Metz, Ph.D.

Maude A. Stuneck, Ph.D.

BEACON HILL PRESS OF KANSAS CITY
Kansas City, Mo.

ISBN 083-410-007X

Printed in the United States of America

41 40 39 38 37

Preface

This book has been written to serve as a textbook for college level survey courses in the Old Testament. It is the result of a long felt need for textbook materials which will provide the beginning student of the Bible the foundation for future reading and more extensive study. Following the outline of Old Testament history, the authors have attempted to use such materials from archaeology, biblical backgrounds, and content as will contribute to an understanding of the Book of Books.

To make the text more adaptable to a typical college classroom situation the book has been divided into 16 chapters, each of which is divided in turn into four or five major sections. The first two chapters are introductory material which may be read rapidly or omitted entirely by teachers who prefer to begin with the study of biblical materials immediately. Chapters III to XV cover the books of the Old Testament following the historical framework. Chapter XVI summarizes some of the major teachings of the Old Testament.

In connection with each chapter dealing with Old Testament content, the Bible portion covered is listed, and a reading assignment of 15 to 20 chapters from the Bible is given. At the close of each chapter will be found a list of recommended readings, together with problems or exercises for further study or discussion. Footnotes have been kept at a minimum, but will be found useful to the student who wishes to refer to other sources. A highly selective bibliography is included, which contains complete bibliographical information concerning the books listed in the recommended readings and in the footnotes.

It must be understood that the inclusion of a book in the recommended readings or in the references *does not* constitute an unqualified endorsement of that volume. All reading in the general field of biblical literature must be done with discrimination, and no statement should be accepted merely on the assertion of its writer. Even books written by scholars whose position is generally conservative may contain items with which the authors of this book could not agree. Reference is made to books by liberal authors for the purpose of pointing out items of value which they contain.

Standard abbreviations have been used throughout, and are listed on page 9 preceding the table of contents. The majority of scripture citations are from the Authorized or King James Version. Whenever a different version is used, the source is indicated by the accepted abbreviation. In quoting some of the poetic passages, the arrangement of lines adopted by the American Standard Version is used but the more familiar and melodic wording of the King James Version is preserved. Such passages may be recognized by the poetic arrangement of lines and the absence of any version designation in connection with the reference.

Two appendices have been included. One is a chronological table covering the Old Testament period, prepared by C. E. Demaray. The other is a thumbnail review of the content of each of the books of the Old Testament, developed by J. S. Blaney of Eastern Nazarene College and used with his permission.

In the preparation of this text, the initial writing of Chapters I, II, VII, and XVI was done by W. T. Purkiser, of Chapters III through VI by M. A. Stuneck, of Chapters VII through XI by D. S. Metz, and of Chapters XII through XV by C. E. Demaray. However the book is, in a real sense, the product of the shared labors of all the group. Each has made a contribution to the whole by way of numerous suggestions. The entire manuscript in final form has been read and approved by each of the collaborators.

It is our sincere prayer that these pages may help to guide young minds in the great task of *Exploring the Old Testament*.

> W. T. PURKISER, *Editor*
> C. E. DEMARAY
> D. S. METZ
> M. A. STUNECK

October, 1955

Acknowledgments

The following publishers have kindly granted permission to use copyrighted materials: Abingdon-Cokesbury Press, quotations from Otto J. Baab, *The Theology of the Old Testament*, and Albert C. Knudson, *The Religious Teaching of the Old Testament;* the Association Press, quotations from Clarence A. Barbour, ed., *The Bible in the World of Today,* and G. L. Robinson, *The Abiding Value of the Old Testament* (copyright, 1911); the Broadman Press and the Sunday School Board of the Southern Baptist Convention, permission to quote from John R. Sampey, *The Heart of the Old Testament,* Revised Edition.

The Christian Century Foundation and the estate of Dr. H. L. Willett, permission to quote from *Our Bible: Its Origin, Character, and Value;* Columbia University Press, from Julius A. Bewer, *The Literature of the Old Testament,* Revised Edition; Harcourt, Brace and Company, from Ann Lindbergh, *North to the Orient;* and Harper and Brothers, from Robert H. Pfeiffer, *Introduction to the Old Testament,* Revised Edition; Ira M. Price, *The Ancestry of Our English Bible,* Second Revised Edition; Kyle M. Yates, *Preaching from the Prophets;* and G. L. Robinson, *The Twelve Minor Prophets.*

Longmans, Green and Company, Inc., permission to quote from Henry Daniel-Rops, *Sacred History;* The Sunday School Times, from Howard A. Kelly, *A Scientific Man and the Bible;* and Zondervan Publishing Company, from Dr. Merrill F. Unger, *Introductory Guide to the Old Testament.* The Fleming H. Revell Company has granted permission to quote from *The Archaeology of Palestine and the Bible,* by William F. Albright.

The quotation from William A. Irwin, *The Old Testament: Keystone of Human Culture,* copyright 1952, is reprinted by permission of the publisher, Abelard-Schuman, Inc. Material from page 80 of *The Authority of the Biblical Revelation,* by Hubert Cunliffe-Jones, copyright 1946, used by permission of the Pilgrim Press. Quotations from G. Ernest Wright, *The Challenge of Israel's Faith,* copyright 1944, by permission of the University of Chicago Press. The quotation

Abbreviations

THE BOOKS OF THE BIBLE

Gen.	Ps. (Pss.)	Mic.	Gal.
Exod.	Prov.	Nah.	Eph.
Lev.	Eccles.	Hab.	Phil.
Num.	Song of Sol.	Zeph.	Col.
Deut.	Isa.	Hag.	I or II Thess.
Josh.	Jer.	Zech.	I or II Tim.
Judg.	Lam.	Mal.	Titus
Ruth	Ezek.	Matt.	Philem.
I or II Sam.	Dan.	Mark	Heb.
I or II Kings	Hos.	Luke	Jas.
I or II Chron.	Joel	John	I or II Pet.
Ezra	Amos	Acts	I, II, or III John
Neh.	Obad.	Rom.	Jude
Esther	Jonah	I or II Cor.	Rev.
Job			

Vulg.	The Vulgate
LXX	The Septuagint
ARV	American Standard Revised Version
RSV	Revised Standard Version
c.	chapter
cc.	chapters
v.	verse
vv.	verses

Table of Contents

CHAPTER I

This Is God's Word

And God spake all these words (Exod. 20:1).

The serious study of the Bible is the most challenging task anyone may attempt. This is because the Bible is like no other book in the world. It is more than our greatest literary masterpiece. It is more than the highest record of heroism and devotion to ideals ever written. It is more than the history of earth's most important culture, or the most elevating philosophy in life men have found. It is because the Bible is the eternal record of God's redemptive purpose for the human race. It is the self-revelation of God to the seeking minds and hearts of men everywhere.

This is God's Word.

I. WHY STUDY THE BIBLE?

The average student today approaches the study of the Bible with one of several different attitudes. The one who is unfamiliar with its content may wonder if he will be able to understand its meaning. He may have heard about difficulties of interpretation, or the endless debates that have been waged about technical points. One who has tried to read the Bible through, only to become discouraged by the detailed descriptions of the sacrifices in Leviticus or the genealogies of Chronicles, may decide that it is dull reading, a Book only for experts.

Others may feel that long familiarity with the Bible at home and in church makes further study of its pages an unnecessary task. Some have always held the Bible in a certain degree of awe, but have not devoted much time or care to its systematic study. It is still a matter of surprise to many to discover that the Bible is a Book to be understood, not just a spring from which to draw temporary inspiration.

Probably the majority will approach the study of the Bible with real anticipation. What little they have learned about it will have whetted their appetites for greater ac-

13

quaintance. They expect to find in it some of the treasures of understanding and devotion which have made it the greatest Book in the world.

1. *The Bible as Great Literature*

It is true that the Bible may be studied for a variety of reasons. It may be studied for its literary value. That the King James Version of the Holy Bible is the greatest literary masterpiece of the English-speaking world has been so often asserted and so clearly proved that its statement now is generally taken for granted.

The literary value of the Bible is shown in many ways. The amazing circulation of the Bible—the "best seller" of the ages—is impressive evidence of its literary power and excellence. Over one billion (1,000 million) copies of the Bible have been printed. W. A. Smart observes, "The Bible has outsold and out-circulated every other book every year since printing began."[1] Recent Gallup polls seeking the most widely read books in America found the Bible well in the lead. Six persons out of every 10 interviewed claimed to have read it.

The facts are that the Scriptures have become a virtual standard of literary expression. Literature is full of biblical allusions and loses much of its beauty and power to those who are ignorant of the source of these references. Scholars have found 550 scriptural allusions in the works of William Shakespeare alone. John Ruskin, an acknowledged master of English prose style, testified, "Whatever I have done in my life has simply been due to the fact that when I was a child my mother daily read with me a part of the Bible, and daily made me learn a part of it by heart." This was seconded by the great American patriot and orator, Daniel Webster, when he said, "If there be anything in my style or thought to be commended, the credit is due to my kind parents in instilling into my mind an early love of the Scriptures."[2]

To list the literary masters whose works are full of biblical references and whose style has noticeably been influenced by their familiarity with the Scriptures seems almost

[1]W. A. Smart, *Still the Bible Speaks*, p. 12.

[2]Quoted by Herbert L. Willett, *Our Bible: Its Origin, Character, and Value*, pp. 209-10.

like naming the great figures of some literary Hall of Fame: John Milton, Wordsworth, Scott, Lord Byron, Shelley, Lord Macauley, Hawthorne, Emerson, Whittier, Longfellow, Dickens, Tennyson, Browning, Matthew Arnold, Eliot, Lowell, Walt Whitman, Swinburne, Stevenson, and Rudyard Kipling.

One scholar claims that there are 15 words or phrases from the Bible in the three short paragraphs of Lincoln's Gettysburg Address, for all time one of the most memorable utterances of men.[3] In a recent display, more than 1,000 successful modern books and plays were counted whose titles are scriptural quotations. Professor Lawrence Nelson, in his book *Our Roving Bible*,[4] cites hundreds of instances where, consciously or unconsciously, literature and modern writing make use of the Bible.

It would be possible to give much more evidence concerning the literary excellence and power of the Bible. However, it has rarely been better summarized than by Professor William A. Irwin, who wrote:

> Merely in terms of its creative influence upon human society, far and away the greatest of the great books is the Bible. And what better criterion of worth is there? Opinions of critics, however high their repute, are only personal opinions. But the test of the ages is irrefutable. Only that which has proven its worth to countless hosts of succeeding generations can live on through the centuries; the weak and the sectarian and the ill-founded fall by the way. Here is the sheer miracle of it: a literature that long antedated our glorious gains in science and the immense scope of modern knowledge, which moves in the quiet atmosphere of the ancient countryside, with camels and flocks and roadside wells and the joyous shout of the peasant at vintage or in harvest—this literature, after all that has intervened, is still our great literature, published abroad as no other in the total of man's writing, translated into the world's great languages and many minor ones, and cherished and loved and studied so earnestly as to set it in a class apart.[5]

2. *The Bible as History*

Again, the Bible may be studied for its historical values. No one can possibly understand the development of Western

[3]Joseph Auerbach, *The Bible and Modern Life*, pp. 96-97.
[4]See bibliography.
[5]William A. Irwin, *The Old Testament: Keystone of Human Culture*, pp. 235-36.

civilization without some knowledge of its roots in the ancient Judaic culture whose story is unfolded in the Old Testament. Our knowledge of the growth of our civilization would be meager indeed were we deprived of the stimulus to historical research which has been provided by the Bible.

It is a well-known fact that present knowledge of the dawn of human life has been greatly increased by the discoveries of the archaeologists whose patient study of buried remains has opened new worlds to our eyes. What is not as well-known is the fact pointed out by Professor H. H. Rowley that archaeological research has been financed and carried on largely by men and women who have been deeply interested in and devoted to the study of the Bible.[6] The Bible has, therefore, a twofold value to the historian. It preserves historical data of untold value, and it stimulates unceasing inquiry into the backgrounds of the earliest human culture.

Unfortunately, it became fashionable about two centuries ago to question the historical accuracy of the Bible. Much of what is called destructive historical criticism was aimed against the truth of the historical data presented in the Bible, particularly the Old Testament. Dr. W. F. Albright, the famed Johns Hopkins scholar who has so notably avoided the fad of questioning biblical accuracy simply on the basis of the critics' opinions, recently summarized the changing attitude toward Bible history which has been brought about by archaeological exploration:

> The excessive scepticism shown toward the Bible by important historical schools of the eighteenth and nineteenth centuries, certain phases of which still appear periodically, has been progressively discredited. Discovery after discovery has established the accuracy of innumerable details, and has brought increased recognition to the value of the Bible as a source of history.[7]

3. The Influence of the Bible on Civilization

Incidental mention has already been made of the vast influence of the Bible in shaping our Western culture. It is impossible to imagine what modern civilization would be like

[6] H. H. Rowley, *The Rediscovery of the Old Testament*, p. 58.
[7] W. F. Albright, *The Archaelogy of Palestine and the Bible*, pp. 127-28.

had we been deprived of the leavening influence of the religion of the Bible. Some clue may be found in the present state of affairs in that portion of the twentieth century world where the Bible and its God have been nationally repudiated. Samuel Coleridge said: "For more than a thousand years the Bible collectively taken has gone hand in hand with civilization, science, law—in short, with the moral and intellectual cultivation of the species, always supporting and often leading the way."[8]

The influence of the Scriptures in civil law is often unrecognized but very real. The first great recodification of Roman law was made by Justinian, and is the basis of the constitution of practically every modern European and American state. This law was shaped on the norm of biblical institutions. Herbert L. Willett has stated:

> The passion for social righteousness, democracy, industrial liberty, universal education, equal suffrage, child welfare, civic purity and international brotherhood are all inspired by the Bible. The reformatory movements, which have removed much of the blight of inhumanity to children, women, criminals, and animals, of intemperance, and the social vices that gnaw at the vitals of the world, owe their inception and progress to the same book.[9]

One of America's leading medical scientists, the noted Baltimore physician and radiologist, Dr. Howard A. Kelly, pointed out that "where the Bible is dishonored, life becomes cheap and science an early victim, or it survives in destructive form."[10] The records of human life and scientific endeavor in both Nazi Germany and Communistic Russia bear out Dr. Kelly's judgment most conclusively.

All forms of art have felt the influence of the Book of Books. In architecture with its Gothic cathedral; in sculpture and painting; and in music with its great hymns, anthems, and oratorios the influence of the Bible is seen. Willett again observes: "The greatest artists have always been interpreters of the moral life. No one can be a really great artist who

[8]"Confessions of an Enquiring Spirit," p. 69; quoted in Clarence A. Barbour, *The Bible in the World of Today*, p. 111.

[9]Willett, *op. cit.*, p. 205.

[10]Howard A. Kelly, *A Scientific Man and the Bible*, p. 55.

lacks the fundamental quality of moral and religious earnestness. Such men have always found the best material for their messages in the biblical narratives."[11]

The witness of Daniel Webster to the value of the Bible for his style has been cited above. He was no less emphatic in his estimate of the importance of the Bible for civic righteousness and prosperity: "If we abide by the principles taught in the Bible, our country will go on prospering and to prosper; but if we and our posterity neglect its instructions and authority, no man can tell how sudden a catastrophe may overwhelm us and bury our glory in profound obscurity."[12]

4. *The Bible as a Norm for Philosophy and Ethics*

The Bible is worthy of serious consideration by today's student because of its admitted philosophical and ethical values. It presents a view of life—its origin, meaning, and destiny—which has no equals and few serious rivals anywhere. Its ethical ideals have been the guiding stars for the greatest lives the Western world has known. Wilbur Wilberforce, the great English social reformer, said:

> I never knew real happiness until I found Christ as a Saviour. Read the Bible. Through all my perplexities and distresses I never read any other book, I never knew the want of any other.[13]

Wherever true nobility has appeared in human life, it has run parallel to the great moral insights of the Bible, even when not directly drawn therefrom. Matthew Arnold, a man far from orthodox in belief and with little faith in the supernatural, yet said:

> As well imagine a man with a sense for sculpture not cultivating it by the help of the remains of Greek art, and a man with a sense for poetry not cultivating it by the help of Homer and Shakespeare, as a man with a sense for conduct not cultivating it by the help of the Bible.[14]

[11]Willett, *op. cit.*, pp. 206-7.
[12]Quoted in Barbour, *op. cit.*, p. 122.
[13]Quoted in Willett, *op. cit.*, p. 212.
[14]Quoted in Barbour, *op. cit.*, p. 108.

Willett declares:

> The Bible is the Magna Charta of human liberty; the Declaration of Independence from the oppression of ignorance and superstition; the Emancipation Proclamation of the soul of man. John Stuart Mill says, "The most important point in the history of liberty was the cross of Christ."[15]

Woodrow Wilson, onetime head of Princeton University and twenty-eighth president of the United States, bore testimony to the ethical value of the Bible in his letter of transmittal printed in servicemen's Testaments during World War I:

> The Bible is the word of life. I beg that you will read it and find this out for yourself—read, not little snatches here and there, but long passages that will readily be the road to the heart of it. You will find it full of the things you have wondered about and been troubled about all your life . . . When you have read the Bible you will know it is the word of God, because you will have found it the key to your own heart, your own happiness, and your own duty.

5. *The Bible and General Education*

It is difficult to see how anyone can claim a liberal education without at least a passing acquaintance with the greatest masterpiece of the English world, the Authorized Version of the Holy Bible. General education seeks to discover and conserve those elements in the culture which should be a part of the experience of every educated person, regardless of his calling or profession. It is a healthy antidote for the disease of overspecialization which has afflicted higher education during the last half-century. The need for a broad base of culture, as well as technical skill, is becoming increasingly clear as modern inventions give us more and more leisure time.

General education stresses the need for educating young people as men and women, as well as educating them as ministers, doctors, lawyers, engineers, teachers, and business people. Here, knowledge of the Bible becomes of greatest importance. A serious study of the Scriptures cuts across all departmental lines. It enlists the aid of and contributes to

[15]Willett, *op. cit.,* p. 213.

the understanding of history, literature, art, ethics, psychology, philosophy, sociology, geography, and many other areas of learning. Dr. William Lyon Phelps, the beloved "Uncle Billy" of the faculty at Yale University for 41 years, has stressed the importance of the study of the Bible in general education as follows:

> Everyone who has a thorough knowledge of the Bible may truly be called educated; and no other learning or culture, no matter how extensive or elegant, can, among Europeans and Americans, form a proper substitute. Western Civilization is founded upon the Bible; our ideas, our wisdom, our philosophy, our literature, our art, our ideals, come more from the Bible than from all other books put together. It is a revelation of divinity and of humanity; it contains the loftiest religious aspiration along with a candid representation of all that is earthly, sensual, and devilish. I thoroughly believe in a university education for both men and women; but I believe a knowledge of the Bible without a college course is more valuable than a college course without the Bible. For in the Bible we have profound thought, beautifully expressed; we have the nature of boys and girls, of men and women, more accurately charted than in the words of any modern novelist or playwright. You can learn more about human nature by reading the Bible than by living in New York.[16]

6. *The Bible and Religion*

The supreme value of Bible study lies in its religious and spiritual meaning. It is the fountainhead and source of both Judaism and Christianity. More than that, it stands alone in its claim, verified in a thousand million lives across 35 centuries, to be the supreme revelation of the redemptive will and purpose of the one true God, Creator, Sustainer, and Governor of this universe. Robert E. Speer, the great missionary-statesman, has written:

> The Bible is one of the solid facts of Christianity. What it is is not affected by what men think of it. Changing opinions about the Bible do not change the Bible. Whatever the Bible was the the Bible is. And what it is it has always been. It is not men's thoughts about the Bible that judge it. It is the Bible which judges men and their thoughts. It has nothing to fear but ignorance and neglect. And the church need have no other fear on its account. The Bible will take care of itself if the church will distribute it and get it read . . .

[16]William Lyon Phelps, *Human Nature in the Bible*, pp. ix-x.

There should not be a home without the Bible. In one sense there cannot be, for it is the Bible from which the ideal of the home is derived and from which the forces for its realization flow.

And what the Bible is for the home it is for men and women one by one—namely, the source of true ideals of character and the fountain of those energies in Christ by which character is won.[17]

Arguments for the truth of Christianity and its Scriptures belong to the study known as apologetics, the logical defense of the Christian faith against all varieties of unbelief. This is a tremendous field in itself, and beyond the scope of our present study. The interested student is referred to the many excellent works on apologetics now available. Here it need only be said that the spiritual value of the Bible lies in its unique place as the historic record of God's redemptive love for man accomplished through Christ and conveyed to the hearts of men through all ages by the Holy Spirit, the Spirit of Truth.

The Bible, thus, is to be regarded as more than a religious book. It is a redemptive Book. *Religion,* in its broadest sense, is man's search for a right relationship with God. *Revelation* is God's self-communication to man. *Redemption* is the meeting of God and man through the central Personality of the Bible, the God-Man, Christ Jesus the Lord. There are many religions, as there are many ways for human beings to seek the Divine. There is only one revelation, the Bible and the Christ who is its theme. And there is only one redemption, that mediated by the Holy Spirit through the belief of the truth embodied in the Bible.

Granting this great faith—and it is essentially the Christian faith—the Bible becomes a Book of unequaled importance. It is the Word of the living God, and nothing could be more vital to man than knowing the Word of the Lord. Every capacity of the mind is challenged by the Bible: the intellect by its truths for understanding and doctrine; the emotions by its unparalleled insights for devotion and inspiration; and the will by its ethical guidance for the conduct of life.

---

[17]Preface to Eric M. North, *And Now . . . In a Thousand Tongues* (brochure for use in the observance of Universal Bible Sunday, December 11, 1938; American Bible Society).

Books born in the minds of men come and go. Of the making of them there is no end. The Bible is the Book for the Ages, always timely because timeless in its eternal verities. No other book can equal its importance. All of them together could never take its place. As John Wesley has put it:

> I am a creature of a day, passing through life as an arrow through the air. I am a spirit, coming from God, and returning to God; just hovering over the great gulf; a few months hence I am no more seen; I drop into an unchangeable eternity! I want to know one thing—the way to heaven: how to land safe on the happy shore. God himself has condescended to teach the way. He hath written it down in a book. O give me that Book! At any price, give me the Book of God! I have it: here is knowledge enough for me. Let me be a man of one book. Here, then, I am, far from the busy ways of men. I sit down alone; only God is here. In His presence I open, I read His book, for this end—to find the way to heaven.[18]

II. The Inspiration of the Bible

The authority of the Bible as a standard for doctrinal truth and ethical practice clearly rests upon the degree to which the Scriptures are more than a human production. The character of the Bible as the supreme revelation from God to man depends upon what is known as its "inspiration." Thus we read, "All scripture is given by the inspiration of God, and is profitable for doctrine, for reproof, for correction, for instruction in righteousness: that the man of God may be perfect, throughly furnished unto all good works" (II Tim. 3:16-17).

Belief in the inspiration of the Scriptures is the primary Christian affirmation about the Bible. The authors of this text give their full support to the strong faith in the complete inspiration of the Bible expressed in the following statement:

> We believe in the plenary inspiration of the Holy Scriptures, by which we understand the sixty-six books of the Old and New Testaments, given by divine inspiration, inerrantly revealing the will of God concerning us in all things necessary to our salvation; so that whatever is not contained therein is not to be enjoined as an article of faith.[19]

[18]Quoted in Barbour, *op. cit.*, p. 110.
[19]*Manual, Church of the Nazarene*, Articles of Faith, par. 4.

1. *The Meaning of Revelation*

The term "revelation" includes all the ways God may make himself known to human beings. Nature itself may serve as a channel through which revelation comes. The Psalmist says, "The heavens declare the glory of God; and the firmament sheweth his handywork" (Ps. 19:1). Reason, experience, and intuition are other ways through which truth about God may come to the mind.

Undoubtedly, the supremely perfect revelation of God is given in the character and personality of His only begotten Son, known in the prologue to the Gospel of John as the "Logos" or the "Word."

A divine revelation would of necessity have a certain twofold character or duality about it. Objectively, it would require a divine self-manifestation. Such a divine self-revelation Christinity finds in the living Word, the personal and eternal Logos, the only true and adequate manifestation of the Father. "No man hath seen God at any time; the only begotten Son, which is in the bosom of the Father, he hath declared him" (John 1:18).

Subjectively, on its other side, revelation is a body of apprehended or known truth, comprising the Christian faith, historically recorded by men of old in the pages of Scripture. Christ, the *living* Word, is the perfect self-revelation of God. The Bible, the *written* Word, is the divinely inspired record of the redemptive nature and work of Christ. It is with this revelation of God as given in the Bible that we are here concerned.

2. *The Meaning of Inspiration*

The *method* by which the revelation of God has been recorded in the Bible is known in Christian doctrine as "inspiration." "To inspire" literally means "to breathe into." When Paul wrote that "all scripture is given by inspiration of God" (II Tim. 3:16), as Moule suggests, he taught that "the breath of God was in each Scripture as man's breath is in his words, making them to be the vehicle of his thought."[20] The Christian doctrine of inspiration affirms that

---

[20]*The Second Epistle to Timothy,* p. 123; quoted in G. T. Manley, ed., *The New Bible Handbook,* p. 8.

God imparted to chosen men truth which they could not otherwise have known, and by His providential control of the formation of the "canon"—about which we shall learn in the next chapter—places His endorsement upon what they have actually set down in words.

Dr. H. Orton Wiley defines inspiration as "the operation of the Holy Spirit upon the writers of the books of the Bible in such a manner that their productions become the expression of God's will." He goes on to list three factors in inspiration which make clear its possibility. The first of these is *superintendence,* whereby the Holy Spirit gives such guidance that the writings of chosen men are kept free from error. The second is *elevation,* in which enlargement of understanding and refinement of thought are given the human minds to whom the revelation is made. The third is *suggestion,* under which a direct communication of thoughts and even words is received from the divine Spirit.[21]

Christianity is the one great world-faith which stresses both divine and human factors. Its Saviour is the God-man, whose humanity cannot be ignored any more than can His deity. Its Scriptures "came not in old time by the will of man: but holy men of God spake as they were moved by the Holy Ghost" (II Pet. 1:21). It was *men* of God who were inspired. They spoke of human feelings—loneliness, sorrow, hope, fear, impatience, anguish—and the triumph given them by God's ever-present grace. As J. Patterson Smyth wrote, "God used human minds as the channels of His truth probably because thus it could be better received and assimilated by the human minds to which it came."[22]

Theologians have offered many proofs of the inspiration of the Bible. Perhaps the most convincing is the Bible itself. It speaks with the ring of incontrovertible authority. An editorial writer in the *London Sunday Times,* commenting on the Graham meetings of 1954 in London, acknowledges this when he says, "The Bible, which has meant so much to the people of this country in past generations, still has an astonishing appeal. There is something about the Bible and about Bible preaching which cannot be explained apart from ac-

---

[21]H. Orton Wiley, *Christian Theology,* Vol. I, pp. 170-74.
[22]J. Patterson Smyth, *How to Read the Bible,* p. 27.

knowledgment of its divine authority and inspiration."[23] Professor Romanes, in his agnostic days, began to examine the Bible, when he suddenly became aware that the Bible was examining him![24] Dr. R. T. Flewelling has said, "I know the Bible is inspired because it inspires me." Dr. Howard A. Kelly, for many years professor at Johns Hopkins University, chief surgeon and radiologist at the Howard A. Kelly Hospital, Baltimore, and author of many books and articles on medical subjects, has eloquently said:

I accept the Bible as the Word of God because of its own miraculous character, born in parts in the course of the ages, and yet completed in one harmonious whole . . . Without the Bible, all God's precious parables in nature, His other book, are utterly lost, and nature, exploited merely for lucre or for the pride of science, is degraded and ruined . . . I testify that the Bible is the Word of God because it is food for the spirit just as definitely as bread and meat are food for the body . . . The Bible appeals strongly to me as a physician, because it is such excellent medicine; it has never yet failed to cure a single patient if only he took his prescription honestly . . .
It is the one book in the world which reveals a God infinitely above our own natural imaginings, worthy of our love and worship, and inexhaustible in His wonderful nature . . . In opposition to false science and false religions it fixes the origin of sin at a particular time and in an individual, Satan, and at the very outset promises sin's cessation forever when that arch traitor shall be rendered forever impotent . . . It reveals God's righteousness in Christ, His judgment of sin, and His great mercy to every sinner who trusts Him . . . It is the one book in the world which is always young and fresh and inspiring . . . Whatever there is in civilization that is worth while rests on the Bible's precepts . . . Everywhere and in all its teachings the Bible claims to be the authoritative Word of God, and as such I accept it.[25]

III. Major Versions of the Bible

A version of the Bible is a translation into some other language than the original Hebrew and Greek. Since the Book of Books is God's Word for all mankind, it is the most translated volume in human possession. All or part of the

[23]Quoted in *U.S. News and World Report*, June 25, 1954, p. 152.
[24]Manley, *op. cit.*, p. 11.
[25]Kelly, *op. cit.*, pp. 51-61.

Bible has been translated into more than 1,100 languages. In many of these languages there have been a number of versions, or different translations.

Since any version is the work of human hands, the translation necessarily falls short of perfection. The value of a version depends upon three major factors. The first is the integrity of the copy of the original from which the translation is made. Unless the text being translated is the best possible, the version made from it will be faulty. Obviously, no version can be better than its original, although it may not be as good.

Second, the worth of a translation is dependent on the knowledge of the languages involved, both the languages of the original and the language into which the text is being translated. There are many examples of defective versions the faults of which are due to lack of intimate knowledge of the Hebrew and Greek originals. There are other examples whose shortcomings arise from lack of complete fluency in the language of the translation.

Third, since translating means determining the meaning of the original, and expressing that meaning in another language, much depends upon the understanding of Scripture possessed by the translator. Every translation is to some degree an interpretation. The chief advantage of Scripture versions which are the work of groups of men lies in the fact that purely private interpretations are kept at a minimum.

We turn now to a brief consideration of some of the outstanding versions of the Bible. By convention, versions made before the discovery of printing in the fifteenth century are known as "ancient" versions, and those made since are called "modern."

1. *Ancient Versions*

The most important ancient versions are four in number.

a. The Septuagint. By far the most significant ancient version is the Septuagint, abbreviated LXX. The name is taken from the Greek term for 70, the supposed number of its translators. It is also called the Alexandrian version, from the place of its completion; or the Greek version, from the language into which it was translated.

The Septuagint is the first translation of any portion of the Scriptures ever made, and is the rendering of the entire Hebrew Old Testament into Greek. The version was made necessary by the fact that the Jews living in Egypt and elsewhere through the Near East in the centuries immediately before the Christian era were no longer able to read and understand Hebrew. The conquests of Alexander and his Macedonian armies had made the Greek language and culture the prevailing language and culture of the Mediterranean world. Jews who spoke only Greek and who accepted Greek ways become known as Hellenistic Jews, and had established synagogues in Jerusalem itself by the beginning of the Christian era (Acts 9:29 RSV).

The origin of the Septuagint is shrouded in uncertainty. The oldest tradition, originating with an alleged letter of Aristeas, an Alexandrian Jew serving under the Ptolemies during the third century B.C., is not highly regarded by scholars at the present time. According to this account, 72 Palestinian Jews, selected from each tribe by the high priest, completed the translation in 72 days, working on the island of Pharos near Alexandria in Egypt. Further embellishments add that each translator worked in his own cubicle, independently of the others, and when the results were compared, each translation was found to be in perfect agreement with all the others.

The facts underlying the tradition would appear to be that the translation was made in Alexandria in the second and third centuries before Christ by a number of different translators, some of whom (if we may judge by their command of Hebrew) were probably Palestinian Jews. The translators were of varying ability, and seem to differ in their underlying purpose in making the translation. Hence, the different portions vary in value. The Torah, which includes the first five books of the Old Testament, is conceded to be the most excellent, and was probably the work of scholars from Palestine.

The importance of the Septuagint can scarcely be overstated. It became the generally used Scriptures of the Jews in Christ's day, and was freely quoted by our Lord and His apostles. It was the Bible of the early Christian Church, and as the New Testament was written its books were added to the Septuagint Old Testament (II Pet. 3:15-16). Except in the case of the Jerusalem Scroll of Isaiah, existing copies of the Septuagint are more than 700 years older than the oldest Hebrew manuscripts of the Old Testament. The oldest and most prized Bible manuscripts in existence, the Vatican Codex, the Codex Alexandrinus, the Codex Sinaiticus, and the Ephraem Rescript, all contain the Septuagint version as the Old Testament portion.

b. The Targums. The second ancient version to be considered is actually a collection of different writings known as the Aramaic Targums, from an Aramaic term meaning "to translate" or "to interpret." As in the case of the Septuagint, the Targums were an answer to a practical need. After the Captivity, Aramaic gradually replaced Hebrew as the popular language. The Targums were first oral paraphrases of the Hebrew Scriptures, given in the synagogues, and eventually committed to writing.

The most important Targums are those of Onkelos or Acquila; of Jonathan on the Prophets; and the Targum on the Hagiographa. Because of their character, the Targums lack the value of an exact translation.

They contain many additions, interpretations, and free paraphrases. They do, however, clarify points of difficulty in the original text used by the scribes with whom the Targums originated. They also reveal the methods of interpretation used by the Jews of the period.

Closely related to the Targums are the Talmud and the Midrash. The Talmud was the collection of explanations, interpretations, and opinions of scholars gathered through the 800 years from the third century before Christ to about A.D. 500. This was the "tradition" of which Jesus spoke in Matt. 15:3. The Midrash was made up of commentaries on the written law, and probably originated in the teachings of the scribes in the synagogues in the period immediately preceding and following the life of Jesus.

c. The Peshitta. The Syriac Peshitta is the third ancient version to be considered. It is the work of Syrian Christians in the early part of the fifth century of the Christian era.

Its name, Peshitta, means "simple" or "literal." Its testimony is of value also in enabling scholars to determine the original Hebrew text from which the translation was made.

d. *The Latin Vulgate.* Jerome's famous Latin Vulgate is the final ancient version we shall consider. The spread of Roman culture throughout the ancient world led to the gradual replacement of Greek by the Latin tongue of the conquerors from the Tiber. By the end of the fourth century, when St. Jerome lived and worked, Greek had become as unfamiliar to the majority of the Christian population as Hebrew had been to the Jews of Jesus' day. This brought about the necessity for translating the Hebrew of the Old Testament and the Greek of the New Testament into the Latin of the common people. Jerome carried through his monumental task in a monastery near Jerusalem during the 20 years between A.D. 385 and 405.

Jerome's work was received with a severe outburst of criticism and opposition. The Septuagint and existing Latin translations were regarded with superstitious awe as divinely inspired, and changes in the familiar readings were bitterly resented. Jerome died in A.D. 420 without ever seeing his work universally accepted. It took three centuries to establish the place of the Vulgate. When once established, however, it remained the Bible of the Roman church and the Western world for a thousand years. It was divided into chapters in the medieval period, and was the first book ever to be printed in movable type (reputedly by Johann Gutenburg in 1456). The first English versions were translations of the Vulgate, rather than of the original Hebrew and Greek. The Vulgate was also the basis for early Italian, Spanish, and French versions. It is still the official Bible of the Roman Catholic church, and most modern Catholic versions are based on it. Jerome's work was magnificently wrought, and has been of great help in getting back to the original languages of the Old and New Testaments.

2. *Modern Versions*

Our notice of translations since the invention of printing will be confined to some of the outstanding English versions. While Wycliffe's work was completed prior to the perfection of the art of printing, it is generally considered to be "modern" by reason of its influence on later English versions.

a. Wycliffe's Version. John Wycliffe (*ca.* 1320-84) was an English scholar, educated at Oxford, and popularly called "the morning star of the Reformation." Active in the struggle of his day against papal supremacy in European politics, he is chiefly noted for his translation of the Bible from the Latin Vulgate of St. Jerome into the English language of his time.

Corruption and false teaching in the existing church, Wycliffe believed, were due to the fact that only the learned could read the Word of God. The best weapon against a corrupt clergy would be the Bible in the language of the common man, available in his own home. Wycliffe was aided in his work by other scholars of equal ability and his organization of a religious order of evangelistic preachers known as the Lollards helped with the spread of the new version of the Scriptures.

Many expressions and phrases used by Wycliffe are still found in the English Bible, such as "strait gate," "make whole," "compass land and sea," "son of perdition," and "enter thou into the joy of thy Lord." How greatly the English language changed between 1382, when Wycliffe's translation was completed, and 1611, when the Authorized Version was published, will be seen in the following quotation from Wycliffe's version of a portion of the Lord's Prayer:

> Our Fadir that art in Heuenes, Halewid by thi name. Thi Kingdom comme to. Be thi wille done as in heuen so in erthe. Gyve to us this dai oure breed ouer other substance; and forgive to us oure dettis as we forgyven to oure dettouris. And leede us not in to temptacioun, but delyvere us fro yvel.[26]

b. Tyndale's Version. William Tyndale (1482-1536) was born just 100 years after the death of Wycliffe, in the midst of the tremendous ferment in the intellectual life of Europe known to us as the Renaissance. Educated at both Oxford and Cambridge, his vigorous mind early brought him into conflict with Catholicism. His vow, made during one of his controversies with the clergy, "If God spare my life, ere many

[26]Quoted in Ira M. Price, *The Ancestry of Our English Bible,* p. 239.

years I will cause a boy that driveth a plough to know more of the Scriptures than thou doest," was literally carried out in his work of translation.

It was Tyndale's purpose to make an English translation of Scripture directly from the original Hebrew and Greek, instead of from the Latin Vulgate, as Wycliffe had done. Beginning his work in London, he was soon forced to flee to the continent of Europe. He spent some time at Wittenberg with Martin Luther, and finally settled at Worms, where he completed the translation and printing of the New Testament. When shipments of the New Testament reached England, it was said to be in tremendous demand by two parties—the people, that they might read it; and the ecclesiastical authorities, that they might burn it! One English merchant actually came to Tyndale, armed with a commission to buy the Testaments at any cost, and said, "William, I know thou art a poor man, and I have gotten thee a merchant." "Who?" asked Tyndale. "The Bishop of London," was the reply. "But he will burn them," said the translator. "Yea, marry," was Packington's smiling response. So, according to the chronicler Hall's account, "Forward went the bargain. The Bishop had the books, Packington the thanks, and Tyndale the money."[27]

Tyndale next began the work of translating the Old Testament out of the original Hebrew. Of this, he completed the Pentateuch, and the Book of Jonah. Returning to Antwerp, through the treachery of a pretended friend and fellow countryman, Tyndale was betrayed into the hands of hostile authorities, and imprisoned near Brussels. While awaiting trial, he is believed to have completed the translation of Joshua to II Chronicles, which was later published by his friend, John Rogers. Convicted at last of heresy, and condemned to death, Tyndale was tied to a stake, strangled, and his body burned. His last utterance, according to Foxe, was the prayer, "Lord, open the King of England's eyes."

The best tribute to William Tyndale's work is to be found in its influence on all subsequent English translations. Portions of the later Authorized Version retain as much as nine-tenths of Tyndale's renderings. His mastery of simple and forceful English and his breadth of scholarship in the original

[27]Cf. James Baikie, *The English Bible and Its Story*, pp. 179-80.

languages enabled him to set a stamp upon both the English tongue and Bible translation which has never been equaled. And, as has been frequently pointed out, his dying prayer that God would open the king of England's eyes was being fulfilled even as he uttered it, in the further work of Miles Coverdale and John Rogers.

c. *Intermediate English Versions.* Between the monumental work of William Tyndale and the Authorized Version of 1611, there are several translations into English which can be mentioned only briefly here.

Miles Coverdale is credited with publishing the first complete Bible in the English language, which appeared in England in 1535 while Tyndale was imprisoned on the continent. This was not a translation from the originals, but from Luther's German and the Latin Vulgate, with heavy reliance on Tyndale's work. Oddly enough, within one year after Tyndale's martyrdom, Coverdale's Bible was printed, bound, and distributed in England with the apparent approval of Henry VIII.

Almost immediately the so-called Matthew Bible followed, also with royal sanction. This was the work of John Rogers, Tyndale's friend of earlier years, and was a compilation of Tyndale's and Coverdale's versions. Next, in 1539, the "Great" Bible was published by Coverdale, embodying the text of the Matthew Bible with variations suggested by comparison with the Latin.

What is known as the Geneva Bible was the result of work by exiled English scholars in Geneva, Switzerland, where they had fled during the persecution of Protestants by the reactionary queen Mary Tudor, during the five bloody years from 1553 to 1558. This was a revision of the Great Bible, and gave England under Queen Elizabeth the best English translation it had yet had. While it did not displace the Great Bible in church use, it soon supplanted the earlier version in popular use. Since the authorities did not fully approve the Genevan edition, another revision of the Great Bible was made by scholars of the Church of England which has come to be known as the Bishops' Bible, from the fact that a number of bishops labored on its pages.

When the Protestant Queen Elizabeth came to the throne of England, the Catholic scholars found themselves in the same position as the Protestants had been under bloody Queen Mary. Some of them took refuge in Flanders, at Douai. Seeing the immense popularity of the Bible in the language of the common people, these Catholic refugees produced an English translation of the Latin Vulgate, the official Catholic Bible. This is known as the Douai Version. Its bondage to the Latin results in a version general unsatisfactory from the point of view of English scholarship.

d. *The Authorized* or *King James Version*. Beyond all debate, the greatest and most historic of the translations of Scripture into English is the King James or Authorized Version of 1611. The Elizabethan era in English history had been replete with significant developments leading up to the production of this great version. Great interest had been manifest in all levels of society in the work of Bible translation. Many of the outstanding literary masters of the centuries lived and worked, bringing their native tongue to a high peak of perfection. Scholarship had advanced to high levels. The king, James I, was by early life and training a student of the Bible, and had even made some personal efforts at biblical translation.

The year after his ascension to the throne of England, James appointed a group of 54 scholars from all segments of the English church, and representing the two great universities at Oxford and at Cambridge, to undertake the work of preparing a revision of the entire Bible. The company was reduced to 47 by the time the work actually began, and was divided into six groups to further the task. The translators agreed to follow the Bishops' Bible in general, but with complete freedom to substitute readings from the other existing versions, or new readings, where the originals demanded it. When the book was completed, it was circulated among the entire group for suggestions and criticisms. The whole enterprise, including the time spent in preliminary planning and individual study, occupied about six years, with the first publication occurring in 1611.

Interestingly enough, the new version, although backed by royal sanction, did not immediately win the field. It soon surpassed the popularity of the Bishops' Bible, but it was almost 50 years before the Authorized Version replaced the popular Geneva Bible. Different editions of the Authorized

Version appeared in 1613, 1629, and 1638 in which minor changes were made, correcting errors discovered by the criticism to which the new work was subjected. In 1762, another edition was brought out at Cambridge; and in 1769, after four years of work, Dr. Benjamin Blayney at Oxford brought out the edition of the Authorized Version which is current today. Dr. Blayney's work was mainly concerned with the modernization of spelling and punctuation, but included some corrections of expression. It was thus 158 years from its first publication until the King James Version assumed its present form.

Dr. Ira M. Price writes:

> For almost three centuries, the Authorized or King James Version has been the Bible of the English-speaking world. Its simple, majestic Anglo-Saxon tongue, its clear, speaking style, its directness and force of utterance have made it the model in language, style, and dignity of some of the choicest writers of the last two centuries. Its phrasing is woven into much of our noblest literature; and its style, which to an astonishing degree is merely the style of the original authors of the Bible, has exerted very great influence in molding that ideal of simplicity, directness, and clarity which now dominates the writing of English. It has endeared itself to the hearts and lives of millions of Christians and has molded the characters of leaders in every walk of life. During all these centuries the King James Version has become a vital part of the English-speaking world, socially, morally, religiously, and politically.[28]

e. Individual Translations. God's truth is eternal and unchanging, but the languages of men are not. The English of today is very different from the English of the Elizabethan era. In addition, biblical scholarship has made tremendous strides in the last three centuries, with the discovery of hundreds of manuscripts throwing much new light on the Hebrew and Greek originals.

These facts made it inevitable that new English versions of the Bible would be attempted. It has been estimated that over 100 new translations, most of them the work of individuals, have appeared since the 1611 publication of the Authorized Version. Mr. H. S. Miller has made a painstaking listing of 38 private versions of all or part of the Bible appearing before the Revised Version of 1881; and of 34 appear-

---

[28]Price, *op. cit.*, pp. 276-77.

ing since 1881. Of this total of 72 private translations, 45 are American.[29]

f. The Revised Version of 1881 and the American Standard Version. In 1870, a committee was set up in Great Britain to prepare a revision of the King James Version which would take account of language changes and advances in biblical scholarship which had occurred in the two and a half centuries since the preparation of the Authorized Version. Numbering more than 50, these scholars were drawn from the major Protestant churches of the British Isles. The committee, dividing itself into Old Testament and New Testament groups, began work with the agreed purpose of introducing as few alterations as possible, consistent with the original texts they were using.

About the time the British scholars were beginning their labors, an American committee was organized, composed of 30 scholars, to work in collaboration with the English group. When the work was finally completed, the two committees were unable to agree on a great many matters. For that reason, the so-called Revised Version represents the work of the British group, incorporating some of the suggestions of the American scholars. By agreement, the American committee refrained from publishing its work until 1901.

The New Testament of the Revised Version (British) was published in 1881. Almost 2 million copies were printed in the first issue, and about 3 million were sold in America and England within a year of publication. Matthew through Romans was telegraphed from New York to Chicago, the longest message ever sent by wire. Four years later, the Old Testament was published, in 1885.

The American Standard Version made its appearance in 1901, after the expiration of the agreement with the British committee. It represents not only the scholarship of the English group, but the added insights of the American scholars who continued their work after the English committee disbanded. Many of the differences between the two revised versions are those of word usage on the two sides of the Atlantic. The English version used "corn" for grain of all kinds, "chapmen" for traders, "occupiers" for merchants, "fat"

[29]H. S. Miller, *General Biblical Introduction*, pp. 385-406.

for vat, "harness" for soldiers' armor, "charger" for platter, and so on.

Scholars are generally agreed that the American Standard Version represents the best English translation for study purposes. It certainly lacks the English grace and style of the Authorized Version, but profits from greater fidelity to an improved text of the original. The use of "Jehovah" as the name for God in place of the hallowed and long-used designation "the Lord" has been criticized. Further, the attempt of the translators to use but one English equivalent for each original term has, on occasion, not only resulted in stilted and unnatural expression but actually in poor translation.

g. Modern-Speech Translations. The discovery of large numbers of Greek papyri, notably in the Fayum in Egypt, which date back to the first century of the Christian era, has led to the recognition that the Greek of the New Testament is not the classical Greek of earlier ages, but the Koine or everyday Greek of the marketplace and home. This, among other factors, has led to the production of a large number of modern-speech translations, particularly of the New Testament. A description and evaluation of these is beyond the scope of this work. Notice will be given primarily to those which include the Old Testament.

The Bible in Modern English appeared in London about 1900, the work of Ferrar Fenton. *The Holy Bible—An Improved Edition,* a translation originally sponsored by the American Bible Union and completed in 1912, among other innovations, uses the expression "baptize (immerse)" consistently throughout the New Testament. Weymouth's *New Testament in Modern Speech* was published in 1902, and together with James Moffatt's translation of the entire Bible represents the Scriptures in what might be called colloquial British English. On the other hand, Smith and Goodspeed's *The Bible—An American Translation* (1931) represents the Scriptures in colloquial American English. In fairness, it should be said that some of these modern works represent paraphrases rather than translations, so free are they in the rendering of the original. The recent work of J. B. Phillips in similarly paraphrasing the Epistles (*Letters to Young Churches*) and the Gospels (*The Gospels*) has aroused much interest.

h. The Revised Standard Version. The efforts culminating in the publication in 1946 (New Testament) and 1952 (Old Testament) of the *Revised Standard Version* began in 1929 when the expiring copyright of the American Standard Version was renewed by the International Council of Religious Education, and a committee of 13 was set up to consider problems connected with the revision of the ASV. The intervening economic depression brought the work to a virtual standstill until 1937, when again the International Council set about to implement "the task of the American Standard Bible Committee" to prepare a "revision of the present American Standard Edition of the Bible in the light of the results of modern scholarship, this revision to be designed for use in public and private worship, and to be in the direction of the simple, classic English style of the King James Version."[30]

The New Testament was published in 1946, and was received with mixed reaction. The committee considered many pointed criticisms, and incorporated a number of them in the second edition, which appeared in connection with the Old Testament in 1952. The most notable of these is probably the return to the consistent use of the terms "sanctify" and "sanctification" in translating the Greek terms *hagiadzo* and *hagiasmos,* instead of the frequent use of the term "consecrate" as in the 1946 edition.

The publication of the entire Bible in 1952 provoked some strong reactions. Many unfair criticisms were made, but some important points were raised. It must be remembered that no translation, being the work of human minds, is perfect, and none can be final. It is to be hoped that the committee in charge of the RSV will be open to suggestion, and that many of the questions raised will be worked out in further editions. When it is recalled that the text of the King James Version did not become settled for many years after 1611, and that it was edited again as late as 1769, there is some reason to hope that the Revised Standard Version may be improved under the impact of thoughtful criticism. While it may never replace the King James Version in the affections of Christian people, it may become a more valuable

[30]From records of the International Council, quoted by Price, *op. cit.,* p. 308.

tool than it now is, especially for the careful student of the Bible who seeks for added illumination through the comparison of various versions.

IV. TOOLS FOR BIBLE STUDY

The study of the Bible is a lifetime occupation. Such a book as this can serve only as an introduction, a sort of orientation within which the student may pursue independent studies as far as his time will permit. It is important, then, that we close this first chapter with a brief description of some of the tools which are of value in further pursuit of the riches to be found in the Book of Books.

Unfortunately, many give lip service to the Bible who do not read it systematically, or with care. Maude Frazer Jackson has noted this attitude in the form of a poetic question:

> *What if I say—The Bible is God's holy Word;*
> *Complete, inspired, without a flaw—*
> > *But let its pages stay*
> > *Unread from day to day,*
> *And fail to learn therefrom God's law;*
> *What if I go not there to seek*
> > *The truth of which I glibly speak,*
> > *For guidance on this earthly way,—*
> *Does it matter what I say?*[31]

First, the Bible must be studied with an open mind, and a heart receptive to its message. Much depends upon the attitude with which one approaches his study of Scripture. Prejudice and a closed mind are sure to result in disappointment. A sincere desire for understanding and guidance is the best key to unlock the treasures of God's Word. This was well put by William Tyndale in the Prologue to his famous translation of the Bible into Elizabethan English:

Though a man had a precious jewel and is rich, yet if he wist not the value thereof, nor wherefore it served, he were nother the better, nor richer of a straw. Even so though we read the Scripture and babble of it never so much, yet if we know not the use of it, and wherefore it was given, and what is there-

[31]In James D. Morrison, *Masterpieces of Religious Verse*, p. 383.

in to be sought, it profiteth nothing at all. It is not enough therefore to read, and talk of it only, but we must also desire God day and night instantly to open our eyes, and to make us understand and feel wherefore the Scripture was given that we may apply the medicine of the Scripture every man to his own sores, unless we intend to be idle disputers, and brawlers about vain words, ever gnawing the bitter bark without, and never attaining unto the sweet pith within.[32]

Second, the Bible should always be studied with the thought in mind that the Book is its own best interpreter. Each verse or incident must be understood in the light of the whole Bible as well as its immediate context. Scripture is like a railroad ticket, "Not good if detached." Always, as someone has remarked, "A text without a context is only a pretext." In the quaint English of John Wycliffe:

It shall greatly help ye to understand Scripture
If you mark
Not only what is spoken or written,
But of whom,
And to whom,
With what words,
At what time,
Where,
To what intent,
With what circumstances
Considering what goeth before
And what followeth.[33]

Third, the student should learn to make use of the helps which are furnished in connection with the Bible text. In most Bibles, marginal references are given between the parallel columns of the text. Usually, small superscript letters are used to call attention to the references in the margin which cite other passages bearing on the same subject. Marginal notes are also included in many Bibles, indicated by small superscript numbers. These notes give alternate translations, meanings of proper names, values of coins and measures, and other items of information. *Italics* are used in the King James Version to indicate words not in the original, but supplied by the translators. Sometimes such additions are necessary to supply the sense which would be

[32]Quoted in Robert R. Dearden, Jr., *The Guiding Light on the Great Highway,* p. 5.

[33]Quoted in Wilbur M. Smith, *Profitable Bible Study,* p. 38.

lost in a direct translation. In some cases, the addition unfortunately obscures the sense.

Fourth, different translations or versions will be found helpful in determining the meaning of the original. Obviously, knowledge of Hebrew and Greek is most helpful in studying the meaning of Bible passages. Lacking such equipment, the ordinary student may gain much new light by comparing various translations.

Fifth, personal interpretations ought to be checked by reference to some of the leading commentaries. A commentary is a book or series of books which takes up portions or verses of scripture and explains or illustrates them. Naturally, each commentary reveals the theological position of its author or authors. The same commentary may be of unequal value in different portions. As is usually true, "in the multitude of voices there is wisdom," and the errors or excesses of one commentator are corrected by others.

Sixth, no one can hope to make any kind of systematic personal study of the Bible without frequent recourse to concordances. A concordance is a volume listing the words of scripture, and giving the reference for each occurrence of each word. Thus by looking in a concordance, one who remembers any of the leading words of a verse can find that verse, as well as others where the same words are used. Some concordances, notably Strong's and Young's, enable the English-speaking student to determine the original Hebrew or Greek term used, together with other usages of that same original term.

Topical concordances, such as *Harper's Topical Concordance,* are arranged by subjects or topics rather than by words. Such a help will give many or all of the references dealing with any selected topic, whether or not these references contain the wording of the topic. In this way, such a topic as "prayer," or "grace," or "faith" may be studied in passages which convey the meaning but may not use the precise words.

Finally, there will be occasions when the careful Bible student will wish to make use of biblical encyclopedias or dictionaries, and a biblical atlas. The Bible dictionary or encyclopedia contains brief articles on the various persons, places, and subjects discussed in the Bible. A Bible atlas is especially necessary for any adequate grasp of the geography of Bible lands.

SUMMARY

In this introductory chapter, we have surveyed the reasons for studying the Bible, the nature of its inspiration, some of its leading versions or translations, and have given some attention to the tools for further Bible study. In the next chapter, we turn to the theme of this text, the Old Testament, and give consideration to some basic matters of importance for its rightful understanding.

> *We search the world for truth: we cull*
> *The good, the pure, the beautiful*
> *From graven stone and written scroll,*
> *From all the old flower fields of the soul;*
> *And weary seekers of the best,*
> *We come back laden from our quest,*
> *To find that all the sages said*
> *Is in the Book our mothers read.*
>
> —Whittier, "Miriam"

RECOMMENDED READINGS

James Baikie, *The English Bible and Its Story*, pp. 113-45, 157-202.

Sidney Collett, *All About the Bible*, pp. 1-44, 75-155.

David Daiches, *The King James Version of the English Bible*, pp. 1-74.

Frank Gaebelein, *Exploring the Bible*, pp. 1-56.

G. T. Manley, *The New Bible Handbook*, pp. 3-18.

H. S. Miller, *General Biblical Introduction*, pp. 16-63, 210-56, 310-406.

Ira M. Price, *The Ancestry of Our English Bible*, pp. 50-316.

Merrill F. Unger, *Introductory Guide to the Old Testament*, pp. 22-43, 148-77.

H. Orton Wiley, *Christian Theology*, Volume I, pp. 167-84.

FOR FURTHER STUDY

1. List any additional reasons for the study of the Bible of which you may be able to think. Why do people today tend to neglect Bible reading and Bible study?

2. Make a list of the titles of books or poems with which you may be familiar which embody scriptural allusions or references.

3. In any of the numerous works on biblical archaeology, look up a few of the many instances where disputed points of Bible history have been confirmed by archaeological finds.

4. Select some outstanding examples of the influence of religion and the Bible in Western art, music, or architecture.

5. How can the study of the Bible be shown to be an essential part of general education?

6. Enlarge on the distinction between religion, revelation, and redemption.

7. How does the Bible challenge every capacity of the human mind? Explain and illustrate.

8. What do you think John Wesley meant by being "a man of one book"?

9. Distinguish clearly between "revelation" and "inspiration."

10. List several reasons for believing that the Bible is the inspired Word of God.

11. If the Bible is God's Word for all human beings, what follows with respect to its translation?

12. What value do ancient versions have for biblical scholarship today?

13. Summarize the contributions of Wycliffe and Tyndale to Bible translation.

14. See if you can find other statements than those given in the text regarding the value and excellence of the Authorized Version.

15. Why are translations by individuals apt to be less dependable than translations by committees or groups?

16. What values do you think may be derived from the study and comparison of different versions of the Bible?

17. Prepare a short list of concordances, commentaries, Bible dictionaries, and Bible atlases in your school or public library.

18. Make an inquiry of some of your Bible-student friends as to their opinions concerning the three most useful books to assist with Bible study.

19. List some of the personal characteristics most essential to the student who would gain most from Bible study.

CHAPTER II

Why the Old Testament?

The reading of the old testament (II Cor. 3:14).

The purpose of this chapter is to consider the place and importance of the Old Testament in the Bible. We shall briefly examine the arrangement of the books of the Bible as we find them today. We shall then turn to the Scriptures of Jesus' day, and study the great story of their origin and preservation down through the ages. You will find here the answers to some of the most common questions about this very important portion of the Holy Bible.

The Bible is actually a library of books, 66 in number. Its name, taken from the Greek *ta biblia*, originally meant "the books." When the term passed into the Latin of the Middle Ages, it became singular in form, *biblia*, or "the Book." No other writing could be known simply as *"the* Book." There is a silent tribute to the uniqueness of the Bible in the very simplicity of its title. Just as for Americans *the* Constitution means only one document, although there are multitudes of constitutions, so for men the world around *the* Book means only one, although there are books almost without number.

I. THE STRUCTURE OF THE BIBLE

The 66 books of the Bible are, of course, divided into two great sections, known familiarly as the Old and New Testaments. The term testament here carries the sense of "covenant" or "agreement." Until well into the Christian era, what we now know as the Old Testament was referred to as "the Scriptures," or "the Law and the Prophets." When the books of our New Testament were written and recognized, the title "Old Covenant" was applied to the Scriptures of that day, and "New Covenant" to the works of the apostles and their companions.

1. *The Unity of the Bible*

Approximately 40 different writers contributed to the formation of the Bible, and their work took a period of about

43

15 centuries, from Moses to John the Revelator. Men of every rank and station in life made their contributions: princes, kings, priests, prophets, herdsmen, farm laborers, fishermen, tax collectors, physicians, lawyers, and teachers. Some wrote without knowing what any of the others had written. Many wrote with knowledge of only a meager portion of the rest. None wrote having at hand all the other books. Yet the whole comprises a unity of theme and purpose which can be accounted for only on the basis that "holy men of God spake as they were moved by the Holy Ghost" (II Pet. 1:21).

The grand theme of the Bible is the story of redemption, conceived in the mind of God, accomplished in the broken heart of Christ, and conveyed by the work and will of the Holy Spirit. From the *creation* recorded in Genesis to the *consummation* or fulfillment described in Revelation, the whole grand scope of human life is described.

The redemptive Cross stands at the heart of the Bible. All of the Old Testament and the bulk of the Gospels look forward to it. All of the New Testament after the Gospels looks back to it as the supreme basis of faith and confidence. The march of the ages, now swift, now slow, from creation to the Cross and onward to the crown, is heard in the measured tread of its pages.

2. *The Order of the Books*

The arrangement of the books of the Bible as we have them now is in part chronological and in part logical. That is, the order is largely historical, in time sequence; and at the same time an arrangement by type of material is provided.

a. Historical. The first books of the Old Testament are in the main historical, and carry the thread of narrative from creation to the return of Israel from captivity in Babylon. Traditionally, these 17 books are divided as follows:

I. The Pentateuch—known as the Five Books of Moses or the Law (Considered in Chapters III, IV, and V of this book)

Genesis	Numbers
Exodus	Deuteronomy
Leviticus	

II. The Historical Books—12 in number
   A. The Period of Tribal Government (Chapter VI)
      Joshua   Ruth
      Judges
   B. The Rise and Fall of the Monarchy (Chapters VII,
      VIII, XI, XII, and XIV)
      I and II Samuel   I and II Chronicles
      I and II Kings
   C. The Return from Exile (Chapter XV)
      Ezra   Esther
      Nehemiah

b. Wisdom and Poetical. Following the historical books, whose record will provide the outline for most of this text, are placed the five books of wisdom and poetry. Most of these were written in, or relate to, the closing part of the period covered by the historical books which precede them, thus preserving something of a chronological order of arrangement.

III. The Wisdom and Poetical Books (Chapters IX and
     X)
     Job   Ecclesiastes
     Psalms   Song of Solomon
     Proverbs

c. Prophetical. The last 17 books of the Old Testament are known as the prophetical books, and again are divided into two groups, as follows:

IV. The Major Prophets (Parts of Chapters XIII, XIV,
    and XV)
    Isaiah   Ezekiel
    Jeremiah   Daniel
    Lamentations

V. The Minor Prophets (Parts of Chapters XI, XIII,
   XIV, and XV)
   Hosea   Obadiah   Nahum   Haggai
   Joel   Jonah   Habakkuk   Zechariah
   Amos   Micah   Zephaniah   Malachi

3. *The New Testament*

A similar pattern of arrangement is found in the New Testament. These books are discussed in the companion volume to this text, *Exploring the New Testament.*

a. Historical. The first five books give the historical narrative and basis of fact upon which the remainder is built. These are:

    I. The Gospels

        Matthew   Luke

        Mark   John

    II. The Book of Acts

b. The Epistles. Following the books of historical emphasis come the Epistles, commonly grouped into two major divisions:

    III. The Epistles of Paul

        Romans   Colossians

        I and II Corinthians   I and II Thessalonians

        Galatians   I and II Timothy

        Ephesians   Titus

        Philippians   Philemon

    IV. The General Epistles

        Hebrews   I, II, and III John

        James   Jude

        I and II Peter

c. Prophetical. The New Testament closes, as does the Old, with a book of which the primary emphasis is on prophecy, directed toward the future:

    V. The Book of Revelation

4. *Parallelism of the Old and New Testaments*

It will be noticed that there is an interesting parallel in the arrangement of the books as they stand in our Old and New Testaments:

	Old Testament	New Testament
a. History	I. The Pentateuch	I. The Gospels
	II. The Historical Books	II. The Acts
b. Interpretation and Application	III. The Poetical and Wisdom Books	III. The Pauline Epistles
		IV. The General Epistles
c. Prophecy	IV. The Major Prophets	V. Revelation
	V. The Minor Prophets	

It should also be noted that the relationship between the structures of the Old and New Testaments is progressive as well as parallel. The New Testament builds upon the Old Testament. The prophecies of the Old Testament, fulfilled in Christ, become the histories of the New Testament. We have, then, a grand ascent through the ages from creation to the Cross to the crown in another great "pentateuch" or fivefold outline.

<table>
<tr><td></td><td>(V) NT Prophecy
(IV) NT Interpreta-
tion</td></tr>
<tr><td>(III) OT Prophecy
(II) OT Interpretation
(I) OT History</td><td>NT History</td></tr>
</table>

The nexus or point of contact is the redemptive life, teachings, and atoning death of Christ.

II. THE IMPORTANCE OF THE OLD TESTAMENT

The Scriptures used by Jesus and the apostles are what we now describe as the Old Testament. This fact alone should show the true importance of this portion of the Bible. The Old Testament can never be replaced by the New Testament. When Jesus said, "The scripture cannot be broken" (John 10:35), and Paul asserted, "All scripture is given by inspiration of God" (II Tim. 3:16), they were certifying the undying value of the Old Testament. As Cunliffe-Jones points out:

> The authority of the Old Testament is more firmly established in the Bible than is the New. The basis upon which both the teaching of our Lord and the testimony of the apostles rests is the acknowledgement of the revelation of God in the law, the prophets, and the Psalms. We destroy the New Testament if we repudiate the Old.[1]

1. *The Old Testament as the Foundation for the New*

A thoughtful Hindu was given the New Testament by a missionary friend. He read it carefully, and came back to the missionary saying, "Please give me the other half."

[1]H. Cunliffe-Jones, *The Authority of the Biblical Revelation*, p. 80.

Curious, the missionary asked him how he knew there was another half. He replied, "The first verse says that this is the book of the generation of Jesus Christ, the son of David, the son of Abraham. I need to know about David and Abraham."

The thoughtful reader of the New Testament quickly senses its dependence upon the Old. For one thing, the authors of the New Testament wrote with minds and hearts saturated with the truths and even the very words of the Old Testament. Much of what they wrote is therefore a closed book to those who are ignorant of the Scriptures so familiar to their thought and so precious to their hearts.

There are more than 250 direct quotations from the Old Testament to be found on the pages of the New. Even more important are the vast number of references and allusions which are not direct quotations, but which draw on the terminology and modes of thought and expression to be found in the Hebrew Scriptures. One scholar lists a total of 1,603 quotations, references, and allusions which link the New Testament with the Old.[2]

The Book of Isaiah is the most frequently used Old Testament book, with a total of 308 New Testament allusions. Psalms runs a close second with 303 references. In the New Testament, Revelation makes most frequent allusions to the Old Testament with 574 references, more than one-third the total number in the entire New Testament. The Book of Acts contains 169, Luke 140, Matthew 135, Hebrews 115, and Romans 103. Only Philemon and the three Epistles of John contain no Old Testament allusions or references. Of Old Testament books, only Ruth, Ezra, Esther, Song of Solomon, Ecclesiastes, and Lamentations are not alluded to in the New Testament. However, all of these were originally joined to other books which are quoted, as we shall see when we study the formation of the Old Testament canon, or list of inspired books.

All of the New Testament writers assumed that God's dealings with man in the history of redemption form a continuous whole, out of which whole came both the Old and New Testaments. A "New" Covenant implies an "Old"

[2]G. T. Manley, *The New Bible Handbook*, Appendix V, pp. 442-55, gives a complete list from which these figures are taken.

Covenant, to which it stands in relation as well as in contrast. Indeed, the idea of fulfillment of the Old Testament in the New means continuity with the past, as well as the introduction of something new. Neither the Old Testament nor the New is fully understandable without the other. Both form two halves of a perfect whole.[3] The Old Testament without the New is like a head without a body. Tertullian said, "In the Old Testament the New is concealed; in the New Testament the Old is revealed."[4]

2. *The Neglect of the Old Testament*

In spite of these facts, the Old Testament is largely a neglected portion of God's Word. In some circles this is due to the influence of the destructive higher critics, who have been especially vigorous in their attacks on the Old Testament. As C. C. Torrey commented, "What was begun with a penknife, was continued with a hatchet."[5] Preoccupation with critical problems has blinded the minds of many to the spiritual and moral values of the Old Testament.

In other circles, the Old Testament has been neglected by those who have esteemed it dull reading, with little or nothing of profit for the average person. However, the law and the prophets still have a message for our day, and one which was never more needed. As Dr. George L. Robinson says:

> The chief enemy of the Old Testament is ignorance of it. For more than two millenniums, the Old Testament has circulated among men, as Dr. Barton expresses it, "revealing the heart of man to himself, holding before human eyes the law of God, awakening the conscience, unfolding the story of the Father's forgiveness in Christ, and forming by its lofty teaching the characters of the saints." And it is destined, I firmly believe, to live on so long as true religion holds sway over human hearts; for, though we may put more knowledge into our worship than did the ancient Hebrews, we shall hardly be able to put in more reality.[6]

[3]Cf. C. H. Dodd, *The Bible Today*, pp. 6-11.

[4]Quoted in Herbert L. Willett, *Our Bible: Its Origin, Character, and Value*, pp. 147-48.

[5]Quoted by Clyde T. Francisco, *Introducing the Old Testament*, p. 1.

[6]"The Abiding Value of the Old Testament," in Clarence A. Barbour, *The Bible in the World of Today*, pp. 145-46.

III. THE SCRIPTURES JESUS USED

The Hebrew Scriptures in Jesus' time contained the same material as is found in our Old Testament, but the arrangement and combination of books was different. Instead of the familiar fivefold grouping of the present English Bible, the Hebrew Scriptures were arranged in three groups, containing in all 24 books. It was to this arrangement our Lord referred when He told His disciples after the Resurrection, "These are the words which I spake unto you, while I was yet with you, that all things must be fulfilled, which were written in the *law of Moses,* and in the *prophets,* and in the *psalms,* concerning me" (Luke 24:44).

1. *Divisions of the Hebrew Scriptures*

Let us look briefly at the arrangement of the books in the Bible of Jesus and the apostles.

a. The *Torah* or Law of Moses. The first division was known as the Torah, or Law of Moses, or more simply, the Law. It contained the same five books which are found in the Pentateuch in the Old Testament, the first five books of the Bible: Genesis, Exodus, Leviticus, Numbers, and Deuteronomy.

The Torah is the oldest portion of the Old Testament, and conservative scholars have strongly contended for its Mosaic authorship. More will be said concerning the authorship of Moses in our next chapter. It will be enough here to note that modern archaeological discoveries have completely discredited the argument of radical critics that Moses could not have written the Pentateuch because writing was unknown in his day. Writing is now known to have been in use as early as 3000 B.C., and extremely common by the time of Abraham, who lived six centuries before Moses. Among the Ras Shamra tablets, discovered as recently as 1929, and dated from the time of Moses, are some written in an alphabetic language closely akin to Hebrew. The "Sinai Hebrew Script," discovered by Sir Flinders Petrie at Serabit on the Peninsula of Sinai in the very locale where Moses was directed to write the law and the work of God (Exod. 17:14 and 34:27), also bears witness to the common use of alphabetic writing in Moses' day.

The earliest writing is now known to have been done on clay tablets, still the popular writing material during the period in which Moses lived, as the Ras Shamra and Tell el-Amarna tablets show. However, the skins of animals, made into long parchment scrolls, and papyrus rolls are known to have been used in Egypt as writing materials as far back as 1,000 years prior to the birth of Moses.

b. The Prophets, or *Nebhiim*. The second division in the Bible of Jesus' day was known as the Prophets. The Hebrew title is *Nebhiim*. The authority of the Scriptures rests in the prophetic office or gift of its authors. Thus, many of what we now describe as the historical books were classed by the Jews with the prophetic writings. This fact also testifies to the conviction of the Jews that God is the God of history, and through historical events makes His will known and reveals His holy character.

The Prophets, in turn, were divided into the Former Prophets and the Latter Prophets. These distinctions probably have to do with the period with which the books are concerned, rather than the period in which they were written.

The Former Prophets included four books, two of which have been divided in our present versions, making six in all. These, it will be noted, are what we classify as historical books. The four Former Prophets provide a continuous record of Israel's history from the crossing of Jordan to the captivity in Babylon. They are Joshua, Judges, Samuel, and Kings.

The Latter Prophets also included four: Isaiah, Jeremiah, Ezekiel, and The Twelve (the Minor Prophets). The division of The Twelve into separate books brings the total number to 15 in our present division and classification.

c. The Writings, or *Kethubhim*. What was referred to as the *Kethubhim* (Hebrew) or *Hagiographa* (Greek) contained the balance of the 39 books in our present Old Testament. These were sometimes called the Psalms because the Book of Psalms stood first in the group (cf. Luke 24:44). The Writings were in turn divided into three subdivisions: Poetical (Psalms, Proverbs, Job); the Five Rolls or *Megilloth* (Song of Solomon, Ruth, Lamentations, Ecclesiastes, Esther); and Historical (Daniel, Ezra-Nehemiah, Chronicles).

2. *Outline of the Divisions of the Hebrew Scriptures*

It will be helpful to summarize in outline form the divisions of the Hebrew Scriptures:

I. The *Torah* (5 books)
   Genesis   Numbers
   Exodus   Deuteronomy
   Leviticus

II. The *Nebhiim*
   Former Prophets (4 books)
      Johua   Samuel
      Judges   Kings

   Latter Prophets (4 books)
      Isaiah   Ezekiel
      Jeremiah   The Twelve

III. The *Kethubhim*
   Poetical (3 books)
      Psalms
      Proverbs
      Job

   The *Megilloth* (5 books)
      Song of Solomon
      Ruth
      Lamentations
      Ecclesiastes
      Esther

   Historical (3 books)
      Daniel
      Ezra-Nehemiah
      Chronicles

The Jewish historian, Josephus, mentions the number of books in the Hebrew Scriptures as 22. This numbering was arrived at by joining Ruth with Judges, and Lamentations with Jeremiah. Apparently Ruth and Lamentations were separated from their original connections because of their use with the other books of the *Megilloth* in the observance of the great religious ceremonies in the Jewish calendar.

3. *Reasons Underlying the Hebrew Division*

Many suggestions have been offered to account for the division followed in the Hebrew Scriptures. It is very likely that the basic principle is to be found in the position of the authors of the various books. Moses was recognized as the lawgiver and a prophet in his own right, prototype of the Messiah (Deut. 18:15-19). The authors of the Former and Latter Prophets, so far as can be determined, were prophets both by office and by gift. The authors of the Writings were prophets by gift, but not by office. The fact that 19 out of the 39 books of the Old Testament are anonymous as to authorship has never caused serious question as to their acceptance in the canon.[7]

A further reason for gathering the Five Rolls together was their use in worship. These were shorter books written on single rolls to be read at the great stated feasts and religious observances of Israel. Thus, the Song of Solomon was read at the Passover; Ruth was read at Pentecost, the Harvest Feast; Ecclesiastes was read at the Feast of Tabernacles; Esther was read at the Feast of Purim; and Lamentations was used in commemoration of the Destruction of Jerusalem.

In the Septuagint, the double books of Samuel, Kings, Chronicles, and Ezra-Nehemiah were separated into two books each. The Book of the Twelve was also divided into the 12 books of the Minor Prophets as we know them. This division and arrangement was preserved in the Latin Vulgate, and has come down to us in our English and other versions. The modern Hebrew Scriptures are divided into 39 books, but the ancient arrangement is preserved—beginning with Genesis and ending with II Chronicles.

IV. THE FORMATION OF THE OLD TESTAMENT CANON

The term "canon" comes from the Greek, *Kanon,* which originally meant "that which measures," perhaps derived from the Hebrew *qaneh,* a reed or measuring rod. Later it came to apply to that which is measured by some standard or rule recognized as authoritative. Apparently its first use in the presently accepted meaning occurred among Christians of the fourth century.

1. *The Nature of the Canon*

The canon, then, applies to those books which are to be accepted as binding and authoritative messages from God to man. Used in this way, both its meanings are appropriate. The canon of Scripture is that list of books measured by a valid standard of inspiration; and its books are the rule and standard which measures men and their doings, and which provides an authoritative guide for faith and practice.

It should be clearly understood that the inclusion of a

---

[7]Cf. Merrill F. Unger, *Introductory Guide to the Old Testament,* p. 50.

book in the canon is not the cause of its inspiration. The canonical Scriptures were as much inspired at the moment of their completion as when their place in Scripture was later seen. Inclusion in the canon means the recognition of inspiration. The Scriptures are therefore the product of a twofold process. First is the work of the Holy Spirit inspiring the production of the book. Second is the activity of the Holy Spirit guiding recognition of the book. As Unger points out:

> God, Who had moved in man's behalf in revelation in giving the message, and in inspiration in causing the message to be inerrantly received and recorded, must so influence and guide His people as to cause them to recognize and receive His Word, rejecting that which laid spurious claim as inspired Scripture, and neglecting none that was genuine. Without this providential interposition the canon could never have been formed. Without further divine activity manifested in miraculously preserving the Sacred Writings the canon would never have been assembled, nor would it ever have been transmitted to us through the vicissitudes of many centuries.[8]

2. *The Need for the Canon*

The need for such a canon to mark off the books accepted as the law and Word of the Lord is readily seen. The inspired literature formed only a fraction of the total produced at any given time. For the Old Testament, the voice of prophecy was heard for about a thousand years—from Moses to Malachi. During that period, many more books were written than are included in the Scriptures. Age or time of writing is never a deciding factor in proof of inspiration, although the lateness of a writing may exclude it from the canon.

Each of the canonical sections of the Hebrew Scripture, that is, the Law, the Prophets, and the Writings, contains references to other books known at the time, books which have since passed into oblivion. More than 15 such are mentioned by name in the Old Testament. For example, in the Law we read of "the book of the wars of the Lord" (Num. 21:14). In the Prophets we read of "the book of Jasher" (Josh. 10:13 and II Sam. 1:18); "the book of the acts of Solomon" (I Kings 11:41), and "the book of the chronicles of the kings of Israel" (II Kings 14:28), obviously not our

[8]*Ibid.*, p. 49.

present book of Chronicles, which records only events relating to the kings of Judah. In the Writings, we read of "the book of Samuel the seer," "the book of Nathan the prophet," "the book of Gad the seer" (I Chron. 29:29); "the prophecy of Ahijah the Shilonite" (II Chron. 9:29), "the book of Shemaiah the prophet," "the book of Iddo the seer" (II Chron. 12:15), and "the story of the prophet Iddo" (II Chron. 13:22), as well as "the sayings of the seers" (II Chron. 33:19).

3. *The Old Testament Canon in New Testament Times*

There is no doubt but that the writers of the New Testament accepted the Hebrew Scriptures in each of their three major divisions as canonical. This is abundantly demonstrated by the large number of quotations, references, and allusions found in the New Testament—over 400 taken from the Torah, 715 from the Prophets, and almost 450 from the Writings.

Parallel testimony is given by Josephus, the noted Jewish historian who lived and wrote in the first century of the Christian era. The following rather lengthy quotation shows clearly how the Jews of Christ's time viewed their Scriptures:

> Every one is not permitted of his own accord to be a writer, nor is there any disagreement in what is written; they being only prophets that have written the original and earliest accounts of things as they learned them of God himself by inspiration . . . For we have not an innumerable multitude of books among us, disagreeing from and contradicting one another, but only twenty-two books, which contain the records of all the past times; which are justly believed to be divine; and of them five belong to Moses, which contain his laws and the traditions of the origin of mankind till his death . . . As to the time from the death of Moses till the reign of Artaxerxes king of Persia, who reigned after Xerxes, the prophets, who were after Moses, wrote down what was done in their times in thirteen books. The remaining four books contain hymns to God, and precepts for the conduct of human life. It is true, our history hath been written since Artaxerxes very particularly, but hath not been esteemed of the like authority with the former by our forefathers, because there hath not been an exact succession of prophets since that time; and how firmly we have given credit to these books of our own nation is evident by what we do; for during so many ages as have already passed, no one has been so bold as either to add any thing to them, to take any thing from them, or to make any change in them; but it is become natural to all Jews immediately, and from their very birth, to esteem these books

to contain Divine doctrines, and to persist in them, and, if occasion be, willingly to die for them.[9]

4. The Completion of the Old Testament Canon

Although the word canon came into use only after the beginning of the Christian era, the recognition of the inspired books runs far back in Israel's history. As Manley observes, "The Old Testament canon was a body of Scripture, continually growing, yet complete at each stage, beginning with the edicts and records of the first lawgiver and increased by the works of each successive prophet."[10]

That the Law was first clearly recognized as authoritative there can be no question. The existence of the Samaritan version of the Pentateuch bears witness that this was very early, at least by the time of Hezekiah (726-697 B.C.) if not much sooner. The Prophets were completed by the time of Zechariah and Malachi, and recognized when it became apparent that the voice of prophecy was no longer heard. We have little light as to when the Writings were first accounted part of the Word of God. It was certainly as early as the second century before Christ, when the Septuagint, which contains them, was translated. Jesus attributed the force of law to the Writings when He quoted from Ps. 82: 6, and said concerning it, "Is it not written in your law?" (John 10: 34) He further called the Psalms "the word of God" and "the scripture" (v. 35). The action of the Jewish council of Jamnia in A.D. 90 in accrediting these books only made official what had been actual for over two and one-half centuries.

5. The Apocrypha

In addition to the canonical books of the Hebrew Scriptures, two other classes of books should be considered. These are the books of the Apocrypha, and what are known to Bible scholars as the Pseudepigrapha.

The term "apocrypha" has come to stand for a group of writings dating after the canonical books from about 200 B.C. to A.D. 100. Originally the word meant "hidden" or "concealed." Its present use dates from about the fourth century of the

---

[9]"Flavius Josephus Against Apion," Bk. I, 7, 8, from *The Life and Works of Flavius Josephus,* translated by William Whiston, pp. 861-62.

[10]Manley, *op. cit.,* p. 29.

Christian era when Jerome stated that other writings apart from those of the recognized canon "must be placed with the Apocrypha."[11]

The Old Testament Apocrypha consists of fourteen books as follows:

> I and II Esdras
> Tobit
> Judith
> The Remainder of Esther
> The Wisdom of Solomon
> Ecclesiasticus
> Baruch (with the Epistle of Jeremiah)
> The Song of the Three Hebrew Children
> The History of Susanna
> Bel and the Dragon
> The Prayer of Manasses
> I and II Maccabees

a. The History of the Apocrypha. The status and value of the Apocrypha have long been the subjects of debate. The Jews have never recognized the books as on a par with canonical scripture. In later copies of the Septuagint, the Apocryphal books were included, and were highly prized by many of the early Christians. However, the New Testament consistently omits any direct quotation from the Apocrypha as inspired scripture, although New Testament writers undoubtedly were acquainted with its pages.

The attitude of the Roman Catholic church toward the Apocrypha has wavered from Jerome's unequivocal rejection of its inspiration to the final inclusion of eleven of the Apocryphal books in the canon as declared by the Council of Trent in 1546 and confirmed by the Vatican Council in 1870. Protestants since the Reformation have unanimously rejected the inspiration of the Apocrypha, while admitting its value for historical information and devotional reading. The early English translations of the Bible included the Apocrypha, as does the English Catholic Douai Version of the present time. Some English printings as early as 1629 omitted these disputed books, and they have been left out of practically all such editions since 1827.

---

[11]Quoted in Unger, *op. cit.,* p. 83.

b. The Apocryphal Books. There are many reasons why we should reject any notion of the inspiration of these books. The Catholic position is based on the false view that the Roman church is final authority in all matters of faith, and boils down to the absurdity that these books are inspired because the church says they are. Unger quotes the Catholic scholar John E. Steinmueller as saying:

> Had the Church accepted the Palestinian canon (that is, without the Apocryphal books), this also would have been binding upon all Christians, but only because of the value placed upon it by her. The Church, however, did not receive this Canon, but rather the Alexandrian, which included the deutero-canonical books and passages (that is, the Apocrypha), and she thereby showed that she is the only legitimate and final authority determining the extent of the Canon.[12]

The Apocrypha abounds in historical inaccuracies and misstatements of fact. It contains teachings at variance with those of the true Scriptures, such as the justification of suicide, and prayers and offerings for the dead (II Maccabees); almsgiving as making atonement for sin, the justification of wrong means by right ends (Ecclesiasticus and Judith); and superstition and magic (Tobit). The leaders of the Ancient Church denied its authenticity. Most conclusive of all, the writers of the New Testament, who make most of their quotations from the Greek Septuagint, avoid all direct quotation from Apocryphal books. The reference in Jude 14-16 to the Book of Enoch does not relate to an Apocryphal book, but to one of the Pseudepigrapha, for which no claims to inspiration have ever been made.

6. *The Pseudepigrapha*

This is a name given to writings dating about the same time as the Apocrypha, but differing in that they purport to be written by well-known ancient writers. No serious claim to a place in the canon has ever been made for these writings. The name means "false writings" and relates to their alleged authorship at a much earlier date.

The majority of these books are apocalyptic in character. That is, they consist largely of visions and prophecies of a

---

[12]*Ibid.,* p. 108.

bright future for the Jewish people. For this reason, they are often known as the Apocalyptic Literature. The fact that these works are supposed to have been written by famous prophets of the past need not be taken as an effort to deceive, as the authors simply followed what was then a very common practice. Included in the Pseudepigrapha are such books as:

The Book of Enoch (quoted in Jude 14-16)
The Secrets of Enoch
The Apocalypse of Baruch
The Assumption of Moses
The Ascension of Isaiah
The Apocalypse of Zephaniah
The Apocalypse of Esdras
The Testament of Adam
The Testament of the Twelve Patriarchs, etc.

No doubt these writings did much to comfort and sustain a people suffering under the yoke of foreign oppression and religious persecution. They testify to the heart hunger of a nation which no longer heard the prophetic voice.

7. *The Bible a Completed Book*

The firm attitude of the Protestant church in rejecting both the Apocrypha and Pseudepigrapha indicates its faith that the Bible is not a loose-leaf book to which additional pages can be added at any time. The general acceptance of the canon shows that the Scripture is a closed Book, a tightly bound volume.[13] God's revelation of himself is complete, and no additions are to be permitted, whether it be a "Book of Mormon" or a "Key to the Scriptures." "But though we, or an angel from heaven, should preach unto you any gospel other than that which we preached unto you, let him be anathema" (Gal. 1:8, ASV).

I testify unto every man that heareth the words of the prophecy of this book, If any man shall add unto them, God shall add unto him the plagues which are written in this book: and if any man shall take away from the words of the book of this prophecy, God shall take away his part from the tree of life, and out of the holy city, which are written in this book (Rev. 22:18-19, ASV).

[13]Cf. Leonard Greenway, *Basic Questions About the Bible*, p. 14.

V. The Text of the Old Testament

The oldest existing copies of the Bible are known as manuscripts, and are handmade copies in the original languages. The writings as first completed by their human authors are known as autographs, and have all long since disappeared. This is probably due to the fragile character of the writing materials used, and to the many waves of fanatical persecution the Word of God has had to endure. That it is also providential may be seen from the incurably idolatrous nature of human beings. A scroll in the handwriting of Moses or Isaiah would soon receive the adoration which should be given to God alone and to His truth.

The original autographs of the Old Testament were written in Hebrew, which was spoken among the Israelites from the fifteenth century B.C. or earlier until the Babylonian captivity early in the sixth century B.C., and which was then gradually replaced by a sister-tongue, Aramaic, the language of Syria (or Aram) and the rest of the Near East. The only exceptions to the use of Hebrew in the Old Testament are brief passages in Jeremiah (10:11), Daniel (2:4—7:28), and Ezra (4:8—6:18; 7:12-26), which appear in Aramaic. This Aramaic, which was spoken by the Jews in the Restoration Period, was in turn gradually supplanted by Greek, so that in New Testament times Greek became the universal language of Bible lands.

1. *Hebrew Writing*

The Hebrew of the Old Testament was written in consonants only, the vowel sounds being supplied by the reader. There were no divisions in the ancient text at all, either into words, verses, paragraphs, or chapters. This was as if we should write the first two verses of the twenty-third psalm,

THLRDSMSHPHRDSHLLNTWNTHMKTHMTLDWNN
GRNPSTRSHLDTHMBSDTHSTLLWTRS

This abbreviated method of writing was economical of space on expensive writing materials, but it often resulted in misunderstanding of the meaning, since much depended on the reader's supplying the proper vowel sounds.

Three types of writing material were in common use during the thousand years the Old Testament was being written: clay tablets; parchment, or the cured skins of animals; and papyrus, a brittle material made from the pith of a reed found plentifully throughout the Near East. From the papyrus we get our word *paper,* and it was the material used by John to which reference is made in II John 12.

The pieces of parchment or papyri were fastened together in long strips which were rolled from each end on rollers. These were known as rolls or scrolls. The use of pages bound together in our accustomed book form originated in the early Christian era. Such a book is called a codex. The writing was arranged in columns in both the scroll and the codex, and was read from right to left—exactly opposite to the way we read.

2. *The Accuracy of the Scribes*

The world has never known more painstaking copyists than the Jewish *sopherim* or scribes. The Talmud, a collection of notes and commentaries on the Scriptures prepared by Jewish rabbis early in the Christian era, gives very detailed regulations for copyists. An example is given in the following quotation,

> An authentic copy must be the exemplar, from which the transcriber ought not in the least to deviate. No word or letter, not even a *yod,* must be written from memory, the scribe not having looked at the codex before him . . . The fifth book of Moses must terminate exactly with a line; but the rest need not do so. Beside this, the copyist must sit in full Jewish dress, wash his whole body, not begin to write the name of God with a pen newly dipped in ink, and should a king address him while writing that name, he must take no notice of him.[14]

In the Masoretic period, from A.D. 500 to 1000, many other devices were used to insure the absolute accuracy of each copy. The Jewish scribes of this period were known as Masoretes, a name which comes from the Hebrew *Masorah,* meaning "tradition." The Masorah were marginal readings, comments, and notes of various kinds, designed to aid the copyist in preserving the uncorrupted text. It was customary to count the words and even the letters of each scroll, noting the middle word and letter, to guard against both omissions and additions of any kind.

[14]Quoted by Sir Frederic Kenyon, *Our Bible and the Ancient Manuscripts,* p. 39.

Between 150 B.C. and A.D. 150, the Hebrew Scriptures were divided into words. Verse divisions began to be made about A.D. 200, and were standardized by Rabbi Ben Asher in the first half of the tenth century A.D. Chapter divisions came later, adopted from the Latin versions about the thirteenth century of the Christian era.

3. Ancient Hebrew Manuscripts

The oldest existing Hebrew manuscripts of any large portion of the Old Testament date back to about A.D. 900. The oldest complete manuscript of the Old Testament in Hebrew was written as late as the eleventh century A.D. However, there are portions that are much older. The famous Nash Papyrus, now dated by Dr. W. F. Albright in the last half of the second century before Christ,[15] was until recently the most ancient bit of scripture manuscript known to exist. The four fragments of this papyrus contain the Ten Commandments and what was known as the Shema, or Deut. 6: 4-9.

A wandering goat was the occasion for the uncovering early in 1947 of "the greatest manuscript discovery of modern times."[16] A shepherd from a small band of Bedouins camped at the spring Ain Feshkha near the Dead Sea was looking for a straying goat when he noticed a small opening in the face of a nearby rock formation, about four feet above the ground. He idly tossed a rock through the hole, and was startled by the resounding crash of breaking pottery. Further investigation revealed a number of pottery jars, each containing an ancient scroll.

When the first of the scrolls reached Jerusalem, their significance was quickly recognized. In the years immediately following, the area was systematically explored and hundreds of manuscripts and fragments were recovered from 11 caves in all. Known by the collective name of Dead Sea Scrolls, the Jerusalem Scrolls, or the Ain Feshkha Scrolls, the finds include Hebrew manuscripts of all or part of every Old Testament book except Esther.

[15]W. F. Albright, *From the Stone Age to Christianity,* pp. 268-69; and *Journal of Biblical Literature,* LVI (1936), pp. 145-76.

[16]W. F. Albright in the *Biblical Archaeologist,* XI, No. 3 (September, 1948), p. 55.

The most important discoveries for Old Testament studies include copies of Leviticus, the Books of Samuel, the Psalms, Isaiah, Daniel, and a commentary on Habakkuk. Careful examination by archaeologists and datings made by the Carbon 14 method have led to the conclusion that these writings come from the first or more probably the second century before Christ. John C. Trever, acting director of the American School of Oriental Research in Jerusalem at the time of the find, was one of the first scholars to study the scrolls. He affirms that the scripture portions are "the oldest existing manuscripts of the Bible in any language."[17]

The practical importance of such a find as this is to be found in the confirmation it gives to our faith in the integrity of the Old Testament text as we now have it. The Dead Sea Scroll of Isaiah is a thousand years older than the oldest Hebrew manuscript known until this discovery. Yet the only variations are extremely minor, and make no difference whatsoever in any doctrinal point. Here in the middle of the twentieth century is striking evidence of the fact that the Old Testament as it has been preserved for us across the ages conveys the Word of the Lord exactly as it was first given through inspired prophets of old.

SUMMARY

In this chapter we have surveyed the structure of the Bible, both as we have it now in our current versions and as it was in Jesus' day. The importance of the Old Testament has been considered, in the light of its contribution to a right understanding of the New Testament. The wonderful providences of God in the formation of the canon and the preservation of His Word across the ages have been noted, and attention given to the nature of the Hebrew text and some of the ancient manuscripts. Having established a few points of reference, we turn now to our interesting task of "Exploring the Old Testament" itself.

RECOMMENDED READINGS

Samuel A. Cartledge, *A Conservative Introduction to the Old Testament*, pp. 13-42.

Sidney Collett, *All About the Bible*, pp. 45-74.

[17]*Bulletin of the American School of Oriental Research*, No. 113 (February, 1949), p. 23.

Clyde T. Francisco, *Introducing the Old Testament*, pp. 1-12.

Sir Frederic Kenyon, *Our Bible and the Ancient Manuscripts*, pp. 3-97.

H. S. Miller, *General Biblical Introduction*, pp. 87-124, 177-89.

J. H. Raven, *Old Testament Introduction*, pp. 17-81.

Merrill F. Unger, *Introductory Guide to the Old Testament*, pp. 45-145.

H. Orton Wiley, *Christian Theology*, Volume I, pp. 185-214.

Edward J. Young, *An Introduction to the Old Testament*, pp. 32-43.

FOR FURTHER STUDY

1. Do you think there is any significance in the fact that the writers of the Bible came from such varied walks of life? State what you think may be implied in the fact that these writers lived and wrote without complete knowledge of what the others had written.

2. Differentiate between a *logical* and a *chronological* arrangement of material. What is meant by saying that the order of books in the Bible is partly logical and partly chronological?

3. Memorize or relearn the order of the 39 books of the Old Testament in their five major divisions: i.e., Pentateuch, Historical Books, Poetical and Wisdom Books, Major Prophets, and Minor Prophets.

4. How is the arrangement of books in the Old Testament related to the order of the New Testament writings?

5. Discuss the value of a knowledge of the Old Testament for the proper understanding of the New.

6. How do you account for the widely prevailing ignorance and neglect of the Old Testament? Discuss: "The Old Testament is timely because its truth is timeless."

7. Compare the order and arrangement of the Scriptures Jesus used with the order and arrangement of the Old Testament as we know it.

8. What has archaeology contributed to our understanding of the authorship of the Pentateuch? Look up additional information about the Ras Shamra and Tell el-Amarna tablets.

9. Do you think there is adequate justification for considering the books of Joshua, Judges, Samuel, and Kings as "prophets"?

10. List the books of the Hebrew Scriptures which were divided to make the present total of 39 in the Old Testament. At what time in the history of the Bible was this division made?

11. What is the practical necessity of a "canon" in relation to the Scriptures? How does the canon relate to inspiration?

12. Describe the attitude of the Jews in Christ's time toward the Scriptures.

13. Look up a copy of the Apocrypha, and read portions of Tobit, Bel and the Dragon, and Maccabees. What is the chief value of the Apocrypha?

14. See if you can find out why the Roman Catholic dogma holds to the inspiration and canonical authority of the Apocrypha.

15. What are the chief differences between the Apocrypha and the Pseudepigrapha? Why were the pseudepigraphical books written?

16. Find a definition of "apocalypse" and "apocalyptic." What portions of the Bible with which you are familiar are apocalyptic in character?

17. Comment on the statement, "The Bible is not a loose-leaf book."

18. Differentiate between "autograph," "manuscript," and "version." Why are there no autographs of Scripture to be found?

19. Describe ancient Hebrew writing and writing materials. When was the Old Testament divided into words? verses? chapters?

20. Tell about some of the devices used by Hebrew scribes to insure the complete accuracy of their copies.

21. See if you can find a more complete description of the discovery of the "Jerusalem Scrolls," and some of the conclusions scholars have formed about them.

CHAPTER III

The Dawn of History

In the beginning God (Gen. 1:1).

Sources: Genesis 1—11

To Be Read: Genesis 1—11

Period: Creation to approximately 2100 B.C. (See summary outline of Old Testament history on page 432.)

In this chapter we are to study the beginnings of human history, the long period before the call of Abraham. If the first 11 chapters of Genesis were to be lost, the rest of the Bible would be very puzzling indeed. These chapters span a longer period of time than all the rest of the Book put together. Before turning to the grand creation epic in the first two chapters of the Old Testament, let us look briefly at what Jesus called "The Book of Moses" (Mark 12:26), in which this record is found.

I. THE PENTATEUCH

The first five books of the Sacred Writings have been given the Greek title "Pentateuch," or "Five Rolls," taken from the Septuagint version. These books, as a unit, trace the origin of both the earth and mankind in general, and then describe the call of God's chosen people. They relate God's dealings with Israel, the nation which was to be the channel through which all mankind might come to know of the one Redeemer. In these five introductory books, we watch the beginnings and development of the chosen nation, as the people were trained and prepared to enter their Promised Land. Genesis explains their origin and beginnings in general; Exodus, their deliverance or "way out" from bondage; Leviticus, their worship, directed by the Levites; Numbers, their organization and wilderness wanderings; and Deuteronomy, the second giving of the Law in preparation for the entrance into Canaan.

The Hebrews called these books the Torah, which was their word for "Law." The original idea of the word was "instruction," either human or divine.[1] Joshua referred to the "book of the law" (Josh. 8:34) or the "book of the law of God" (Josh. 24:26); and in the time of Jehoshaphat (ca. 872-48 B.C.) Judah was taught from the "book of the law of the Lord" (II Chron. 17:9). In the New Testament, Jesus also called it the "law" (Matt. 12:5) because of the great amount of legislation in it. Luke referred to it as the "law of the Lord" (Luke 2:23); and Paul called it the "book of the law" (Gal. 3:10).

1. *Mosaic Authorship of the Pentateuch*

In regard to the writer of the Pentateuch, the Bible itself bears witness to the authorship of Moses. In Old Testament times David referred to it as the "law of Moses" (I Kings 2:3); and in the New Testament era Luke uses the same title (Luke 2:22). Jesus also when He was speaking to the Sadducees called it the "book of Moses" (Mark 12:26).

In spite of frequent references to Moses in relation to the Torah, there are those critics who contest the Mosiac authorship of this portion of scripture. The extreme critical view holds that it is a composite of four or more ancient documents edited long after the reign of King David. The extreme conservative view states that Moses alone wrote the entire book exactly as it exists in the present Hebrew Bible.

Various names have been given to the theory of the liberal critics. It has been called the "Developmental Hypothesis," the "Documentary Theory," the "Modified Document Hypothesis," the "Critical Hypothesis," or the "New Critical School." The use of abbreviations has led to the designation "JEDP Theory," from the letters or symbols assigned to the documents which are supposed to have been put together to make up the Pentateuch.

The JEDP theory identifies four different manuscripts in the composition of the Torah, not written by Moses, but supposed to have been produced at different dates ranging from the ninth to the fifth century B.C. The *J* manuscript was named from the writer's use of the divine word *Jahweh* or *Jehovah*, and was alleged to have been written about 850 B.C. The *E* manuscript was so called from the author's use of the

---

[1]Francis Brown, S. R. Driver, and Charles A. Briggs, *Hebrew and English Lexicon of the Old Testament*, p. 435.

word *Elohim* when speaking of God. This was supposed to have been written a century later, about 750 B.C. The *D* manuscript includes the major part of Deuteronomy, and was believed to have been discovered in 621 B.C. and therefore written in the seventh century B.C. The *P* manuscript was the work of a "priestly" writer, and makes up the body of the Pentateuch. It is alleged to have been written between 500 and 450 B.C. The present form is supposed to have been the work of editors combining these various sources about 400 B.C.

2. *Weakness of the Liberal View*

A careful examination of these alleged documents shows that the theory of the critics is not sound. For example, several of the arguments are based on assumed differences in diction and style. One notable argument concerns the use of different names for God. Such arguments are certainly inconclusive. As the subject matter changes, why should not the diction and style change, and the author give to God an appropriate title in each particular context?

Genesis 1 and 2 are assigned to separate authors by the critics—Genesis 1 to *P* and Genesis 2 to *J*. But these accounts are not two separate accounts, neither can anything be omitted without losing the thread of the story. The first chapter is a general account of creation, and the second supplies the necessary details. Dr. Free suggests that the popular method of modern writers offers a parallel. They often make a "passing remark" which is developed later with the details.[2]

There is no valid reason to dispute the Mosaic authorship. The Scriptures uphold it, and the style of the Pentateuch is in harmony with other records originating at an earlier date than the beginnings of the Hebrew monarchy. As religious history it omits any annals and information which would be of no value in the study of redemption. Besides, it is altogether possible that Moses used earlier documents and annals, such as the "Ten Generations" described below, and compiled them into one account. Suffice it to say, whether it was compiled or originally composed, Moses was guided by the Spirit, as the Bible indicates, to write a redemptive or religious history of "first things."

[2]Joseph P. Free, *Archaeology and Bible History,* p. 15.

3. *The Book of Genesis*

The first book of the Bible derives its name from the title it bears in the Greek Septuagint, *genesis,* which means "beginning" or "generation." This word occurs in the title of each of the 10 sections of the book which begin with the expression, "These are the generations of . . . ," or, "The books of the generations of . . ."[3] Even in the creation account we read, "These are the generations of the heavens and of the earth" (Gen. 2:4). In the Hebrew the title is *Bereshith,* which means "in the beginning." The idea of beginnings or origin underlies the entire book.

Genesis naturally divides into three major sections:

   I. The Creation Hymn (1:1—2:3)

  II. Human Life Before Abraham (2:4—11:26)

 III. The Beginnings of the Hebrew Nation (1:27—50:26)

Sections I and II will be considered in this chapter. Section III will be considered in Chapter IV. We turn now to what has been called "The Creation Hymn," "The Epic of Creation," or "The Poem of the Dawn."

II. THE CREATION

1. *The Epic of Creation* (Gen. 1:1—2:3)

The Epic of Creation answers man's first inquiry, Whence came I, and to whom am I responsible? Its first verse sublimely announces an intelligent Creator, the great First Cause of all things, the One who has devised and ordered all affairs in heaven and on earth. "In the beginning God created the heaven and the earth." Everything begins with God. With the grandeur of simplicity, no proof is given for the existence of God any more than a human author prefaces his book by

[3]A listing of these generations is as follows:

    (1) Gen. 2:4—Generations of Heaven and Earth.
    (2) Gen. 5:1—Generations of Adam.
    (3) Gen. 6:9—Generations of Noah.
    (4) Gen. 10:1—Generations of the Sons of Noah.
    (5) Gen. 11:10—Generations of Shem.
    (6) Gen. 11:27—Generations of Terah.
    (7) Gen. 25:12—Generations of Ishmael.
    (8) Gen. 25:19—Generations of Isaac.
    (9) Gen. 36:1—Generations of Esau.
  (10) Gen. 37:2—Generations of Jacob.

proving his own existence. God has no beginning: He is "from everlasting to everlasting." As the Psalmist says:

Lord, thou hast been our dwelling-place
In all generations.
Before the mountains were brought forth,
Or ever thou hadst formed the earth and the world,
Even from everlasting to everlasting, thou art God.

(Ps. 90:1-2, ASV)

This passage is the answer to the agnostic, who declares that God's existence and the origin of the universe are unknowable. It contradicts the atheist, who denies the very existence of a Supreme Being. It eliminates pantheism, which is the belief that the universe itself is God. It answers the argument of polytheism, which upholds a plurality of gods instead of the one supreme God.

Once the creative purpose of God is affirmed, the beginnings of all finite things may be explained. This simple but sublime account of the creative period traces the formation of earth and man, but not of the entire universe. The Bible does not say how long a period of time might have elapsed between the beginnings of heaven and earth in verse 1 and the creative processes described in the rest of the passage. Nor is such a statement necessary, for the purpose of the account is religious. We are next informed of the preparation of earth for man's abode, together with his relation to the other orders of creation. The earth had no form until the Spirit of God entered and became the energizing force which "moved upon the face of the waters" (1:2) for six creative days. The Word of God spoke, and all forces obeyed His command. Three words, "And God said," occur 10 times in this first chapter.

a. The Six Creative Days. At the beginning of each day came the divine command, "Let there be," and it was done. On the *first* day God commanded the light to appear, the prime essential for all nature. On the *second*, He produced the firmament or expanse which He called heaven. He separated the clouds and vapors from surface waters by an atmosphere. The *third* day He rolled the waters into seas, and divided them from the dry land, which He called earth. Then He clothed the hills and the valleys with all kinds of vegetation, trees, plants, and grass, each one yielding "seed after its kind," reproducing only its own kind. Even horticulture cannot change the "kind" although it may change the variety. The various families of vegetables cannot blend any more than the numerous families of animals. The *fourth* day He caused the sun, moon, and stars to appear that they might regulate the calendar and measure the years for eras in history. He divided day and night, caused moon and sun to influence tides on the sea, provided a starry universe for the astronomer, latitude and longitude for the sailor, and seasons for the farmer. The *fifth* day God created the lower animals, the birds of the air, and the fish of the sea. On the *sixth* day He proceeded in orderly progress to create the higher animals on land, and to prepare for the introduction of man, the crowning act of creation.

"Creepers" and all lower animals were formed from the earth with constituent elements much the same as those forming the bodies of human beings. All animal species bear evidence of the same design of an intelligent Creator, for each family is "after his kind." God closed the sixth day by fully accomplishing His divine intention, when He created man in the image of the Creator.

b. *The Creation of Man.* "And God said, Let us make man in our image, after our likeness: and let them have dominion over the fish of the sea, and over the birds of the heavens, and over the cattle, and over all the earth, and over every creeping thing that creepeth upon the earth" (1:26, ASV). "And God created man in his own image, in the image of God created he him; male and female created he them" (1:27, ASV). Here was created the first couple to be the first parents of the first family.

From Gen. 2:7 we learn that man's physical body was formed from the "dust of the ground," and that "God breathed into his nostrils the breath of life; and man became a living soul," possessed of immortality. Man is a complex being. His *physical* nature makes him akin to all inferior creation, yet even here he represents the goal and height of creation in the ultimate design of the Creator. All animals on earth, and the plants which are rooted in the soil, minister to his material needs out of the very earth to which he returns. His physical good requires an *intellect* capable of understanding himself and the elements in the world as they affect him. The senses, as feeling, sight, hearing, taste, and smell, meet this need through the nervous system. But man has something even greater than these. Animals have instinct, feelings, and desires; but man has a *moral* nature and a capacity for the *spiritual* which is the image of his spiritual Creator.

In the creation of man, God's supreme gift was spirit. As such, man's image in the highest sense is "the image of God." It is this divine image which makes man responsible to the Sovereign of creation, although he himself dominates all lower creation. With intellectual and moral resources, man can partly understand God's character and ways. But the essential characteristic of man centers about the decisions of which he is capable, as a creature endowed with both reason and conscience. In the fact of moral responsibility lies the essential nature of human personality. It carries with it the possibility of a personal relationship with the Creator in whose image the human soul is fashioned.

c. The Sabbath. The closing scene in the great Epic of Creation is the institution of the Sabbath on the seventh day (2:2-3). There is no evidence of any new creations since that first great Sabbath. By example, God himself ceased to work (*shavath*) on the seventh day, and He "blessed" it and "sanctified" it, or made it holy.

d. Parallel Accounts of Creation. There are interesting parallel accounts of creation which have come to us from Babylonia and Assyria. Some of these were found on tablets unearthed by Layard and Rassam in 1850 to 1854 in their excavation of Ashurbanipal's Royal Library at Nineveh, a collection which dates back to the seventh century B.C. "The Epic of Creation" is a Semitic-Babylonian account originally written on seven tablets. The story tells how the gods first appeared "before the beginning of things" and framed the heavens above and the earth beneath, and then appointed Anu to be ruler of the sky. Conflict ensued between Marduk, a god of light, and Tiamat, a goddess of the "deep" or chaos. Marduk then took one-half of Tiamat's body to cover the heavens, and the other half to make the earth. He also furnished the heavens with the stars and signs of the zodiac. On the sixth tablet, the creation of man was recorded.

The Babylonian Epic of Creation is comparable to the Hebrew in some respects. It is written on seven tablets corresponding to the seven days of Genesis. The order of the creative stages is much the same. Order wins the victory over chaos; and the Babylonian goddess of the deep, Tiamat, corresponds with the Hebrew *Tehom*, which is translated "the deep" or "abyss" in Gen. 1:2. These similarities suggest that in the Babylonian parallels we may have a corrupted form of the same true account given in Genesis.

There are many contrasts, however, between the Babylonian and Hebrew Epics of Creation. The polytheism of the Babylonian account contrasts with the true monotheism of the account in Genesis. In the Babylonian account the creation was partly the result of a blind force and conflict between divinities; but in Genesis, the one supreme God made all things with no conflict, His Spirit moving "upon the face of the waters." The Old Testament account is far superior; it preserves the record without the superstition and crude polytheism of the Babylonian tradition. However, the very existence of such ancient parallels bears witness to the factual source from which the corrupt tradition came.

b. *The Babylonian Sabbath.* The Hebrew institution of the Sabbath is often compared with a Babylonian text citing special observance of the seventh, fourteenth, nineteenth, twenty-first, and twenty-eighth days of the month. With the exception of the nineteenth day, these correspond in number to the Jewish Sabbath. Sayce says that the seventh day was observed as a day of rest among Babylonians, and even called the Sabbath.[4] However, the Babylonian tablets prohibited only certain classes of people, as shepherds, seers, physicians, and kings, from breaking the Sabbath; whereas the observance of the Hebrew Sabbath was to be universal. This parallel also confirms the Genesis account, since doubtless the Babylonian practice came from the same original observance, instituted in the beginning of the race.

2. *Man in the Garden of Eden* (Gen. 2:4-25)

It is at this point in the inspired record that we are first introduced to the name of God as He later revealed it to Moses (Exod. 3:13-14). In all the previous descriptions of His great

---

[4]A. H. Sayce, *Fresh Light from Ancient Monuments*, pp. 28-29. Also by the same author, *Babylonians and Assyrians, Life and Customs*, p. 245.

works in creation, He bears the name *Elohim,* the Hebrew term for the mighty God of transcendent power. With the might of His word, He had displayed His sovereignty. The world has no independent existence apart from Him. Nothing is self-made.

a. *The God of His People.* When we reach the fourth verse of chapter 2, we find that this God is more than a God of power. He is the "Lord God," *Jehovah,* who came down in person and with love to create man in His own image. He "so loved the world" (John 3:16) that He personally supervised the creation of man. He not only created in mighty power, but He also cared for the man whom He created; and He was to provide a means of redemption for man when sin should enter human experience.

b. *The Garden of Eden.* Thus in chapter 2 we are given a detailed account of the creative work of a loving God, the Father of all. After He had placed vegetation upon the earth and had provided water for it from the mist that then arose from the ground (vv. 5-6), He "planted a garden eastward in Eden," where His newly created human beings might live. In the midst of the garden were two specially designated trees: the tree of life, and the tree of the knowledge of good and evil.

Four rivers watered the garden. The first was the Euphrates, the name of which means "fruitful." The name of the second, Hiddekel, is the Hebrew name for the Babylonian Idiglat which appears on Babylonian clay tablets and refers to the river now called the Tigris.[5] The names for the third and fourth rivers, Pison and Gihon, correspond with two Babylonian names, Pisanu and Guhana, which appear in a list of irrigating canals in Mesopotamia.[6]

The location of the Garden of Eden has been the subject of much debate. A tablet discovered in Babylonia in 1885 reads "Sippar in Eden," and it is now generally agreed that the oldest known civilization centered about the region of Mesopotamia, "between the rivers."[7]

[5]William Harper, *Hebrew Method and Manual,* p. 90. Also, Free, *op. cit.,* p. 30.

[6]Ira M. Price, *The Monuments and the Old Testament,* p. 110.

[7]J. McKee Adams, *Ancient Records and the Bible,* p. 12; and W. F. Albright, *From the Stone Age to Christianity,* p. 6.

The Lord God made Adam caretaker of this garden, and gave him the privilege of eating from every tree except the tree of the knowledge of good and evil. This was the only restriction, and any disobedience was to be followed by death.

Also among the Babylonian inscriptions there is an account of a sacred garden containing a tree of life which bore fruit of life-giving qualities. Entrance was granted only to the gods or noted personages. Prominent people used seals with the design of this sacred tree, and often it was carved in the royal palaces in alabaster relief on the wanscoting.[8] This is another testimony to the ancient tradition handed down among nations which did not possess the inspired Scriptures.

   c. *The Institution of the Family.* Man had a definite place and task in the world, but God knew that he needed companionship. "It is not good that the man should be alone," said He; "I will make him a help meet for him" (2:18, ASV). Symbolic of the unity of marriage, God made the woman "bone of his bones, and flesh of his flesh." The pair were to live in the beautiful garden which was adapted to their needs and happiness, while a relationship of holy fellowship between Creator and creature was to be maintained by simple obedience. Here was the beginning of the first family, which God blessed and enjoined to multiply or increase upon the earth. The Hebrew word *ma-le,* translated "replenish" in Gen. 1:28, means to "fill" the earth, but not to "refill" it. The first marriage was performed by Jehovah God himself. The man and woman were to be as one flesh and to cleave to one another.

III. The Fall

For a time everything was pleasant with Adam and Eve. They lived in an atmosphere of primitive holiness, in obedience to the simple commandments God had given them. But the capacity for righteousness through obedience implies the capacity for evil through disobedience. The image of God means the power of self-direction, the ability to choose between alternatives. There could be no personality, no selfhood,

⁸Price, *op. cit.,* p. 111.

without the capacity for choice, and therefore there could be no holiness without the *possibility* of sin. This does not mean that sin was necessary. It does mean that in a moral universe evil is possible.

1. *The Temptation* (Gen. 3:1-5)

As Eve walked in the garden and looked at the beautiful fruit, the serpent recognized his victim. Knowing the best way to deceive her, he first asked a question in a doubtful tone, "Yea, hath God [*Elohim*] said, Ye shall not eat of every tree of the garden?" (3:1) Jehovah God had placed but one restriction on man's dominion (2:17). Yet by the misleading character of his question, the seducer caused Eve to distrust the truth of God's warning. When she quoted it, she omitted the name of the *Lord* God, Jehovah, and repeated only the name *Elohim* (God of power), which had been used by the serpent.

As she looked at the fruit, Eve's desire grew. Satan saw his opportunity and, adding falsehood to doubt, insisted, "Ye shall not surely die; for God [*Elohim*] doth know that in the day ye eat thereof, then your eyes shall be opened, and ye shall be as gods, knowing good and evil" (3:4-5). This treacherous adversary (John 8:44; Rev. 12:9) acknowledged God merely as a God of wisdom and power. He deceived, lied, and appealed to Eve's pride until her human will was in conflict with the known will of God. She made her choice, disregarded her divine Lord, and yielded to the temptation of Satan, heedless of the costly results which were to follow.

2. *The Beginning of Sin* (Gen. 3:6-13)

Eve not only ate of the fruit; she also gave it to Adam, who shared in the disobedience. With their new knowledge of good and evil came a sense of shame. They could not face Jehovah God, so they "hid themselves." They felt a sense of alienation from the Lord Jehovah. They had violated His holiness and love. But the Lord found them in the garden "in the cool of the day," and examined them with the searching question, "Where art thou?" Guiltily they acknowledged their reason for hiding. When questioned again, the man blamed the deed upon his wife, and she in turn traced it to the serpent.

3. *Judgment on Sin* (Gen. 3:14-24)

Judgment was first pronounced upon the serpent, who had been instrumental in the temptation. His curse was to crawl upon the ground for all future time. Then the woman was to suffer the penalty of multiplied sorrows, with enmity existing forever between the serpent and herself and her posterity (3:14-15). Turning to Adam, God said:

> *Because thou hast hearkened unto the voice of thy wife, and hast eaten of the tree, of which I commanded thee, saying, Thou shalt not eat of it all the days of thy life; thorns also and thistles shall it bring forth to thee; and thou shalt eat the herb of the field; in the sweat of thy face shalt thou eat bread, till thou return unto the ground; for out of it wast thou taken: for dust thou art, and unto dust shalt thou return* (Gen. 3:17-19).

Lest Adam and Eve might now partake also of the tree of life and "live for ever," the Lord banished them from the Garden of Eden. "At the east of the garden" God placed two symbols to guard against their return. First were the *cherubim*, which were "living creatures" (Ezek. 10:18-22) and, in Hebrew theology, beings of celestial and sacred nature. They were keepers or guards against any approach to Paradise, stationed there to vindicate God's holiness when outraged by sin. The other symbol was the flaming sword, or literally "the flame of the sword turning itself every way." William G. Blaikie suggests that this eastern gate of Eden, where God's presence was manifested (Gen. 4:14), was the sanctuary where the first couple presented their offerings.[9]

4. *Parallel Accounts of the Fall*

A Babylonian parallel for the fall of man has been found in the Adapa myth on four Babylonian fragments, three of which came from the library of Ashurbanipal at Nineveh, and the fourth from the archives of King Amenhotep IV of Egypt at Tell el-Amarna.[10] The Babylonian Adapa compares with Adam in gaining knowledge which would include divine

[9]William G. Blaikie, *A Manual of Bible History*, p. 25.
[10]Price, *loc. cit.*

attributes but not immortality. Each hero was tempted; each could obtain immortality by eating a certain kind of food. At the close of the story, toil, suffering, and punishment were inflicted upon the man and woman for disobedience in eating food which opened their eyes. Adam and Eve were clothed with skins, and Adapa received a special clothing.

Again, the Old Testament account is far superior. The monotheistic record in Genesis contrasts with the Babylonian polytheism. The Babylonian gods do not possess unity of purpose or action, and the god Ea tells a falsehood to accomplish his purpose. In the Old Testament account, Jehovah is the omnipotent and righteous God, whose nature and will are the law of right for all moral beings.

So-called "Temptation Seals" have also been unearthed in the vicinity of Nineveh. In 1932, the University of Pennsylvania expedition, under the leadership of E. A. Speiser, found an old seal with a picture of a man, a woman, and a serpent.[11] Another unusual seal cylinder, found still earlier, shows a tree in the middle, with a woman on the left and a man on the right. Behind the woman stands a serpent, which "appears to whisper in her ear," while the woman is plucking some fruit.[12] E. J. Banks calls this a date tree.[13] Like parallel accounts of creation, these records imply a widespread tradition based upon the facts recorded in the Scriptures.

5. A Foreshadowing of Redemption

The story of the Fall does not end without some ray of hope. When God pronounced the curse upon the serpent, He added, The seed of the woman "shall bruise thy head, and thou shalt bruise his heel" (Gen. 3:15). We find a statement of the fulfillment of this first prophecy of Christ in Gal. 4:4, "God sent forth his Son, made of a woman"; and in Heb. 2:14, that "through death he might destroy him that had the power of death, that is, the devil."

God clothed Adam and Eve with the skins of animals (3:21). Since meat was not eaten as food until after the Flood, the animals seem to have been slain for sacrifice. At least the shedding of blood was necessary to provide a cover-

---

[11]G. A. Barton, *Archaeology and the Bible*, p. 46.
[12]Price, *op. cit.*, pp. 115-16.
[13]Edgar J. Banks, *The Bible and the Spade*, p. 24.

ing for those so keenly conscious of their sin. As we turn to the study of the next generation of mankind, we find that Cain and Abel possessed some knowledge of what an acceptable sacrifice should be.

IV. DEGENERATION

After the Fall, conscience awoke in man to distinguish good as obedience and evil as disobedience to the known will of God. The record of Genesis 4 and 5 is the story of the soon-appearing fruit of sin.

1. *The Second Generation* (Gen. 4:1-16)

In the second generation, the elder Cain and his younger brother Abel presented their offerings to the Lord. The words "In process of time," or literally, "At the end of days," (4:3) indicate a stated time or appointed occasion which had been set for offering sacrifices. The two brothers were a decided contrast in every way. Cain was a "tiller of the ground," and Abel a "keeper of sheep." Cain brought as his offering the fruit of the ground, a thank offering which did not express any sorrow for sin. Abel offered a sacrifice from his flock, and in the shedding of blood presented a sin offering. The laws of sacrifices in the Old Testament all point forward to the final sacrificial death of Christ on Calvary. Abel's lamb was the first lamb of sacrifice. Christ was the last: "Behold the Lamb of God, which taketh away the sin of the world" (John 1:29). Christ was the "Lamb without spot," "slain before the foundation of the world" (I Pet. 1:19-20); and He gave "himself for an offering and a sacrifice to God" (Eph. 5:2).

a. The First Murderer. We read in Heb. 11:4, "By faith Abel offered unto God a more excellent sacrifice than Cain, by which he obtained witness that he was righteous, God testifying of his gifts." Cain did not have the faith of Abel. Therefore God could not accept Cain's offering as He did Abel's (4:4-5). This angered the jealous Cain, and "his countenance fell." Jehovah showed the love of a kind Redeemer. "Why art thou wroth?" He asked, "and why is thy countenance fallen?" (4:6) In a mild rebuke, He still reminded Cain of the opportunity of turning to the right way: "If thou doest well, shalt thou not be accepted?" But the self-willed Cain would not be corrected. In jealous rage he killed his brother Abel. Here, in the second generation, hatred made Cain the first murderer, and loyalty to God made Abel the first martyr.

b. *The Exile of Cain.* For Cain's crime, he was "cursed from the earth" and banished as a "fugitive and vagabond" (4:12). "My punishment is greater than I can bear," he said, fearing the vengeance he might meet. Therefore the Lord placed a mark on Cain to give him unusual protection and pronounced a sevenfold vengeance on anyone who would slay him. Here is suggested the early prevalence of blood revenge which later become so firmly established among the Arabic tribes. If any member of a clan received violence, it was the duty of any other member to take vengeance on the offending clan. If the murderer was a member of the same clan as the slain, the penalty was banishment. Therefore we read, "Cain went out from the presence of the Lord, and dwelt in the land of Nod [or land of wandering], on the east of Eden" (4:16).

It is interesting to note that in the time of the judges a tribe of nomads called Kenites (the same Hebrew root-term as Cain) joined the Israelites (Judg. 1:16). If Cain was the ancestor of the Kenites, as the Hebrew implies, then the tribe would receive special protection from other hostile tribes. A. R. Gordon suggests that the cry, "Cain shall be avenged sevenfold," may have become an old Kenite war cry.[14]

2. *The Beginnings of Civilization* (Gen. 4:16-26)

After Cain's banishment, the Cainite population rapidly increased, and the beginnings of an agricultural and cultural civilization appeared.

a. *The Cainite Civilization.* Cain was the builder of the first city, which he named "Enoch" after his son. This marked the beginning of urban life. In the sixth generation, Lamech had three sons: Jabal, Jubal, and Tubal-cain.

Jabal, who was the father of tent dwellers and shepherds, began to develop agriculture and cattle raising.

Jubal, the "father of all such as handle the harp and the

---

[14]A. R. Gordon, *Early Traditions of Genesis*, p. 191. Other scholars hold that "Kenite" is derived from the Hebrew "Smith."

organ" (*'ughav*, flute or pipe), was the herald of culture in music (4:21). The harp represents the stringed instrument, and the organ or flute is a wind instrument often identified with the old pastoral pipe of Pan. Evidence of early music on both harp and lyre has been furnished by archaeology from excavations at Ur of the Chaldees.[15] The early harp was represented on old Babylonian and Egyptian monuments with Semitic musicians. It was a portable lyre, enclosed in a framework of special wood such as sandalwood, and supported by a kettle-shaped sounding box. Over this were stretched three to six strings which were either picked with the fingers or stuck with a metal plectrum.

Tubal-cain was "instructor of every artificer in brass and iron" (4:22), becoming the father of metalwork of various kinds. Ancient cutting instruments of bronze and iron used for war and for agriculture have been found in Mesopotamia.[16]

Although rapid strides were made in material civilization, any true religious feeling was sadly lacking. Therefore we are not surprised when we learn that the Cainite civilization, with all its culture, finally found its highest expression in the so-called "Song of Lamech" or "Song of the Sword" (4:23-24).

b. *Early Poetry.* The "Song of Lamech" is a song of revenge in which Lamech sang his praise of the sword as a more effective weapon of vengeance than even divine aid. These six lines of Hebrew poetry are composed with neither rhyme nor meter, but have a form of Oriental parallelism which is a "kind of measured rhythm in lines, reflecting an inner rhythm of thought or feeling." A. R. Gordon says this fierce lay of Lamech was doubtless chanted to "strongly-marked rhythm."[17] With these lines, the record of the career of Cain's descendants comes to an end because they did not contribute to the development of God's plan of redemption.

c. *Abel's Successor.* After the death of Abel, God

---

[15]O. R. Sellars, "Musical Instruments of Israel," *Biblical Archaeologist*, Vol. 4, No. 3 (September, 1941), pp. 33-39.

[16]William F. Albright, "Present State of Syro-Palestine Archaeology," *Haverford Symposium on Archaeology and the Bible*, pp. 9-10. Also Millar Burrows, *What Mean These Stones?* p. 158.

[17]A. R. Gordon, *Poets of the Old Testament*, p. 51.

raised up a new spiritual successor to become the ancestor of the Messiah. This was Seth, a younger son of Adam and Eve (4:25-26). Hence it is Seth's name which stands at the head of the genealogies leading to Christ.

3. *The Families of Cain and Seth* (Gen. 5:1-32)

As the genealogies of Cain and of Seth are recorded, we notice the contrasting character of the two ways of life represented. The line of Cain lists six generations. Cain, the first, was a murderer; and Lamech, the last, was the second recorded murderer, the first polygamist, and the first outspoken promoter of blood revenge. Although the Cainites excelled in material civilization, not one "walked with God." After six generations, the Cainite line was dropped from the sacred records.

In contrast, the line of Seth (5:6-32) carries on the spiritual emphasis. Ten names are listed here of those who became founders of religious worship. Enoch was the first after the Fall to be mentioned for his fellowship with God. His devotion, his spirituality, and his entrance into eternal life without passing through the experience of death are told in simple and stately language: "And Enoch walked with God; and he was not; for God took him" (5:24).

Another characteristic is the length of life noted in the family of Seth. Seth himself lived 912 years, and the others named lived for more than 900 years with the exception of Mahalaleel, Enoch, and Lamech. Methuselah lived to be the oldest man, according to the Hebrew records. Similar records of longevity have been found on Babylonian tablets. This would indicate a longer span of life before the Flood, before the harmful effects of sin and disease had spread too far.

The tenth and last name in the line of Seth is Noah, who became God's representative in the days of moral degeneration as the Deluge drew near. As Lamech, last of the wicked Cainites, had three sons, so Noah, last of the virtuous Sethites, also had three sons. These became ancestors of the three great races of mankind.

V. NOAH AND THE FLOOD

After the lapse of 10 generations, a widespread corruption existed upon the earth. Cainites and Sethites had reached great heights in civilization, yet compromise and degeneracy had done its evil work. As the population increased, the sons of Seth, known as the "sons of God" (6:2), married the daughters of Cain, called also the "daughters of men." From these alliances arose giants, or "mighty men" (*Nephilim*) in physical power. God declared that His Spirit should "not always strive with man" (6:3), and that the span of life should be limited to 120 years. So great was human depravity that God changed His course of action ("repented") with regard to man. Kindness and warnings had been of no avail, so judgment at last must come in the form of a flood which should destroy all life from the earth. Only Noah and his family, who had proved their loyalty by obedience, were to be saved.

1. *Instructions Before the Flood* (Gen. 6:1—7:5)

God instructed Noah to make an ark, or bargelike vessel, of gopherwood or pitchwood, with three stories divided into rooms, and covered with pitch on the outside and on the inside. The length was to be approximately 450 feet, the width 75 feet, and the height 45 feet (reckoning 18 inches to the cubit). There was to be one window at the top, and one door at the side. At God's command, Noah was to bring into the ark his wife, his three sons, and their wives, a total of only eight human beings. He was also to bring into the ark one pair of each of the unclean animals, and seven pairs of all clean animals for sacrifice or food. The distinction between "clean" and "unclean" animals is thus seen to have been made long before the Mosaic law given in Leviticus 11. Animals were classified as "clean" or "unclean" according to whether they were "proper" or "improper" for sacrifice and food. Provisions for 12 months were to be stored for all in the ark.

Taking the dimensions of the ark as here described, Dr. J. P. Free has calculated that the three floors could accommodate 43,000 tons. The ordinary ocean liner of today can carry only about 25,000 tons, or a little over half the capacity of the ark. "There would have been plenty of room in the three decks of the ark for Noah, his family, the animals, and their food."[18]

[18]Free, *op. cit.*, pp. 41-42.

2. *The Flood* (Gen. 7:6—9:17)

Noah was obedient in "all that God commanded him" (6:22). When he and his family entered the ark, he had reached the age of 600 years. It was in the second month of that year when "all the fountains of the great deep [were] broken up, and the windows of heaven were opened" (7:11). The rain fell in torrential floods, and the ark floated upon the waters. On the seventeenth day of the seventh month, it was miraculously grounded on one of the mountains of Ararat, in what is now Armenia. In the tenth month the mountain peaks appeared; and after another 40 days Noah began to send out the raven and then the dove "to see if the waters were abated from the face of the ground" (8:6-8). When the dove finally returned with an olive leaf, Noah knew that the floodwaters had receded. When at last the dove did not return, he knew the earth was almost dry. He still remained in the ark until God commanded him to leave with all his household and their belongings. Altogether Noah spent one year in the ark.

a. Noah's Sacrifice. As Noah left the ark, his first act was to build an altar to the Lord and offer burnt offerings of every clean beast and fowl (8:20). God showed His approval, and promised never to smite the earth thus again, but that "seedtime and harvest, cold and heat, and summer and winter" should continue as long as the duration of the earth (8:21-22). There is a Jewish tradition that Noah built his altar in the same place where Adam had first built an altar, also used by Cain and Abel.[19]

b. The First Covenant. Now that the Flood was over, there were many changes both in nature and in human life. In the atmosphere, with the coming of seasons, and heat and cold, the way was open for heavy storms and for the appearance of the first rainbow. Before that time, the direct rays of the sun apparently did not pierce through the "watery canopy" above to scatter in the form of a beautiful rainbow. In accepting Noah's sacrifice, God made His first covenant with man, using the rainbow as a symbol of His everlasting mercy. Included in the covenant were (1) the pledge of no other universal human destruction by a flood, (2) man's

[19]Adam Clarke, *Commentary on the Holy Bible,* I, 77.

increase and dominion over animal life, (3) the use of animal food, and (4) a death penalty for murder (9:1-17).

3. Parallel Accounts

There are many Babylonian accounts of a flood in the Mesopotamian area. The great Gilgamesh Epic was inscribed on 12 tablets and once belonged to the Royal Library of Ashurbanipal at Nineveh. The story on the eleventh tablet most closely resembles that of Genesis. In each case, a divine revelation of an impending calamity was given to only one man. The events were much the same, but the purpose of the flood was different. The Babylonian gods had their differences and sent the flood because of a passing whim. In excavations at Ur, a deposit of eight feet of clay was found between the later and earlier civilizations. Here is supporting evidence that the Flood extended to include all civilization in the inhabited earth. These records point to a common origin for the flood story, but the Old Testament shows that "the light of a true knowledge of God has never been wholly extinguished among men."[20]

4. Noah and His Three Sons (Gen. 9:18-29)

After the Deluge, Noah took up agriculture and cultivated a vineyard. Many believe that Noah's drunkenness was due to the fact that he knew nothing of the effects of fermented wine before he drank it. Certainly there is no record of his continued drinking.

Noah's final benediction upon his three sons is the earliest "triumphal ode," so called from its expression of "national hope and aspiration."[21] The character of each son was revealed. Shem, the Hebrew hope, received the greatest blessing. He and his posterity were to be the ancestors of the Christ, and to bear a special relationship to the Redeemer Jehovah. The "Lord God" of Shem had been the "Lord God" of Adam, and was later to be the "Lord God" of Abraham (24:7). Japheth was to be enlarged, as he became the ancestor of those nations which are most progressive in government, science, and art. He was to "dwell in the tents of Shem," by accepting the worship of the "Lord God" of Shem. The curse

[20]Banks, *op. cit.*, p. 33.
[21]A. R. Gordon, *Poets of the Old Testament*, p. 37.

was upon Canaan, the son of Ham, and is often thought to be related to the idolatrous tendencies of the Canaanites. The Canaanites were later subjugated by the Israelitish descendants of Shem when they took possession of their promised land of Palestine. The poem bears the popular name, "The Curse of Canaan."

VI. The Beginning of Races and Languages

The "Generations of the Sons of Noah," in the tenth chapter of Genesis, traces the ethnic and geographic relations of mankind. Broadly considered, from these descend the three great races: the white, the black, and the yellow. Their geographic settlement is sometimes delimited as Europe, Africa, and Asia. Dr. Ira M. Price identifies these as the northern zone of Japheth, the southern zone of Ham, and the middle zone of Shem.[22]

1. *The Beginning of Races* (Genesis 10)

The seven sons of Japheth include the Caucasian peoples of Europe, among them the Greeks, Romans, Spaniards, and Anglo-Saxons, who have been rulers for 2,500 years. The four sons of Ham seem to have located around the lower Euphrates at first, and in the valley of the Nile in Egypt. The "mighty hunter," Nimrod, extended his kingdom to include the cities of Babel, Erech, Accad, and Calneh, from Babylonia to Assyria. The five sons of Shem peopled western Mesopotamia and Syria. Shem was called "the father of all the children of Eber" (10:21), from which statement many have derived the word "Hebrew." However, this is usually thought to be connected with the pilgrimage of Abraham, since the word means "one from the other side," "a crosser," or nomad. The Semitic family has given to the world its three great monotheistic religions: Hebrew, Mohammedan, and Christian.

2. *The Beginning of Languages* (Gen. 11:1-9)

As the families of Noah's three sons slowly migrated, they were still speaking one language. When they reached the plain of Shinar (or Sumeria) in the lower Tigris-Euphrates valley, they decided to build a capital city with a mammoth

[22]Ira M. Price, *A Syllabus of Old Testament History*, pp. 38-39.

tower which should "reach the skies." In egotism and self-will, they planned to prevent any future dispersion.

However, they reckoned without the Lord. As the building progressed, God's judgment fell upon the unity of their language. He confounded their language so that they could no longer understand one another, and scattered them abroad throughout the earth. The very name "Babel" is typical of this confusion of languages. In Arabic and Assyrian, it signifies "the Gate of God." While human ambition was trying to reach the Gate of God, the Lord rebuked this willfulness. Even the word for "Gate of God" in Assyrian was confused with the Hebrew *balal,* which means "confusion."

Many remains of ancient towers or ziggurats have been unearthed in Babylonia. Each city was built around the temple of its local god, and on top of this temple was a tower or shrine for the worship of that god. The Babylonian ziggurat was constructed of either burnt or sun-dried bricks, with three to seven stories, often in colors. Each story or stage had steps leading to the next story, both straight and winding stairways being used. The record of the destruction of one ziggurat reads as follows: "The building of this temple offended the gods. In a night they threw down what had been built. They scattered them abroad and made strange their speech."[23] The remains of these towers fell into the posession of later peoples in Mesopotamia, and became forerunners of the Mohammedan mosque.

3. The Generations of Shem (Gen. 11: 10-32)

"The generations of Shem" logically continue the "generations of Adam" in chapter 5. Adam's line was traced to Noah and his three sons, Shem, Ham, and Japheth. "The generations of Shem" are recorded as far as Abraham, where they reach their culmination in the history of primitive men as individuals, and their beginning in the history of God's chosen people. They form a transition from "general" history to Hebrew history, wherein the patriarchal era begins.

SUMMARY

The Bible opens with the sublime account of creation, the best answer ever offered to man's perennial questions,

---

[23]S. L. Caiger, *Bible and Spade,* p. 29.

"Whence? Whither? Why?" The first words, "In the beginning God," give the key to unlock all the Old Testament. The early chapters of Genesis take us back into the dawn of human existence, and help us understand many of its most puzzling mysteries. Although sin marred God's plan for man, we see the first steps taken toward the redemption of the race. The selection of Seth, of Noah, and of Shem, in the midst of the rapid moral degeneration of humanity, points ahead to the fulfillment of God's redemptive purpose through a chosen people. In the next chapter, we see the further development of this divine purpose in the lives of the patriarchs.

RECOMMENDED READINGS

Blaikie and Matthews, *A Manual of Bible History,* pp. 1-33.

Alfred Edersheim, *The Bible History,* Volume I, pp. 17-72.

Joseph P. Free, *Archaeology and Old Testament History,* pp. 11-47.

J. A. Huffman, *Voices from the Rocks and Dust Heaps of Bible Lands,* pp. 48-72.

James C. Muir, *His Truth Endureth,* pp. 9-33.

R. L. Ottley, *A Short History of the Hebrews to the Roman Period,* pp. 1-22.

Ira Maurice Price, *The Dramatic Story of the Old Testament History,* pp. 43-55.

L. R. Ringenberg, *The Word of God in History,* pp. 15-39.

J. R. Sampey, *The Heart of the Old Testament,* pp. 15-27.

———, *Syllabus for Old Testament Study,* pp. 66-71.

Merrill F. Unger, *Archaeology and the Old Testament,* pp. 26-104.

FOR FURTHER STUDY

1. By what names or titles are the first five books of the Bible known? What are the conservative and liberal views of their authorship?

2. Review the first 11 chapters of Genesis, and list all of the "beginnings" you can find there: e.g., the beginning of matter, light, life, the family, sin, etc.

3. What do you think the "Epic of Creation" teaches concerning the nature of God? What great questions does it answer?

4. Look up definitions for atheism, agnosticism, pantheism, polytheism, and monotheism.

5. How many times does the word "create" occur in Genesis 1? The word "made" or the phrase "let there be"? What is the difference?

6. In what sense is man "a creature of two worlds"? What do you think is meant by "the image of God" in the creation of man?

7. What is the capacity which most clearly distinguishes man from the animal species?

8. What is the bearing of the Babylonian creation myths and Sabbath laws upon the Mosaic record?

9. Comment on the difference between Elohim and Jehovah as names for God. See if you can discover the difference in the way these names are translated in the Authorized Version by comparing Genesis 1 and Genesis 2.

10. Where is Eden thought to have been located?

11. In what sense does the capacity for choice imply the possibility of evil? If Adam and Eve had been incapable of sin could they have been capable of righteousness?

12. What parallels can you find between the temptation of Adam and Eve in the garden, and the temptation of Christ in the wilderness (Matt. 4:1-11)? Also compare the first Adam's attitude toward God's will in the Garden of Eden with that of the second Adam (I Cor. 15:45) in the Garden of Gethsemane.

13. Discuss the relationship between the garments of skins with which the first couple were clothed and their sin.

14. Describe the "way of Cain" about which Jude speaks in Jude 11.

15. What were the major developments in the Cainite civilization? How is it contrasted with that of Seth's descendants?

16. Who are the "sons of God" and the "daughters of men" in Gen. 6:2?

17. What would you say to be the meaning of Christ when He said, "As it was in the days of Noe, so shall it be also in the days of the Son of man" (Luke 17:26)?

18. Look up some of the archaeological material that verifies the account of the Flood (see material listed above in recommended reading).

19. What racial and geographical divisions are represented by the three sons of Noah?

20. What do you think were the motives of the builders of the Tower of Babel?

21. What has been the character of the history throughout the first 11 chapters of Genesis? How does it compare with that which follows?

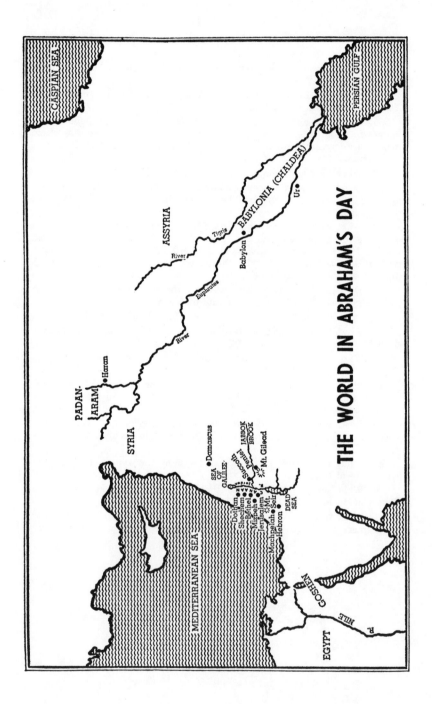

THE WORLD IN ABRAHAM'S DAY

CHAPTER IV

The Age of the Patriarchs

By faith Abraham . . . went out, not knowing whither he went
(Heb. 11:8).

Sources: Genesis 12—50

To Be Read: Genesis 12—13; 15; 17; 22; 24; 27—32; 37;
39—45; 49—50

Period: Approximately 2100 B.C. to 1850 B.C.

With the twelfth chapter of Genesis, we enter a new era
in Bible history. After the very earliest days, the Scriptures
make no attempt to report the history of the entire human
race. However, much more attention is given to the development of civilization at large in the opening chapters of Genesis
than in the remainder of the book. We now take up the story
of Abraham, and those of his descendants whom God chose
to be the "channel of blessing" for all nations. The first eleven
chapters of Genesis covers a period of more than 2,000 years
of human history. The remaining 39 chapters cover the lives
of four men in a period of about 250 years.

I. ABRAHAM, THE FAITHFUL

About 21 centuries before Christ, God began the unfolding of His divine purpose. The first events took place in
the famous city of "Ur of the Chaldees," mentioned in the
Hammurabi Code,[1] and located on the Euphrates in southern
Mesopotamia near the Persian Gulf. With all its culture, art,
and learning, this great city was the center of rank paganism
and nature worship. Its religion demanded the worship of
many gods, with the sun and moon and other heavenly bodies
as the leading divinities.

In this environment, a family of the "sons of Shem" had
settled under the leadership of their shepherd-father Terah,
in the eighth generation from Noah. Terah had three sons,
Abram, Nahor, and Haran, the latter meeting an early death.

[1]Robert Francis Harper, *The Code of Hammurabi*, p. 5.

Although Abram's name is mentioned first, he is generally thought to have been the youngest. Terah's family seems to have been very close-knit. Abram took a marked interest in his nephew Lot, the only son of his deceased brother, Haran; and he even married his half sister Sarai (20:12). As Abram followed pastoral life and farming, his rapid increase in possessions soon demanded a large number of servants, all of whom seemed to manifest unusual loyalty to their master. Abram was God's choice to become the pilgrim father of the Hebrew people, in whom all nations of the earth should be blessed.

1. *First Period—The Call of Abram* (Gen. 12:1-3)

"The God of glory" (Acts 7:2) appeared to Abram, giving him a call which could not be mistaken: "Get thee out of thy country, and from thy kindred, and from thy father's house, unto a land that I will shew thee: and I will make of thee a great nation, and I will bless thee, and make thy name great; and thou shalt be a blessing: and I will bless them that bless thee, and curse him that curseth thee: and in thee shall all families of the earth be blessed" (12:1-3).

This call was the first of a series of marvelous appearances of God to man, leading at last to the Incarnation. For Abram, who was 75 years of age at the time, it marked the beginning of a new era and established a basis for his entire future. The key to his life was now obedience, separation, and friendship. Separation from his family and former friends was to win for him the unique title of being "the friend of God" (Jas. 2:23). Just now this call involved the hardship of leaving home, country, and associates for the great unknown. But "he obeyed . . . not knowing whither he went" (Heb. 11:8).

According to Josh. 24:2, 14, Terah had already been influenced by the idolatry of his neighbors. The Jewish tradition relates that Abram had been persecuted by many of the Chaldeans for not comforming to their pagan worship. Perhaps for these reasons, the family of Terah, including Abram, Lot, and probably Nahor, had left Ur and moved to Haran, a city some 600 miles northwest of Ur, in an area which came to be known as Padan-aram. Located on a branch of the Euphrates, Haran had become a center of Babylonian trade and of moon-worship, with laws and customs resembling those of Ur. The two cities of Ur and Haran were at the two extremities of Mesopotamia. For the most part, the family of Terah settled at Haran, and Terah himself lived there the remainder of his life.

2. *The Great Migration* (Gen. 12: 4—14: 24)

After the death of his father, Terah, Abram, in obedience to the call of God, set forth on his long pilgrimage. This meant leaving his brother, Nahor, and his family. It also meant transporting a great household with dozens of servants, many tents of dark camel's hair, hundreds of camels, and perhaps several thousand sheep and cattle. One with less faith would certainly have staggered at the command. Taking Sarai and his nephew Lot, Abram followed the highway southward from Haran through the Syrian desert, the long road through the Lebanon and Anti-Lebanon valleys toward Damascus, which was the gateway to Canaan. Henceforth this area which became known as the "Fertile Crescent" was to be the center of the Old Testament world.

When the caravan stopped at Shechem in the plain of Moreh, about 30 miles north of the later site of Jerusalem, God again appeared unto Abram. The Lord had said before, "Get thee out . . . unto a land that I will shew thee" (12:1-3). Now God appeared with the definite promise of this particular land for the family inheritance. Abram erected his first altar near Shechem by an oak or terebinth tree. Later he moved his camp to a mountain east of Bethel, where again "he called upon the name of the Lord" (12:8). These places and many others in Abram's journey have been excavated, and the sacred spot of Abram's sacrifice at Bethel is still revered today.

a. The First Famine—a Test. As Abram left Bethel and continued his southward journey, a severe drought and famine struck the land. The test was more than Abram's faith could stand. Had not God pointed out this country for his inheritance? Was this parched terrain the Promised Land? Blinded by difficulties, Abram's courage failed, and he did not consult the Lord for guidance. As did many other Asiatic Semites of his day,[2] he left for distant Egypt.

When Abram arrived in Egypt, he became fearful for his life. The Pharaoh had been known to force a beautiful woman

[2]James H. Breasted, *A History of Egypt*, p. 188.

into his court, and then to order the murder of her husband.[3] Abram persuaded Sarai to pose as his sister. When the Egyptians expressed their admiration for her beauty, Pharaoh took Sarai and gave Abram courteous treatment until his land was afflicted with plagues from Jehovah, and the deception was discovered. It was then Pharaoh's turn to be fearful. "What is it that thou hast done to me?" he said in reproof to Abram. "Take thy wife and go thy way." With Pharaoh's assistance, Abram and his household returned to Bethel, and again "called on the name of the Lord" (13:4).

b. *Lot's Choice*. As Abram and Lot became more wealthy in flocks and herds, the shortage of good pastureland caused disputes among the herdsmen. To avoid trouble, Abram took the initiative, offering Lot his choice of land, either the fertile lowlands of the Jordan valley or the more austere highlands of Canaan. Lured by the prospect of easy riches, Lot chose the "well watered" plain of the Jordan, and "pitched his tent toward Sodom," a center of notorious wickedness. But Abram took God's choice and "dwelled in the land of Canaan." The Lord at this time gave him again His promise: "Lift up now thine eyes . . . all the land which thou seest, to thee will I give it . . . Arise, walk through the land in the length of it and in the breadth of it; for I will give it unto thee" (13:14-17).

c. *Abram the Hebrew*. In an early genealogy (10:21), Shem was called "the father of all the children of Eber." Now Abram, when at last he had settled at Hebron in the Promised Land, is first called "the Hebrew." Both terms are thought to be derived from the same Hebrew root meaning "to pass over." At least, Abram was thus distinguished from a Babylonian *Abarama,* whose name has been found on Babylonian tablets in connection with the business transactions of a small farmer.[4]

d. *The First War Recorded in Scripture*. While Abram was in Hebron, a refugee informed him that a foreign confederacy of four Mesopotamian kings had invaded the Jordan plain and Lot and his friends had been captured. To rescue Lot, Abram secured some of the neighboring Amorites as his

[3]Blaikie and Matthews, *Manual of Bible History,* pp. 40-41.
[4]Ira M. Price, *The Monuments and the Old Testament,* p. 169.

allies, and took 318 of his household servants. Together they pushed their way across the hills and up the Jordan valley until in a surprise night attack the enemy was routed. Lot and his friends were recaptured at Damascus, and the spoils recovered.

In the monuments, there is a striking resemblance between four names of Mesopotamian kings there inscribed and those recorded in Gen. 14:1. These are Hammurabi of Shinar or Babylon, Ericku of Larsa, Kudurlachgumal of Elam, and Tudchula of Gutim in north Babylonia.[5]

The priest Melchizedek, king of Salem, is first introduced at this time. On Abram's return home, Melchizedek met him and presented to him and his soldiers bread and wine, the memorials of sacrifice. As a priest of God, he blessed Abram in the name of the "most high God, possessor of heaven and earth." In return, Abram gave tithes of his booty to Melchizedek. Heb. 6:20 names Christ "a high priest for ever after the order of Melchisedec."

3. *Settled Life* (Gen. 15:1—21:34)

From this time, Abram began to lead a more settled life at Hebron. God appeared to him again by night, and renewed the covenant promise. This is the first time in which God's revelation is called "the word of the Lord," as later given in John 1:1. It is also the first conversation expressed in words between God and man after the Fall in the Garden of Eden. Abram of late had been fearful. He had sacrificed much to obey God. Yet he had no son of his own, and no heir except his servant Eliezer. God began the conversation, brushed aside the legal inheritance of Eliezer, and definitely promised Abram a child of his own. Outside the tent, He showed Abram the stars, which indicated how numerous would be his descendants. Abram "believed in the Lord," and God "counted it to him for righteousness." Paul, in Rom. 4:1-5, uses this event as one basis for the doctrine of justification by faith. Abram had no merit by works, but his faith was the basis for his righteousness.

a. Ratification of the Covenant. To ratify the covenant, Abram was ordered to sacrifice three full-grown animals,

[5]James C. Muir, *His Truth Endureth,* p. 43.

each three years old, a heifer, a she goat, and a ram; and then two young birds, a turtledove and a young pigeon (15:9). This list includes all the animals which were acceptable for sacrifice in the later Mosaic law (Leviticus 1). As the death of the animal signified punishment, so the sacrifice indicated atonement to God.

Jehovah gave Abram a glimpse of the future. Abram's descendants would serve in a foreign land for four centuries, but would be released in "the fourth generation." As for Abram himself, he would go to his "fathers in peace," and would "be buried in a good old age." Adam Clarke sees in this the immortality of the soul in a spiritual world, a place separate from the burial of the body.[6]

b. *The Birth of Ishmael.* After Abram had lived in Canaan for 10 years, he became impatient waiting for the promised son. In accordance with an old law of the country which they had left, Sarai gave her bond servant Hagar to Abram for a secondary wife.[7] This was her own idea, not in the plan of God; and this act was destined to bring only trouble to Abram. At the age of 86, Abram became the father of Ishmael, the son of the maid Hagar.

c. *Abram Called Abraham.* At the age of 99, Abram was given renewed assurance that Sarai would be the mother of the son God had promised. Abram could hardly believe the words of the almighty God. His love of Ishmael, then a lad of 13 years, cried out, "O that Ishmael might live before thee!" It was in connection with this renewed promise that Abram's name was changed to Abraham, "father of a multitude," and Sarai became "Princess" Sarah.

The institution of circumcision was now given as a seal of the covenant. Circumcision was to be the outer symbol of separation from pagan worship. No evidences of the rite have been discovered in Babylonia, but many instances are found in Egyptian tombs and reliefs.[8]

d. *The Deliverance of Lot from Sodom.* Soon three angelic guests stopped at the door of Abraham's tent in Mamre. The promise of a son to Sarah and Abraham was

[6]*Op. cit.,* I, 108.
[7]Harper, *op. cit.,* p. 51, Law No. 145.
[8]Joseph P. Free, *Archaeology and Bible History,* p. 60.

repeated. When two of the guests left for Sodom, the other Divine Guest informed Abraham of the impending destruction of the wicked cities, Sodom and Gomorrah. Abraham was much concerned. Would not Lot be destroyed? Alone, Abraham interceded for Sodom. "Wilt thou also destroy the righteous with the wicked?" he prayed. Six times he persisted, but not even 10 righteous persons could be found in the doomed cities.

The two angels arrived at Sodom toward evening, and found Lot sitting in the gate of the city, where a group might often be seen on the built-in seats of the city gate.[9] Abraham's prayer for his nephew had prevailed. In the morning the angels led Lot and his family from the city with the injunction, "Look not behind thee." The cities of the plain were soon in flames. Lot and his daughters escaped, but Lot's wife looked back and "became a pillar of salt." The doom of the cities is often cited in the Old Testament to warn others who are "pitching their tents" near Sodom. It is believed today that the cities are covered by the southern waters of the Dead Sea. Christ referred to the event when He said, "Remember Lot's wife" (Luke 17:32). As Lot and his family escaped, they settled the eastern highlands "above the Jordan" and became ancestors of the two tribes Moab and Ammon (19:37-38). Though related to Israel, the Israelites looked down upon both tribes.

e. Abraham at Gerar. Abraham now moved southward to Gerar near Kadesh. Through fear, as formerly with Pharaoh, he called Sarah his sister, and the word reached the Philistine king Abimelech, who took her into his harem. But God warned the king in a dream, and he restored Sarah to Abraham. A treaty was made between the two, later ratified by a covenant at Beersheba.

In due time Abraham realized the fulfillment of God's promise in Isaac, his son and legal heir. The boy was named Isaac, "laughter," because his father and mother had laughed at the idea of having this son. On the eighth day Isaac was circumcised, and when he was weaned, "Abraham made a great feast." The conduct of Ishmael at this time betrayed his jealousy, for he taunted his young half brother, and pre-

[9]George A. Barton, *Archaeology and the Bible*, p. 170.

sumed to be the rightful heir. His mother, Hagar, had previously displayed the same presumptuous spirit toward Sarah, and one time had even been driven away by Sarah's severe treatment. A provision is found in the Code of Hammurabi dealing with a slave girl who would try to rank with her mistress.[10] Accordingly, both Hagar and Ishmael were exiled, at Sarah's request, never to return. It was a sad day for Abraham when, the next morning, he took them to the wilderness of Beersheba and left them there in God's providential care.

4. *Abraham and Isaac* (Gen. 22:1—25:18)

Since the first divine summons to Abraham, he had met the demand for separation three times: first, from country and kindred; second, from Lot; and third, from Ishmael, the son of the flesh. Now came Abraham's fourth and supreme test. The Lord said, "Take now . . . thine only son Isaac, whom thou lovest, and get thee into the land of Moriah; and offer him there for a burnt offering upon one of the mountains which I will tell thee of" (22:2).

a. The Supreme Test. Why sacrifice this only son of promise? It was true that the Phoenicians and other pagan nations offered human sacrifices, especially their firstborn, who were regarded as sacred to their gods.[11] But this seemed contrary to God's teaching. However, Abraham did not falter. He did exactly as Jehovah required, meeting the test by faith. Father and son made the three-day journey to Mount Moriah, built an altar, and Isaac was bound upon the wood. As Abraham's hand was raised the voice of the Lord broke the tense silence, "Lay not thine hand upon the lad." God had required only obedience; He had himself provided a ram as a substitute, in accordance with the later law given with regard to the firstborn of the Hebrews (Exod. 34:20). The ram stands as a type of Christ, who became the Substitute for us in redemption. The covenant was renewed, the promise strengthened, and father and son returned first to Beersheba and then to Hebron. There is still a rock altar at Jerusalem on Mount

[10]Harper, *op. cit.,* p. 51, Law No. 145; cf. Hittite Code, Law No. 31 in Barton, *op. cit.,* pp. 409-10.

[11]Barton, *op. cit.,* p. 216.

Moriah, now within the Mosque of Omar, where sacrificial victims were offered in Solomon's and Herod's Temple.[12] Later the Redeemer, the only Son of God, offered himself near this same place as a supreme Sacrifice for all humanity.

b. *The Burial of Sarah at Machpelah.* Sarah died in Hebron at the age of 127 years. She is the only woman whose age is recorded in Scripture. She was the first occupant of the Machpelah cave which Abraham bought from Ephron the Hittite as a burial place. The purchase price of 400 shekels of silver was not coined as today, but "weighed." By this transaction Abraham proved his faith in the promise of God that the land should be his, and belong to his descendants. Today a Moslem mosque stands at this site, having been partly investigated by a British officer under Lord Allenby during World War I.[13]

c. *The Marriage of Isaac.* When Isaac was 40 years of age, Abraham instructed his faithful steward Eliezer to go to Haran to secure a wife for Isaac from Abraham's kindred. He made the journey with camels and gifts, calling upon God for guidance. At the village well in the city of Nahor, and in direct answer to prayer, Eliezer met Rebekah, granddaughter of Nahor, who was Abraham's brother. She provided drink for the camels, and invited the stranger to spend the night with her people. The family welcomed him, and the next morning the lovely Rebekah consented to go with Eliezer to become the bride of Isaac. Isaac, walking and meditating in the fields, met the returning caravan. Rebekah "became his wife; and he loved her: and Isaac was comforted after his mother's death." In this beautiful story many find a type of Christ in Isaac, of the Church in his bride, and of the Holy Spirit in Eliezer.

d. *Abraham's Closing Years.* After the death of Sarah, Abraham married Keturah and became the ancestor of the Midianites and other Arabic tribes. But he "gave all that he had unto Isaac" except a few remembrances for his other children whom he sent away as he had done with Ishmael. At the age of 175 Abraham died and was buried at Machpelah by his two sons, Isaac and Ishmael. At the death of their father,

[12]*Ibid.*, p. 213.

[13]Free, *op. cit.*, p. 67.

all differences were laid aside by the son of promise and the son of law.

"The generations of Ishmael" (25:12-18), the seventh list of generations in the Book of Genesis, records the 12 sons and one daughter of the great desert sheik, who himself lived to be 137 years of age. But with this genealogy the Ishmaelite line was dropped from the history, as it made no contribution to God's purpose in redemption.

II. ISAAC, THE HUMBLE

The sacred record now turns to the "generations of Isaac" (Gen. 25:19 ff.). This is the eighth in the list of 10 "generations" which trace Jehovah's redemptive purpose from Adam through the patriarchal era and on to the 12 tribes of Israel. The account of Isaac's life is interwoven with that of his father, Abraham, for 60 years, and then with his son Jacob for 120 years. We admire this peace-loving, submissive man who offered himself on Abraham's altar, who respected his mother's influence while she lived, and proved such an understanding companion for his wife, Rebekah. We find him walking in the footsteps of his father, cherishing the same lofty faith in Jehovah, who often renewed the Abrahamic covenant with him.

1. *Isaac and His Sons* (Gen. 25:19-34)

Nineteen years after his marriage, which had been childless, Isaac interceded with God for a son to fulfill the promises the Lord had made. God answered, and Rebekah gave birth to twin boys: Jacob, to be the ancestor of the chosen race; and Esau, to be the ancestor of a second nation. This is somewhat similar to Abraham's experience with Isaac and Ishmael. Although Esau was the elder, God's choice fell to Jacob, and it was predicted, "The elder shall serve the younger" (25:23). Even as young men, these two displayed different types of character. "Esau was a cunning hunter, a man of the field; and Jacob was a plain man, dwelling in tents" (25:27). A spirit of rivalry existed between the brothers, which was fostered by their parents and continued on in their posterity. Although Jacob possessed at first a very treacherous nature, he responded to spiritual interests in a way his brother did not.

One day Esau, the favorite of his father, Isaac, returned hungry from the hunt, and bargained with Jacob for a serving of lentils. It was the custom of the day for persons to sell their rights of inheritance for some treasured object.[14] Accordingly, Esau made the sale of his birthright legal with an oath, finished his meal, and "went his way." The unstable Esau had sold all his opportunities for covenant blessings for a mere trifle (Heb. 12:16).

2. Isaac in Gerar of the Philistines (Genesis 26)

When a famine seized the land of Canaan, Isaac took refuge in Gerar in Philistine territory, where another by the name of Abimelech was king. He followed the example of his father by calling Rebekah his sister, without the half-truth which had saved Abram from an outright falsehood. When Abimelech learned the truth, he respected the God of Abraham and Isaac, and protected the chosen family from harm. But Isaac's prosperity incurred the envy of the Philistines, who seemed to feel that his gain was at their expense. They filled with dirt "all the wells which his father's servants had digged in the days of Abraham," contrary to the solemn treaty between Abraham and the former king Abimelech. Finally, the old agreement was renewed, and the well of Beersheba was reopened. During these testing days, God renewed His covenant to Isaac, and Isaac responded by erecting an altar to Jehovah.

3. Jacob and Esau (Gen. 26:34—27:40)

When Esau reached the age of 40, he took two wives from the nearby Hittites: Judith, daughter of Beeri; and Bashemath, daughter of Elon. This was a constant source of grief to Isaac and Rebekah.

The time came for Isaac to pronounce his patriarchal blessing upon his son and heir. Contrary to the divine purpose indicated in the children's birth-song (25:23), Isaac had determined to bestow the blessing upon Esau. As such religious ceremonies were accompanied by eating, Isaac requested Esau to prepare him some "savoury" venison. Rebekah overheard the request and conspired to secure the blessing for her

[14]Edward J. Young, *Introduction to the Old Testament*, p. 64.

favorite younger son. She prepared the "savoury meat," and clothed Jacob "in hairy raiment" to simulate Esau. Isaac, after some hesitation, gave his blessing to the deceitful Jacob. The younger twin should receive the fertile fields and vineyards, and also rulership over the surrounding nations and his mother's posterity. Then came the added blessing spoken in poetic form, and once given to Abraham, "Cursed be every one that curseth thee, and blessed be he that blesseth thee."

Scarcely had Jacob left when Esau entered with the meat he had prepared. The truth dawned upon Isaac. However, the oral blessing in that day was legal and binding.[15] Remorse and anger overcame Esau. "Is not he rightly named Jacob?" said the defrauded brother, "for he hath supplanted me these two times . . . Hast thou not reserved a blessing for me?" Isaac then bestowed a secondary blessing upon Esau. He promised that after a long submission to his brother's people, he would break that yoke. This incident caused a persistent hatred in Esau, destined to divide the two families of Edom and Israel.

4. *Separation of Jacob and Esau* (Gen. 27:41—28:9)

Esau's hatred led to the thought of vengeance. He said, "The days of mourning for my father are at hand; then will I slay my brother Jacob." Rebekah realized Esau's smoldering anger, and prevailed upon Jacob to flee to her brother, Laban, and her father's people until his "brother's fury had abated." Isaac consented to this, once more pronounced the "blessing of Abraham" upon him, and instructed him to seek a wife from his mother's relatives in Padan-aram of Haran. This would unite the families of Abraham and Nahor for the second time. Jacob now must flee for his life from the vengeful hatred of the brother whom he had twice defrauded, leaving the father whom he had deceived and the intriguing mother whom he loved.

Esau saw that his father did not wish his sons to marry "the daughters of Canaan," so he too left to join his uncle Ishmael, where he took as another wife "Mahalath the daughter of Ishmael Abraham's son." He then settled in the region

---

[15]Free, *op. cit.*, p. 70.

of Mount Seir and by other marriages formed alliances with nomad tribes. From this point the story of Isaac drops into the background and becomes absorbed in the eventful life of Jacob.

5. *Isaac's Death and Burial* (Gen. 35:27-29)

Years later when Jacob had returned to Hebron, Isaac died, having reached the age of 180 years. He was buried in the cave of Machpelah by his two sons, Esau and Jacob, united for the moment at least in paying their last respects to their peace-loving father. This reminds us of the burial of Isaac's father, Abraham, in the same place by his two sons, Ishmael and Isaac, who were so unlike. The redemptive purpose of God through the patriarchs is now continued through Isaac's son Jacob.

III. JACOB, THE TRANSFORMED

Jacob's early life was closely linked with that of his father, Isaac, and his mother, Rebekah. By birth, Jacob was entitled to neither birthright blessing nor inheritance. His aspirations were good, but his methods were wrong. It was due to God's goodness and overruling purpose that Jacob received the blessings which he schemed to secure. It was not necessary for him to practice deception upon his blind father, hypocrisy in dressing like Esau, falsehood in denying his name, nor what is still worse, blasphemy by associating the name of God with his intrigue.

1. *Jacob's Flight to Haran* (Genesis 28)

After Jacob had left his childhood home, he had time to ponder on the memories of his early life. Where now was the covenant God of Abraham and Isaac? Would He also be the "God of Jacob"? Weary at the close of the first day's journey, at a place called Luz, Jacob made a pillow from the stones at his feet and lay down to rest during the darkness of night.

God was ready to reveal himself to the tired traveler. In a vision, Jacob saw a "ladder set up on the earth, and the top of it reached to heaven." The angels were ascending and descending upon it; and the Lord Jehovah was standing above. He assured Jacob that He was the covenant God of Abraham and Isaac, and that the same covenant should be extended him. At dawn when the traveler awoke, he realized the import of the divine visitation. "Surely the Lord [Jehovah] is in this place;" said he, "and I knew it not." As a memorial of his vision Jacob set up his stone pillow as a pillar, anointed it with oil, and named the place Bethel, or "House of God." He made a vow that Jehovah should be his God, and that he would pay tithes of all the Lord would give him.

2. *Jacob in Exile* (Gen. 29:1—30:43)

Jacob continued his journey, retracing the path which Abraham had once traveled from Haran into Canaan. As he was nearing the home of Laban, his mother's brother, a scene greeted him such as Eliezer had found just a century before. Rachel, the daughter of his uncle Laban, appeared with her sheep at the well and invited Jacob into their home, in the same friendly manner displayed previously by Rebekah.

Jacob loved Rachel at once, and agreed to serve as shepherd to Laban for seven years in order to secure her for his wife. We are told that this "seemed unto him but a few days, for the love he had to her" (29:20). At the end of the seven years, Jacob began to reap a portion of the deceit he had practiced on others. He met his equal in trickery when he tried to cope with Laban, who surpassed him in that art on the very day which was to be Jacob's wedding day. After seven years of service for the one he loved, the "supplanter" was given the older daughter, Leah, in marriage instead of his beloved Rachel. This was not difficult for Laban to arrange, for the Eastern bride was heavily veiled. His excuse was that custom demanded the marriage of the elder sister first. Jacob agreed to serve another seven years, in return for which he was to have the hand of Rachel also. Later Jacob also took Bilhah, Rachel's maid, and Zilpah, Leah's maid, as secondary wives. Eleven sons and one daughter were born in Padanaram, and a twelfth son, Benjamin, later in Canaan.

After the birth of Joseph, Rachel's first child, Jacob's possessions were sufficient for him to become his own master. But Laban persuaded him to stay and work "on shares," dividing the profits according to certain markings on the animals. It was God's purpose, not Jacob's scheming, which bettered Laban in all his efforts to outdo the younger man.

Jacob thus completed 20 years in servitude: 14 years for his wives and six years for his herds.

3. Homeward Bound to Canaan (Gen. 31:1—33:17)

At the end of this period, the "God of Bethel" appeared to Jacob in a dream, bidding him to return to the land of his youth. Realizing the growing jealousy of Laban and his sons, Jacob fled secretly from Padan-aram with all his household and possessions. Laban was shearing sheep at the time and was not aware of Jacob's departure until the third day. By this time he had crossed the Euphrates, and had begun the tedious journey southward across the desert and through the eastern plain of Damascus, toward Bashan and Mount Gilead.

a. Laban's Pursuit. Quickly Laban summoned his kindred, and together they pursued Jacob for seven days, overtaking him at Mount Gilead. Laban's anger had been made still greater by his discovery of the loss of his household gods (the teraphim). Jacob did not know that Rachel had stolen them and hidden them in the saddle of her camel. According to the law of the day, a son-in-law who had these family images in his possession could appear in court and claim the inheritance of his father-in-law's estate.[16] When Laban caught up with Jacob, he searched in vain but could not find the teraphim. Moreover, the night before God had warned Laban in a dream not to molest Jacob. So the two made a covenant, God being their Witness, and Jacob offered sacrifice. They named the place Mizpah (the watchtower), saying, "The Lord watch between me and thee, when we are absent one from another."

b. Jacob's Prayer at Peniel. As never before, Jacob realized his helplessness. Before this last meeting with Laban, he had found himself between his two enemies, his father-in-law behind him and his brother, Esau, before. At Mizpah he had realized that legally his wives and children belonged to Laban. But God had intervened for him with Laban. Now he was to meet his other enemy, Esau, whom he had wronged, and who was advancing toward him with 400 men. What should he do? He decided to send messengers and gifts ahead

[16]*Ibid.,* p. 71.

to the land of Seir, and then divided his household and herds into two groups for greater protection. In the valley of the brook Jabbok he remained alone on the north side to watch until morning. Jacob now approached God in prevailing prayer, reminding Him of His promises. The angel of the Lord began to wrestle with Jacob as God prepared this son of promise to enter the land of promise. Jacob, still in the training process, declared, "I will not let thee go, except thou bless me." The Lord touched his thigh, reminding Jacob of his humanity.

It was dawn when the struggle ended. The voice of the divine Wrestler announced, "Thy name shall be called no more Jacob, but Israel: for as a prince hast thou power with God and with men, and hast prevailed" (32:28). The "supplanter" was transformed into the prince. This was a new name for a new man. It was the turning point in the life of the third patriarch. From this time on, Jacob never deceived nor lied, although he suffered the deception and falsehoods of others. From Israel were to arise the 12 tribes, descendants of the 12 sons who were to bear his name. In memory of this decisive event in his life, Jacob named the place Peniel or "the face of God," for he said, "I have seen God face to face, and my life is preserved." This experience of Jacob is recognized by many as a type of entire sanctification, a second crisis in the life of the child of God.

c. *The Meeting with Esau.* At sunrise Jacob saw Esau coming from the south with his band of warriors. He arranged his household so that Rachel and Joseph should be protected, and advanced toward Esau, bowing seven times according to the Oriental custom. Esau ran to meet him, embraced and kissed him, and they wept together. After a most friendly interview, the twin brothers separated once more.

4. *Jacob's Return to Canaan* (Gen. 33:18—36:43)

As Esau returned to Mount Seir, Jacob continued his journey westward, through Succoth to Shechem. Here he bought his first Canaanite tract of land from the Amorite Hamor, and erected an altar to "God, the God of Israel," in memory of his own new name. Centuries later, Jesus sat on the edge of Jacob's Well at Sychar or Shechem (John 4:4 ff.) and expounded His gospel to the Samaritan woman.

When a violent feud broke out between Jacob's sons and the inhabitants of Shechem, God directed the patriarch to return south to Bethel and erect an altar. Here God had given him the vision of the ladder as he fled from Esau 20 years before. Jacob now ordered his household to "put away the strange gods" which they had brought from Haran, and to "be clean" and change their garments as they approached Bethel.

The patriarch followed the familiar trail which Abraham had traced more than a century before. At Bethel he built an altar to El-bethel, or the "God of Bethel," acknowledging the personal God who had appeared to him there, rather than the mere place called Bethel. This indicated great spiritual progress for the man now named Israel. Again God renewed His covenant promises, and Jacob set up a stone pillar. Upon this he poured the first drink offering on record.

As the caravan continued on from Bethel and neared Bethlehem, Rachel, Jacob's favored wife, died leaving a newborn son, Benjamin. Jacob erected a pillar over her grave, and even today there is a memorial called Rachel's Tomb in the vicinity of Bethlehem. The bereaved patriarch continued his journey "beyond the tower of Edar" until he reached Hebron, where his father lived. The remainder of Jacob's life is inseparably connected with that of his favorite son, Joseph.

"The generations of Esau" are merely enumerated, and the genealogy closes with the simple statement, "He is Esau, the father of the Edomites." Edom often appears as the enemy of Israel.

IV. JOSEPH, THE TRUE

With a brief reference to "the generations of Jacob," the tenth and last genealogy of Genesis introduces Joseph, the most outstanding of the sons of Jacob. Joseph was born in Haran, the first son of the beloved Rachel. He possessed the faith and patience of Abraham, the meekness of Isaac, and the foresight of Jacob, and showed a patient and lovable nature. The incidents told concerning him while living as a shepherd lad with his family near Hebron are among the most interesting of his remarkable career.

1. *Early Life* (Gen. 37: 2-36)

After Rachel's death, Jacob's partiality for Joseph increased. Joseph, on his part, began to report the questionable conduct of his brothers, especially the sons of the secondary wives, Bilhah and Zilpah. When Joseph was 17, his father gave him a brilliant "coat of many colors." This suggested that Jacob had chosen Joseph as the prince and priest for the family, and intended to transfer the birthright to him. This naturally enough aroused the resentment and hatred of the older brothers.

Joseph now had two unusual prophetic dreams. In the first, he saw 11 sheaves of corn bowing to a twelfth sheaf which belonged to him. In the second, sun, moon, and 11 stars "made obeisance" to him. When he told the dreams, his brothers said, "Shalt thou indeed rule over us?" Even his father rebuked him, yet Jacob remembered the incident. Fuel was added to the fire of his brothers' envy.

One day while the older brothers were searching for pasture land about 50 miles northward at Shechem, Jacob sent Joseph to investigate their whereabouts and bring back a report to him. When Joseph overtook them at Dothan, about 20 miles beyond Shechem, his brothers, seeing him at a distance, said, "Behold, this dreamer cometh. Come now therefore, and let us slay him, and cast him into some pit . . . and we shall see what will become of his dreams." Only the persuasion of Reuben, the eldest brother, kept them from taking his life immediately.

Instead of killing Joseph outright, the brothers placed him in a dry pit, stripping him of his coat. While Reuben was gone, the others sold him for 20 pieces of silver to a passing band of Ishmaelite traders traveling down the Dothan road to Egypt. When Reuben returned and found the lad gone, he tore his clothes in grief, but it was too late. The treacherous brothers then dipped the hated coat in the blood of a kid and returned it to the grief-stricken father. "Joseph is without doubt rent in pieces," he wailed, and he "refused to be comforted."

2. *Servitude in Egypt* (Gen. 39: 1—41: 37)

Once in Egypt, Joseph was sold to Potiphar, captain of the king's guard, and "found grace in his sight." Syrian slaves were considered valuable, and Joseph was well treated by his master until he was falsely accused by Potiphar's sensual wife. Then, without a trial, he was cast into prison. But we read, "The Lord was with him," and the keeper of the prison soon recognized his ability and promoted him.

Joseph's bearing inspired confidence, and soon he was asked to interpret dreams for two former servants of the Pharaoh. "Do not interpretations belong to God?" he said. "Tell me them." One, who had been the king's butler, had seen three branches of a vine in his dream; the other, a baker, had dreamed of three white baskets. Joseph prophesied the restoration of the butler to the king's favor within three days, but the execution of the baker at the same time. Both predictions were fulfilled on the king's birthday three days later.

Two years later, the Pharaoh himself was disturbed by two mysterious dreams. Seven fattened kine coming up from the river were devoured by seven lean cattle behind them. Next, seven full ears of corn were swallowed up by seven thin ears. None of the sacred scribes or magicians were able to give an interpretation. Suddenly the chief butler remembered that he had promised to help Joseph when he was restored to his position at the court. He reported the prison incident, and the young slave was summoned at once. Giving glory to God, Joseph meekly replied, "It is not in me: God shall give Pharaoh an answer." The seven fattened kine and the seven full ears of corn represented seven years of plenty. The seven lean kine and the seven lean ears represented seven years of famine to follow. Joseph's advice was, "Let Pharaoh look out a man . . . and set him over the land of Egypt . . . and take up the fifth part . . . in the seven plenteous years . . . that food shall be for store to the land against the seven years of famine" (41:33-36). Pharaoh was so impressed with this unusual foresight and religious reverence that he appointed Joseph as administrator. At the age of 30, after 13 years of slavery, Joseph was exalted from prisoner to prince.

3. *Ruler in Egypt* (Gen. 41:38—46:34)

Pharaoh made Joseph the second ruler in his kingdom, giving him his ring, the seal of the kingdom, and fine flowing garments of linen. All were ordered to give him respect, and his name was changed to Zaphnath-paaneah, "revealer of secrets" in the Egyptian language. He was given an Egyptian bride, Asenath, daughter of the priest of On. The name of his first son, Manasseh, "forgetting," indicates his happiness; and the name of the second, Ephraim, "doubly fruitful," shows his prosperity.

During the seven years of plenty, Joseph wisely stored one-fifth, or a double tithe, of the corn in each city of Egypt. The usual royal land tax was one-tenth. Through Joseph's orderly administration, the surplus corn was carefully stored until the famine began. Then he "opened all the storehouses . . . And all countries came into Egypt . . . to buy corn." Jacob and his family were still living at Hebron in Canaan. After two years of famine, they too began to feel the shortage of grain. Keeping Benjamin at home, Jacob sent his 10 remaining sons to Egypt to buy food.

a. The First Interview with the 10 Brothers. When the 10 brothers appeared before Joseph in Egypt, he recognized them, although they did not suspect his identity. To test them, he accused them of being spies from Canaan, and by this means learned that his father and Benjamin were still living. After holding them for three days, Joseph sent them back to their father with the grain they had come to buy, keeping Simeon as a hostage to insure their return with Benjamin. Reuben, on the side, reminded them that they were reaping some of the harvest of the past sins which they had committed against Joseph.

On their return trip each man found his money in his sack. Mystified, they did not know that Joseph's steward had been ordered to return their money. When they recounted the events of their trip to their father, Jacob was distressed over Simeon, and refused to allow Benjamin to go. Even at Reuben's pledge to be security for the boy, Jacob said, "Ye shall bring down my gray hairs with sorrow to the grave."

b. The Second Trip to Egypt. When the supply of corn was again almost exhausted, Jacob requested his nine sons to make a second trip to Egypt for provisions. Remembering the governor's stern injunction, they refused to go without Benjamin. Faced with the desperate choice between the possible loss of Rachel's only remaining son on the one hand and starvation for all on the other, the reluctant Jacob at last consented to entrust the lad to Judah's care. Again the brothers started out with gifts of nuts, spices, honey, and balm, besides a double amount of money.

When they came to Joseph, he invited them to dine with him. As they informed the steward of the money found in their sacks, he assured them that God had given them the treasure. During the banquet, one table was set for Joseph, one for the 11 brothers, and a third for the Egyptians. Joseph sent portions of food from his table to his brothers, sending five times as much to Benjamin as to any of the others.

When at last they were ready to depart, Joseph's steward enclosed their money in each sack as before, adding a silver cup, a royal treasure, to Benjamin's sack. The following morning the steward was instructed to overtake the Israelites outside the city, and to accuse them of stealing the silver cup. The search began with the eldest and ended with the youngest. When the cup was found in Benjamin's sack, he was doomed to be Joseph's servant. In utter dismay, the brothers returned to the governor. Judah begged Joseph to allow him to substitute for his youngest brother, for the aged father's life was "bound up in the lad's life." This plea was more than Joseph could bear.

c. *The Reconciliation.* Joseph commanded everyone except his brothers to leave the room. Then came that memorable scene in which Joseph revealed himself to his 11 brothers. He kissed Benjamin and then the others, wept with all of them, and forgave them. With the aid of Pharaoh, he sent treasures from Egypt to the aged patriarch, and wagons to carry all their possessions down to Egypt. Jacob was unable to believe the tidings his returning sons brought. However, at the sight of the wagons and gifts, unbelief soon gave way to anticipation and eagerness to start out. At Beersheba, Jacob sacrificed to God, who bade him, "Fear not to go down into Egypt." There his people should become a great nation, and Jacob would once more see Joseph.

As the caravan of 66 persons and their possessions entered the land of Goshen, with Judah leading, Joseph came out in a chariot to meet them. After an interval of over 22 years, the lad who had been stripped of his "coat of many colours" was transformed into a man wearing the royal purple, Egypt's supreme ruler, next to the Pharaoh himself. But he was still the same affectionate son. Father and son were so overjoyed at this reunion that Jacob said, "Now let me die, since I have seen thy face."

4. *Settled in Egypt* (Gen. 47:1—50:26)

After Joseph presented the family of Israel to Pharaoh, they were given an abundance of supplies for the remaining years of famine. At the end of 17 years in Goshen, Jacob called Joseph and his two sons to him. He blessed each son, but gave the greater blessing to the younger, as Isaac had once done. Then the final blessing was pronounced on his own 12 sons, who were to become the heads of the 12 tribes of Israel. Three of these were noteworthy. Reuben, the eldest, was unstable and would not excel. Judah, who had saved Joseph's life, would be the ancestor of the Redeemer. "The sceptre shall not depart from Judah, nor a lawgiver from between his feet, until Shiloh come" (49:10). For Joseph, the special favor of God would continue. Jacob died at the age of 147 years, after instructing his sons to bury him in the Machpelah family sepulcher. Joseph mourned 70 days for his father, who was embalmed according to the Egyptian custom. The 12 sons of Israel then carried him to Machpelah, as he had wished, and buried him there beside Abraham and Isaac. After the burial of Israel, Joseph assured his brothers and their families of protection and sustenance. Not one sign of resentment at their earlier mistreatment had he ever shown.

When Joseph had lived to see the third generation of his sons, he made this prophecy, "God will surely visit you, and bring you out of this land unto the land which he sware to Abraham, to Isaac, and to Jacob." He also exacted the promise that when the people of Israel left Egypt they would carry his remains with them for final burial in Canaan. At the age of 110 years, Joseph died in Egypt, and his body was embalmed there. Many years later, the coffin was brought to Shechem and buried in the parcel of land Jacob had first purchased in Palestine (Josh. 24:32).

SUMMARY

The patriarchal era begins the unfolding of God's redemptive purpose in the choice of Abraham and his covenant family. Abraham's ready answer to God's call led to the life of faith which made him the father of the Hebrew nation. Isaac was noted for his patience, self-denial, and meek submission to Jehovah. Jacob wrestled with the corruption of an inner heart and an outer world, but won the victory and received the name of Israel, "Prince of God." Joseph possessed the good characteristics of his predecessors, receiving wisdom from a close fellowship with God. In Egypt, the 12 tribes of Israel became a separate people, a covenant community which God trained for the Promised Land. The crowning glory of the Hebrew race belonged to Judah, and was centered in the Hope of Israel, the promised Messiah.

RECOMMENDED READINGS

Blaikie and Matthews, *A Manual of Bible History*, pp. 34-63.

Alfred Edersheim, *The Bible History*, Volume I, pp. 72-190.

Joseph P. Free, *Archaeology and Old Testament History*, pp. 48-83.

James C. Muir, *His Truth Endureth*, pp. 35-59.

R. L. Ottley, *A Short History of the Hebrews to the Roman Period*, pp. 23-52.

G. F. Owen, *Abraham to Allenby*, pp. 17-30.

Ira M. Price, *The Dramatic Story of the Old Testament History*, pp. 56-88.

John H. Raven, *Old Testament Introduction*, pp. 85-135.

L. R. Ringenberg, *The Word of God in History*, pp. 44-57.

Merrill F. Unger, *Archaeology and the Old Testament*, pp. 105-28.

FOR FURTHER STUDY

1. See what you can learn about the civilization of Ur of the Chaldees during Abraham's time.

2. In an atlas of Bible lands, check the distance in miles between Ur and Haran, and between Haran and Canaan.

3. Look up and locate other place names indicated in this chapter: e.g., Shechem, Bethel, the Jordan River, the Dead Sea, Hebron, Gerar, Kadesh, Machpelah, Beersheba, Peniel, and Dothan.

4. Discuss Abraham's statement to the Egyptians that Sarah was his sister.

5. What is implied in Lot's choice of territory in which to live? What were some of the unhappy results of this choice?

6. In what way does the writer to the Hebrews in the New Testament apply the meeting of Abraham and Melchizedek? (See Heb. 6: 20— 7: 19.)

7. Note the application Paul makes of the relationship between Ishmael and Hagar, and Isaac and Sarah (Gal. 4: 22-31).

8. How does Jesus make application of the escape of Lot from Sodom? (See Luke 17:28-30.)

9. Indicate as many points as you can find which make the sacrifice of Isaac a typical incident. See what you can find out about the "mountains of Moriah," and what happened there 1,900 years later.

10. At what point in Christian experience does the New Testament apply Esau's sale of his birthright? (See Heb. 12:14-17.)

11. What do you think were some of the results for Rebekah of her part in deceiving Isaac and gaining the patriarchal blessing for Jacob?

12. Review Jacob's experiences at Bethel and at Peniel, and suggest how they illustrate the two crises in Christian experience.

13. What do you find in Jacob's life to illustrate the saying, "Chickens come home to roost"? (See also Gal. 6:7.)

14. How does Gen. 31:9 help explain Jacob's prosperity in spite of Laban's changing methods of payment?

15. Joseph has often been taken as a type of Christ. How many points of resemblance can you find?

16. In view of the strong feeling of antipathy between the Egyptians and foreigners, how can you account for Pharaoh's readiness to give so much authority to Joseph?

17. What reasons can you assign for the Israelites' settling in Goshen?

18. Why was Joseph so partial to Benjamin?

19. What predictions have you noticed that Israel's stay in Egypt was not to be permanent?

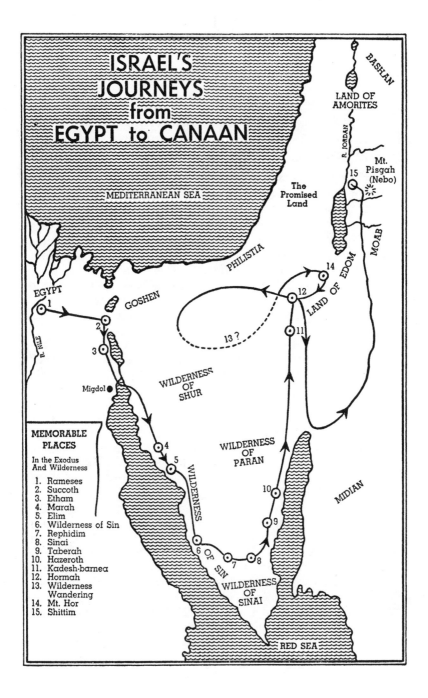

ISRAEL'S JOURNEYS from EGYPT to CANAAN

MEDITERRANEAN SEA

BASHAN

LAND OF AMORITES

R. JORDAN

Mt. Pisgah (Nebo)

15

The Promised Land

PHILISTIA

EGYPT

GOSHEN

1

2

3

R. NILE

Migdol

WILDERNESS OF SHUR

13 ?

12

14

LAND OF EDOM

MOAB

11

4

5

WILDERNESS OF PARAN

WILDERNESS OF SIN

10

9

MIDIAN

6

7

8

WILDERNESS OF SINAI

RED SEA

MEMORABLE PLACES

In the Exodus And Wilderness

1. Rameses
2. Succoth
3. Etham
4. Marah
5. Elim
6. Wilderness of Sin
7. Rephidim
8. Sinai
9. Taberah
10. Hazeroth
11. Kadesh-barnea
12. Hormah
13. Wilderness Wandering
14. Mt. Hor
15. Shittim

CHAPTER V

Moses and the Law

Did not Moses give you the law? (John 7:19)

Sources: Exodus; Leviticus; Numbers; and Deuteronomy

To Be Read: Exodus 1—4; 12; 20; Leviticus 19; 26; Numbers 21; Deuteronomy 1; 4; 6—8; 18; 30-34

Period: Approximately 1525 B.C. to 1400 B.C.

The closing verses of Genesis leave the Israelites enjoying the favor and bounties of Egypt. The opening chapter of Exodus reveals a very different situation. During the long years the descendants of Jacob had lived in Egypt, the original small group had increased in number and in wealth until "the land was filled with them." Then "there arose up a new king . . . which knew not Joseph" (Exod. 1:8), and who chose to forget Joseph's past benefits to the nation of Egypt. From a position of royal favor, Joseph's people were reduced to serfdom.

Jacob's family had settled in Egypt at a time when the land was governed by the friendly Hyksos or "Shepherd" Kings (*ca.* 2100-1580 B.C.). These were rulers of Semitic origin who had gained control of Egypt's government. About 1580 B.C., the native Egyptians expelled the "foreign" Hyksos, and placed Ahmose or Ahmosis I on the throne. He is thought to be the "new king" of the Eighteenth Dynasty who did not know Joseph. He became alarmed at the increase in Semitic population within his territory. How could he manage them in case an Eastern army should invade Egypt and secure these Hebrews as their allies?

For these reasons, the new Egyptian policy toward the Hebrews became one of oppression, with the attempt to crush their spirit and physical powers by enforced labor. Rigid taskmasters were appointed to supervise the making of brick and building. The severity of the toil was steadily increased. The midwives were ordered to destroy all the male children. When this did not succeed, Pharaoh commanded the people to throw all newborn boys into the Nile. But God had heard the cry of His people, and already was preparing a deliverer.

The chronology of the Egyptian bondage and the Exodus

116

is based upon the statement in I Kings 6:1 that Solomon's Temple was begun 480 years after the Israelites left Egypt. Since the building of the Temple is generally thought to have begun in about 967 B.C., the Exodus would then be dated approximately 1450 B.C. This date has the added confirmation of the archaeologists who set the date of the fall of Jericho at about 1400 B.C.

I. Moses, the Deliverer

According to Stephen's speech recorded in the seventh chapter of Acts, the life of Moses was divided into three periods of 40 years each: (1) 40 years in Egypt as the son of Pharaoh's daughter, Exod. 2:1-15; Acts 7:23; (2) 40 years in Midian, Exod. 2:15—4:19; Acts 7:30; and (3) 40 years from Egypt to the crossing of the Jordan, Exod. 4:20—Deuteronomy 34; Acts 7:36.

1. *Birth and Preparation* (Exod. 2:1-15)

Moses was the son of Amram and Jochebed, both of the tribe of Levi, who had two older children, Aaron and Miriam. At the time of Moses' birth in about 1525 B.C., the Egyptians were attempting to destroy all Hebrew male children as soon as they were born. Jochebed concealed her infant son in the home for three months. When this was no longer possible, she placed him in a waterproof reed basket "by the river's brink."[1] His sister, Miriam, was standing watch when the daughter of Pharaoh came to the river's edge and discovered the infant. The baby cried and the princess "had compassion on him." She accepted Miriam's quick-witted offer to secure a Hebrew nurse for the child, and Miriam ran for Jochebed. Thus it came about that the Hebrew baby was adopted by Pharaoh's daughter, who called him Moses, "because," said she, "I drew him out of the water." The name Moses is derived from a Hebrew term meaning "to draw out."[2] Moses therefore grew to be "learned in all the knowledge of the

[1] A Babylonian inscription describes the abandonment of Sargon of Agade, whose mother placed him in a reed basket waterproofed with bitumen, and set him adrift on a river, where he was found and raised by a farmer named Akki. See G. A. Barton, *Archaeology and the Bible,* p. 375.

[2] Brown, Driver, and Briggs, *op. cit.,* p. 602.

Egyptians" (Acts 7:22), but he also grew in the spiritual knowledge of Jehovah under the apt tutelage of his own mother.

When Moses "was grown," he began to realize the gulf between court life in Egypt and the slavery of his Hebrew kinsmen. "By faith Moses, when he was grown up, refused to be called the son of Pharaoh's daughter; choosing rather to share ill treatment with the people of God, than to enjoy the pleasures of sin for a season" (Heb. 11:24-25, ASV). He began now to live for the deliverance of his people from servitude.

One day, observing his people struggling with their burdens, Moses struck and killed an Egyptian who was brutally mistreating a Hebrew, and hid the body in the sand. The next day he found that he had lost the confidence of the very people whom he was striving to help. More than that, he had incurred the wrath of Pharaoh to such an extent that the king was seeking to have him killed.

2. *Exile in Midian* (Exod. 2:15—4:31)

Moses now fled to the land of Midian, east of the Red Sea. As he sat down by a well, the seven daughters of the priest Jethro (also known as Reuel) came to water their flocks. Bedouin shepherds tried to drive the sisters away, but Moses championed their cause, as he had tried to do earlier for his Hebrew brothers. When this deed of kindness was reported to the priest, Moses found refuge in the home of Jethro. Here he became shepherd of the flocks, and later married one of Jethro's daughters, Zipporah.

The Midianite country was located in the vicinity of rugged Sinai, where Moses was to spend 40 years in exile. As a shepherd, he could roam the valleys and wilderness, seeking water, food, and shelter for his herds. With his previous understanding of people in Egypt, he could study the customs of the Bedouin tribes with which he would have to deal later. Moses now received the training which he needed for the great task that awaited him in the last 40 years of his life.

a. *The Call of Moses.* After Moses had been in Midian 40 years, and was 80 years old, the Lord appeared to him at Horeb, "the mount of God," in a burning bush which was not consumed. "I am the God of thy father, the God of Abraham, the God of Isaac, and the God of Jacob," Moses heard the Voice say. The people of Israel were crying unto the Lord for deliverance from their taskmasters in Egypt. God was now calling Moses. The commission was unmistakable. "Come now therefore, and I will send thee unto Pharaoh, that thou mayest bring forth my people the children of Israel out of Egypt" (3:10). God renewed the covenant He had made with Abraham, giving to Moses the commission which once had been given to the patriarchs. As Moses hesitated, God assured him that, when He brought the Hebrews out of Egypt, they should worship on that same holy mountain. God revealed His redeeming name of Jehovah, that Moses might be accepted by his people when he went to them in the name of the God of their fathers.

Moses objected that the people would not believe him, and that he was not eloquent in speech. The Lord promised him his brother, Aaron, three years his senior, as a spokesman. He was also bidden to take his rod, with which he would work mighty wonders in the deliverance of his people from Egypt.

b. The Return of Moses. After a favorable interview with Jethro, his father-in-law, Moses "took the rod of God in his hand" and departed for Egypt. At "the mount of God" he met Aaron, who had been commanded to meet him in the wilderness. Together they made the journey to Egypt. When they arrived, they summoned the elders of the tribes of Israel, and announced to them God's purpose to deliver His afflicted people. Moses and Aaron confirmed their mission with miraculous signs, and the people gratefully accepted their leadership.

3. *The Exodus* (Exod. 5:1—15:21)

The next step was to confront Pharaoh. Moses and Aaron made the request that Pharaoh allow the Hebrew people to make a three days' journey into the wilderness in order to sacrifice to the Lord their God. This *first* attempt not only failed, but Pharaoh increased the amount of work required of the Israelites. As Moses met the bitter reproaches of his people, God appeared to him and once more renewed the covenant which had been made with Abraham, Isaac, and Jacob. A *second* time Moses made the same request, and when Aaron cast down his rod it became a serpent. The magicians imitated this miracle, but Aaron's "rod swallowed up their rods." The *third* demand was also refused, whereupon the miracle was wrought which was the beginning of the 10 plagues visited by the hand of God upon the people of Egypt.

  a. The Plagues. The plagues inflicted upon the rebellious Egyptians represented more than a contest between Moses and Pharaoh, or even a contest between a nation in slavery and its oppressors. They had a deep religious significance, and the outcome was to be a victorious conquest by Jehovah of Egypt's pagan gods. The very nature of the plagues was obnoxious to the Egyptian who worshiped idols and animals, and who prided himself on being ceremonially clean. Even the Nile River was sacred, as was the soil which was cultivated for food. Many of the plagues involved pests which were known in Egypt. But their progressive order and increasing intensity served to bring about God's purpose in the deliverance of His people.

  The first nine plagues may be grouped into three series, with three plagues included in each series. The *first* series brought plagues of (1) blood, Exod. 7:14-25; (2) frogs, Exod. 8:1-15; and (3) lice, Exod. 8:16-19. The *second* series was marked by plagues of (4) flies, Exod. 8:20-32; (5) murrain, Exod. 9:1-7; and (6) boils, Exod. 9:8-12. In the *third* series, there were plagues of (7) hail, Exod. 9:13-35; (8) locusts, Exod. 10:1-20; and (9) darkness, Exod. 10:21-27.

  At the beginning of each series, the first miracle was announced to Pharaoh "in the morning" beside the river (7:15; 8:20; and 9:13). The second was declared to him in his royal palace. The third smote the Egyptians without any warning at all. In the first series, Aaron's rod was used; in the second, no rod at all; and in the third series, Moses' rod. In the first two plagues the magicians of Egypt attempted to compete with Aaron. They imitated the plagues of blood and frogs, but Pharaoh still had to call for Moses and Aaron to deliver him from the frogs. The third plague of lice they acknowledged to be "the finger of God," and withdrew from the contest. After the third plague, Egyptians alone were afflicted. Israel's protection was announced each time except before the pestilence of boils and locusts. Pharaoh appealed to Moses for help after the plagues of frogs and flies, and then all during the plagues of the third series. Each plea was with increasing eagerness, but never did the stubborn monarch yield to the Hebrews' request for more than a short time.

b. *The First Passover.* At last the climax was at hand. The tenth judgment was impending. At midnight the death-blow was to fall on all the firstborn of both man and beast. In the meantime, the Hebrews demanded of their Egyptian neighbors jewels of gold and silver, poor enough pay for years of slave labor. When, at midnight, the Lord smote the eldest son of every Egyptian family, Pharaoh said, "Go, serve the Lord . . . Also take your flocks and your herds . . . and be gone; and bless me also" (12: 31-32).

Just before the midnight execution of Egypt's firstborn, the ceremony of the first Passover was observed by the Hebrews. Each household killed a yearling lamb "without blemish" and sprinkled its blood upon the lintel and doorposts. This sign indicated the house belonged to an Israelite, and the promise was that the angel of the Lord would "pass over" and spare the eldest son of the Hebrew. The lamb itself was roasted and eaten the same night with unleavened bread and bitter herbs. Exod. 12: 14-20 established the Passover ceremony as a great annual observance of the chosen people, to commemorate the deliverance of the nation from its bondage in Egypt, and to point ahead to "the Lamb of God, which taketh away the sin of the world" (John 1: 29).

In the terror of the Egyptians at the slaughter of their firstborn, the people of Israel began their exodus from Rameses to Succoth that memorable night in the month of Abib, or April, about 1450 B.C. The Lord "went before them by day in a pillar of cloud, to lead them the way; and by night in a pillar of fire, to give them light" (13: 21). He guided them through the wilderness where it would be possible to cross the northern tip of the Red Sea and escape the Egyptian fortifications. Once across the Red Sea, they would be out of danger from Egyptian armies. From Succoth they went through Ethan, "in the edge of the wilderness," to a place near Migdol. By this time Pharaoh had again changed his mind and led his army in swift pursuit.

c. *Crossing the Red Sea.* At the seashore, the Hebrew refugees found themselves between their enemies and the sea. "Fear ye not," said Moses, "stand still, and see the salvation of the Lord" (14:13). As Moses lifted his hand over the sea, the waters separated, and the Israelites crossed on dry ground into the wilderness of Shur. When the Egyptians followed, their chariots and horsemen were engulfed in the waters; and "Israel saw the Egyptians dead upon the sea shore" (14:30).

Moses and the Israelites then sang the great song of victory which expressed their triumphant gratitude to the Lord and their faith in their possession of the land of promise. The "Song of Moses" is often called the "Song of Triumph." It is written in ancient poetic style,[3] and is answered by the prophetess Miriam, who led the women in a brief "Song of Deliverance" (15:20-21).

4. *From the Red Sea to Sinai* (Exod. 15:22—19:2)

After the miraculous crossing of the Red Sea, the Israelites again lived as nomads, like the patriarchs before them. They made a three-day journey southward "into the wilderness of Shur," which was on the northeast coast of the sea. They found no water until they reached Marah, and there discovered that the water was unfit for drinking. Now began the many murmurs of a people with little faith. However, the waters of Marah were sweetened when Moses, at God's direction, cast a tree into them. The people next came to Elim, an oasis where they found 12 wells of water and a grove of 70 palm trees.

a. The Wilderness of Sin. In the middle of May, the tribes entered the wilderness of Sin, which was south of Shur along the coast. Provisions began to fail, and hunger and thirst faced them in this sandy desert. God then began His daily provision for their needs, quail each evening for meat, and manna each morning for bread.[4] For 40 years the supply of food did not fail. Christ referred to the miracle of the manna in His great discourse on the Bread of Life, and concluded, "I am the bread of life: he that cometh to me shall never hunger" (John 6:31-35).

---

[3]Cf. Samuel R. Driver, Introduction to the Literature of the Old *Testament*, p. 30.

[4]Cf. Free, *op. cit.*, pp. 102-3.

The next encampment was at Rephidim, where the wanderers again suffered from thirst and again complained to Moses. At God's command, Moses struck a rock in Horeb, and water appeared. At Rephidim, the advance of the people was challenged by the descendants of Amalek, grandson of Esau, a hostile Edomite tribe. Joshua makes his first appearance in the battle which followed. While he and his warriors fought the Amalekites, Aaron and Hur held up Moses' hands in prayer. After the victory, Moses recorded the event in a book, and erected an altar to Jehovah as a memorial.

b. *Jethro's Visit to Moses.* Moses' father-in-law, Jethro, Midian's king-priest, heard of the wonders accomplished in Egypt, and came into the wilderness to meet Moses. He brought Moses' wife Zipporah, with their two sons, Gershom and Eliezer, to visit the Hebrew camp, and acknowledged that "the Lord is greater than all gods" (18:11). When he saw the immense task which Moses had undertaken in administering justice to such large numbers, Jethro advised the delegation of authority to representative leaders. This is the earliest instance of governmental organization among the Hebrews, and was an important step toward the later organization of the nation at Sinai into a theocracy (a government in which authority is derived from the command of God). Rulers of tens, fifties, hundreds, and thousands were appointed, and provisions made for orderly processes of appeal.

Next Moses led the Israelites through towering mountains into the wilderness of Sinai, and they encamped on an extensive plain at the base of the "mount of God." This was to be the birthplace of the Hebrew nation.

II. LEGISLATION AT MOUNT SINAI

Israel had escaped physical bondage in Egypt, but there was still much to be gained in moral and spiritual discipline. Moses was to be God's representative in establishing a permanent covenant relationship for the Hebrew nation. This was the task of the year which was spent at Sinai. In the third month after the Exodus, God summoned Moses to the peak of Sinai. Here He promised to make Israel "a peculiar nation," and then commanded the people to prepare for the receiving of the Law with ceremonies of purification.

1. *The Decalogue* (Exod. 20:1-17; cf. Deut. 5:6-21)

Early on the third day of the encampment at Sinai, lightning began to flash and thunder resounded out of a dense cloud which enveloped the holy mountain. The Lord descended, and the Israelites came from their tents and stood at the foot of Sinai. The voice of God summoned Moses and Aaron into the mountain, where God again established His covenant with His people, and laid its foundation in the moral, judicial, and ceremonial law which He there gave to the nation.

The Decalogue (from the Greek, "10 words" or "10 sayings") given at Sinai was a *moral code* of 10 commandments written on two tables of stone. It is commonly supposed that the first four commandments were written on one tablet and the last six on the other. Thus, the first tablet set forth the duties of a holy people to a holy God; and the second asserted the ethical duties of man to his neighbor. The commandments, as arranged on the two tables, may be summarized as follows:

(1) Thou shalt have no other gods before Me.
(2) Thou shalt not make unto thee any graven image.
(3) Thou shalt not take the name of the Lord thy God in vain.
(4) Remember the Sabbath day to keep it holy.
(5) Honor thy father and thy mother.
(6) Thou shalt not kill.
(7) Thou shalt not commit adultery.
(8) Thou shalt not steal.
(9) Thou shalt not bear false witness.
(10) Thou shalt not covet.

Jesus made this same distinction between duties to God and duties to man when He summarized the commandments thus:

> *Thou shalt love the Lord thy God with all thy heart, and with all thy soul, and with all thy mind. This is the first and great commandment. And the second is like unto it, Thou shalt love thy neighbour as thyself. On these two commandments hang all the law and the prophets.* (Matt. 22:37-40; cf. Deut. 6:5 and Lev. 19:18)

The importance of this moral code is emphasized in other New Testament passages. For example, Paul reminds us that "the law was our schoolmaster to bring us unto Christ" (Gal. 3:24). Jesus stated, "Till heaven and earth pass, one jot [the smallest Hebrew letter] or one tittle [the smallest part of a letter] shall in no wise pass from the law, till all be fulfilled" (Matt. 5:18).

2. *The Book of the Covenant* (Exod. 20:22—23:33)

The Book of the Covenant (24:7), which follows the Decalogue in the Exodus account, contains chiefly *judicial* statutes pertaining to Israel's new national life, as growing out of the *moral* requirements of the Decalogue. First, Israel's worship should be at an altar which Jehovah would indicate, reducing the temptation to idolatry. Second, the value of human life should be recognized in the administration of justice to all, including slaves, and in retribution in general. Similar laws may be found in the Code of Hammurabi. These, however, are purely civil in character and lack the strong religious tone of the biblical code.[5] Finally, as an item of *ceremonial* legislation, three annual festivals or feasts were commanded: Unleavened Bread, Firstfruits, and Ingathering. In Leviticus, others were added (see page 130).

Moses read the Book of the Covenant to the people, and in ratification of its terms sprinkled the blood of a sacrifice on the people and upon the altar which had been constructed. The people said, "All that the Lord hath said will we do, and be obedient." There followed then directions for the construction of a Tabernacle which would be a visible sign of God's covenant presence with His people.

III. THE TABERNACLE AND ITS WORSHIP

When Moses went into the mountain again, he fasted and waited six days for God's voice. On the seventh day, the Lord spoke through the cloud and commanded him to have a sanctuary or Tabernacle constructed. Forty days and nights were spent in receiving the pattern for this structure. The Temple was later built along the same lines.

[5]Robert F. Harper, *The Code of Hammurabi*, pp. 13-89; Laws No. 6-20; 42-65; 112-19; 195-214; 241-56.

1. The Sanctuary (Exod. 25:1—31:18; 35:1 ff.)

The materials for the Tabernacle were to be contributed by Israelites only. Three metals were needed: gold, silver, and brass. Three kinds of skins were acceptable: goats' skins, rams' skins, and badgers' or seal skins. Other materials were: linen, acacia wood, oil, spices, onyx, and other precious stones. The colors were to be purple, scarlet, blue, and white.

a. The Arrangement of the Tabernacle. The Tabernacle was to be placed at the center of the camp of Israel. Its court was an open yard of 75 by 150 feet which was enclosed with white linen curtains suspended on 60 posts, 7½ feet high. The gate, also of linen, faced the east and was 30 feet high.

Toward the rear of the court stood the Tabernacle proper, a tent of oblong shape, 15 by 45 feet in area, and 15 feet high. Its framework was of acacia boards overlaid with gold and set in silver sockets, then covered with white linen curtains in which figures of cherubim were interwoven in purple, scarlet, and blue. The outside door was a white linen curtain embroidered in the same three colors. The ceiling of the tent was a white linen curtain with the colored embroidery, making a beautiful inside canopy. Over this, for shelter from the elements, there was a threefold covering or tent: goats' hair cloth, rams' skins dyed red, and badgers' or seal skins.

The tent was divided into two rooms. The first was known as the "holy place," and was 30 feet long and 15 feet wide. The inner room was called the "most holy," or "holy of holies," and was a perfect cube, 15 feet in length, width, and height. Between the two rooms was a veil embroidered with cherubim.

b. Worship in the Tabernacle. The men of the tribe of Levi were chosen to be the custodians of the Tabernacle and its worship. The priests were Aaron and his descendants. Only the priests could enter the Tabernacle proper, and only the high priest might enter the holy of holies. The other members of the tribe were known simply as Levites, and took care of the many tasks connected with the Tabernacle and its order of service. The tribe of Levi encamped immediately about the Tabernacle, the other tribes surrounding them: Judah, Issachar, and Zebulun on the east; Reuben, Simeon, and Gad on the south; Ephraim, Manasseh, and Benjamin on the west; and Dan, Asher, and Naphtali on the north.

In offering a sacrifice the priest entered the court through the eastern gate, and performed the sacrificial rite at the brazen altar just inside the gate. He then washed at a copper laver before entering the Tabernacle proper. There were three symbolic articles of furniture in the holy p l a c e. Light was furnished by a seven-branched golden candlestick on the left, or south side. This was lighted each evening and extinguished each morning. Opposite, on the right side, was the golden table of shewbread, called the "bread of Presence," with 12 cakes of unleavened bread arranged in two piles of six each, and crowned with frankincense. Each Sabbath these were eaten by the priests, and replaced with fresh loaves. The golden altar of incense was at the rear in the center. On this the priest set a censer of fire brought from the outside altar, and crumbled incense upon it, while the fragrant smoke filled the holy place and penetrated the holy of holies.

c. *The Holy of Holies.* Within the holy of holies the only furniture was the "ark of the covenant." This was a rectangular chest, covered and lined with gold, which contained the two tables of the Law, a golden bowl filled with manna, and Aaron's rod. The lid, or mercy seat, was a golden slab adorned with a golden cherub at each end, spreading its wings and facing the center. At the center of the mercy seat the presence of God was symbolized by a brilliant light known as the Shekinah. The furniture in the entire Tabernacle was arranged in the form of a cross, which seemed to cast its shadow backward through the veil.

The author of the Book of Hebrews in the New Testament devotes three chapters to the Tabernacle and its worship (cc. 8—10), pointing out striking types of the life and ministry of Christ.

2. *The Priesthood and the Offerings* (Lev. 1:1—10:7; 16:1-34)

The people of Israel were prone to lose the consciousness of God's presence in their midst and to turn their attention to other gods. Even while Moses was in the mountain, the people of Israel fell into idolatry by worshiping a golden calf.

Only the remarkable intercession of their leader (Exod. 32: 30-32) saved them from complete destruction. When the sanctuary was finished according to the instructions given, it was dedicated to God, and the people were made to feel that God was actually dwelling in their midst. Now that the Tabernacle was constructed and a central place of worship set up, there was need of a guidebook for the priests, and the people must receive instruction for worship at the Tabernacle. Leviticus develops and enlarges upon the ceremonial laws recorded in Exodus, and becomes the basis for later developments in Judaism.

The first 16 chapters of Leviticus provide instruction in (1) *the way of access* to God through the various sacrifices prescribed. The last 11 chapters are concerned with (2) *the way to maintain fellowship* with God. The sacrifices were gifts brought to a holy God, serving the twofold purpose of illustrating the need of atonement for sin and consecration to God. They were object lessons in holiness, given to the people during a stage in their spiritual development when they could best learn by having the abstract concepts of righteousness and purity acted out before them in beautiful ceremony and symbolism. The utter abhorrence with which God views sin and pollution, the sublime truth that without the shedding of blood there can be no remission of sins, and the absolute necessity of scrupulous holiness on the part of those who would worship Jehovah are all set forth in most striking fashion. The key to Leviticus is *holiness,* a word not used until after the crossing of the Red Sea. The demand for holiness is expressed in a key verse, "Ye shall be holy: for I the Lord your God am holy" (19:2).

God's requirements concerning the sacrifices and sin offerings in the first 16 chapters of Leviticus reveal the great fact that man must first have all defilment removed before he can have fellowship with a holy God. There are five main types of offerings, as follows:

a. *The whole burnt offering.* (Lev. 1:1-17; 6:8-13) was an expression of worship and devotion, a symbol of dedication of oneself to God. The worshiper sought no blessing for himself, but offered his best to Jehovah, and waited at the altar until he saw his gift consumed by fire. Acceptable animals for this sacrifice were to be clean and without blemish. They might be oxen, sheep, goats, or pigeons, the latter being available even to the poor man.

b. The *meal* offering (Lev. 2:1-16; 6:14-23) was a thank offering possible for the lowliest worshiper. A few small cakes or wafers were baked upon the hearth, made with finely ground meal, oil, salt, but without leaven.

c. The *peace* offering (Lev. 3:1-17; cf. 7:11-38) indicated fellowship with God. A portion of the offering was burned at the altar, and the remainder was reserved for a feast which the worshiper and his guests might enjoy.

d. The *sin* offering (Lev. 4:1-35; 6:24-30) was an acknowledgment of guilt, and unlike the first three was not said to be "a sweet savour unto the Lord." For all sins committed through ignorance, whether by a priest, a ruler, or any individual, a sacrificial animal was required, with confession of the sin committed.

e. *The trespass* offering (Lev. 5:1—6:7; 7:1-7) was for an intentional offender. This involved more than was required for sins of ignorance. The guilty one must not only offer sacrifice, but must also make restitution with added compensation to the one wronged. Both the sin offering and the trespass offering were made as an atonement for sin.

The Day of Atonement (Lev. 16:1-34) was the climax in the system of offerings which showed the way of access to God by sacrifice. The high priest entered the Tabernacle alone and sacrificed a bullock for a sin offering and a ram for a burnt offering. He cast lots over two goats to decide which should be sacrificed as a sin offering and which should escape into the wilderness. After the sacrifice of the bullock for himself and his household, he sacrificed the one goat for the sins of the nation and sprinkled its blood for the purification of both Tabernacle and altar. Placing his hands upon the live goat, known as the "scapegoat," he confessed the sins of the nation. The goat was then taken away into the wilderness, there to bear away the sins of the people.

3. *A Holy God and a Holy People* (Lev. 10:8—15:33; 17:1—26:46)

The covenant community was charged to keep certain laws of ceremonial cleanness, that there might be a "difference between holy and unholy, and between unclean and clean" (10:10). A holy God called His chosen people to be a holy nation. The nation was to be consecrated to Jehovah, and to regulate life and conduct by the ideal furnished in His law.

In order to maintain fellowship with the Lord, man must honor God on the Sabbath, observe total abstinence from wine in the Tabernacle, and refrain from any idolatry or superstition. Since human life was sacred, no human offering should be made. The blood of sacrifices was not to be eaten. Domestic and commercial life was regulated. Intermarriage with close relatives was forbidden. Rules restricting diet were set forth, and requirements of sanitation established. Honesty in business relations and mercy to the aged and afflicted were required. Matters which would now be commonplace had to be taught, in the infancy of the nation, "precept upon precept; line upon line."

Special regulations governed the priesthood. Moses consecrated Aaron and his sons to the priesthood with suitable ceremonies of purification and sacrifice, and anointed Aaron as high priest. Nothing ordinary or profane was to be allowed to desecrate God's holy sanctuary. A vivid lesson in the need for careful obedience on the part of the priests was given in the death of Nadab and Abihu, Aaron's sons, who presumed to place ordinary fire on the altar (10:1-7). As representative of the holy God, the high priest wore the words, "Holiness to the Lord," upon his brow. As Israel's intercessor, he bore the names of the 12 tribes upon his breastplate.

4. *A Calendar of Holy Days* (Lev. 23:1—25:55; Deut. 16: 1-17)

At each season of the year, special festivals were set up. The weekly observance of the Sabbath was first in importance, but seven annual holy seasons were provided.

a. *The Spring Festivals.* In the spring, emblematic of a new life, there were four feasts. On the fourteenth day of the first month the *Passover Feast* was held, reminding the people of their deliverance from Egypt, and looking forward to "Christ our passover" (I Cor. 5:7). Next was the *Feast of Unleavened Bread,* just one day after the Passover, symbolizing a holy walk with the Redeemer. The *Festival of First-fruits* was to begin after the people had entered the Promised Land and had reaped their first harvest. A sheaf of the firstfruits waved "before the Lord" has often been thought to be a symbol of the Resurrection. At *Pentecost,* called also the Feast of Weeks, just 50 days later, the wave loaves were baked with leaven, symbolic of the human tendency toward sin. In the New Testament, Pentecost was the birthday of the Church.

b. *The Autumn Festivals.* There were three holy days in the autumn season. The *Feast of Trumpets,* on the first day of the seventh month, was the beginning of the new civil year. The *Day of Atonement* followed on the tenth of the same month. The *Feast of Tabernacles,* also known as the Feast of Ingathering, was to be the crowning event of the year, a great homecoming time with all its joys of family reunion and the harvest-home festival. In one night, hundreds of booths were built from the branches of trees for temporary shelter near the Tabernacle of Jehovah. Commemorating their long pilgrimage, the people of Israel dwelt in their "tabernacles" for seven days.

c. *Sabbatical Years.* Two laws related to years grouped into sevens or "sabbaths." The first one involved a "sabbath year." The land was to be cultivated for six years, but the seventh year was to be "a sabbath of rest unto the land" (25:4). In the second law, the year following the seventh sabbatic year, or the fiftieth year, was called the "year of jubilee." At that time, lands and houses which had been sold were to be returned to the families whose inheritance they were, and slaves were to be given their liberty.

IV. FROM SINAI TO THE JORDAN

The Book of Numbers receives its name from the two numberings or occasions for taking census which are described in its pages. This was a custom prevalent among ancient nations.[6] The content of the book, however, is primarily concerned with the journey from Sinai to Moab. After a year at Sinai, the people were now ready to resume their march toward Canaan.

---

[6]Free, *op. cit.,* p. 113.

1. *Preparations for the Journey* (Num. 1:1—10:10)

The first census was taken just one month after the Tabernacle was erected. It included only fighting men of 20 years of age and up, listed according to tribes, but excluding the Levites. The total number was 603,550 men (1:46), from which it has been estimated that the total population must have been two or two and a half million people.

The provisions of the law which had just been given were now put into effect, as the people made ready to move toward Canaan. Provision was made for a special vow of consecration known as the "law of the Nazarite." The beautiful and well-known Levitical benediction is given at the close of this section (cc. 5—6) of special regulations:

> *The Lord bless thee, and keep thee:*
> *The Lord make his face shine upon thee,*
> *And be gracious unto thee:*
> *The Lord lift up his countance upon thee,*
> *And give thee peace* (Num. 6:24-26).

The tribe of Levi was now appointed to take the place of the firstborn from each tribe, since at the first Passover in Egypt the life of the first child in each house had been spared and declared to be consecrated to God. The 12 princes representing the 12 tribes brought a special offering of oxen and wagons to be used in the transportation of the Tabernacle and its equipment. The official consecration of the Levites took place, the Passover was celebrated, and Moses made two silver trumpets as signals of alarm, or to call together the assembly.

2. *From Sinai to Kadesh* (Num. 10:11—13:33)

Suddenly "on the twentieth day of the second month, in the second year," the cloud was lifted from the Tabernacle, the trumpets were sounded, and the entire camp was set in motion. Preceded by the sacred ark and Hobab, the guide, the entire host began to move in the direction of the Promised Land. Each tribe with its prince was marshaled under its own standard. Moses began the journey with a warning song, "Rise up, Lord, and let thine enemies be scattered; and let them that hate thee flee before thee" (10:35; cf. Ps. 68:1).

At evening the people sang, "Return, O Lord, unto the many thousands of Israel" (10:36).

a. *Murmuring of the People.* When the travelers left Sinai, they made a three days' journey into the wilderness of Paran. As they penetrated the barren desert, the people complained and God sent a fire which consumed those "in the uttermost parts of the camp." At the intercession of Moses, the fire was quenched; but the name of the place was called "Taberah" or "burning." Soon the people again became discontented and rebellious because they had only manna, and no meat to eat. Moses said to the Lord, "I am not able to bear all this people alone, because it is too heavy for me" (11:14). In reply, the Lord directed the appointment of 70 elders, upon whom He placed the Spirit of wisdom and prophecy which had rested upon Moses. Soon thereafter, God sent an abundant supply of quails, but punished the rebellious spirit of the nation by permitting a plague to kill many of them. The camp at Taberah therefore gained another name, *Kibroth-hattaavah* or "graves of lust."

At the next encampment at Hazeroth, Miriam and Aaron showed a deep-seated spirit of jealousy toward Moses. "Hath the Lord indeed spoken only by Moses?" they asked. Their complaint not only questioned Moses' right of leadership, but also an Ethiopian marriage which is not mentioned elsewhere. It is not known whether this refers to Zipporah or to a later marriage, perhaps after Zipporah's death. God swiftly vindicated his chosen leader, and Miriam was stricken with the disease of leprosy, so much dreaded in Eastern lands. Healed in answer to Moses' prayer, Miriam was quarantined without the camp for seven days, after which the journey was resumed.

b. *The Report of the 12 Spies.* Yet another problem awaited Moses at Kadesh. God commanded him to send the chief of each tribe northward "to spy out the land of Canaan" and to bring back a report to the people. After exploring thoroughly, the spies came to the brook of Eshcol, where they cut off a cluster of grapes so large it had to be carried on a staff by two men. They found pomegranates, figs, milk, and honey; and returned to Kadesh after an absence of 40 days.

With the "fruit of the land" in their hands, they acknowledged the fertile soil and the good produce. However, 10 of the spies feared the giant inhabitants of the great walled cities. Israel, said the pessimistic 10, would be like grasshoppers in their sight. Caleb and Joshua did their best to encourage the people in spite of this faithless report, but they alone believed that God would enable His people to conquer the country.

3. *The Failure at Kadesh and the 40 Years of Wandering* (Num. 14: 1—20: 13)

The entire company of Israelites now broke out in open rebellion and threatened to elect a new captain and return to Egypt. Joshua and Caleb "rent their clothes" in anguish, and continued to plead until the people tried to stone them. The glory of the Lord appeared and God threatened to disinherit the nation, making a greater and mightier people with the descendants of Moses. Again Moses interceded for his wayward people. Never before had they deliberately refused to go forward, although many times discouraged. Never before had they turned back toward Egypt and bondage. They had gone too far, and God decreed that all above 20 years of age, except Joshua and Caleb, should die before their "little ones" reached Canaan. Israel should wander about for 40 years in the wilderness, a year for each day that had been spent in the exploration of Canaan. The 10 spies who brought the evil report were victims of a plague. The people quickly repented, but it was too late. Against Moses' warning, they attempted to do in their own strength what they had refused to do with God's help. An ill-timed invasion of the Promised Land was attempted, but Amalekite and Canaanite warriors easily drove them back as far as Hormah.

For a generation God's people were nomadic wanderers because they had refused to obey Him at Kadesh, a term which interestingly enough means "holiness" (Hebrew, *Qodesh*). These years are passed over with few details. Three events of note are mentioned. First, judgment was visited upon a Sabbath breaker, and as a result the people were directed to place blue fringes and cords on their garments to remind them to keep the Law.

The second event was the rebellion of Korah, challenging both the religious and civil authority of Aaron and Moses. Korah, a Levite, with Dathan and Abiram of the tribe of

Reuben, secured a following of some 250 leaders of the people. Together they challenged Aaron's priesthood and Moses' authority in civil affairs. When the issue was tested, Korah and his fellow leaders in the conspiracy were swallowed up by an opening in the earth, and fire destroyed the 250 princes. Jude, in the New Testament, refers to Korah as a type of those religious leaders who attempt to usurp authority not rightfully theirs. Continued murmuring brought another pestilence. Aaron took his censer, stood between the dead and the living, and "made an atonement for the people." The plague claimed 14,700 victims in addition to those who lost their lives in Korah's rebellion.

The third event proved Aaron's divine calling to the priesthood. Each of the 12 princes was directed to bring a rod bearing the name of his tribe, and place it in the Tabernacle overnight. In the morning, the rod of Levi, Aaron's rod, had "brought forth buds, and bloomed blossoms, and yielded almonds" (17:8). This was the rod which was placed in the ark of the covenant in the holy of holies.

As the 40 years approached an end, about 1400 B.C., God's chosen people again returned to Kadesh, where they had once turned their backs on Jehovah and the Promised Land. Two incidents took place during this last encampment at Kadesh. Miriam died, and was buried there. Moses was bidden to speak to a rock to secure water for his murmuring people. In impatience, he went ahead of the Lord, and struck the rock twice. Because of this disobedience, Moses was not allowed to go into the land of promise, although he led the people to its borders.

4. *The Approach to Canaan* (Num. 20:14—21:35)

Instead of proceeding north directly into Palestine, the Israelites sought to turn east in order to follow what was known as the King's Highway through Edom and on up the east side of the Jordan. However, when Moses sent messengers to the king of Edom, asking permission to pass through the country, he was refused. As a result, the people were forced to detour southward around the mountain range stretching from the Dead Sea to the tip of the Red Sea. This brought them east of Edom, approaching Moab from the south, on the east side of the river Jordan.

At Mount Hor, Moses, Aaron, and Eleazar were directed to ascend to the summit of the mountain. Here Eleazar was invested with the robes of the high priest, and Aaron died and was buried. The people remained in mourning for Aaron for 30 days at Mount Hor. An attack by Arad, a Canaanite chieftain whose tribesmen inhabited the territory south of Kadesh, was repulsed and his tribe subjugated.

During the long march around the mountains, the complaining spirit of people was again manifested. An invasion of poisonous serpents with venom that burned like fire was used this time to bring them to repentance. But Moses was ordered to make a serpent of brass and set it on the top of a pole in the midst of the camp. Anyone who was bitten might look at the brazen serpent, and live. Jesus applied this to himself in His conversation with Nicodemus as recorded in John 3:14-16. As the Israelites were stricken by the deadly serpent, so the world is infected with sin, the wages of which is death. As Moses lifted up the serpent, and those who looked might live, so Christ was lifted on the Cross that those who look to Him in faith "should not perish, but have everlasting life."

As the company approached the territory east of the Jordan, Moses sent messengers to the Amorite King Sihon, asking permission to pass through his territory on the established roads. Instead of permitting a peaceful passage, Sihon led his army out to give battle to the Israelites. He was defeated and killed, and his land possessed. The country of Bashan to the north and east was ruled by the giant, Og. He also attempted armed resistance, but was slain and his army routed.

5. *On the Banks of the Jordan* (Num. 22:1—36:13)

With these conquests, the people of Israel neared their goal. They now descended into the valley of the Jordan, opposite Jericho, on the plains of Moab. Here they pitched their last camp before entering the land of promise.

Balak, king of Moab, sent in desperation for a famous Eastern prophet by the name of Balaam to come and place a curse on the Israelites. Balaam was apparently a polytheist, a worshiper of many gods, and recognized Jehovah as the God of Israel. He insisted that he could not answer Balak's

call without permission from the Lord. However, his greed
for the promised reward overcame his caution, and he attempted to invoke a curse upon the invaders. Even as he
tried to curse the chosen people, his curses turned to blessings,
including the beautiful Messianic prophecy, "There shall come
a Star out of Jacob, and a Sceptre shall rise out of Israel"
(24:17).

Before he left Moab, Balaam advised the pagan king to
send Moabite and Midianite women into the camp of Israel
to entice the people into immorality and idolatry, knowing
that this would bring down upon them the wrath of God
(31:16). So successful was this ruse that 24,000 Israelites died
in the plague which followed. Phinehas, son of Eleazar, strongly championed the cause of God or the loss to Israel would
have been much worse. Balaam paid dearly for his trickery,
for when the Israelites later captured Midian, he was among
those put to the sword (31:8). In the New Testament (II Pet.
2:15; Jude 11), Balaam is cited as an example of false prophets
who are more interested in personal gain than in serving
their people unselfishly.

Following the plague brought about through Balaam's
evil counsel, the second census or "numbering" of the people
was made. The number of fighting men had diminished
slightly to 601,730, with only two names that had appeared on
the original list, those of Joshua and Caleb (26:65).

With the completion of the eastern conquests the tribes
of Reuben and Gad and the half-tribe of Manasseh were
given their inheritance in the district once ruled by Sihon
and Og. They promised, however, to assist the remaining
tribes with the conquest of the territory west of the Jordan.
A total of 48 cities were allocated to the Levites, including
six which were to be known as "cities of refuge" to which
an unintentional killer might flee for shelter from vengeance.
A number of additional laws were also established at this
time.

V. The Last Messages of Moses

The Book of Deuteronomy, "the second law," consists
mainly of three great addresses by Moses, delivered to the
people of Israel as they camped just east of the Jordan at
Shittim. Another generation had grown up who had been

children or yet unborn at the time when the law was first given on Mount Sinai. They needed to learn of God's dealings with His people, and of the requirements of their new life in the land they were about to enter.

In the *first address* (Deuteronomy 1—4), Moses reviewed God's faithful guidance from Horeb to their present location on the plains of Moab, despite the failure of their faith at Kadesh. He emphasized God's love and mercy, and exhorted them to obey His holy law.

In the *second address* (Deuteronomy 5—26), Moses gave a noteworthy interpretation of the moral law, or "The Repetition of the Law," from which the book takes its name. He restated the Ten Commandments, with the additional, "Thou shalt love the Lord thy God with all thine heart, and with all thy soul, and with all thy might" (6:5). The religious training of children should begin in the home; the sacred seasons must be observed; and the priests were urged to read the Law to the people once every seven years from the central sanctuary. All idolatry was forbidden; and many civil and judicial statutes were proclaimed, with a strong exhortation to faithful obedience.

The third address (Deuteronomy 27—30) looked ahead toward the future. Upon their arrival in Canaan, the people should renew and ratify the covenant, gathering in the valley between Mount Ebal and Mount Gerizim, two opposite mountains in the vicinity of historic Shechem. Upon Mount Ebal they were to build an altar and set up a monument on which the Law should be inscribed. From Mount Gerizim should be proclaimed the blessings obtained by obedience: they would be blessed in the city and in the field, in basket and in store; their enemies would flee before them; heaven would give its rain, and the earth its increase; they would lend to many nations, and not borrow; they would be the head, and not the tail. From Mount Ebal were to be proclaimed the curses which would result from disobedience: the heaven above would be as brass, and the earth as iron; they would become an astonishment, a proverb, a byword among the nations; if they refused to serve the Lord with joyfulness, they would serve their enemies with sorrow, in hunger, thirst, and nakedness; their very land would become as desolate as Sodom and

Gomorrah. Moses concluded his address with the solemn charge, "I call heaven and earth to witness against you this day that I have set before thee life and death, the blessing and the curse: therefore choose life, that thou mayest live, thou and thy seed" (Deut. 30:19, ASV).

At the age of 120, Moses gave his last public charge to his people, commending them to God's unfailing care. Joshua was ordained to succeed him as Israel's captain. Moses then finished the writing of the Law, and commanded that it be placed in the ark of the covenant. As poet and prophet, he composed the ninetieth psalm and the prophetic song recorded in Deuteronomy 32, adding a tribal blessing as Jacob had done before him. God summoned him then to Mount Pisgah or Nebo, and gave him a full view of the Promised Land. There he laid down his mission and his life, and no one has ever discovered his sepulcher. He was seen at the Transfiguration in company with Elijah and Jesus (Matt. 17:2-6), the lawgiver with the prophet and the Redeemer. It would be very difficult to overestimate the contribution of Moses' life and work. He was a great general, a great statesman, a great legislator, a great religious organizer, a great author, a great prophet, and a great intercessor.

SUMMARY

The four great books we have surveyed in this chapter lead us far along the road toward the full revelation of God's redemptive purpose. The giving of the Law made plain the exacting requirements of God's holiness, and the prescribed sacrifices pointed forward to the redemptive work which was to fulfill the righteousness thus demanded. Moses was God's man to deliver His people from enslavement and bondage and to transform them into an organized nation. He protected and interpreted Israel's priceless heritage of redemption, and built a sanctuary to root the worship of the one God firmly in the hearts of the chosen people. The Decalogue which Moses received at Sinai became the foundation of all law in the Western world, 10 centuries before the famous Twelve Tables of Rome. The New Testament recognizes the "Law of Moses" (Luke 2:22) and Jesus declared, "Think not that I am come to destroy the law, or the prophets: I am not come to destroy, but to fulfil" (Matt. 5:17).

RECOMMENDED READINGS

Blaikie and Matthews, *A Manual of Bible History*, pp. 64-111.

Alfred Edersheim, *The Bible History*, Volume II, pp. 9-200.

Joseph P. Free, *Archaeology and Old Testament History*, pp. 84-123.

James C. Muir, *His Truth Endureth*, pp. 59-86.

R. L. Ottley, *A Short History of the Hebrews to the Roman Period*, pp. 53-82.

G. F. Owen, *Abraham to Allenby*, pp. 31-39.

Ira M. Price, *The Dramatic Story of the Old Testament History*, pp. 89-131.

John H. Raven, *Old Testament Introduction*, pp. 85-148.

L. R. Ringenberg, *The Word of God in History*, pp. 61-114.

Merrill F. Unger, *Archaeology and the Old Testament*, pp. 129-57.

FOR FURTHER STUDY

1. See what you can learn about the Hyksos or "Shepherd Kings" and relate this information to the Bible record of the Israelites in Egypt.

2. What did Moses give up when he "refused to be called the son of Pharaoh's daughter"?

3. What evidence does Moses' life provide to establish the fact that "great leaders are never made by shortcut methods"?

4. List Moses' objections to God's call at the burning bush. What do they indicate of his character?

5. What, if any, was the religious significance of the Egyptian plagues?

6. Look up and make a list of Pharaoh's four compromise offers to Moses and Aaron (Exodus 8 and 10).

7. In what sense was the annual Passover observance of the Jews both a memorial and a prophecy?

8. On a map, note the route followed in the Exodus. What reason is given for not taking the more direct land route? (Exodus 13.)

9. Point out the similarities you can find between the deliverance of Israel from Egypt and the Christian's deliverance from sin.

10. What was accomplished during the year spent at Mount Sinai?

11. What do you think is implied in the breaking of the first two tablets of stone on which the Decalogue was written? (Exodus 32.)

12. Look up other New Testament passages, besides the statement of Jesus, which summarizes the commandments of the Law in Christian love.

13. Draw a floor plan of the Tabernacle to approximate scale, indicating the location of the holy of holies, the ark of the covenant, the holy place, the veil, the table of shewbread, the golden candlestick, the altar of incense, the laver, and the brazen altar.

14. What part do you suppose the many sacrifices and ordinances of the Tabernacle and Temple played in the religious training of the chosen people?

15. List the great annual festivals of the Jews. Which of these are prominent in the New Testament?

16. What foolish prayer of the people at Kadesh-barnea was quickly answered? (See Numbers 14.) Why was the period of 40 years to be spent in the wilderness?

17. How do you account for the fact that Moses' "minor" disobedience in striking the rock (Numbers 20) resulted in his exclusion from the Promised Land, while others guilty of much more "serious" sins were allowed to enter?

18. List the points of resemblance you can discover between the brazen serpent and the atoning work of Christ.

19. Describe the character of Balaam. Of what, in our day, is he typical? (See Jude and II Peter 2.)

20. Give your estimate of the contribution of Moses to his people and to the world.

PALESTINE
in the Time
of the Judges

SCALE OF MILES

CHAPTER VI

Possessing the Promised Land

A good land and large . . . a land flowing with milk and honey
(Exod. 3:8).

Sources: Joshua; Judges; Ruth; and I Samuel 1—8

To Be Read: Joshua 1—6; 24; Judges 1—2; 7; 16; Ruth
1—2; I Samuel 1—3; 7

Period: Approximately 1400 B.C. to 1050 B.C.

The Israelites had been a people without a homeland for
over 400 years. Delivered from the bondage of Egypt, they
had camped for 40 years in the wilderness between Egypt
and the land which God had promised to give to Abraham and
his heirs. The time had come at last for the chosen people to
possess their promised land.

The period covered in this chapter includes the conquest
of Canaan, and the constant struggle of the tribes to retain
their precarious position during the three and a half centuries
before the establishment of a central monarchy. The record
is given in the books of Joshua, Judges, Ruth, and the first
part of I Samuel.

The Book of Joshua traditionally is believed to have
been written by the man whose name it bears, and continues
without interruption the story begun in the Pentateuch. This
book has sometimes been grouped with the first five books
of the Bible and called the Hexateuch, or "six rolls." But it
would seem to be better to consider it with the historical books
which follow and to which it bears greater resemblance.

The Book of Judges traces the checkered history of the
people of Israel from the death of Joshua until the era of
Samuel, covering a period of about three centuries. Tradition
assigns its authorship to Samuel, and internal evidence seems
to indicate its early origin (Judg. 1:21; cf. II Sam. 5:6-8).
Left without a leader, the people desired a king such as the
adjoining nations had. Instead, during this period, God provided deliverers who were called judges, to meet each emergency as it arose.

143

144 144 • *Exploring the Old Testament*

Joshua and Judges interpret God's dealings with His people in what is called a theocratic form of government, or the rule of God through representatives He has chosen. They form a connecting link between Israel's earlier nomad tribal life and the settled national life of the period of the monarchy.

The Book of Ruth, possibly also written by Samuel, belongs to the period of the judges. The first eight chapters of I Samuel close the period of the judges. Samuel, the last judge, anointed the first king, Saul, and became the first of the prophets.

I. The Land of Promise

The "Land of Promise" is the title frequently given to the country which God's chosen people received as their inheritance. "Canaan" was the name usually applied to this land between the Jordan River and the Mediterranean Sea until after the time of the judges (Exod. 6:4; Deut. 32:49). Other Bible names were "the land of the children of Israel" (Josh. 11:22) and "the country of the inheritance of Israel" (Judg. 20:6). Other peoples called the country Palestine, a Greek form of Philistia, especially after 586 B.C.

Palestine as we know it today lies between Asia and Africa, about 180 miles from north to south, and approximately 30 to 50 miles in width between the Mediterranean and the Jordan. The boundaries as given to Abraham (Gen. 15:18), to Moses (Exod. 23:31), and by Moses to Israel (Num. 34:3-15; Deut. 1:7-8), reached the Euphrates, a total area of perhaps 10,000 to 12,000 square miles, just a little larger than Maryland or Vermont and about half the size of West Virginia. After the period of the judges the limits were usually given as extending from "Dan to Beer-sheba" (Judg. 20:1).

The country west of the Jordan falls into three natural divisions: the north, the central, and the south. From east to west, the mountain ranges running from Dan in the north to Beersheba in the south provide five natural divisions:

1. The maritime plain, with Sharon at the north and Philistia in the south.

2. The foothills, or Shephelah, a range of lower hills back of the coastal plain.

3. The central mountain range, from the extreme north to the desert of the wanderings.

4. The Jordan valley, from Mt. Hermon to the Dead Sea.

5. The East Jordan plateau, the section east of the Jordan River, known as Gilead.

Strategically, Palestine was situated on the major trade routes between Egypt and the countries to the east (Gen. 37:25), near the western end of the fertile crescent.

When the Hebrews invaded Canaan they found many small city-kingdoms with a well-defined civilization.[1] The country was in a transitional period in its history. It was still vulnerable to wandering tribes and unable to make a united defense of its borders. The Amarna Letters, written by Canaanite kings of this period to their Egyptian rulers about 1400 B.C., speak of a formidable people called Habiri who were invading the land. These tablets give a valuable record of the conquest from the viewpoint of the Canaanites.[2]

Although the term Canaanite is often used in a general sense for all inhabitants of Palestine, it frequently is used to denote one tribe dwelling "by the sea, and by the coasts of Jordan" (Num. 13:29). In addition, Josh. 3:10 speaks of six other tribes inhabiting the land: the Hittites, the Hivites, the Perizzites, the Girgashites, the Amorites, and the Jebusites. Of these, the Hittites are well-known as invaders from the north who had settled around Hebron. The Jebusites lived in the neighborhood of Jerusalem. The Amorites had settled east of the Jordan.[3]

II. Joshua, Moses' Successor

After the death of Moses, Joshua became the leader of Israel. He had been Moses' aide and trusted companion for many years, and now became his successor. His was to be the great task of leading his people into their promised land.

Joshua was the son of Nun and was of the tribe of Ephraim. His original name, Oshea (Num. 13:8, 16), meaning "helper," had been changed to Joshua, or "Jehovah the Helper," a name which appears in the Amarna Letters about 1400 B.C.[4] Shortly after the Exodus, Joshua had been ap-

[1] Joseph P. Free, *Archaeology and Bible History*, p. 136.
[2] *Ibid.*, pp. 136-37.
[3] G. A. Barton, *Archaeology and the Bible*, pp. 74-92, 146.
[4] Free, *op. cit.*, p. 125.

pointed by Moses to be commander in the battle with the Amalekites (Exod. 17:8-16). He had accompanied Moses to Mount Sinai (Exod. 24:13; 32:17); and as Moses' "servant" (Exod. 33:11) was left in charge of the Tabernacle after the people had sinned in worshiping the golden calf. When Moses sent the 12 spies into Canaan, Joshua had been chosen to represent the tribe of Ephraim (Num. 13:6, 8; 14:6, 38). He and Caleb were the only ones who had confidence that God would enable the people to possess the land.

Just before the death of Moses, God spoke to Joshua and said, "Be strong and of a good courage: for thou shalt bring the children of Israel into the land which I sware unto them: and I will be with thee" (Deut. 31:23). This divine appointment was confirmed later when God commissioned Joshua to assemble the people and lead them across the Jordan (Josh. 1:2-9) into the land Moses had been allowed only to view. Jehovah reassured Joshua that He would be with him as He had been with Moses, and that no one could withstand him in the task ahead (Josh. 1:6).

1. *On the Border of the Promised Land* (Josh. 1:1—2:24)

Israel had been camping on the east side of the Jordan River opposite Jericho since the last days of Moses. Plans were now formulated to attack this strongly fortified city. Joshua sent two spies from the camp at Abel-shittim, which was six miles from the river to get information about the approaches to the city, the nature of its fortifications, and the morale of its inhabitants. The spies found no difficulty in entering Jericho and secured lodging with an innkeeper named Rahab. She asserted her belief in the God Jehovah who had "dried up the waters of the Red Sea" (2:10) and had given mighty victories over the Amorites. When the king of Jericho heard that two Israelite spies were in the city, he demanded that Rahab surrender them. Instead she hid the men among the "stalks of flax" drying on her roof.

a. The Scarlet Thread. Rahab, realizing that all the inhabitants of Jericho were doomed to destruction, demanded that her visitors give her their pledge of safety and protection for herself and her family. The spies agreed to this, but warned her that her life depended upon their escape in safety. Rahab's house was built on the town wall (2:15) with a window overlooking the countryside beyond. Darkness had fallen and the city gates were closed. Rahab therefore let the men down to the ground outside the wall by a scarlet cord suspended from her window. This "scarlet thread" was to be the sign to indicate Rahab's house and household, which was to be spared when the city was attacked. Explorations at Jericho have shown that houses in that city were built upon the walls in just such a way as Rahab's house is described in the Bible.[5]

b. *The Report of the Spies.* Traveling by night and hiding by day, the spies returned to Joshua with this report, "Truly the Lord hath delivered into our hands all the land; for even all the inhabitants of the country do faint because of us" (2:24). This report was very different from that of the 12 spies sent out from Kadesh by Moses. The children of Israel had become panic-stricken before, but now it was the Canaanites who were filled with fear. They had heard of the victories over the Amorite kings, Sihon and Og, and were terrified.

2. *Entrance into Canaan* (Joshua 3—6)

With the report of the spies Joshua made a proclamation to break camp from Shittim and march forward. It was during the harvest season, about the tenth day of the first month, and the melting snow from Lebanon was already flooding the plains of the river. The priests marched ahead with the ark, followed by the host of Israel at an interval of about one-half mile. Reaching the bank of the river, the people spent three days in preparing for the crossing, sanctifying themselves before the Lord. On the third day the priests bearing the ark marched to the brink of the river. Not until the soles of their feet touched the water was the river rolled back, leaving the dry bed of the stream for the column to cross. Faith that had faltered 40 years before at Kadesh was now tested much more severely. At the Red Sea, God honored Moses when the foe was *pursuing* the tribes; at the Jordan, He parted the waters with the foe *confronting* them, in order to instill faith in himself and His appointed leader.

a. *The Camp at Gilgal.* The people went on to Gilgal, where they made their next encampment within sight of

[5]Jack Finegan, *Light from the Ancient Past,* p. 134.

Jericho, setting up a memorial pillar made with 12 stones taken from the dry bed of the river. Located in the plain halfway between Jericho and the Jordan, Gilgal became the permanent camp and central base for the conquest of Canaan. At Gilgal the nation observed the rite of circumcision, which had been neglected during the wanderings of the previous generation. This was a sign of their acceptance and the renewal of the covenant which had been made with Abraham (Gen. 17:7-14). "The Lord said unto Joshua, This day have I rolled away the reproach of Egypt from off you" (5:9). The first Passover in Canaan was observed on the next day. The day after the Passover the people of Israel began to eat food found in their new homeland, the "old corn of the land"; and on the second day following the sacred feast the manna ceased to fall.

b. The Fall of Jericho. As Joshua was about ready to lead his army against Jericho, he met the angel of the Lord standing with sword drawn for conquest. The Divine Visitor said, "Loose thy shoes from off thy foot; for the place whereon thou standest is holy." Joshua obeyed, as Moses had done at the burning bush. As Jericho was located in a strategic position, it really formed the gateway to Canaan. Instructions were given Joshua for the capture of this important stronghold. Obeying the divine command, the Israelites marched around the city. Seven priests bearing seven trumpets carved from rams' horns led the company, carrying the sacred ark. This was done for six consecutive days. On the seventh day they marched around seven times. Then the priests blew their trumpets, finishing with one "long blast," whereupon the people gave a great shout. The walls fell flat and Jericho was in the hands of Joshua and his host. As commanded, the Israelites completely destroyed the city, burning everything except the gold and silver, which was deposited in the "treasury of the house of the Lord" (6:24). Archaeologists excavating the site of Jericho have confirmed the date of the city's destruction at approximately 1400 B.C., and the fact that "the walls fell outward so completely that the attackers would be able to clamber up and over their ruins into the city."[6] Only Rahab and her household were saved and ad-

---

[6] John Garstang, *Joshua, Judges,* p. 146.

mitted into the Hebrew community. Rahab later married Salmon, of the tribe of Judah, and became the mother of Boaz, who in turn married Ruth and in whose family lineage David came, one of the forefathers of Christ (Matt. 1:5).

3. *Completion of the Central Campaign* (Joshua 7—8)

Just west of Jericho was Ai, the "key city" to central Canaan. Joshua sent out spies, who returned with the report that the city could easily be taken by two or three thousand men. In their first attack, the Israelites were beaten off. In dismay Joshua and the elders fell down before the ark and prayed to Jehovah. God answered: there was transgression in the camp, and He would not give victory until the sin was removed and atonement was made. In the morning Joshua gathered the people, lots were cast to determine where the guilt lay, and the lot fell upon Achan. He confessed his theft of 200 shekels of silver, 50 shekels of gold, and a Babylonian garment from Jericho. Achan's sin cost him his life and the lives of his family, who were doubtless in collusion with him. The Israelites erected a mound of stones at the spot and named it the valley of Achor, meaning "trouble."

a. *The Capture of Ai.* God now instructed Joshua to make another assault on Ai. He divided his army, placing part of the force in ambush on the west side, and the remainder in the valley before Ai. When the king of Ai saw the Israelites in the valley, all of the inhabitants came out to counterattack. Joshua's men pretended to flee as before. When the Canaanites reached the valley, they looked back toward the city which had been set on fire by the Israelites in ambush. Caught between the two divisions of the Hebrew army, 12,000 inhabitants of Ai were killed. The city was burned, but the spoils and the cattle were given to the Israelites.

b. *Israel's First Altar in Canaan.* In gratitude and worship, Joshua erected an altar of unhewn stone at Shechem, as Moses had directed in his last message to Israel (Deuteronomy 27). There in the narrow valley between Mount Ebal on the north and Mount Gerizim on the south, Joshua called the people together. Here was renewed the solemn covenant given to the patriarchs in this same historic territory. Joshua sacrificed burnt offerings and peace offerings on the stone altar. The Levites stood in the valley and pronounced the blessings and curses commanded by Moses. The six tribes on Mount Gerizim responded with an "Amen" to each blessing promised for obedience; and the six tribes on Mount Ebal replied "Amen" to each of the curses. The law was not only read but a memorial stone was erected with this portion of the law inscribed upon it.

4. *The Southern Campaign* (Joshua 9—10)

The miraculous victories of the Israelites caused such terror among the Canaanites that the kings west of Jordan formed a confederacy against their common enemy. The next city in Joshua's path was Gibeon, about six miles northwest of Jerusalem and opposite the valley or pass of Ai. It was one of the four chief cities of the Hivites.

a. The Strategy of Gibeon. The Gibeonites realized the necessity for immediate action. Knowing that they would not receive an interview with Joshua if he recognized them as people in an adjoining city, they disguised themselves as tired, ragged travelers, ambassadors from a far country, with only a few morsels of moldy food. As part of their deception they praised Israel's God and pretended to desire a league with His people. Joshua believed these crafty Canaanites and readily accepted a treaty agreeing to spare their lives, without consulting "the oracle before the ark." Three days later Joshua marched toward Gibeon and was about to attack it when the people identified themselves and reminded him of his treaty. It was too late to remedy the mistake. However Joshua did reduce them to slavery. When the five Amorite kings of Jerusalem, Hebron, Jarmuth, Lachish, and Eglon discovered that Gibeon had abandoned their cause and had united with Israel, they turned to attack their former ally, laying siege to the city. The Gibeonites hurriedly sent to Joshua for help.

b. The Battle of Beth-horon. Joshua made a forced march by night from his camp at Gilgal and suddenly appeared before the city at dawn. He attacked the confederate Amorites and drove them over the plateau up to Beth-horon's height, where they were completely routed. As the Amorites fled down the hill of Beth-horon, a great hailstorm was sent from heaven, in which the majority of the Amorite warriors perished (10:11). The remaining Canaanites were pursued down the valley of the Ajalon to Makkedah in the foothills. After the hailstorm, the sun was low in the horizon, and Joshua needed more time to complete the annihilation of his terror-stricken foe. He prayed, "Sun, stand thou still upon Gibeon; and thou, Moon, in the valley of Ajalon" (10:12). Jehovah answered the prayer of His captain, and the sun "hasted not to go down about a whole day." By that time Joshua had completed the rout of the enemy and returned to Gilgal.

The account of this famous "long day" was given in a poem in the lost book of Jasher (10:13; II Sam. 1:18). The portion quoted here appears to be a fragment of an old ballad commemorating Israel's great victory.

After Joshua's return to camp, news reached him that the five kings had fled for refuge to a cave at Makkedah and were in hiding there. He had the refugees executed and buried in the cave in which they had hidden. This victory extended the territory held by the Israelites beyond Makkedah to Libnah, Lachish, Eglon, Hebron, and Debir. Archaeologists excavating these sites have discovered evidence of their violent destruction, and have dated their conquest at about 1400 B.C.[7]

5. *The Northern Campaign* (Josh. 11:1-15)

Another Amorite confederacy was formed in northern Palestine. Joshua had been moving so rapidly that Jabin, king of Hazor in northern Galilee, had not had time to join forces with the southern league. He now led the forces of the northern allies to the waters of Merom, north of the Sea of Galilee (11:5). According to Josephus he had 300,000 infantry, 20,000 chariots, and 10,000 cavalry.[8] But the Lord said to Joshua, "Be not afraid because of them: for tomorrow about this time will I deliver them up." Encouraged, Joshua surprised his foe at Merom and completely scattered them. Some fled westward to Sidon on the coast, and some eastward across the Jordan into Gilead. The destruction of the enemy hordes was swift. Horses, mentioned earlier in Genesis and Exodus, were disabled; but the other spoils of war, cattle and

[7]Free, *op. cit.*, p. 137.

[8]Josephus, *Antiquities of the Jews*, 5:1; 18.

cities, were reserved for the Israelites. Only Hazor was burned. Like the cities mentioned in the central and southern campaigns, the site of Hazor has been excavated and its destruction dated in the fifteenth century before Christ.[9]

With the battle at Merom, united resistance to the Israelites came to an end. The separate tribes still carried on minor conquests in their various territories. The Canaanites were not entirely driven out. Even until the era of the monarchy there were pockets of resistance against the rule of the conquerors.

6. Inheritance in the Promised Land (Joshua 13—21)

Joshua's work was not finished with the major conquest of Canaan. He must now direct the Israelitish tribes in their division of and settlement in the land. The ground must be cleared, cultivated, and developed. Nomadic warriors must become farmers in order to hold and improve the territories won.

a. The Levites. The tribe of Levi was not given a separate portion of the new homeland. Instead, the Levites were distributed among the other tribes in 48 towns or cities of their own, including six cities of refuge. The support of the Levites came from the tithes of the other tribes. Three of the cities of refuge were on the east side of the Jordan: Golan of Manasseh, Bezer of Reuben, and Ramoth of Gilead. The other three on the west side of the Jordan were Kadesh of Naphtali, Shechem of Ephraim, and Hebron of Judah. There were still twelve tribes to be given allotments of land, however, since the tribe of Joseph was divided into the two tribes of Ephraim and Manasseh (cf. Gen. 48:17-20).

b. Trans-Jordanic Tribes. The tribes of Reuben, Gad, and half of the tribe of Manasseh had chosen their inheritance east of the Jordan before the conquest of the west side. Reuben's territory lay in the extreme south toward the Arnon, and was bordered on the east and south by the Moabites. Gad received the land north of Reuben including part of Gilead, with the Ammonites for their eastern and southern neighbors. Half of the tribe of Manasseh settled to the north in Gilead and Bashan.

[9] Free, *op. cit.*, p. 136.

c. *The Western Tribes.* The land west of Jordan was divided naturally into three distinct areas by two rows of Canaanite cities. Between the northern and central districts were Dor, Megiddo, Taanach, and Bethshean. Between central and southern Palestine were cities like Gezer and Ajalon, and a range of hills.

In the south, Judah received the first assignment of territory. This was just north of the wilderness and later known as the "hill country of Judah." Here the people remained quite unmolested until the time of Samson. Caleb, at the age of 85, was given Hebron at his own request. Simeon was assigned the district adjoining Judah on the southwest, but never rose to a position of any importance (cf. Gen. 49:7). Dan settled northwest of Judah, and together with Simeon possessed some of the territory of the Philistines, a warlike people who were never entirely subdued by Joshua. A colony of Danites later moved to the extreme north and founded the city of Dan (Judges 18). Benjamin, the fourth southern tribe, was assigned a section just north of Judah. Although the smallest tribe, Benjamin made some outstanding contributions to the nation, including its first king. Saul's capital at Gibeah in Benjamin has recently been excavated by Professor W. F. Albright.[10]

The central tribes, Ephraim and the other half of Manasseh, were located north of Benjamin. Ephraim, the tribe to which Joshua belonged, early took a position of leadership in the north like that of Judah in the south. Shiloh in Ephraim was the first sacred capital of the Israelites, for here the Tabernacle was set up (18:1). Joshua's personal inheritance was in Timnath-serah in the hill country of Ephraim, some 10 miles northwest of Shiloh.

The remaining four tribes were given their portions in northern Palestine. Issachar (19:17-23) settled in the plain of Jezreel, known as Esdraelon in modern times. Zebulon, Asher, and Naphtali were allotted sections still farther north.

7. *Return of the Trans-Jordanic Tribes* (Josh. 22:1-34)

Although Reuben, Gad, and half of Manasseh had been given land east of the Jordan, their warriors had assisted with

---

[10]W. F. Albright, *Archaeology of Palestine and the Bible*, p. 47.

the conquest of Canaan. When the task was done, these soldiers started back for their own territories. Giving them his blessing, Joshua urged them to serve the Lord and be faithful to Him. As they approached the river, they erected an altar to Jehovah as a memorial of their loyalty and unity with the rest of the Israelites. When the news of the building of this altar reached the western tribes, the latter misinterpreted their motives and suspected them of erecting an idolatrous altar. A tribal war was threatened until the priest Phinehas and 10 of the princes investigated. Satisfied that no evil was intended, the men from the Trans-Jordanic tribes were permitted to go their way in peace.

8. *Joshua's Last Days* (Joshua 23—24)

At the age of 110 years, Joshua summoned the leaders of Israel for two final exhortations. In his first address (23: 1-16) he charged Israel to obey the Lord, who had fought for them and given them an inheritance. As Moses had done, he warned them of the dangers of association with the Canaanites and of worshiping their gods. At a tribal assembly at Shechem, Joshua reviewed the history of Israel and God's dealings with His people from the beginning. The Lord had given them possessions for which they had not labored (24: 13), and they should serve Him only. He warned them of punishment arising from apostasy. "Choose you this day whom ye will serve . . . ," he said, "but as for me and my house, we will serve the Lord" (24:15). Joshua set the example by committing his household to the service of Jehovah, and the people pledged their loyalty: We will "serve the Lord, for he is our God" (24:18). Israel's national covenant with the Lord was renewed. Joshua gave them statutes and ordinances, and "wrote these words in the book of the law of God" (24:26). He set up a stone memorial as a witness to the covenant under an oak tree in Shechem "by the sanctuary of the Lord."

Soon after the gathering at Shechem, Joshua died and was buried "in the border of his inheritance in Timnath-serah, which is in mount Ephraim" (24:30). Immediately afterwards the priest Eleazar, Aaron's son, died and was buried beside his son Phinehas in Mount Ephraim. Joseph's bones, which had been brought up from Egypt, were buried "in Shechem, in a parcel of ground which Jacob bought of the sons of Hamor" (24:32; Gen. 33:19; 50:25). Joshua's influence continued as a blessing to his people for many years. Nowhere is there record of any sin against God in his life. It was his name, translated into Greek as "Jesus," which was given to our Lord by the angel who appeared to Joseph (Matt. 1:21).

III. THE PERIOD OF THE JUDGES

At the death of Joshua, Israel was at least partially established in the land of promise. The tribes had settled in the districts assigned to them. However the Lord had said to Joshua, "There remaineth yet very much land to be possessed" (Josh. 13:1). Unconquered Canaanites surrounded Israel's borders and also separated the central tribes from the northern and southern groups. The Hebrews were living in open camps and villages similar to those of their wanderings and frequently fell into contact with the Canaanite peasants. It was not long before God's people began to assimilate the culture, language, and pagan religion of their neighbors who were worshipers of Baal. Local victories were won by several of the tribes (Judg. 1:1-36), but these did not check for long the spread of idolatry among the Israelites.

God's mercy and unceasing care were displayed in the assurance that He would never break His covenant with Israel and that He would never fail them (Judg. 2:1). However the Canaanites still living among them would be as thorns and "a snare" to them (2:3). With no central government and no appointed leader to succeed Joshua, the widely separated tribes began to go their own ways and rapidly degenerated morally. Forgetting past blessings of deliverance, conquest, and possession, they were soon out of harmony with God, first neglecting and then forsaking the Lord. The keynote of Judges is, "Every man did that which was right in his own eyes" (Judg. 17:6; 21:25).

1. *Six Cycles of Judges* (Judg. 3:5—16:31)

The Book of Judges deals with a period in the history of Israel in which there was only a very loose confederacy among the tribes. A succession of six apostasies, six periods of bondage to foreign nations, six prayers for deliverance, and six deliverances form the cycles which recurred during the period of the judges.[11] In each case, the Lord raised up a judge or deliverer to rally some or all of the tribes in armed resistance against the enemy oppressors. Fifteen such deliverers are named altogether, although not all authorities recognize all of these as judges. The outstanding judges are Othniel, Ehud, Deborah and Barak, Gideon, Jephthah, and Samson. They were not chosen because of family connections, rank, or position, or even on the basis of moral character. They were military leaders raised up by God to meet an emergency in the life of their people.

a. First Cycle (3:5-11). The first apostasy of Israel brought the tribes under the oppression of the Mesopotamian King Chushan-rishathaim for eight years. The Mesopotamian invasion came from the northeast. Continued oppression led the Israelites to repent and pray for deliverance. God raised up Othniel, Caleb's nephew in the tribe of Judah, as the first judge. "The spirit of the Lord came upon him," and under his leadership the invaders were driven out. During the remaining 40 years of Othniel's life the land enjoyed a period of peace.

b. Second Cycle (3:12-31). After the death of Othniel, Israel again lapsed into idolatry. This new apostasy was punished by a Moabite invasion from the southeast. King Eglon of Moab, with the help of the neighboring tribes of Ammon and Amalek, crossed the Jordan and captured Jericho, "the city of palm trees" (3:13). This oppression continued for 18 years until God raised up Ehud, a left-handed Benjamite, as the second judge and deliverer. Sent with tribute money to Eglon, Ehud schemed to gain secret access to the king and assassinated him. He locked the door and escaped unnoticed to Mount Ephraim, where he assembled an army of his fellow tribesmen. Blocking the fords of the Jordan where the Moabites had to cross the river, the men of Israel destroyed the entire fleeing enemy force of 10,000 men. Once more the yoke of bondage was broken and a period of 80 years of peace followed. It should be noted that there was some overlapping in these periods of oppression and peace, since a few of the actions were local and did not affect all of the tribes.

[11]Free, *op. cit.*, p. 140, lists seven apostasies by including the period of Abimelech's authority (8:33-35).

A third judge, Shamgar, the son of Anath (3:31), defended his people during an invasion by the Philistines from the southwest. Single-handed he killed 600 men with an oxgoad.

c. *Third Cycle* (4:1—5:31). Another period of religious corruption in Israel brought God's judgment in the form of an invasion of Canaanites from the north. For 20 years, King Jabin of Hazor[12] with a great army and 900 chariots of war held the people of Israel in virtual slavery. At length the prophetess Deborah, from Mount Ephraim, appealed to Barak, a man of Naphtali living at Kedesh, to rally an opposing force. He agreed on condition that Deborah would accompany him on the expedition. These were Israel's fourth and fifth deliverers. Barak gathered men from the tribes of Zebulun and Naphtali, an army of 10,000 warriors. With these he pitched camp on Mount Tabor, looking down on Esdraelon's level plain.

Hearing of the impending revolt, Jabin's general, Sisera, assembled his forces near Megiddo on the banks of the Kishon, which flowed across the plain. Directed by Deborah, Barak bravely descended with his less numerous troops, and with a furious onslaught drove Sisera's cavalry and chariots into confusion. A sudden storm caused the Kishon to overflow, so that Sisera's horses and heavy iron chariots were impeded on the muddy ground. Many were carried away by the torrential current (5:21). "The stars in their courses fought against Sisera" (5:20). Sisera himself managed to escape from his chariot and fled to the tent of a friendly Kenite chief named Heber, a descendant of Jethro. But when he fell asleep he was treacherously murdered by Heber's wife, Jael, who took a stone hammer and drove a "nail into his temples" (4:21).[13] Victory over the Canaanites on the northern border was thus assured for the next 40 years.

Deborah's *Song of Triumph* (Judges 5) commemorates this deliverance in one of the most ancient war-ballads known to Hebrew literature. The ode, though fierce and crude in its moral level, exalts courage and faith as it censures cowardice and idleness. It is a combination of religious fervor and

[12]Ira M. Price, *The Monuments and the Old Testament,* p. 237.
[13]Barton, *op. cit.,* p 194.

patriotic enthusiasm for tribal unity in the cause of freedom. This valuable memorial of Israel's crisis is one of the best examples of early Oriental poetry.

d. Fourth Cycle (6:1—8:32). After 40 years of freedom from foreign foes, Israel again went back to evil practices and apostasy. Divine punishment came in the form of an invasion from the east this time, from the Midianites together with the Amalekites and kindred tribes as numerous "as grasshoppers." For seven years they and their herds crossed into Palestine just at the harvest season. The outnumbered Hebrews sought refuge in caves and in dire need again "cried unto the Lord" (6:6). Jehovah's sixth deliverer was Gideon, son of Joash, of the tribe of Manasseh, whose brothers had been slain in a previous Midianite raid (8:18-19). As Gideon was secretly threshing wheat at his father's house in Ophrah, the angel of the Lord commanded him to destroy Baal's altar which his father, Joash, had built. Gideon obeyed, and erected an altar to Jehovah and offered sacrifice upon it as the angel directed him. The men of Ophrah resented the insult to Baal, but Joash protected his son, saying, "Let Baal plead against him" (6:32). From this incident Gideon received another name, Jerubbaal, "Let Baal plead."

As the multitudes from Midian encamped in the valley of Jezreel, Gideon collected 32,000 men from Manasseh, Zebulun, Naphtali, and Asher near the base of Mount Gilboa, just south of the Midianites' camp (6:36-40), the Lord commanded him to reduce the number of men with him. All who were fearful and afraid were to be permitted to return to their homes. Twenty-two thousand availed themselves of this privilege. In a test at a nearby stream, only 300 qualified to go with Gideon (7:4-7).

Secretly exploring the hostile camp with his armor-bearer, Gideon was greatly encouraged by overhearing a Midianite gloomily predicting the victory of Israel. He divided his band into three groups of 100 each with lamps, pitchers, and trumpets as their weapons. At Gideon's signal the men blew their trumpets, broke their pitchers within which the torches were hidden, waved their torches, and pierced the darkness with a great shout, "The sword of the Lord, and of Gideon" (7:20;. Panic-stricken, the Midianites attacked one another in the dark and the few who escaped to the ford of the river were intercepted at Beth-barah, where their chiefs, Oreb and Zeeb, were slain. A detachment of 15,000 escaped, but Gideon vigorously pursued them and captured and killed the chiefs, Zebah and Zalmunna, who had shown no mercy to his brothers previously (8:18-19). After the conquest, Gideon punished the Gileadites who had refused him assistance on the march. When the Ephraimites complained of the minor part given them in comparison with Manasseh, he flattered them with a reminder of their more important work at the ford across the Jordan. For future protection the central tribes wished to make Gideon their king, but this he refused, consenting only to serve as their judge. After 40 years Gideon died, leaving 70 sons, and was buried in the sepulcher of Joash in Ophrah (8:32). His achievements are mentioned by the Psalmist (83:9-12), by Isaiah (10:26), and in the Book of Hebrews (11:32).

At the death of Gideon, when national confusion again led to apostasy, Abimelech, one of Gideon's sons, decided to trade on his father's reputation to secure a kingdom for himself. Although Gideon had refused the crown (8:23), Abimelech appealed to his mother's people, the Shechemites, and persuaded them to declare him king. Was it not better for them to be ruled by one man, a Shechemite, than to be ruled by 70? They provided him with money from the temple of Baal-berith (9:4) and a band of desperadoes, with whom he marched to Ophrah and slew his 68 brothers. The one brother who escaped, Jotham, fled to Mount Gerizim and delivered a famous speech to the Shechemites, upbraiding them with the parable of the trees (9:7-20) and reminding them of their debt to his father, Gideon. Abimelech, son of a bond servant, had no title to the throne; Jehovah was the only King. Jotham pronounced a curse upon Abimelech and the Shechemites; and this was finally fulfilled in the burning of the tower at Shechem and at Thebez, where the skull of Abimelech was crushed by a fragment from a millstone hurled from above.

The imposter king Abimelech ruled for three years, and has sometimes received the title of seventh judge. During the period following his downfall, other judges are named. Tola of Issachar was the eighth (10:1-2); and the ninth was Jair, a Gileadite, who ruled for 22 years (10:3-4).

e. Fifth Cycle (10:6—12:15). Another period of social and religious decline was followed by a second invasion from the east. The Ammonites pressed westward across Jordan and invaded the territory of Judah, Benjamin, and Ephraim. After 18 years of servitude, again the Israelites "cried unto the Lord" and confessed their sinful worship of Baal. The Lord at first refused to heed their plea. "I will deliver you no more," He said. "Go and cry unto the gods which ye have chosen" (10:13-14). But after testing them and receiving a more sincere confession, the Lord "was grieved for the misery of Israel" (10:16). The tenth judge was Jephthah, an illegitimate son of a man named Gilead. His brothers had driven him from home to exclude him from any possible inheritance, and he moved to the land of Tob, where he became the captain of a band of warriors. Upon the invitation of the Gileadite chiefs, he agreed to muster the army of Israel against the Ammonites, with the understanding that he would afterwards be appointed chief of the inhabitants of Gilead. At a battle near Aroer, the former scene of Moses' victory over Sihon, he accomplished the utter defeat of Ammon.

But a personal tragedy followed this triumph. Jephthah had made a solemn vow that if he were successful in the battle he would sacrifice to the Lord whatever he should first meet on his return home to Mizpeh. It was his daughter and only child who first greeted him. Some have charitably supposed that Jephthah did not actually offer a human sacrifice, forbidden by the law, but redeemed the child with money and consecrated her to a life of virginity. The Hebrew in Judg. 11:40 will admit the translation, "The daughters of Israel went yearly to talk with, or sympathize with, the daughter of Jephthah the Gileadite four days in a year."

Jephthah's troubles were not over. The jealous tribe of Ephraim confronted him with the complaint that he had not asked their assistance in the war against Ammon. Jephthah did not return a flattering reply to their insolence, as Gideon had done. He reminded them of their refusal to respond to his call in the earlier conflict. Consequently the hotheaded Ephraimites and Gileadites met in a decisive battle in Gilead, where the Ephraimites suffered total defeat (12:4-7). The Gileadites blocked the fords of the Jordan, where they caught the fugitives. The scheme used to detect an Ephraimite was to require the pronunciation of the word shibboleth, meaning "a stream or flood." Because of a difference in local dialects, the Ephraimites dropped the *h* and pronounced it "Sibboleth," thus betraying their tribal identity. The death of 42,000 Ephraimites in this senseless struggle placed the tribe of Ephraim in relative obscurity for many years.

Jephthah judged Israel for six years before he died and was buried in Gilead. Three less important judges are mentioned between the time of Jephthah and Samson. The eleventh judge, Ibzan, a Bethlehemite, governed for seven years and died at Bethlehem (12:8-10). The twelfth judge, Elon, of the tribe of Zebulun, judged the nation for 10 years, and at his death was buried in Aijalon of Zebulun (12:11-12).[14] The thirteenth judge, Abdon, was a Pirathonite, who ruled for eight years in Pirathon in Ephraim (12:13-15).

f. Sixth Cycle (13:1—16:31). Israel again lapsed into idolatry, especially the tribes in the southwestern section, and the Lord allowed the Philistines to become their masters and oppressors for 40 years. These new oppressors came from the southwest and their first incursion fell upon Dan and Judah. The early victory of Shamgar (3:31) had warded off serious difficulties for a time, but now the Philistines oppressed Israel more than ever. A deliverer was raised up in the person of Samson, a Danite, whose birth had been promised by an angel of the Lord. His father, Manoah, and his mother reared him as a strict Nazarite (Num. 6:1-21). Although he was a man of great physical strength, Samson's moral weakness proved to be a fatal flaw.

Since Samson often visited the Philistine country, in his youth he chose a wife from Timnath. Nearby he strangled a lion and threw the dead body into a stretch of woods. Later finding bees and honey in the carcass, he propounded the famous riddle: "Out of the eater came forth meat, and out of the strong came forth sweetness" (14:14). His bride revealed the answer to the Philistines, and Samson left her and returned to his father's house. When he reconsidered and went back to reclaim her, he found that her father had given her in marriage to another. The father offered him a younger daughter for a wife. Samson, however, was so in-

---

[14]Price, *op. cit.*, p. 236.

censed at all Philistines that he caught 300 foxes, tied their tails together, and placed a firebrand between the tails of each pair. He then set them loose in the grain fields among the shocks of grain which were just ready for harvest. The Philistines took vengeance on his wife and her father by burning them.

Another remarkable deed was Samson's massacre of a thousand Philistines at Enhakkore with the jawbone of an ass. Later when the Philistines were seeking to capture him at Gaza, he ran against the city gates, tore them and the supporting posts loose, then carried them on his shoulders up to the crest of a hill nearby.

It was easy enough for Samson to pick up the gates of Gaza; but when he met the beautiful Philistine woman Delilah of Sorek, he did not have the moral courage to resist her charms, although he knew God had forbidden marriage with the Canaanites. This beautiful but treacherous wife was bribed to obtain from Samson the secret of his superhuman strength. At last she teased it from him. Learning that his strength would be continued only as long as his Nazarite vow was kept and his hair left long, Delilah quickly called her confederates. When Samson fell asleep, his hair was cut off, and he was bound. With no more strength than an ordinary man, he was easily subdued and his eyes put out. He was then set to grinding grain in the prison, a pathetic object of derision and scorn. When a feast day came, the Philistines brought Samson into the temple dedicated to their idol Dagon to ridicule and make sport of him. Samson's hair had begun to grow and a last desperate prayer to God brought a temporary return of the old strength. Pushing over the two key pillars supporting the temple roof, Samson brought it crashing down upon himself and his foes. "So the dead which he slew at his death were more than they which he slew in his life" (16:30).

2. *The Fruit of Anarchy* (Judges 17—21)

The days which followed were filled with civil and religious confusion. Two episodes afford examples of the idolatry, apostate priests, and civil war among the widely separated tribes when "there was no king in Israel" (18:1; 19:1).

a. Micah and His Images. There was a man of Ephraim

named Micah who had made two household gods called "teraphim" together with an ephod or priestly robe, and had set up a place of worship in his house. Seeking a priest for his idolatrous shrine, he hired Jonathan, a Levite from Bethlehem who had left his native village seeking employment. However when a band of men from the tribe of Dan, seeking more territory, passed Micah's house, they persuaded young Jonathan to go with them, taking Micah's images without heed to his protests.

Journeying north to the headwaters of the Jordan, the Danites conquered the city of Laish or Leshem and renamed it Dan after the name of their tribe (Josh. 19:47; Judg. 18:29). In the new settlement of Dan they reestablished Micah's form of worship, adapting their shrine in imitation of the sanctuary at Shiloh. The location, the ritual, and the priesthood were all contrary to Hebrew law, and Dan later became one of the two main centers of idolatry in northern Palestine.

b. *Benjamin's Tragedy at Gibeah.* The second episode relates to a tragedy in Benjamin. A Levite was returning home from Bethlehem to Mount Ephraim with his wife and stopped for the night in Gibeah, a town of Benjamin. A vicious mob surrounded the house and finally murdered the woman. Investigating the affair, the remaining 11 tribes arose as one man demanding vengeance. They sent tribal representatives "through all the tribe of Benjamin" to demand the surrender of the perpetrators of the deed, but the Benjamites refused. Civil war followed between Benjamin and the 11 tribes, resulting in the burning of Gibeah and the virtual annihilation of the tribe of Benjamin with the exception of 600 men who fled to the wilderness and took refuge in Rimmon (20:47). To avoid the loss of one of the 12 tribes, wives were later found for the surviving Benjamites. However, it was many decades before the people of Benjamin regained their former prestige.

The Book of Judges closes with the summary statement, "In those days . . . every man did that which was right in his own eyes" (21:25).

IV. THE STORY OF RUTH

The Book of Ruth takes its name from its main character and is written in the form of a pastoral idyll with its setting near Bethlehem. It is an interesting sequel to the Book of Judges, and its description of King David's ancestry makes it a connecting link with the later historical books. Its historicity is confirmed in the Old Testament by David's friendship with Moab (I Sam. 22: 3-4) and in the New Testament in the genealogies of Christ (Matt. 1: 5; Luke 3: 32).

1. *Naomi and Ruth* (Ruth 1: 1-22)

Elimelech and Naomi were Ephrathites of Bethlehem who migrated to Moab with their two sons, Mahlon and Chilion, during a time of severe famine in Palestine. Mahlon married a Moabitess named Ruth, and Chilion married another Moabite girl known as Orpah. After 10 years, the father and sons died, leaving the three women widows with no children. Naomi decided to return home and both daughters-in-law started with her. Realizing the lonely life ahead for women of a foreign country, Naomi entreated them to turn back. Orpah returned, but Ruth's devotion impelled her to accompany her mother-in-law to Judah and Jehovah's people. "Intreat me not to leave thee," she said, "or to return from following after thee: for whither thou goest, I will go; and where thou lodgest, I will lodge: thy people shall be my people, and thy God my God" (1: 16).

2. *Ruth and Boaz* (Ruth 2: 1—3: 18)

It was springtime in Bethlehem during barley harvest when Naomi and Ruth returned. Seeking work, Ruth went to glean in the field of a wealthy Ephrathite by the name of Boaz, a relative of her husband's family. Boaz favored Ruth, allowing her to eat with the Jews, contrary to Hebrew custom (Deut. 23: 3), and soon came to love her. Naomi furthered Boaz' interest by seeking to arrange a marriage in conformity with a Hebrew levirate law (Deut. 25: 5-10), which was similar to laws found among the Assyrians and Hittites.[15] It permitted a childless widow to marry her husband's brother or nearest kinsman in order to perpetuate the dead husband's name. Ruth's nearest relative renounced his obligation and transferred it to Boaz by removing his shoe and handing it to the other man in the presence of witnesses (Deut. 25: 9-10;

15Barton, *op. cit.*, pp. 424, 432.

Ruth 4: 7-8). This enabled Boaz to redeem the inheritance of Naomi's family and paved the way for his marriage with Ruth.

3. *The Ancestress of Christ* (Ruth 4: 1-22)

Obed, the son of Ruth and Boaz, was the grandfather of David, of whose royal line the Babe of Bethlehem was born 13 centuries later. Ruth was thus recorded in Jewish-Christian annals as an honored ancestress of David, Mary, and Jesus. The fact of Ruth's Gentile ancestry may suggest the importance of Christ's mission to the Gentiles and to the entire world.

V. SAMUEL

The Books of Samuel receive their name from the principal figure of their opening section. Samuel was Israel's last judge and first prophet. The first eight chapters of I Samuel close the period of the judges, and prepare for the coronation of Saul and the coming of the kingdom.

1. *Samuel and Eli* (I Sam. 1: 1—4: 22)

Samuel was born in answer to the prayer of his mother, Hannah. In gratitude for his birth Hannah dedicated him to the Lord. He was trained in the temple at Shiloh by the priest Eli. God personally called Samuel during his childhood, speaking to him during the night hours and revealing to him the impending destruction of Eli's household. Since Israel, including Eli's two sons, had lapsed into idolatry, God sent judgment upon the nation in a battle with the Philistines at Aphek. Eli's two sons were killed and the ark of the covenant was carried off to Dagon's temple in Ashdod. The news stunned Eli as he sat on his judgment throne at the city gate, so that he fell upon the stones below and broke his neck. He died at the age of 98 after judging Israel 40 years.

2. *Samuel, the Judge* (I Sam. 5: 1—7: 17; 25: 1)

The capture of the ark brought nothing but trouble to the Philistines. Each morning while it was in the temple of Dagon in Ashdod, the idol was found lying face downward before the ark, and the inhabitants of the town suffered severe plagues. When the ark was removed to other Philistine cities, the result was the same. Finally in desperation the Philistines determined to return the ark to the people of Israel. They placed it in a new cart, drawn by two milch cows, put with it a golden offering, and watched as the animals pulled the cart directly back to the land of Israel. It came at last to the home of Abinadab in Kirjath-jearim, where it remained for many years.

After the disastrous battle in which the ark was captured by the Philistines, Samuel became recognized as the judge and leader of his people. He made his home in Ramah, where he had been born and was later buried, and from which he made an annual tour throughout the land, instructing the people and leading them in worship.

When Samuel felt that the people were sufficiently sincere in their repentance for the idolatry into which they had fallen and in their desire to serve the Lord, he called a convocation at Mizpah to offer sacrifice and renew the covenant. Hearing of the gathering, the Philistines marshaled their forces and marched to attack. God heard Samuel's prayer, and a great thunderstorm so confused the attacking army that they were quickly defeated by the Israelites. So complete was this victory that the Philistines never dared attack Israel again during the period of Samuel's strong leadership.

The later life of Samuel is closely connected with the establishment of the kingdom and the anointing and coronation of Saul, and will be considered in the next chapter. It should be said, however, that few men have exercised a greater influence on the religious life of their times than Samuel. No family feast was thought to be complete without his presence, so great was the honor and respect given to him. His benediction was sought for every enterprise, and his counsel was considered in all matters. Around him, at Ramah, was gathered one of the first companies or "schools" of young prophets, assisting in the work of instruction and reform. His death was a time of national mourning (25:1).

SUMMARY

In this chapter we have traced the fulfillment of the prophecy made to Abraham concerning the return of his descendants to Palestine after their sojourn in Egypt. The lessons of this period are many. During the days of Joshua, and as long as the people were loyal to the God of their fathers, Israel was invincible. However, idolatry and the adoption of Canaanite ways brought anarchy and defeat to the people of God. The beginning of better things is seen in the greater national unity brought about by Samuel's vigorous leadership.

RECOMMENDED READINGS

Blaikie and Matthews, *A Manual of Bible History*, pp. 112-64.

Alfred Edersheim, *The Bible History*, Volume III, pp. 11-191.

Joseph P. Free, *Archaeology and Old Testament History*, pp. 124-45.

James C. Muir, *His Truth Endureth*, pp. 87-111.

R. L. Ottley, *A Short History of the Hebrews to the Roman Period*, pp. 83-123.

G. F. Owen, *Abraham to Allenby*, pp. 40-47.

Ira M. Price, *The Dramatic Story of the Old Testament History*, pp. 132-80.

John H. Raven, *Old Testament Introduction*, pp. 150-62.

J. R. Sampey, *The Heart of the Old Testament*, pp. 89-104.

————, *Syllabus for Old Testament Study*, pp. 84-92.

Merrill F. Unger, *Archaeology and the Old Testament*, pp. 158-96.

Westminster Atlas, pp. 43-46.

FOR FURTHER STUDY

1. What can be said of the authorship of the books of Joshua, Judges, and Ruth?

2. List the main geographical divisions of Palestine from north to south and from east to west.

3. Look up some additional information about the Tell el-Amarna Tablets in recent archaeological manuals or reference sources.

4. In what manner had Joshua served God and his people before he became Moses' successor?

5. Recalling the retreat of the Israelites from Kadesh-barnea, can you see any greater challenge to their faith in the crossing of the Jordan opposite Jericho than they had at Kadesh?

6. See what you can find concerning archaeological confirmation of the Bible account of the destruction of Jericho.

7. Can you think of any lessons for the Christian life in the surprising defeat of the Israelites at Ai?

8. In what way, if any, was Joshua at fault in making his peace treaty with the Gibeonites?

9. Describe Joshua's overall strategy in his campaign of conquest in Canaan.

10. How did the inheritance of the tribe of Levi differ from the inheritances of the other tribes? Can you think of any good reasons for this arrangement?

11. Note the positions of the tribes in the division of the land, particularly of Judah and Ephraim.

12. Summarize the contribution of Joshua's life to his nation.

13. What is the keynote of the period of the judges? Tell what you think is meant by the term "judge" in this context.

14. Make your own list of the judges, and write a sentence characterization of each.

15. How is Gideon's testing of God's leadings commonly used today?

16. Can you find any modern usages of Jephthah's "Shibboleth" test?

17. What would you say was Samson's fatal character flaw?

18. What incidents illustrate the lawlessness of the period of the judges?

19. What light would you say the Book of Ruth sheds on this period?

20. Two women of other nationalities entered the ancestral line of Christ during this period. Who were they? Has this fact any significance for the gospel?

CHAPTER VII

Establishing the Kingdom

Thy kingdom shall be established (II Sam. 7:16).

Sources: I and II Samuel; I Chronicles 10—29; Psalms
32 and 51

To Be Read: I Samuel 8—15; II Samuel 5—12

Period: 1050—970 B.C.

During the period of the judges Israel was constantly
in danger of falling into complete anarchy. The tribes were
divided and frequently oppressed. The dedicated life of Samuel temporarily lifted the people to a place of unity. But when
his decline and approaching death became apparent, the people clamored for a king. Reluctantly Samuel granted them
their desire, crowning Saul as Israel's first king. While showing great promise, Saul was a tragic failure. He was succeeded
by David, who forged Israel into a mighty and prosperous
nation. Under these two kings Israel completed the transition
from a confederacy of independent clans to an established and
powerful kingdom.

The establishment of a kingdom was highly significant,
for it was not only a fateful experiment in politics, but also a
radical departure from a concept of government dating back
to Moses five centuries before. William F. Albright points
out some fundamental causes of this shift from a theocratic
(rule of God) type of government to the monarchial type.
The constant struggle between the Israelites and the surrounding groups was slowly but surely hammering them into
national unity. As soon as one foe was defeated, another,
more powerful and menacing, confronted them.[1]

A further influence was the type of government surrounding Israel. While the Israelites maintained their loose
federation, depending for leadership upon occasional judges,
the surrounding nations were all highly organized. Edomites,
Moabites, and Ammonites all had kings who were absolute
in their power. The Philistines likewise had lords who seem
to have been tyrants with unquestioned authority.

[1]William F. Albright, *From the Stone Age to Christianity*, p. 221.

169

170 Exploring the Old Testament

Since the fate and fortunes of the kingdom are so inextricably bound to the kings who ruled them, we treat the establishment of the kingdom by highlighting the lives of Saul and David, the two kings responsible for its founding.

I. Saul, Israel's First King

Saul is one of the great tragic figures of history. Blessed with natural graces and talents, selected by God, enjoying the confidence of the people, he degenerated into a psychopathic condition in which his powers were sapped and his kingdom weakened. Rejection, defeat, and suicide were the inevitable and historic results.

1. *The Establishment of the Monarchy* (I Samuel 8—10)

The coronation of Saul as Israel's first king was the climax of a desire which had existed for nearly 200 years. Two centuries before, the Jews had attempted to make Gideon king. He wisely refused, reminding them that the Lord should rule over them (Judg. 8:22-23). But during the intervening years the desire for a monarch had been growing until it was almost a nationwide obsession. The lofty and wise leadership of Samuel had temporarily checked the desire. But as the venerable prophet approached his end, the people's demand for a king increased.

a. Reasons for Desiring a King. Three reasons may be given for this pressure for a monarchy. First, the people wanted a leader to direct them in time of war (8:20). The Philistines at this time had become a serious menace. They had carried away the sacred ark of the covenant and had levied taxes on the people of Israel. In addition the Hebrews were denied the privilege of forging weapons of war and even of possessing iron tools and implements. While this enemy had been checked for the time under the leadership of Samuel (7:10-11), yet the peril was ever present.

Another reason for the request for a king was the advanced age of Samuel. If a leader was not chosen before Samuel died, his death would open the gates of anarchy again, as in the days of the judges, when each "did that which was right in his own eyes" (Judg. 17:6). Both of Samuel's sons, Joel and Abiah, had been trained to succeed their father, but they disqualified themselves when they "turned aside after lucre, and took bribes, and perverted judgment" (8:3).

A third reason was the desire for the pomp and ceremony of a royal court—to be like other nations. As long as the people were wandering, unsettled nomads, they cared little what other nations did. But when they became firmly established in their new homeland they felt the eternal urge to be "like others." A delegation came to Samuel's home at Ramah to present the request that he appoint a king to rule over them (8:20).

b. *Warning Against Kingship*. It was a trying moment for Samuel. The aim of his life's work had been to restore the theocratic ideal as instituted by Moses and to train his sons to insure this restoration of the kingship to God. Now it seemed that the people were to reject both God and the two sons of Samuel. We are told, "The thing was evil in the sight of God." This was the cause of Samuel's reluctance, for "at his age, and with his spirit, we cannot suppose him to have been much concerned at the loss of his own power."[2] But Samuel placed the welfare and unity of the nation above his individual feelings, and when God sanctioned the choice of the people, he did his utmost to bring about a smooth transition in the government.

Using all the persuasion and talent acquired in a lifetime of public service, he pointed out in graphic language and vivid detail the dangers involved in the insistence on a king to rule over the nation. The cherished equality of all before God would be lost, and the liberty of each family would be weakened if not destroyed. The king would draft the finest young men for his chariots and servants. He would demand free labor to cultivate the king's fields, and to make arms and implements of war. In addition he would select young women to assist in household duties. He would levy taxes, and requisition land and cattle as he desired. In extreme cases, Samuel pointed out, the king might become a lawless despot who would make the people of the nation his slaves.

Disregarding these warnings, the people insisted, "We will have a king over us" (8:19). When Samuel saw their stubborn insistence he worked wholeheartedly to select the

[2]William Smith, *Old Testament History*, p. 381.

proper man for the vastly important task of being Israel's first king.

c. *The Choice of Saul.* The choice fell upon Saul, an obscure member of the tribe of Benjamin, the smallest of the 12 tribes of Israel. Saul had shown no signs of ambition and self-advancement. His clan, that of Matri, was one of the smallest in the tribe; but his father, Kish, had a reputation as a courageous and a wealthy man.

The young Benjamite farmer was sent by his father to round up some stray donkeys. Failing to locate the strays, he decided to appeal to Samuel, the seer, for assistance. But when they met, Samuel had more urgent business than giving directions for locating wandering animals. Saul was amazed to learn that on him rested "all the desire of Israel" (9:20).

To his unassuming mind it was incredible that one so insignificant as he should be selected as the ruler of Israel (9:21). But the extreme respect and deep courtesy of Samuel convinced him. The old prophet and the young king-to-be enjoyed a feast of celebration at which Saul was given the chief seat in the presence of 30 of the leaders of Israel. After the feast Samuel invited Saul to spend the night with him. Early the next day Samuel anointed Saul king, and then advised him to return home to await developments.

d. *Saul's Selection Confirmed.* Returning home, Saul was given further confirmation of God's choice. Two men in the neighborhood of "Rachel's sepulchre" informed him that the stray donkeys were found. At the historic oak near Tabor three men going to Bethel to worship gave him, as a token of respect, two loaves of bread, three choice pieces of meat, and a container of wine. Finally, at Gibeah, where the Philistine tax collector was accustomed to station himself, Saul met a group of prophets returning from the offering of sacrifices. The singing and contagious spirit of these men inspired Saul. The Spirit of God came upon him and he prophesied (10:10).

This unusual demonstration of prophetic power and emotion by such an unlikely young farmer astonished the bystanders; but to Saul it was a crisis in his spiritual life. Prior to this, religious tendences had been dormant in his life; but from this time on, religion became a ruling factor in his thinking. Now he felt he had been entrusted with a divine commission to lead and deliver his people, although as yet he kept his secret, not even informing his family of these thrilling events.

e. Saul, the Man. The man selected to be Israel's first king was about 40 years old, and had a grown son, Jonathan. Saul was a man of fine stature, in the prime of life, and "noble alike in features and bearing." To the men of Israel he represented the ideal of royalty. Men thought of him fondly, after his death, as the roe or gazelle of Israel, the symbol of swiftness and grace, of beauty and gentleness. But his spiritual life was as weak as his physical being was strong. Courageous when facing the enemy, he feared to displease his friends. Though able at first to take his place among the prophets, he later lost his spiritual balance and starved his inner life. He was a creature of impulse: often kindly, as in his love for David and Jonathan; often noble, as in his patriotic zeal for God; but always lacking the control of steady principle.

f. The Coronation. In order to secure public approval and support, a great national convention was held at Mizpeh, that Samuel might present "the chosen of God" to the people of Israel, to be accepted as their king. Momentarily overwhelmed with panic at the tremendous responsibility about to be placed upon him, Saul fled to a hiding place among the baggage nearby. But the enthusiastic people searched him out and hustled him to the place of coronation. Once presented to the expectant throng, his magnificent presence won the instant allegiance of the people and for the first time in Israel's history the shout went up, "God save the king."

2. *Enlarging the Borders* (I Samuel 11—14)

While Saul was thrilled at the honor so unexpectedly thrust upon him, he was fully aware that accompanying the honor were staggering responsibilities. The political situation in Israel was most discouraging. Although the Hebrews had been in Palestine for 300 years, they had been able to conquer very little of the Promised Land. In fact, at this time they were practically at the mercy of their enemies and in danger of losing entirely their national existence.

The people were completely disarmed. Even the use of

tools was restricted; for sickles, coulters, axes, and goads could be sharpened only in towns governed by the Philistines. Saul and his son Jonathan alone had swords (13:19-22). Tax collectors representing the conquerors were ever present, as were occupation troops. Some, as in Saul's own tribe of Benjamin, were forced into enemy armies to fight against their countrymen. Only a king enjoying God's blessing could hope to drive out the enemy.

a. Saul's Good Beginning. Saul's first test came as a result of pressure from the people of Ammon, east of the Jordan. Here among the thickly wooded hills of Gilead, was situated the town Jabesh. It was the center of a fertile farm district. An old blood tie bound it to Benjamin, Saul's tribe, for 400 of its young women had become wives of the survivors of the intertribal warfare in the time of the judges.

Runners brought the news that Nahash, king of Ammon, had laid siege to Jabesh, and had threatened to display his utter contempt for Israel by putting out the eyes of all those in the city. Great men rise to great occasions. The news fanned the spark of leadership in Saul into a flame. He immediately killed the two cattle he was driving home, carved the animals into 12 pieces, and dispatched one piece to each of the 12 tribes with the command to rally to the defense of Jabesh-gilead. To disobey meant to meet the fate of the slain animals. For the first time since the days of Gideon the response to an emergency was nationwide.

Large numbers of volunteers from all the tribes rallied to the designated meeting place (11:8). Attacking directly across the Jordan, the Hebrews launched a three-pronged assault on the Ammonites. After a brief but futile attempt to defend themselves, the enemy fled in panic. Saul had firmly entrenched himself as the king.

His triumph was graced by an act of kingly mercy. The people requested that Samuel put to death the men who had despised the new-made king. But Saul revealed his generous humility by declaring that not a man should be put to death on that day in which Jehovah had saved Israel (11:13). To celebrate the notable victory a great throng assembled at historic Gilgal, and with great popular joy once again anointed Saul king (11:15).

b. Samuel's Farewell Address. This joy was sobered,

however, by the retirement of Samuel from public life. The venerable prophet, testifying to his integrity from boyhood, reminded them of all God had done for them from the time that Jacob went down to Egypt till that hour. He warned them that by their own request they had been given a king, and it would depend on them whether his kingdom should be established. If they would honor God and be loyal to Him, they would realize permanent blessings and growth. But if they became rebellious and stubborn, God's hand would be against them.

Then with prophetic passion he pointed to the brilliant eastern sky and. asked that his words be confirmed with a thunderstorm. The people bowed before this divine manifestation and begged Samuel to pray for them that they might not die. With pathos the retiring leader promised to pray continually for Israel, and to give them the benefit of his wisdom and experience.

c. Preparations for War. The smashing triumph over Ammon did not pass unnoticed by the other enemies of the Hebrews, particularly the Philistines. These warlike people, holding the most fertile part of Palestine, were at the height of their power. In farming, commerce, and military affairs the Philistines were aggressive and prosperous. Any increase of Israel's power would threaten their homes and the profitable trade routes which they controlled. Both Israel and the Philistines began preparations for war.

Saul had assembled a handpicked band of 3,000 men to serve as the hard core of his fighting forces. Two-thirds of these men were stationed at Michmash among the hills of Bethel, and the other thousand camped at Gibeah with Saul's son Jonathan. Jonathan made a successful surprise raid on the Philistine garrison on the hill of Geba. Encouraged by this triumph over the renowned soldiers of Philistia, Saul summoned the fighting men of Israel to Gilgal. The Philistines answered the challenge with an immense army, made up of 30,000 chariots (the ancient counterpart of tanks) and 6,000 cavalrymen, in addition to hordes of foot soldiers.

d. Signs of Weakness. Before going into battle Israel was accustomed to offering sacrifices to God and to seeking His blessings and favor in the coming fray. It would appear that Samuel had instructed Saul to wait until he, Samuel, came to offer the sacrifice, and had appointed the seventh day for that purpose. However, the appearance of the vast Philistine army struck panic among the Israelites, and Saul's soldiers were rapidly deserting. Thinking that it was necessary to act at once, Saul assumed the role of priest and offered the sacrifice with his own hands.

He had barely finished when Samuel arrived, and asked what he had done. Saul justified his actions by pointing out the danger of the Philistines' attacking at once. The prophet sorrowfully yet sternly declared that he had acted with sinful folly. He further intimated that this deed, added to other acts of disobedience, would result in the eventual loss of the kingdom.

e. A Partial Victory. An unexpected deliverance resulted from the daring and courage of Jonathan, the king's son. This intrepid young warrior, accompanied only by his armor-bearer, made a lightning foray against the outpost of the enemy army at Michmash from which Saul had withdrawn. Taking a small outpost by surprise, Jonathan fell on them with an intensity that caused confusion among the band. An earthquake spread the confusion to other parts of the army. Soon the Philistines were fighting blindly among themselves. Seeing the turmoil in the enemy's camp, Saul marshaled his forces for a hasty attack and succeeded in completely routing the foe. The pursuit continued down the pass of Bethaven and would have been a total victory except for another foolish and impulsive act of Saul. He made a rash vow, placing a curse on anyone who ate before sundown. As a result the Hebrews were too exhausted to achieve a complete victory.

3. *Saul's Brief Glory* (I Samuel 15)

Two great military victories had strengthened Saul's position and secured for him the loyalty of the people. These triumphs were followed by a series of victories over other enemies—Moab, Ammon, Edom, and the kings of Zobah. This is the period of Saul's greatest glory. He now assumed his full royal state. His standing army of 3,000 men was commanded by his uncle Abner, one of the greatest warriors in the annals of Hebrew history. A bodyguard of Benjamites, chosen for their beauty and stature, attended the king on all occasions. In recruiting these guards the king acted in the arbitrary manner which Samuel had predicted: "When Saul saw any strong man, or any valiant man, he took him unto him" (14:52). In royal fashion Saul gathered herds and flocks. Even the high priest obeyed the orders of the king (21:2).

a. Saul's Great Test. Although Saul had twice shown himself unfitted for his task, he was given a third opportunity to prove his obedience. The great Bedouin tribe of the Amalekites continued to cast a shadow over the rising Jewish kingdom. In the past, at Sinai, in the wilderness wanderings, and in the days of Gideon, this group had repeatedly attacked the Israelites. Saul now received a special commission to destroy this vicious, idolatrous people. He was specifically commanded to put to the sword every living thing.

The king responded immediately. Mustering a force of 200,000 infantrymen, in addition to 10,000 from Judah, Saul marched to the south. With the shrewdness of a seasoned general Saul surprised the Amalekites, now weakened by the loss of their Kenite allies, who had been warned to leave the doomed tribe. The victory was decisive. Saul's army annihilated the entire tribe except the very few who managed to escape. Only Agag, the king, was taken alive.

In addition the Jews captured enormous quantities of plunder which the Amalekites had stolen from the trade caravans passing between the Euphrates and Egypt. Vast flocks of sheep and goats and great herds of oxen and camels came into the Amalekites' possession. According to the command of Samuel, all this should have been destroyed. But such a rich treasure proved too tempting to the Israelites, who convinced themselves and Saul that they deserved the rewards of their success.

Agag, the captured king, was led back in chains to serve as the prize showpiece in the triumphal procession. Saul's early humility now gave way to personal pride at the achievement of such a monumental exploit. In order to remind posterity of the glorious occasion Saul erected a memorial in the oasis near Carmel.

b. Rejection of Saul. In the meantime Samuel had been directed to meet Saul at Gilgal with the announcement that God had completely rejected him. The warmhearted Samuel was grieved and "cried unto the Lord all night" (v. 11), re-

luctant to deliver such a shattering message. But in the
morning he prepared to fulfill his duty. The meeting between
the two is profound in its moral significance, as well as tragic
in its results. Acting as though nothing had happened, Saul
confidently informed the prophet that he had fulfilled his
commission. With his dull spiritual perception he no doubt
had rationalized his actions to the point of believing them just.

Saul stated that the best of the cattle had been saved in
order to offer them as sacrifices to God. But Samuel cut short
the king's excuses by uttering one of the greatest spiritual
principles of the Bible: "Hath the Lord as great delight in
burnt offerings and sacrifices, as in obeying the voice of the
Lord? Behold, to obey is better than sacrifice, and to hearken
than the fat of rams" (15:22). Then came the terrible sentence: "Because thou hast rejected the word of the Lord,
he hath also rejected thee from being king" (15:23).

Overwhelmed with guilt and remorse, the humbled king
now confessed the simple truth, that he had been afraid of
the people. He begged Samuel to return to the altar with
him, probably so that the Israelites would not learn of his
rejection. Samuel refused and turned from the stricken
monarch. As he turned, Saul seized the prophet's mantle to
gain further time to present his cause. But an added omen
of doom resulted, for the mantle or cape of the prophet was
torn down the middle. Then Samuel said, "The Lord hath
rent the kingdom of Israel from thee this day, and hath given
it to a neighbour of thine, that is better than thou" (15:28).

4. Fear and Failure (I Samuel 16—31)

This meeting between Samuel and Saul was a turning
point in the latter's life. The elation of victory had been
changed to the despair of defeat. His mind echoed the words
of Samuel that he was forsaken and rejected of God. The
hand that had been so reluctant to take up the scepter of
kingly power now clutched it with a determined, defiant
grasp. If God had rejected him, then he would try to insure
his position by winning the people more completely. But
although Saul determined in his heart to retain his position,
fear and suspicion began to undermine his mental stability.

a. A Fearful King. It soon became evident to Saul's
servants that he was developing a severe case of melancholy.

They requested permission to send for a singer whose music might dispel the king's moods (16:16). David, a talented young shepherd lad from Bethlehem, was chosen for this task and remained with Saul until he was much improved. David later impressed Saul by his single-handed defeat of the Philistine giant, and was given command of the standing army (18:5).

David led his men on periodic raids against the Philistines and won fame and popularity. However, his success aroused Saul's jealousy, and when the women sang that "Saul hath slain his thousands, and David his ten thousands," Saul's affection for David turned to hatred. He realized that he had promoted the very one whom he dreaded most—the one who would succeed him as king. From that hour Saul devoted the cunning of a warped mind to unceasing attempts to do away with this dangerous rival.

b. Saul's Hate and David's Love. After twice failing to murder David, Saul excluded him from the palace. But since he could not highhandedly dismiss such a public favorite, Saul reduced him to the position of captain over 1,000 men. Hoping to see David become a battle casualty, Saul promised to give one of his daughters, Michal, to David in marriage if he should personally kill 100 Philistines. David doubled the number of victims and returned to claim his bride.

Frustrated in this scheme, Saul ordered his men to murder David. But the unselfish friendship of Jonathan, Saul's son, and the protecting love of Michal helped David escape the traps of the king. Saul's insane desire to kill David caused him to commit ruthless and irrational deeds, such as killing the 85 priests at Nob who had innocently given aid to David. The instability of Saul is seen from his outburst of gratitude and friendship when David spared his life in the wilderness of Engedi. But in a short while he took up the pursuit again with 3,000 soldiers. After a second such gesture on David's part, Saul seems to have accepted the inevitable and made no further attempts on David's life.

c. Saul's Tragic Death. Saul's eventual death on the fields of Gilboa was a tragic end to a tragic career. The Philistines had decided to wage a decisive war with Saul. Fearful and disheartened, Saul turned to a fortune-teller, the witch of Endor, for information and guidance. This unfortunate experience left Saul in a more distracted state than ever. Perhaps the discouragement of Saul was reflected in the fighting of his soldiers, for they were easily defeated by the Philistines. Fleeing with a few survivors, Saul was wounded and his three sons Jonathan, Abinadab, and Melchishua, were killed. Rather than be captured alive and tortured, Saul committed suicide by falling on his own sword.

II. DAVID—SECOND KING OF ISRAEL

Israel's first king had failed. Saul had been offered a priceless opportunity. But "his rashness and self-will, his want of spiritual sympathy with the prophet, and his gross and superficial conceptions of religious duty, proved him unfit to advance the high aims designed for Israel, and tended to found a mere worldly kingdom."[3] If Saul had possessed true spiritual insight and sound spiritual principles, his instincts would have guided him aright. But his fear of men and his regard for outward ceremony stifled his best self until he became a frantic, frightened, half-demented leader whose ungodly course ended inevitably in suicide.

1. *A New Champion* (I Samuel 16—17)

Long before Saul's death the finger of God was pointing to his successor. While Samuel was regretfully pondering the erratic course of Saul, God has spoken to him and said: "How long wilt thou mourn for Saul, seeing I have rejected him from reigning over Israel? fill thine horn with oil, and go, I will send thee to Jesse the Beth-lehemite: for I have provided me a king among his sons" (16:1). The place to which Samuel was sent was a small town in Judah about five miles south of Jerusalem. Bethlehem was "of lowly reputation" (Mic. 5:2), but rich in spiritual history. In the neighborhood was the tomb of Rachel, wife of Jacob. In nearby grain fields Ruth had gleaned after the reapers of Boaz. On the slopes of the hills outside the city David had watched his father's sheep.

a. David's Training Ground. David's experiences at Bethlehem were an ideal training for a future king and

[3]Cunningham Geikie, *Hours with the Bible*, III, 123.

spiritual leader. No occupation could have been more con-
ducive to the development of the qualities "of prudence,
promptitude, and prowess which his after life required, than
that of a shepherd."[4] As with Moses, the solitude would
direct him to the companionship of God. His long night
vigils would make the grandeur of the stars an ennobling
experience.

In addition, he would be familiar with the fury of the
storm, the blessings of the seasons, and the mystery of life
which everyone near to nature senses. His unceasing labors
and occasional conflicts with wild animals from the neighborhood would give him courage, confidence, and physical
strength. The nearness of his home to the tribe of Benjamin
would challenge him to compete with these skilled marksmen
"who could sling stones at an hair breadth and not miss"
(Judg. 20:16). But most important of all, this work and its
wholesome environment afforded abundant opportunity for
the development of David's musical ability and his capacity
to understand spiritual truths.

b. Samuel Anoints David. Commissioned to anoint a
king in place of disobedient Saul, Samuel went reluctantly
to Bethlehem. Arriving there he requested Jesse, grandson
of Boaz, to gather his sons, eight in number, for a sacred
sacrificial ceremony which ended with a feast. As they were
about to sit down, Samuel intently examined each of the
sons to see which of them was the Lord's anointed.

The eldest attracted his attention because of his stature
and countenance. But God, perhaps reminding him of the
same attractive features in Saul, indicated that he was not the
choice. In rapid succession the other sons were passed over.
Finally Samuel asked if there were any other sons. Upon being told that the youngest son was out in the fields the prophet
insisted that he be brought in. When David appeared Samuel
immediately anointed him, and God's Spirit came upon the
young man.

From the time of his anointing the advance of David
was rapid. Recommended to play his harp before the fitful
Saul, he completely won the monarch's heart and was soon
made his armor-bearer (16:21). His presence seemed to have

[4]William H. Taylor, *David, King of Israel,* p. 15.

been a tonic for the king, who appears to have recovered temporarily, for David soon returned to his sheep.

c. *David and Goliath.* David emerged again into public life when the Philistines made one of their frequent raids on Israel. Goliath of Gath, a giant of tremendous stature some 9½ feet tall, was their leader. Goliath was probably one of the Anakims (Num. 13:33; Josh. 11:22), a strain of men of huge stature whom Joshua had driven out of Hebron and who had taken refuge among the Philistines. David, bringing food to his brothers on the battle line, was amazed at the fear which paralyzed the warriors of Israel. Not willing to see his nation ashamed and embarrassed, the young shepherd accepted the challenge and vanquished the giant and the Philistine army.

David's glory was immediate and widespread. As he entered Gibeah the women ran out to meet him, singing with their tambourines the refrain:

> *Saul hath slain his thousands,*
> *And David his ten thousands* (I Sam. 18:7, ASV).

2. *Preparation for Kingship* (I Samuel 18—31; II Samuel 1)

David had been designated as king, but before he ascended the throne he had to serve a long apprenticeship. He could learn from Saul's example the disastrous results of ignoring God's will, and of acting hastily without consulting God. With rare and exemplary restraint David waited, refusing to lift a hand against half-crazed Saul. Even when Saul was finally removed, instead of exulting that the way to the throne was now clear, David lamented his tragic death.

a. *David at Court.* Saul had promised his daughter to the man who should defeat Goliath. The king, after further tests, reluctantly permitted David to marry one of his young daughters, Michal. Is addition to the marriage to the king's daughter, David formed a lasting and historic friendship with Saul's son, Jonathan. From this time a series of strange incidents occurred between the king and his popular lieutenant. One day when David was playing the harp before him, Saul impetuously seized a spear and threw it at him. The alert and agile David eluded it. In the army Saul assigned David to difficult and dangerous missions. But David, with

God's blessing, was able to perform every mission with God's help and grew in power and popularity.

b. *David Becomes an Outlaw.* After a number of such experiences, David fled from Saul's presence and went to be with Samuel at Ramoth. Jonathan, the son of Saul, proved his friendship for David by keeping him informed of the jealous king's plans. Jonathan was the logical successor to his father as king; but realizing that David was the chosen of God, Jonathan, a truly great soul, stepped aside and actually helped David toward the kingship.

But even this affection between David and Jonathan, which has become a classic example of friendship, could not divert Saul's murderous intent.[5] When it became clear that the king was not to be placated, David left Saul's court permanently.

At the historic shrine at Nob, David and a few followers induced Ahimelech the priest to give them shelter and bread. Saul ordered the massacre of all the hapless priests at Nob, 85 in number, in vengeance for their innocent help to the refugees. David himself escaped from Nob and took refuge at Adullam, a high, isolated hill full of caves. The cave at Adullam is said to be situated about six miles southeast of Bethlehem, on the site of the wide gorge at el-Kureitum. It is a large natural cavern in the side of a cliff. So difficult are the approach and entrance that from within it a few sturdy defenders could easily hold an army at bay. This cave may have been a favorite rendezvous for David as a boy.

Making this stronghold his headquarters, David began to collect a band of loyal followers. These followers of David during the dangerous period of his outlaw life no doubt formed the hard core of his army later. Psalms 34 and 62 should be read with this stronghold in mind, for "the Adullam fortress doubtless was the occasion for the analogy of God as a rock, as a refuge, and as a secure hiding place, so common in the Psalms."[6]

C. *David Spares His Enemy.* As the result of a warning by a prophet of God, David moved to the woods of Hareth. Here in a deadly game of hide-and-seek occurred two in-

[5]Carl S. Knopf, *The Old Testament Speaks,* p. 141.
[6]Loyal R. Ringenberg, *The Word of God in History,* p. 147.

cidents that reveal the true greatness of David's spirit. Twice
he had Saul completely at his mercy, yet refused to harm
him. On the first occasion David and his men secretly surrounded Saul in a cave (24:3). The second time they stole
silently into Saul's camp while he was asleep (26:4-12). On
both occasions David refrained from taking vengeance on the
man who had so hatefully abused him. In addition he threatened with death anyone who should harm Saul, for he was
the Lord's anointed. In David's action of refusing to injure
one who had been selected and anointed by God there is a
lesson of far-reaching import. It is at one's own peril that he
lightly uses sacred things or spitefully misuses God's divinely
anointed and commissioned servants.

d. *David's Wanderings.* The outlaw life of David was
a strange but profitable training for his kingship. As Carl S.
Knopf writes, "There is a genius for leadership and popularity
in David's character. Far from being a robber, David established a sort of private police force."[7]

Upon being informed that the Philistines were besieging
Keilah, David hurried to the rescue of the city, drove off
and scattered the enemy, and for a short period made this
his base of operations (23:1-6). However, Saul maintained
a persistent pursuit and forced David to flee again (23:7-14).
But these wanderings had not been completely to David's
disadvantage. His prestige had drawn 600 to his support.
In addition he had married a rich widow, Abigail, the widow
of Nabal, a wealthy sheep owner of Carmel (25:2-42).

Finally David left the kingdom entirely and sought
refuge among his former enemies, the Philistines. With the
consent of Achish, king of Gath, he established his headquarters at Ziklag for over a year (27:1-7). During this time
David gained the friendship of the Philistine king by supporting his men in their raids on the tribes to the south in
the wilderness of Shur (27:8-12). When the Philistines decided to wage an all-out war against Saul, however, they
refused to let David participate, questioning his sincerity in
fighting against his own people.

e. *David's Lament for Saul and Jonathan.* The sad tidings
of the death of Saul and his sons were brought to David at

[7]Knopf, *op. cit.*, p. 142.

Ziklag by an Amalekite, who arrived with clothes torn and earth upon his head—the sign of mourning. David fasted until evening. A person of less stature would have rejoiced at the removal of such a dangerous and persistent enemy. But when evening came he took his harp and poured out a most beautiful and touching lament:

> *Saul and Jonathan were lovely and pleasant in their lives,*
> *And in their death they were not divided* (II Sam. 1:23, ASV).

Together they were celebrated as "swifter than eagles" and "stronger than lions." The mourner described the joy of the Philistines over the mighty who were fallen in memorable words:

> *Thy glory, O Israel, is slain upon thy high places!*
> *How are the mighty fallen!*
> *Tell it not in Gath,*
> *Publish it not in the street of Ashkelon;*
> *Lest the daughters of the Philistines rejoice,*
> *Lest the daughters of the uncircumcised triumph* (1:19-20, ASV).

The realm of nature is called to share the sorrow of Israel by suggesting a curse for the region where the tragedy occurred.

> *Ye mountains of Gilboa,*
> *Let there be no dew, nor rain upon you, neither fields of offerings,*
> *For there the shield of the mighty was vilely cast away,*
> *The shield of Saul, not anointed with oil* (1:21, ASV).

The daughters of Israel, who once aroused Saul's jealousy by singing in David's honor, are now called upon to weep for their fallen king:

> *Ye daughters of Israel, weep over Saul,*
> *who clothed you daintily in scarlet,*
> *who put ornaments of gold upon your apparal* (1:24, RSV).

But the grand outburst of love and grief is reserved for Jonathan:

> *Jonathan is slain upon thy high places.*
> *I am distressed for thee, my brother Jonathan* (1:25-
> 26, ASV).[8]

3. David as King (II Sam. 2:1—5:5)

With the death of Saul the pathway to the throne of Israel seemed clear for David. He was just past 30 and had shown kingly characteristics in every way. His courage was unquestioned; his ability to lead hardy men had become a legend; his magnanimous spirit was recognized by the entire nation; he was the anointed of God. But the transition was not as smooth as the situation indicated. Judah, David's native tribe, readily accepted him as king. But Saul's general, Abner, refused to recognize David, placing instead a son of Saul, Ish-bosheth, on the throne as ruler over most of Israel (2:8-9).

a. David as King over Judah. David's ability was first recognized by his own tribe of Judah, with its capital at Hebron. He was declared king (2:4) and reigned at Hebron for seven and one-half years. During this period David's strength and fame continued to grow, while the house of Saul grew weaker and weaker (3:1). David himself seems to have been satisfied to again await God's time, for he gave no indication of aggression toward Saul's son. But beneath the surface bitter and ruthless intrigue was carried on between the rival military factions.

Abner, general of Ish-bosheth, had killed a young man named Asahel, brother of David's leading commander, Joab. Noting the growing weakness of his position, Abner attempted to affect a reconciliation with David and Joab by once again uniting the two kingdoms. His efforts failed when Joab tricked Abner into a secret meeting, and under pretense of speaking with him, assassinated his foe.

Another deed of violence was performed when two young men of Judah, disguised as farmers or merchants, killed Ish-bosheth, Saul's son, as he rested at noonday. When David

---

[8]Smith, *op. cit.*, p. 420.

learned of this he ordered the execution of the assassins. Now all Israel, except Judah, was bereft of leadership. Swallowing their pride, these leaderless groups sent a delegation to Hebron (5: 3) to request that David be their king.

It was a marvelous triumph for David. He had waited for at least 10 years with rare patience for the words of Samuel to be fulfilled. No act of enmity or hate marred his record. No spirit of rebellion or disobedience was ever manifested.

b. David, King over All Israel. The circumstances connected with David's coronation are significant. In the first place, the coronation assembly was not made up of the elders or delegates alone, but it was virtually a convention of the entire nation. The particular numbers present from each tribe are given in the Book of Chronicles (I Chron. 12: 23-40). All the tribes were present in force, except Issachar, which sent only 200 men. The entire number was 280,000. Thus David, in his thirty-eighth year, in the prime and vigor of his manhood, ascended the throne of the united kingdom of Israel.

4. *David's Achievements* (II Sam. 5: 6—10: 19)

The shepherd boy with remarkable talents lived up to his promise as a king. His achievements were brilliant and permanent. First he founded a national capital at Jerusalem. Then he systematically defeated all Israel's enemies, resulting in almost a century of peace for the nation. Not forgetting the importance of spiritual interests, he had the ark returned to Jerusalem and reestablished the worship of Jehovah. Then he completed his achievements by enacting notable social reforms.

a. Jerusalem—the City of David. Hebron could never be the capital of an important and powerful kingdom in Palestine. It was poorly located for the purpose of defense, and it would be unacceptable to the tribe of Benjamin. Likewise a northern capital would be unacceptable to Judah in the south. If the kingdom was to enjoy a stable government, it must have a central capital which could be developed into a symbol of national prowess. Twenty miles to the north of Hebron, on neutral ground between northern and southern tribes, lay the strongest fortified city of the region. This city, Jebus, David selected for his capital.

Jebus, the city of the Jebusites, occupied a strategic site. It was the focal point where the routes from Gaza, Jaffa, Shechem, Jericho, and Bethlehem crossed. Yet it was remote enough for security. Built on three hills, it had sections of wall 40 feet thick. The Jebusites were so smug in their security that they believed the blind and the lame were able to defend the walls (5:6). David accepted the challenge, promising great rewards to the first one entering the city. Joab was the hero. The Israelites had located an underground waterway that opened into the heart of the city. Joab scaled the rocks, entered the watercourse, and surprised the defenders. Within modern times, in the course of excavations at Jerusalem, an English lieutenant repeated this bold adventure without difficulty.

The city was now given its former name, Jerusalem, and was made completely independent of the Israelite tribal system. It owed allegiance only to the king. Its people were largely the king's personal attendants, who had abandoned their original loyalties, and devoted themselves to the service of their royal master. David's strategic choice of Jerusalem as his capital was an evidence of his political genius.[9]

b. Military Achievements. The principal military task of David was to break the power of the Philistines. Since Saul had died on the slopes of Gilboa this enemy had dealt roughly with Israel. Beginning with sporadic raids David began to whittle away at the military giant. He moved about the countryside like a scourge. Eventually the Philistines determined to have a showdown, and marched their army up the valley of Rephaim, which leads toward Jerusalem from the southwest. In two pitched battles David shattered the Philistine forces so completely that they never again were a threat to Israel (5:17-25).

Shrewd soldier that he was, David pressed his advantage to the limit. Moab, Edom, Ammon, Zobah, and Syria felt the power of his might and submitted to his taxation (8:2-8;

II Sam. 21:15-22). God gave His leader victory after victory. Garrisons were placed in the outer areas of Syria and Edom; several ports came under his control; in the north, the plain of Esdraelon was recaptured. David was the instrument who brought into reality the ancient promise of God to Abraham: "I will give unto thee . . . all the land of Canaan, for an everlasting possession" (Gen. 17:8).

c. Religious Achievements. Another notable feat of David was the centralization of religion in the new capital. Shiloh, Mizpah, and Gilgal had served as religious centers in the past. Each had noble traditions and sacred memories in the life of the nation. However, each might become a rallying point for contending factions. With the ark in Jerusalem all eyes would center on the capital for final authority.[10] The ark, since it had been carried off by the Philistines in the days of Eli, had remained in a private home in a small town with a big name, Kirjath-jearim.

An elaborate tabernacle, or tent, was prepared for it on Mount Zion and a great national assembly was called, which all tribes were invited to attend. Excitement spread over all Israel. Such an elaborate festival had never been seen before by these people. When the Levites entered the gates of Jerusalem, David expressed the joy of the entire nation by dancing "before the Lord with all his might." With the coming of the ark, Jerusalem became not only "the city of David," but the "holy city," the center of the worship of Jehovah.

d. Social Improvements. David had vanquished his enemies and established a new capital. He had given the people a religious center which they would ever cherish. Now he turned his attention to organizing the government and improving social conditions. To care for the complex activities of government the king appointed overseers, men who had proved their fitness for such tasks. These men became a private council, or king's cabinet. Several of them, with the offices they filled, are mentioned by name. These men were appointees of the king and responsible to him only.

Industrial activity flourished. Armies of workmen and tons of building material arrived. Foreign architects and master builders were secured from among the Phoenicians,

[10]Knopf, *op. cit.,* p. 151.

experts in the art of building. Workmen from surrounding countries came to share the prosperity of Israel. Some of the poorer Canaanites, and even Hebrews, became virtual slaves of the king. The military machine was perfected and overshadowed every activity of the nation. Central authority over all Israel had now become an actual fact. David was supreme in his own land, and respected and feared in other lands.

5. *Twilight and Evening Star* (II Samuel 11—24)

One historian observed that Abraham Lincoln died in time to be great—that, if he had lived, his greatness might well have been tarnished with mistakes. David did not die at the peak of his power and achievement. He lived to make his greatest mistake and commit his great sin.

a. David's Great Sin. David was taking an evening stroll on an elevated terrace of his palace when he looked down and saw a woman bathing. He made inquiries about her and found she was the wife of an army officer named Uriah, who was serving in a distant area fighting the Ammonites. David's lust conquered his nobler sensibilities and he soon entered into an illicit relationship with the woman, Bath-sheba. To cover his sin and avoid scandal David ordered his general, Joab, to place Uriah in a position in battle where he was certain to be killed. Shortly Joab sent a terse report that the king's wish had been accomplished. Now both adultery and murder were indelibly recorded in the career of Israel's greatest king.

b. Nathan Denounces David. God directed the prophet Nathan to go and denounce the king for his sin. This was an extremely dangerous mission, as the monarch held the power of life and death over his subjects. But the courageous prophet went to the palace and quickly gained the ear of the king with the parable:

> *There were two men in one city; the one rich, and the other poor. The rich man had exceeding many flocks and herds; but the poor man had nothing, save one little ewe lamb, which he had bought and nourished up: and it grew up together with him, and with his children; it did eat of his own morsel, and*

*drank of his own cup, and lay in his bosom, and was
unto him as a daughter. And there came a traveller
unto the rich man, and he spared to take of his own
flock and of his own herd, to dress for the wayfaring
man that was come unto him, but took the poor man's
lamb* (12:1-4, ASV).

David sensed the injustice. His anger rose. "The man that
hath done this thing shall surely die: and he shall restore the
lamb fourfold" (12:5-6). Nathan shot the arrow home, saying, "Thou art the man . . . thou hast killed Uriah the Hittite
with the sword, and hast taken his wife to be thy wife"
(12:7, 9). Both the king and the prophet knew it was the
voice of God. David's bigness of soul is shown by his humble
confession, "I have sinned against the Lord." He knew that
he would be punished for his sin.

c. *The Wages of Sin.* The punishment predicted by
Nathan was swift in coming. It came in the form which
struck David hardest—in his own home. Amnon, a son of
David, seduced by force one of his half sisters, Tamar. Absalom, a brother of the girl, killed Amnon. David banished
the hot-tempered Absalom, allowing him to return only after
a three-year interval. Returned from his exile, Absalom set
to work to undermine his father, perhaps having learned that
his younger half brother, Solomon, was being favored as
David's successor. So successful was Absalom's traitorous
scheme that he was soon able to go to Hebron, set himself up
as king, and rally to his banner the majority of the nation.

Hearing of the rebellion, David and his immediate followers fled in dismay. His friend, Hushai, by pretending
allegiance to the new king was able to give wrong counsel
to Absalom and to keep David informed of what was afoot.
Absalom himself led a large army in pursuit of his father.
However, his amateur leadership was no match for David's
experienced generals, and Absalom and his army were soon
routed. Caught by his hair in an oak tree during flight,
Absalom was killed by Joab, who sent word to David. The
violent death of another son threw the aging king into the
depths of despondence, from which only Joab's sharp words
could rouse him.

David now returned to his capital and his authority was

never again seriously challenged. A premature rebellion led by a man named Sheba, of the tribe of Benjamin, was quickly suppressed. Provoked by Satan, David later ordered an illegal census taken, which brought a serious plague upon the nation. Even to the last, strife within his household and the ambition of another of his sons threatened the aged king's peace of mind. He died at the age of 70, having ruled as king of Judah for seven years and king over all Israel for another 33 years.

David was in every way a remarkable man. He was as human as he was great. He had a boundless love for God, an unshakable faith in and loyalty to Him, and a true hunger to know and do God's will. He reflects in many ways the weaknesses and characteristics of a harsh age. In spite of this, he stands as a spiritual monument. Daniel-Rops has succinctly stated his evaluation of David in these words:

. . . what ability, what power, and what grace! As a soldier full of valour, a poet whose work has come down to us, decisive in politics, and chivalrous in war, determined in his undertakings, feeling deeply in his personal relationships, he has every quality that makes a man lovable.[11]

SUMMARY

The kingdom was firmly established at the end of David's reign. During the life of Saul some notable achievements were made, in spite of his vacillating loyalties. Most of the progress was in the form of sporadic and indecisive victories over the persistent enemies along the borders. Because of his presumptuous sins Saul was rejected and David was selected to replace him.

At Saul's death David was accepted as king over Judah but the major portion of the nation preferred a son of Saul, Ish-bosheth. After seven and a half years all Israel accepted the shepherd-king as ruler. He ruled the united kingdom 33 years. Under David a central capital was established; religious worship was centered in Jerusalem; Israel's enemies were defeated and her borders enlarged; and great social advances were made. Although his inexcusable sin marred his work and resulted in rebellion, heartbreak, and bloodshed, David's work was solid and lasting. When his son Solomon came to

[11]Henry Daniel-Rops, *Sacred History*, p. 191.

the throne he found a strong, respected, and fairly prosperous nation. Solomon lifted the nation to its highest level of political power and prosperity.

RECOMMENDED READINGS

Blaikie and Matthews, *A Manual of Bible History*, pp. 165-95.

William J. Deane, *Samuel and Saul: Their Lives and Times*, pp. 79-213.

————, *David: His Life and Times*, pp. 1-222.

Alfred Edersheim, *The Bible History*, Volume IV, pp. 35-196.

Joseph P. Free, *Archaeology and Bible History*, pp. 150-61.

James C. Muir, *His Truth Endureth*, pp. 113-38.

G. Frederick Owen, *Abraham to Allenby*, pp. 48-59.

David R. Piper, *Youth Explores the Bible*, pp. 89-104.

Ira M. Price, *The Dramatic Story of the Old Testament*, pp. 181-229.

Henry P. Smith, *Old Testament History*, pp. 106-55.

William Smith, *Old Testament History*, pp. 379-472.

FOR FURTHER STUDY

1. What changes were involved in the transition from a tribal confederacy to a monarchy?

2. Why did God agree to the people's demand for a king, when His plan was for a theocracy?

3. Discuss Samuel's warning against a king. In what ways was it fulfilled?

4. What characteristics or talents did Saul have which fitted him for the throne? What were his weaknesses?

5. Can you note any factor common to all of the sins associated with Saul's rejection by God as king?

6. What famous example of friendship is found in I Samuel? List other famous Bible friendships. List friendships in life and literature.

7. Describe Saul's death. How can you account for the scene in the cave of Endor?

8. Explain the political situation at Saul's death.

9. Of what tribe and lineage did David come? Why is this important?

10. How did David make his debut into public life?

11. List and discuss the traits in David's personality that made him a success.

12. Why did David refuse to harm Saul? What opportunities did he have to injure the older man? How did Saul react to David's kindness?

13. By what process, or steps, did David become king over all Israel?

14. What was the advantage in making Jerusalem the capital city? How was this achieved?

15. What religious advances were made under David? What was the significance of returning the ark to Jerusalem?

16. What were the results of David's great sin as seen in his own life and in the lives of others?

17. What is your estimate of Nathan's courage and tact in confronting David with his great sin?

18. Is there any record of David's repentance elsewhere than in II Samuel?

19. What contributions did the reign of David make toward the strength and stability of the nation?

PALESTINE
in the Time of
the Divided Kingdom

0   10   20   30

SCALE OF MILES

Gebal

Berothai ●

Heibon ●

Chun ●

Zedad ●

Hazar-enam ●

Sidon ●

Damascus ●

River Abana

Zarephath ●

PHOENICIA

Mt. Hermon

Pharpar

Tyre ●

Ahel ●   ● Dan

Waters of Merom

Accho ●

● Cabul

Sea of Galilee

● Ashtaroth

MEDITERRANEAN SEA

Mt. Carmel

Dor ●

ISRAEL

● Edrei   ● Nobah

● Megiddo

● Jezreel

Ramoth-gilead ●

Dothan ●

Tishbeh ●

● Mahanaim

Salcah ●

● Samaria

Shechem ●

Plain of Sharon

River Jordan

Brook Cherith

River Jabbok

AMMON

● Joppa

Gilgal ●

Bethel ●

Gibeah ●   ● Ai   Jericho ●

● Gilgal

● Rabbath-ammon

● Anathoth

Heshbon ●

Mt. Nebo

Ashdod ●   Gath ●

Jerusalem ●

● Medeba

Askelon ●

Lachish ●

● Beth-peor

Gaza ●

● Etam

● Tekoa

● Dibon

● Gerar

JUDAH

● Hebron

Dead Sea

MOAB

Beer-sheba ●

● Ar

● Kir-haraseth

ARABIAN

DESERT

PHILISTIA

Bozrah ●

● Kadesh-barnea

Punon ●

EDOM

Sela ● ● Teman

CHAPTER VIII

Solomon and the Temple

Solomon in all his glory (Luke 12:27).

Sources: I Kings 1—11; II Chronicles 1—9

To Be Read: I Kings 1—11; II Chronicles 3—5

Period: Approximately 970-931 B.C.

The century between the coronation of Saul and the death of Solomon was the period of glory of Israel. In that century the kingdom was established, reached its highest point of power and prosperity, and began to decline. David bequeathed to Solomon a nation firmly entrenched in Palestine and prepared to further its interests. For a brief time the succession to the throne seemed doubtful, but the aged David won his final victory by insuring Solomon's right to the throne.

In the beginning Solomon, like Saul, humbly walked with God. With the exception of a campaign against Hamath in the far north (II Chron. 8:3), Solomon secured his position by brilliant diplomacy, forming alliances with surrounding nations. Then he embarked on a gigantic building program, beginning with a spectacularly beautiful temple. But he drifted from God into idolatry. When he died he left a nation rotten at the core and ripe for disaster.

I. Stepping-stones to the Throne

When Solomon was born the kingdom was at peace. David had seen enough of war. This is indicated by the fact that he gave to his youngest son by Bath-sheba the stately name of Solomon—"the peaceful." Nathan was immediately informed of the birth, and the child was placed under his sponsorship and care (II Sam. 12:25). The prophet, too, hailed the birth of the child as a sign that God had restored to David the favor which had been promised to him in answer to his repentance. He therefore gave to Solomon the more sacred name of Jedidiah—"beloved of the Lord." This name, however, is never mentioned again, for it was not to be used in common life. The name Solomon was like a prophetic intimation of the ideal and the history of the brilliant, unwarlike king.

Though Solomon was the first Jewish king "born in the purple," it was by no means certain that he had been destined from the first to be David's heir. Appointing a successor was a complex and dangerous affair, as pointed out by F. W. Farrar:

> To make it generally known while Solomon was a child would have been to awaken the turbulent jealousies of his powerful and unscrupulous rivals, and to mark him out for almost certain destruction.[1]

Adonijah, an older brother of Solomon, was a strikingly handsome man who had always been treated indulgently by his father (I Kings 1:6). Deciding to take advantage of David's increasing feebleness, he formulated plans to make himself king. When he thought the time was ripe, he invited a select group to a great banquet at the rock of Zoheleth, near Enrogel. Here, at the height of the gaity of the festival, the cry was made, "Long live King Adonijah."

Nathan, the prophet, and Bath-sheba, the mother of Solomon, learned of the connivings of Adonijah and hastily informed David. Summoning his remaining strength and calling upon his political acumen, David had Zadok, the high priest, declare Solomon king. When the usurper, Adonijah, learned of the action of David he fled to the Tabernacle for safety, but Solomon assured him clemency and sent him to his home.

David gathered all the leaders of the people together, at which time he delivered a solemn charge to the congregation and to the new king. With great dignity and reverence he delivered to Solomon the plans for the house of God, and the materials he had collected for the building. After David had offered thanksgiving and prayer for Solomon, all the people feasted together. Then Solomon was inaugurated as king a second time, while Zadok was publicly anointed as high priest. By the swift and decisive actions of David, the

[1] F. W. Farrar, *Solomon, His Life and Times,* p. 12.

new king was established in power and in favor with the people. "And Jehovah magnified Solomon exceedingly in the sight of all Israel, and bestowed upon him such royal majesty as had not been on any king before him in Israel" (I Chron. 29:25, ASV).

II. THE STATESMAN—MILESTONES TO GLORY

Solomon's early reign gave evidence of much promise. He appears as a humble and capable ruler, whose first desire seemed to be the welfare of his people. After establishing himself firmly as monarch, he turned his attention to many projects, all of which contributed to the glory of his early reign. Yet, while the young king exhibited qualities of statesmanship in negotiating alliances and conquering enemies, in building programs, in commerce, and in internal organization, his work was not enduring. Foolish and sinful choices undermined the foundations of the nation and brought about its eventual collapse.

1. *Initial Troubles of Solomon's Reign* (I Kings 2:13-46)

The decisive action of David had secured the throne for Solomon, but the initial days of his reign were occupied with a persistent threat to his leadership. The source of the trouble was in the smoldering desire of Adonijah to be king. This young prince and his fellow conspirators, Joab and Abiathar, were finally executed. Only then did Solomon's kingship become stable and strong.

a. The Second Plot of Adonijah. Soon after the death of David, Adonijah renewed his efforts to gain the kingdom for himself. In this plot he was doubtless assisted by Joab, military leader under David, and by Abiathar, the high priest. No doubt they thought it would be easy to outwit the young and inexperienced king.

The first stage of the plot, which was to be the springboard for further action was that Adonijah should marry Abishag, the nurse of David. This young woman, who had been chosen for her beauty to care for the aged and enfeebled David, was a native of Shunem, a town on the northern side of the Plain of Esdraelon. She was nominally and legally David's wife, though in reality she was nothing more to him than a nurse (I Kings 1:1-4). A king's wives are usually passed on to his successor, so it would indicate that Adonijah had a claim to the throne if he could marry Abishag. To gain his end Adonijah went to Bath-sheba and requested her to intercede with Solomon, that he might be permitted to marry Abishag. When the queen mother presented the request to her son, Solomon interpreted it as an attempt to gain the throne and vowed that the request would cost Adonijah his life. The threat was speedily carried out, for Benaiah, captain of the guard, was ordered to strike down the conspirator on the very day the request was made.

b. *The Execution of Joab.* The news of Adonijah's execution was at once relayed to Joab, who fled to the Tabernacle at Gibeon. When Solomon learned that Joab had sought safety at the altar in the ancient Tabernacle, he sent Benaiah to put him to death. The stalwart captain was reluctant to perform the execution at such a sacred place, but the relentless Solomon insisted and the gory old warrior was dispatched. Thus the blood-thirsty and brutal man of intrigue met a fate similar to that which he had so frequently meted out to others.

c. *A High Priest Rejected.* While punishing with death Adonijah and Joab, Solomon was more merciful to the third of the conspirators, Abiathar, the high priest. Solomon was unwilling to put Abiathar to death because of the long and intimate relationship of the priest with David. But the king did deprive him of his office and banished him to his native town of Anathoth, which was located about three miles northeast of Jerusalem.

In ejecting Abiathar from the high priesthood, Solomon fulfilled a warning God had issued to Eli by a prophet at Shiloh more than a century before (I Sam. 2:27-36). The house of Eli was doomed for its unfaithfulness. Though the divine purpose might seem for many years to miscarry, yet in the course of events it was carried out to the letter.

d. *The Death of Shimei.* Shimei, the Benjamite who had so bitterly denounced David while the king was fleeing from Absalom's rebellion, was placed under strict probation. He was warned against leaving Jerusalem under any pretext, and when he violated his probation, was also put to death.

2. *Solomon's Choice of Wisdom* (I Kings 3—4; II Chron. 1:1-12)

Having eliminated all contenders for the throne, Solomon went in solemn procession to the altar at Gibeon, about five and a half miles from Jerusalem, where the ancient Tabernacle still stood. Here the new king celebrated an elaborate religious festival in which he offered the enormous sacrifice of 1,000 burnt offerings on the venerable and sacred altar which Bezaleel had constructed nearly five centuries before.

a. Solomon's Dream. That same night with thoughts of the empire on his mind and thanksgiving to God in his heart, Solomon had a dream in which God appeared and promised to grant him any request he would name. Passing over the lower and more personal objects of smaller minds, Solomon asked for wisdom, or understanding, to rule his people. Because his choice was so appropriate he was assured wisdom surpassing any of the past and eclipsing any of the future (I Kings 3:12). In addition he was promised manifold riches and multiplied honors for which he had not asked.

Solomon awoke and realized it was a dream. However, he recognized that God had spoken to him in this way. He returned from Gibeon to the altar on Mount Zion, where he stood before the ark, offered fresh burnt offerings and thank offerings, and celebrated a great feast (I Kings 3:15) as a sign of his gratitude.

b. Solomon's Wisdom. The sacred historian, after relating the dream at Gibeon, gives an example of the extraordinary sagacity of the young king. Shortly after his return to Jerusalem he was confronted by a problem which seemed impossible to solve. Two mothers came, bearing two infants, one living and one dead, each claiming the living child as her own. Solomon commanded one of his soldiers to cut the living child in two, giving each woman half. Then the agonized wail of the mother's heart came: "O my lord, give her the living child, and by no means slay it." This cry revealed the true mother, who now was given the child.

But Solomon's claim to wisdom went beyond practical shrewdness in everyday affairs. Illustrations of his wisdom are given in scientific knowledge, and in literary ability (I Kings 4:29-34). He is credited with 3,000 proverbs, of which only a portion have come down to us. Such prolific literary production in the midst of his many administrative duties and building projects indicates a mind of the highest intellectual power.

3. *Foreign Alliances* (I Kings 3:1; 5:1-18)

Israel had been called to be a distinct and separate people. God himself had purposed to be their Leader. He proposed to enlarge, prosper, and protect them. But their desire for a king had replaced God with an earthly monarch. Now this monarch set out to gain security and prosperity by forming alliances with other nations.

a. Egypt. The first of these alliances was with Egypt. Egypt's power was waning, and her days of supreme glory were past, but she was still a model of order, building interests, and military equipment. The biblical record (3:1) describes this alliance as Solomon's first act of foreign policy. It was made stronger by the marriage of Solomon to an Egyptian princess. Such a union not only amounted to a departure from Hebrew tradition, but also was an innovation in Egyptian custom, for Egyptian women were not given in marriage to foreigners. It must, therefore, be assumed that the marriage was regarded by both states as a political act of the first order.[2] Solomon brought his wife to the city of David, where eventually a palace was built for her near the Temple. With this alliance a dangerous potential enemy south of Israel was eliminated.

b. Phoenicia. In the north, there was no need of a change of policy, for David had already formed a strong friendship with the Phoenician king Hiram I, who lived in Tyre. Hiram I and Solomon were kindred spirits. Neither was primarily a warrior. Both took pleasure in methodical building, artistic accomplishment, political stability, and economic progress. Though the voyages of his merchant ships had made him extremely wealthy, Hiram needed the grain, fruit, oil, and wine from Palestine. For Solomon, the alliance meant a supply of skilled craftsmen and materials to carry out his building program. According to an ancient tradition, the

[2]Frederic Thieberger, *King Solomon,* p. 196.

bond of friendship was sealed by Solomon's marriage to a daughter of Hiram.

4. *Solomon's Building Projects* (I Kings 7:1-12; 9:15-19)

Solomon had the passion for building characteristic of many ancient kings. His great masterpiece was the Temple, but he also supervised the building of walls for defense of cities, palaces for himself and his wives, and even entire cities (9:17-19).

a. Temple and Palace. First came the erection of the Temple, which David had planned, but was not permitted to build. Then came the building of a magnificent palace, which required 13 years (7:1). The old palace on Mount Zion seemed completely inadequate for an Oriental despot like Solomon. The main part of the new palace was a large dwelling and reception area, called "the house of the forest of Lebanon."

In front of this striking building was an equally impressive porch. Since it was in the form of a colonnade, 75 feet long and 45 feet wide, it was called the Porch of Pillars. Adjoining this rose the porch proper, which served as the throne room, or Hall of Judgment. It was completely wainscoted with cedarwood, and was the King's Gate, from which he administered justice. In this hall stood the regal throne, which was the wonder of the age. Separated from these structures by a court stood the palace proper, or residence.

b. Military Building. Jerusalem was fortified and strengthened so that no vulnerable point might be left in the circuit of the city (I Kings 11:27). Solomon protected his entire domain by a chain of forts built at every point of chief access.

The fortification of the old Canaanite capital Hazor, at the foot of Lebanon (Judg. 4:6), gave security to Naphtali and the north from any possible attack from Rezon, king of Damascus. Gezer, the town which Pharaoh had conquered and given to him, protected his domain on the west of Ephraim (I Kings 9:16). The walls of Beth-horon dominated one of the natural passes to Jerusalem, while Baalath, on the borders of Dan, overawed the Philistines. He also built several cities to house provisions and cities to accommodate his cavalry and horses. Solomon's empire was now extended from the Arabian Desert to the Mediterranean, and from Egypt to Syria.

5. *Solomon's Commerce* (I Kings 10:14-29; II Chron. 9: 13-28)

Nothing is more remarkable in Solomon's reign than the immense and sudden development of a widely extended commerce by both land and sea.

a. Land Commerce. The land traffic with Tyre was founded chiefly on the needs arising out of Solomon's building program. He could have built neither the Temple nor the palace without the aid of the skilled wood-carvers and metal-casters of Phoenicia. The Tyrians supplied the world with the scarlet robes of kings. Silver, gold, and copper were the staple items of their trade. In return they received the agricultural produce of Israel.

Another phase of Solomon's land traffic was with mysterious Arabia. From this fabulous area must have come the supply of spices which became so popular in Jerusalem during this period. From this source also came a great part of the royal jewels and precious stones.

Egypt became a vitally important factor in Solomon's foreign commerce. The major traffic with Egypt was in horses and chariots, for which the land of the Pharaohs became famous. Business was carried on by large caravans. Solomon maintained a large stable to supply the 4,000 horses for his 1,400 chariots, and chargers for his 12,000 horsemen (9:25). Extensive excavations have verified the king's interest in horses, for large stables have been found at Megiddo.[3] Surplus horses and chariots were sold to Hittite and Aramean kings at a handsome profit.

b. Sea Commerce. The business enterprise of Solomon was also strikingly displayed at sea. He constructed a fleet of ships at Ezion-geber on an arm of the Red Sea. From this port he built a lucrative trade with Ophir, probably in southern Arabia, from which were brought algum or sandalwood trees and precious stones and as much as 420 to 450 talents of gold yearly (I Kings 9:28; II Chron. 8:18).

[3]Jack Finegan, *Light from the Ancient Past*, p. 152.

There was also a royal fleet in the Mediterranean which went with the ships of Hiram to Spain and returned every three years with gold, silver, ivory, apes, and peacocks (I Kings 10:22; II Chron. 9:21). Solomon appears to have given Hiram the privilege of sharing with him the trade of Ophir in exchange for the privilege of sharing with Hiram the trade with Tarshish.

As a result of his business skill and commercial aggressiveness Solomon lifted Israel to a peak of wealth and prosperity. The historian reports: "And the king made silver to be in Jerusalem as stones, and cedars made he to be as the sycamore trees that are in the vale, for abundance" (I Kings 10:27).

6. *In All His Glory* (I Kings 4:7-8; 10:1-29)

History, poetry, and legend unite to describe and magnify the glory of Solomon. Surrounded by breathtaking splendor, reveling in pomp and ceremony, giving free reign to every appetite and fancy, he provides the classic example of a worldly kingdom at its climax.

a. Public Appearances. When Solomon first became king, he appeared in public riding a mule, as had David, his father, before him. But later he never rode in public except in one of his glittering Egyptian chariots. It was drawn by swift horses, magnificently harnessed, and was followed by a parade of archers, riding on sturdy war horses. These handpicked men were selected as the king's bodyguard for their beauty and stature. They were uniformed in robes of Syrian purple, over which hung glittering weapons.

b. Palace Entertainment. The wealth and splendor of the royal feasts and entertainments contributed to the glory of Solomon. All the drinking and other vessels in the palace were of pure gold (10:21). The provisions for the single day were "thirty measures [335 bushels] of fine flour, and threescore measures [670 bushels] of meal, ten fat oxen, and twenty oxen out of the pastures, and a hundred sheep, besides harts, and gazelles, and roebucks, and fatted fowl" (4:22-23, ASV).

His servants and messengers were dressed in expensive and attractive uniforms. He seems to have had an obsession for gold, using it liberally for plating in his buildings and furniture as well as for his tableware. In addition to the 300 shields of gold which adorned the great hall of the palace, there were evident everywhere curious and costly articles which had been presented to Solomon by foreign princes and tributary kings.

c. *Administration of the Kingdom.* To maintain such a palace and direct such a nation required efficiency of the highest order. That Solomon possessed this talent in a marked degree is shown by his plan for supplying the royal table with regular and adequate supplies.

This was achieved by dividing the land into 12 districts with an officer over each. It was the duty of each officer and district to send a month's supply of provisions to the palace each year. These 12 officers were under the supervision of one of the princes of the court, Azariah, the son of Nathan. The names of these 12 officers and their districts are given in I Kings 4: 7-19.

d. *Solomon's Yearly Income.* "Now the weight of gold that came to Solomon in one year was six hundred threescore and six talents of gold, beside that which the traders brought, and the traffic of the merchants, and of all the kings of the mingled people, and of the governors of the country" (10: 14-15, ASV). While the exact value of the Hebrew talent cannot be stated with finality, it is possible to estimate Solomon's income between $15 million and $20 million per year. In addition to the 666 talents of gold, Solomon had a large revenue from the other sources referred to. Little wonder the historian remarked: "So king Solomon exceeded all the kings of the earth for riches and for wisdom" (10: 23).

e. *The Royal Throne.* No account of Solomon in all his glory would be complete without a description of the "royal throne." It was carved from solid ivory, inlaid with gold. It was approached by six steps, on each side of which stood a golden lion, symbol of the tribe of Judah, and the accepted emblem of sovereignty. In addition to these 12, each of the massive arms of the chair was guarded by a golden lion. The king's feet rested on a golden footstool. Upon this throne, dressed in scarlet or purple, sat the king to dispense justice.

f. *The Visit of the Queen of Sheba.* Even a period of such unexcelled brilliance as the reign of Solomon must reach a climax. The culminating point for Solomon was the visit of the Queen of Sheba, or as she is called in the Gospel of Matthew, "the queen of the south." Sheba was located in southern Arabia, at the straits of Bab el Mandeb, the entrance into the Red Sea.

This woman was a great queen in her own land and had prided herself on the splendor of her own court and capital. But when she heard the wisdom of Solomon and saw the house that he had built, and the performance of his servants and ministers, she readily admitted that "the half was not told me: thy wisdom and prosperity exceedeth the fame which I heard" (10:6-7).

The visit ended in an exchange of costly presents. The queen presented Solomon with "an hundred and twenty talents of gold, and of spices very great store, and precious stones: there came no more such abundance of spices as these which the queen of Sheba gave to king Solomon" (10:10). In return for her generosity "king Solomon gave to the queen of Sheba all her desire, whatsoever she asked, beside that which Solomon gave her of his royal bounty" (10:13).

III. THE TEMPLE—KEYSTONE OF NATIONAL FAITH

Sacred to all Jews and prominent in all their literature is the Temple. It exerted a profound influence on the life of the Israelites for many centuries. As soon as there began to be kings and palaces, it was felt to be incongruous that the ark of the Lord should still be housed in wood and in curtains. David had planned to build a temple in Jerusalem, but was not permitted to realize his cherished dream. As Farrar says:

> The voice of Nathan did but interpret for him his own sense of religious fitness when it assigned the building of the House of God to a son, whose course should have been less chequered by moral failure, whose hands should have been less stained with blood.[4]

1. *Building the Temple* (I Kings 5—6; 7:13-51; II Chronicles 2—6)

David had done everything possible to prepare for the erection of the Temple. He assembled stonemasons and con-

[4]Farrar, *op. cit.*, p. 72.

struction workers and amassed a gigantic building fund. Before he died he challenged his son Solomon to proceed with the work, which Solomon did with enthusiasm.

a. *Location of the Temple.* The location selected for the Temple was Mount Moriah at Jerusalem. At present this site is occupied by the Mosque of Omar. It was on this same hill, centuries before, that Abraham prepared to sacrifice his son of promise, Isaac. After Abraham's time the place fell under the control of the Amorites, whose principal city, Jebus, occupied a hill westward from Moriah.

In the early reign of King David, who conquered the Jebusites, it was consolidated into the city of Jerusalem. David himself built an altar here that was used for many years. In deciding to build the Temple on this sacred spot, Solomon carried out the wishes of his father. A broad, level site had to be prepared for the Temple and its surrounding courts, so Solomon filled in the area with huge stones 20 to 30 feet in length. In some places this "fill" was as much as 150 feet deep. This spot remains perfectly identified after nearly three thousand years.[5]

b. *Value of Material and Cost of Construction.* It is estimated that Solomon's Temple cost more than twice the debt of World War I. The enormous wealth expended, based on present-day standards, throws some light on the gigantic task involved in the work of construction. The lavish use of gold and the amounts mentioned are almost beyond belief.[6] However, "it was nothing accounted of in the days of Solomon" (I Kings 10:21).

In addition to vast amounts of gold and silver must be added the value of the "brass and iron without weight; for it is in abundance" (I Chron. 22:14). There were also precious stones, onyx stones, semiprecious stones, great stones, marble, woods, fine linens, fabrics, skins, etc. Even the cost of labor added much to the value of the completed Temple.[7]

c. *Materials Used in the Temple.* The stone used in the construction of the Temple was obtained partly from the Lebanon Mountains, partly from the vast quarries which

[5]Percy H. Sykes, *A Brief History of King Solomon's Reign*, p. 30.
[6]John Wesley Kelcher, *A Description of Solomon's Temple*, p. 5.
[7]Sykes, *op. cit.*, p. 31.

have been discovered under the northern part of Mount Moriah, and according to the Mishna, partly from the neighborhood of Bethlehem.[8] It was a form of white limestone, and is sometimes called "Jerusalem marble." The scriptural accounts state that "the house, when it was in building, was built of stone made ready before it was brought thither: so that there was neither hammer nor axe nor any tool of iron heard in the house, while it was in building" (I Kings 6:7). The statement of Josephus is as follows:

> Now the whole structure of the temple was made, with great skill, of polished stones, and those laid together so very harmoniously and smoothly, that there appeared to the spectators no sign of any hammer, or other instrument of architecture, but as if, without any use of them, the entire materials had united themselves together . . .[9]

Outside the walls of the city, to the north and west of the Temple site, are vast underground quarries, which extend south under the city. This tremendous cavern is known as the Royal Quarries. It was accidentally discovered in 1855. The entrance is about fifty yards east of the Damascus gate, outside the city wall. The largest room in the cave is about 750 feet long, 100 feet wide, and 30 to 40 feet high. The immense piles of chippings found in the quarry indicate that the stones were not only quarried, but were also polished and finished there, as the Bible account states.[10]

Next to the immense quantity of stone used, the cedar logs from Lebanon furnished most of the material for the Temple. These were obtained by permission of Hiram of Tyre from the forests that covered the slopes of the Lebanon Mountains. The labor necessary to cut the trees on the mountains, to drag them several miles to the sea, to lash them together in rafts, to float them 75 miles along the shore of the Mediterranean, to lift them up the steep cliff at Joppa, to haul them nearly 40 miles across country up a tortuous roadway, and to cut them by hand for their designated use—all this compares with the labor of building the pyramids.

The beauty of the cedarwood, its pleasing fragrance, and above all, its durability, recommended it as a highly useful

---

[8]Ernest C. Stinson, *The Temple of King Solomon,* p. 68.
[9]William Whiston, trans., *The Works of Flavius Josephus,* p. 244.
[10]Stinson, *op. cit.,* p. 69.

material for the Temple. In addition to cedar special use was made of fir, olivewood, and algum or sandalwood. The metals used throughout the building for the furniture and decorative features were gold, silver, iron, and brass.

d. The Workmen. The people of Israel had first been slaves, then nomads, then farmers and warriors. At no time were they able to develop the skilled workmen needed to construct such an intricate building. So King Solomon, taking advantage of the long-standing friendship with Hiram of Tyre, requested the services of expert craftsmen from Sidon and Tyre.

The chief engineer was another Hiram of Tyre (not to be confused with the king of that name). He was a widow's son of the tribe of Naphtali (I Kings 7:13-14) and his father was a man of Tyre. He is described as: "Skilful to work in gold, and in silver, in brass, in iron, in stone, and in timber, in purple, in blue, and in fine linen, and in crimson; also to grave any manner of graving, and to find out every device which shall be put to him" (II Chron. 2:14). A man richly endowed by nature in wisdom and knowledge, he was uniquely qualified for the demanding task.

e. The Plan of the Temple. The Temple as a whole consisted of a series of terraces built around Mount Moriah, the highest point of which was crowned by the Great Porch, the Temple proper, and a three-storied building on two sides and the rear. The first terrace, surrounding the mount, was a rectangle, 1,600 feet long and 800 feet wide.

All the splendor of the Temple was concentrated inside. The only outer decoration was in the form of two huge copper pillars right and left of the entrance. Each rose to a height of 32 feet, just a little lower than the building itself. Each was like a tremendous stand, on whose top was set a copper or bronze vessel, from which lily-shaped leaves projected and which appeared to be held together by a copper network. Round about this network there were two rows of chains, each with 100 pomegranates.

A spacious door led into a room 15 feet deep and 30 feet wide. It was completely empty of furniture, as though to suggest a proper spiritual preparation before entering the holy place. In the middle of the wall facing the entrance porch a magnificent, double-leaved door, gleaming in the most varied tones of brilliance, attracted all attention to itself. It was 15 feet wide, made of cypress wood and decorated with carved flowers, palms, and cherubim, all overlaid with very fine gold. It led to the holy place.

f. The Holy Place. Only the officiating priests were allowed to enter the holy place. It was exactly twice as long as it was wide, 60 by 30 feet, and paneled all over, so that no stone was seen. The walls were covered with cedar, the finest wood obtainable, and famed for its fragrance. Here again there was carving everywhere—palms, flowers, and cherubim, all plated with gold. The floor was laid with cypress wood lest the priests, who walked here barefoot, should break the peace by the sound of footsteps.

At one end of this room stood a table about five feet high and three feet long and wide, with the hornlike corners characteristic of a place of sacrifice. It was the altar of incense, richly overlaid with gold plating. Near to it stood a table, also gold-plated, with the 12 shewbreads. On either side of the incense altar, five candlesticks were mounted on stands. They filled the room with solemn brightness day and night.

g. The Holy of Holies. Back of the holy place was the sanctum sanctorum, or holy of holies, sometimes called the oracle. It was 30 feet square and 30 feet high—a perfect cube. In this inner sanctuary two mighty cherubim stood side by side, carved out of wood, overlaid with gold, rising to half the height of the room. The two wings of each of the cherubim were spread out, so that the tips of the outer wings reached the side walls, and the inner wings touched one another. Under the shelter of these wings there stood the single wooden chest, the ark, which contained the stone tables of Moses. All the splendor of the holy of holies, of the holy place, and of the remainder of the Temple was designed and created for the sake of this ark and these tablets of stone.

2. *Dedication of the Temple* (I Kings 8; II Chronicles 7)

The day appointed for the ceremonial dedication of the Temple occurred in the harvest month, in which the Feast of Tabernacles was celebrated. The elders of Israel and the heads of the tribes and clans were invited to Jerusalem, and many others came from all parts of the land. The emphasis

on the old tribal organization was intended to remind everyone
of the national significance of this great historic occasion.

Many sacrifices were offered when the ark at last was
placed within the holy of holies. At the same instant, "The
house was filled with a cloud, even the house of the Lord;
so that the priests could not stand to minister by reason of
the cloud: for the glory of the Lord had filled the house
of God" (II Chron. 5:13-14).

a. Prayer of Solomon. Solomon, like his father, David,
before him, assumed the role of high priest as well as king
and proceeded to bless the congregation of Israel, who stood
reverently before him. Finishing his words of blessing, he
went forward to the massive altar. Here, instead of the usual
standing posture in devotion, he knelt before the Lord (I Kings
8:54), the first example in the Bible of this attitude.

Lifting his hands toward heaven, he uttered a prayer
of rare sublimity and passion. He prayed that in all the difficulties of the nation or its citizens, at home or in foreign
lands, God might hear and answer the cries directed towards
this holy hill. We read,

> *Now when Solomon had made an end of praying,*
> *the fire came down from heaven, and consumed the*
> *burnt offering and the sacrifices; and the glory of the*
> *Lord filled the house. And the priests could not enter*
> *into the house of the Lord, because the glory of the*
> *Lord had filled the Lord's house* (II Chron. 7:1-2).

b. Significance of Solomon's Prayer. The prayer offered
by Solomon at the dedication of the Temple is remarkable
for its comprehension of the greatness and infinity of God.
This wise man was aware that God did not dwell in one
locality on the earth, for even the "heaven and heaven of
heavens cannot contain thee" (I Kings 8:27). This insight
into God's nature is a striking refutation of modern critics
who say that Israel had no conception of God as a Supreme
Being until the eighth century before Christ. Here is no
proud reference to a tribal deity, but a humble recognition of
a universal God.

The dedication prayer also reveals an exalted concept of
fellowship and communion with God. Solomon is amazed,
yet confident, that the God who surpasses the universe does

actually condescend to commune with man. Turning from this picture of a benign, universal God, Solomon recognizes that any departure from the precepts of God will result in swift punishment and eventual oblivion (I Kings 8:31-32).

c. *Feast of Dedication.* To climax the occasion of the dedication Solomon announced a 14-day feast. The feast was in reality part of the act of offering sacrifices, of which there was an abundance. The total number of animals sacrificed was 22,000 oxen and 120,000 sheep. As fixed by the Law, however, only a small part of each sacrifice was consumed by fire; the rest was given to the people, that they might participate and rejoice in the great sacred feast.

IV. STUMBLING STONES AND FAILURE

The outward splendor of Solomon reached its zenith during the visit of the Queen of Sheba. His brilliance appears at that time to have shone in an unclouded sky. For a brief period after the visit of the queen the glow of luxury and prosperity continued. However, two deadly evils, leading to others, lurked behind the superficial brilliance of the court. These evils were the curse of polygamy and the curse of dictatorship. They brought spiritual ruin to both king and people.

Solomon evidently was fully aware of the condition on which his success and prosperity rested, for he reminded the people, after he had offered the dedicatory prayer in the Temple, "Let your heart therefore be perfect with the Lord our God, to walk in his statutes, and to keep his commandments, as at this day" (I Kings 8:61). But to know is one thing and to do is another. As one has said, "It is one thing to have a vivid recognition of great truth in youth, or in peculiarly solemn circumstances, and another to have it in advanced years or in the ordinary course of human life."[11] Great truths are frequently forgotten or ignored amid the distractions and allurements of the world.

1. *The Sins of Solomon* (I Kings 10:23—11:8)

Three things had been specifically forbidden to the theocratic ruler in the law of Moses (Deut. 17:14-20). All three things Solomon did deliberately, and on a large scale.

[11]Thomas Kirk, *Solomon: His Life and Works,* p. 168.

a. He had been forbidden to multiply horses. Horses were the sign and symbol of militarism, while Israel was supposed to be an instrument of peace. Acquiring horses also meant trade with Egypt, and God had said, "Ye shall henceforth no more return that way." Solomon's traffic in horses and the profit he made by reselling them to the kings of the Hittites and of Syria were among the outstanding features of his land commerce.

b. He had been forbidden to amass gold and silver. This could be done only by the impoverishment of his people. But Solomon made it a part of his glory to make silver as common as stones in Jerusalem.

c. He had been forbidden to take numerous wives because of the danger of "turning away his heart." In particular, marriage with women of other nations was explicitly forbidden (Exod. 34:11-16; Deut. 7:3). Yet "king Solomon loved many strange women beside the daughter of Pharaoh, women of the Moabites, Ammonites, Edomites, Zidonians, and Hittites" (I Kings 11:1, marg.). Some have suggested that these were simply political marriages in order to satisfy Solomon's thirst for power and prestiage. But the sacred writings state that "Solomon clave unto these in love" (I Kings 11:2).

The number of wives ascribed to Solomon is not only unparalleled but almost incredible. He had, we are told, 700 wives and 300 concubines. It was probably in the last decade of his reign, when he was about 50 years of age, that Solomon openly sponsored the heathen worship of his foreign wives.

It is stated that he went after Ashtoreth, the goddess of the Sidonians, and after Milcom, or Molech, the abomination of the Ammonites (I Kings 11:5), and that he built two high places on the Mount of Olives—one for Chemosh and one for Molech (I Kings 11:7). The discovery of a seal at Bethel pictures the goddess Ashtoreth and indicates how widespread idolatry had become.[12] It is also stated that he made similar arrangements for the remainder of his idolatrous wives (I Kings 11:8).

2. *Divine Displeasure* (I Kings 11:9-40)

Solomon could break the commands of God without compunction, but not without consequences. Luxury, indolence,

[12]Joseph P. Free, *Archaeology and Bible History*, p. 173.

and lust had done their work in the hearts of the people of Israel. Their land was full of silver and gold, and their treasure houses were bulging; their land was full of horses, and there was no end to the number of chariots. Their land was also full of idols and idolatry. Divine displeasure was the inevitable result.

a. A Prophet of Doom. It was in times such as this that the prophet Ahijah, known as the Shilonite, appeared. Jeroboam, to whom Ahijah was sent, was the son of Nebat and Zeruah. As Jeroboam is called "a mighty man of valour," he appears to have distinguished himself for his leadership during the building of the fortifications around Jerusalem. Because of his diligence and ability he had been promoted to a key position.

As Jeroboam journeyed from Jerusalem he was met by Ahijah. The prophet took the young official aside into a field. Taking his prophet's mantle he tore it into 12 pieces, stating that God would take the kingdom from Solomon, giving 10 tribes to Jeroboam. Then, having indicated that the predicted rupture of the kingdom was due to the idolatry of Solomon and his house, Ahijah stated that this division would not take place in the lifetime of Solomon.

b. Treason at the Court. Apparently Jeroboam was too impatient to wait for his master's death. In some way or other "he lifted up his hand against the king." No doubt the ambitious Jeroboam had revealed the prophet's message to friends and was hurried into premature rebellion. His plot came to the king's attention, who immediately sent to arrest the traitor. Jeroboam fled to Egypt, where he remained until Solomon's death.

3. *Solomon's Death* (I Kings 11: 41-43)

Because Solomon had forsaken God, God forsook him, and warned him that his son should be heir to only a portion of the kingdom. But although the full measure of punishment was not immediately realized, Solomon himself did not go personally unpunished and his punishment came in a form which would be especially galling to the king.

His commerce depleted, his popularity dimmed, his body

prematurely aged, Solomon became the prey of enemies he would have utterly disdained in his day of power. Yet he was powerless to control or punish those who harried him. After Jeroboam's rebellion nothing further is recorded in Scipture concerning him. The story of his reign ends with the statement that "Solomon slept with his fathers, and was buried in the city of David his father; and Rehoboam his son reigned in his stead." Solomon was probably about 58 years old when he died.

SUMMARY

In review, Solomon's life falls into three periods. The first is the early part of his reign, in which he is still, in the fullest sense, Jedidiah, the beloved of the Lord, and worthy of his twofold destiny as monarch and builder of the Temple. God seems to have showered upon him every gift—princely beauty, great intelligence, noble aims, and an understanding heart. To these was added brilliant wisdom in administering the affairs of government.

In the second stage of his history Solomon reached his height of glory. He built the Temple, fragrant with precious woods, glittering with costly metals and priceless stones. He built city after city, and palace after palace. His coffers were filled with gold; his name was a byword around the world. Even the magnificent Queen of Sheba was breathless at the splendor she saw in Jerusalem. In the midst of all this glitter moved Solomon's foreign wives.

In the third stage of the history the glory had vanished. There was a sudden collapse. The gold became dross, the prosperity vanished, the pomp and ceremony began to fade. The builder of the Temple became an idolatrous polytheist. The splendid youth became a dissipated, spent, and disillusioned old man. The well-beloved prince was replaced by a despised tyrant.

Solomon had unparalleled opportunities to guide the destiny of his nation into channels of spiritual greatness. Instead of taking advantage of these opportunities, he squandered his talents and his nation's wealth and left his nation ripe for disaster and division.

216 • *Exploring the Old Testament*

RECOMMENDED READINGS

W. Shaw Caldecott, *Solomon's Temple, Its History and Its Structure,* pp. 1-70.

F. W. Farrar, *Solomon, His Life and Times,* pp. 2-165.

Fleming James, *Personalities of the Old Testament,* pp. 149-65.

Charles Foster Kent, *A History of the Hebrew People,* pp. 169-206.

John Wesley Kelchner, *A Description of King Solomon's Temple and the Tabernacle in the Wilderness,* pp. 5-65.

Thomas Kirk, *Solomon, His Life and Works,* pp. 2-188.

Theodore H. Robinson, *A History of Israel,* pp. 239-65.

Frederic Thieberger, *King Solomon,* pp. 3-145.

FOR FURTHER STUDY

1. Who were some of Solomon's competitors as successor to the throne of David?

2. Describe the events surrounding the coronation of Solomon as king.

3. What lessons may be learned from the death of Joab?

4. Of what significance was Solomon's choice of wisdom?

5. Even though he had unique wisdom, Solomon failed. Is there any gift superior to wisdom?

6. Discuss the various areas in which Solomon revealed qualities of leadership. In which did he excel?

7. Why was David not permitted to construct the Temple? What was his contribution to the building of the Temple?

8. Discuss the significance of the building of the Temple.

9. What contributions did other nations make to the building of the Temple?

10. Who was permitted to enter the holy of holies? How often?

11. How does the building of the Temple compare with other building projects of ancient history?

12. Does the difference in the number of years required to build the Temple and the palace have any meaning?

13. With the transfer of worship from the Tabernacle to the Temple, worship became more elaborate and formal. Is it possible to be formal and spiritual? Are there any dangers in informal worship?

14. Read Solomon's prayer at the dedication of the Temple (I Kings 8:26-54), and from it discuss Solomon's ideas of religion.

15. Why was the Temple built on Mount Moriah?

16. List some examples of the prosperity of Solomon. Can a person live in luxury and retain deep spirituality?

17. When did Solomon reach the peak of his prosperity and power?

18. How old was Solomon when he began to show signs of spiritual decay by sponsoring idolatry? Do particular ages have special problems?

19. What specific sins did Solomon commit? What part did each of these play in his decline?

20. What would you say was the measure of Solomon's success?

CHAPTER IX

Hebrew Poetry and the Psalms

The sweet psalmist of Israel (II Sam. 23:1).

Sources: The Psalms, with examples of poetry to be found in Genesis, Deuteronomy, Judges, Job, Song of Solomon, etc.

To Be Read: Psalms 1; 8; 15; 19; 22—24; 27; 32; 34; 37; 40; 46; 51; 63; 68; 78; 84; 91; 103; 116; 119; 121; 125; 139

Period: Indefinite (approximately 1050-500 B.C.)

In our English Bible the third main division of the Old Testament is composed of the very important books known as the Poetical and Wisdom Books. These books, five in number, are Job, Psalms, Proverbs, Ecclesiastes, and the Song of Solomon. In this chapter, after a brief discussion of Hebrew poetry in general, we turn to a study of the Book of Psalms, beyond all doubt the greatest and most immortal expression of religious song.

I. HEBREW POETRY

Experiential religion, the kind that is felt deeply, has always found expression in poetic imagery and utterance. The place which hymns hold in the religious life of our own time bears witness to this fact. Poetry among the Hebrews was a very ancient art, and played a vital part in the development of the Old Testament faith. While Hebrew poetry reached its climax in David and the psalmist of his own and a later day, classic examples of poetic expression are found in an earlier age.

1. *Early Expressions of Hebrew Poetry*

The lament of Lamech (Gen. 4:23-24) is the first example of poetry to be found in the Old Testament, dating back to the infancy of mankind. The prophecy of Noah (Gen. 9:25-27) is expressed in poetic form. The blessing of Isaac (Gen. 27:

218

27-29, 39-40) bestowed upon both of his sons rises to a high level of poetic utterance. Jacob's predictions of the future careers of his 12 sons and their descendants (Gen. 49:2-27) is rich in poetic feeling and expression.

The song of Moses and Miriam (Exod. 15:1-18, 21) is a beautiful hymn, containing words later used in the psalms:

> *The Lord is my strength and song,*
> *And he is become my salvation:*
> *He is my God, and I will prepare him an habitation;*
> *My father's God, and I will exalt him* (v. 2).[1]

Moses is also credited with writing one of the psalms (Psalms 90). The utterances of Balaam, when he vainly strove to curse the children of Israel, are set to poetic form (Num. 23:7-10, 18-24; 24:3-9, 15-24). The farewell of Moses is a beautiful song (Deut. 32:1—33:29). Joshua's command to the sun (Josh. 10:12-13) is in poetic form. The triumph of Deborah and Barak (Judg. 5:2-31), composed by the prophetess Deborah, has few peers in the poetry of any people. The prayer of Hannah (I Sam. 2:1-10) is poetry of unequaled beauty:

> *My heart rejoiceth in the Lord,*
> *Mine horn is exalted in the Lord:*
> *My mouth is enlarged over mine enemies;*
> *Because I rejoice in thy salvation.*
> *There is none holy as the Lord:*
> *For there is none beside thee:*
> *Neither is there any rock like our God* (vv. 1-2).

Not only are there passages of rare poetic power in the Pentateuch and historical books, but many of the prophetical books also contain passages uttered in the typical poetic form of the Hebrews. The psalm of Hezekiah (Isa. 38:10-20), the lamentations of Jeremiah (Lamentations), the prayer of Jonah (Jonah 2:2-9), and the prayer of Habakkuk (Hab. 3:2-19) are examples. In addition there are prose orations that rise to the heights of beautiful poetic imagery.

---

[1]The poetical arrangement throughout this chapter follows the ASV. Unless otherwise noted, the text is that of the AV.

2. Characteristics of Hebrew Poetry

The poetry of the Bible is characterized by a rhythm of thought expressed in graphic language. This rhythm of thought is usually characterized by a basic parallelism of structure which is its foundation. The epic and dramatic elements are not often found. The poetry of the Bible consists of expressions of the spiritual genius of a nation whose ultimate hope rested upon its relationship to God.

a. Rhythm. Rhyme and meter, in the Western sense, are absent from ancient Hebrew poetry. Present-day poetry, with its lines of measured length consisting of a definite number of metrical units or "feet," is more rhythmic and musical. But the psalms and other Hebrew poetry have a stately rhythm of thought and grandeur of expression unsurpassed in any literature.

The Hebrew poem and psalm are divided into lines which are approximately the same length. The lines are further arranged in couplets, triplets, or quatrains, which are sometimes called verses. These then may be combined into strophes, or stanzas, with a number of stanzas making up the whole poem. The result is a balance or rhythm of thought, not of sound or syllable. The lines are so arranged that the thought is expressed in different ways, by repetition or amplification, contrast, or response.

The irregularity of the Hebrew poem, or psalm, forms a middle ground between the strict order of meter on the one hand and the still greater irregularity of musical prose on the other. It has a beauty and charm of its own. Davison describes it in these words:

> The thought proceeds not directly, but as by the "beat of alternate wings"; or rather, like the progress of a bird, which advances by a series of spiral flights, circling in the air as it rises skywards, or drops gently and gradually into its nest in the young April corn.[2]

b. Parallelism. Much of the beauty and cadency of Hebrew poetry is due to the use of parallelism. An example of this characteristic is the couplet, in which the first line ex-

---

[2]W. T. Davison, *The Praises of Israel,* p. 72.

presses a thought, then the thought is repeated or balanced in the second line with variations. These parallelisms are arranged in various forms, the most frequent of which is the two-line form known as the distich.

(1) Synonymous parallelism. In this form the same thought is expressed in two parallel lines, with the second line echoing or expanding the first, and saying virtually the same thing in different words. This is the most familiar form of parallelism, and is seen in the following examples:

The heavens declare the glory of God;
And the firmament sheweth his handywork (Ps. 19:1).

Hear my voice, ye wives of Lamech,
Hearken unto my speech:
For I have slain a man to my wounding,
And a young man to my hurt (Gen. 4:23).

Pharaoh's chariots and his host hath he cast into the
* sea:*
His chosen captains also are drowned in the Red sea
(Exod. 15:4).

(2) Synthetic or constructive parallelism. A second kind of parallelism is synthetic parallelism, in which the construction of the two lines is similar but the second adds a variation, or supplement, in thought. In this form of parallelism part of the first line is amplified or explained on the second. Thus, only a part of the first statement is parallel in the second, and then by way of enlargement.

The law of the Lord is perfect, converting the soul:
The testimony of the Lord is sure, making wise the
* simple* (Ps. 19:7).

For I know that my redeemer liveth,
And that he shall stand at the latter day upon the
* earth* (Job 19:25).

The eternal God is thy refuge,
And underneath are the everlasting arms (Deut. 33:27)

(3) Analytical parallelism. Here, the second line gives a consequence of the first. What is implied in the first line is drawn out and made explicit in the second.

> *The Lord is my shepherd;*
> *I shall not want* (Ps. 23:1).

> *He is the Rock, his work is perfect:*
> *For all his ways are judgment* (Deut. 32:4).

> *The Lord is my portion, saith my soul;*
> *Therefore will I hope in him* (Lam. 3:24).

(4) Antithetic parallelism. In this form the second line is in direct contrast or opposition to the first.

> *For the Lord knoweth the way of the righteous,*
> *But the way of the ungodly shall perish* (Ps. 1:6).

> *Weeping may endure for a night,*
> *But joy cometh in the morning* (Ps. 30:5).

(5) Tautological parallelism. Here for rhetorical reasons the same words are exactly, or almost exactly, repeated.

> *Lord, how long shall the wicked,*
> *How long shall the wicked triumph?* (Ps. 94:3.)

(6) Climactic parallelism. In this form the same words are repeated for effect and the thought is gradually built up to a climax.

> *O come, let us sing unto the Lord:*
> *Let us make a joyful noise to the rock of our salvation.*
> *Let us come before his presence with thanksgiving,*
> *And make a joyful noise unto him with psalms.*
> *For the Lord is a great God,*
> *And a great King above all gods* (Ps. 95:1-3).

(7) Other forms of parallelism. While the distich, or two-line verse, is the basic form, frequently tristichs, or three-line units, are found. The four-line verse, or tetrastich, and occasionally the five-line, or pentastich, are also found in

Hebrew poetry. The hexastich is a combination of three distichs or two tristichs into a six-line verse. An example of the tristich is the familiar reading:

> *Blessed is the man that walketh not in the counsel of the ungodly,*
> *Nor standeth in the way of sinners,*
> *Nor sitteth in the seat of the scornful* (Ps. 1:1).

3. Main Types of Hebrew Poetry

There are three main types of Hebrew poetry familiar to the Bible student. Best loved and most frequently found is the familiar lyric, or song type. The Psalms consist chiefly of lyric poetry, and most of the poetic passages found in the historical books and in the prophecies are lyrics. While there had been lyric poetry even before Moses, the form grew in beauty and sensitivity until it reached its highest point of perfection in David, the "sweet singer of Israel." After David's time poetic expression in Israel gradually declined in beauty and grandeur.

In addition to lyric poetry the Hebrews produced didactic or gnomic poetry of the teaching type. Proverbs and Ecclesiastes furnish excellent examples of this. As the lyric poem is the expression of the poet's desire to communicate his feelings, didactic poetry is the expression of his desire to instruct. The didactic poetry of the Old Testament is not concerned with abstract reasoning, but is the expression of observations about life and of insights into duty and the moral order of the universe.

A third type of Hebrew poetry is the dramatic form, as found in Job and, to a lesser extent, in the Song of Solomon. In dramatic poetry among the Hebrews the action is a movement of ideas rather than of persons or events. An interplay of thought provides the plot. Thus there is no necessity for stage settings or external trappings.

II. The Book of Psalms

The Book of Psalms was originally the hymnbook of the Hebrew nation. Both the tradition of the Jews and the title which the book carries indicate that this collection was a book

224 • Exploring the Old Testament

of hymns used to praise and worship God. The Hebrew title is *Tehillim*, which means "praises," or songs of praise. Our familiar English title "Psalms" is a word derived from the Greek and simply means "songs set to music." The historic, but not so familiar, term "Psalter" is derived almost letter for letter from the Greek word for stringed instrument, revealing that these poems of spiritual aspiration were sung with musical accompaniment. In the New Testament the Psalter is referred to as "the book of Psalms" (Luke 20:42; Acts 1:20), a title adopted from the Septuagint, and later commonly accepted and used in the Christian Church.

Not only is the Book of Psalms the hymnbook of the Hebrews; it is the hymnbook of the Bible and of the Christian Church. Music and religion are inseparable. For when man reaches a state of spiritual exaltation in which he feels at one with the eternal God, he naturally expresses himself in poetry and song. And when man is burdened with grief or guilt he pours song from his inmost being, expressing his longings, hopes, and desires.

The psalms, sacred songs of the Hebrews, are a mirror into which one can peer and see himself and his emotions reflected. This is why the psalms are so important, for in them we find not only a profound revelation of the inner spiritual life of the Hebrews, but also a striking picture of the inmost religious life of all sincere followers of God. Here, as Martin Luther so aptly put it in his Second Preface to the Psalter, "we can look into the hearts of all the saints."

These sacred lyrics, 150 in number, have for centuries exerted a tremendous spiritual influence upon both Hebrew and Christian worship. Included in the Psalms are songs from the time of Moses down to the close of the Old Testament period. The majority of psalms are ascribed to David, but the problem of time and authorship of each individual poem is still a source of disagreement among scholars. In structure the Book of Psalms has no doubt undergone numerous revisions before finding its present form in the Bible. The profound and divinely inspired truths of these songs relate to repentance and redemption, holiness and purity, praise and thanksgiving, sin and retribution, God and nature, national pride and historic mission.

1. Origin and Characteristics of the Psalms

H. Wheeler Robinson, the English Bible scholar, writes: "The book of Psalms is one of the most important and at the same time one of the most difficult books of the Old Testament."[3] It is one of the most important because it is a reflection of the religion of Judaism in terms of personal experience and living language. It is also the most varied and diverse of the 39 Old Testament books, revealing the influence of many courses of development. Partly because of this variety, and partly because of a lack of definite reference to historical incidents, the book is also one of the most difficult to interpret.

a. *Authorship of the Psalms.* The authorship of the Psalms is a problem which has occupied students of the Bible for a long time. But "in spite of ingenious explanations of generations of biblical scholars, the question of the authorship and date of the Psalter, of its purpose and the circumstances under which the different psalms were composed, is still an open one."[4] Tradition attributes the whole collection of the psalms to King David. Liberal scholars deny the Davidic authorship of nearly all the psalms, dating them for the most part in the period after the Exile. Conservative scholarship would credit David with the majority, but not all, of the psalms.

The inscriptions which appear at the head of the individual psalms assign 73 to David, one to Moses (90), two to Solomon (72 and 127), 12 to Asaph (50, 73—83), 11 to the "sons of Korah" (42—49, 84, 85, and 87), one to Heman (88), and one to Ethan (89). Forty-nine are "orphan psalms," or without inscription. At least one scriptural passage gives authority to assign certain of the psalms to an authorship other than David. In II Chron. 29:30 it is said that "Hezekiah the king and the princes commanded the Levites to sing praises unto the Lord with the words of David, and of Asaph the seer."

b. *Divisions of the Psalms.* The Book of Psalms in its present form is divided into five divisions or books. Each

[3]H. Wheeler Robinson, *The Old Testament, Its Making and Meaning,* p. 133.

[4]A. S. Rappoport, *The Psalms,* p. 11.

section closes with a doxology. Book one ends at Psalm 41 with the words,

> *Blessed be the Lord God of Israel*
> *From everlasting, and to everlasting.*
> *Amen, and Amen* (v. 13).

Book two (Psalms 42—72) closes with a longer doxology,

> *Blessed be the Lord God, the God of Israel,*
> *Who only doeth wondrous things.*
> *And blessed be his glorious name for ever:*
> *And let the whole earth be filled with his glory;*
> *Amen, and Amen* (vv. 18-19).

The third book (Psalms 73—89) closes with

> *Blessed be the Lord for evermore.*
> *Amen, and Amen* (v. 52).

Book four (Psalms 90—106) ends,

> *Blessed be the Lord God of Israel*
> *From everlasting to everlasting.*
> *And let all the people say, Amen.*
> *Praise ye the Lord* (v. 48).

Psalm 150 forms a doxology to book five (Psalms 107—150) and to the entire Book of Psalms. It closes with the words,

> *Let every thing that hath breath praise the Lord.*
> *Praise ye the Lord* (v. 6).

While this division is not original, it is very old. An ancient commentary (The Midrash), which predates Christian tradition, opens with a glowing comparison between the law-giver and the king, between the five books of the Torah and the five books of psalms, between the blessings of Moses and the blessings of David. The Septuagint also recognizes the fivefold division.[5]

---

[5]Frederick G. Eiselen, *The Psalms and Other Sacred Writings*, p. 41.

2. Types of Psalms

As varied and diverse as life itself, the psalms "are tossed together in the same kaleidoscopic manner as life's experiences themselves."[6] Rowland E. Prothero says:

> The Book of Psalms contains the whole music of the heart of man, swept by the hand of his Maker.

Then he adds:

> In it are gathered the lyrical burst of his tenderness, the pathos of his sorrow, the triumph of his victory, the despair of his defeat, the firmness of his confidence, the rapture of his assured hope.[7]

Another has said that in the Psalms we find sunrise and sunset, birth and death, promise and fulfillment—the whole drama of humanity. St. Ambrose stated his concept of the Psalms in these words:

> All portions of Divine Scripture breathe the grace of God, yet sweet beyond all others is the Book of Psalms; history instructs, the Law teaches, prophecy predicts, rebukes, chastens, persuades; in the book of Psalms we have the fruit of all these and a sort of medicine for the salvation of all men.[8]

In this book we find national psalms, historical psalms, royal or Messianic psalms, nature psalms, penitential psalms, imprecatory psalms, psalms of trust, wisdom and communion psalms, and hallelujah psalms.

a. National Psalms. To the Hebrews, religion and politics were inseparable. God was vitally concerned about the welfare of nations, particularly Israel. Many times He wonderfully delivered Israel from national disaster. Such a deliverance inspired the great hymn of faith and trust recorded as Psalm 46. The opening line, "God is our refuge and strength," inspired Luther's immortal hymn "A Mighty Fortress Is Our God."

Not all of the national psalms are triumphant testimonies to victory. Some are lamentations in disaster. Israel's history

[6]Julius A. Bewer, *The Literature of the Old Testament*, p. 341.

[7]Rowland E. Prothero, *The Psalms in Human Life*, p. 1.

[8]Quoted in J. J. S. Perowne, *The Book of Psalms*, I, 26.

is not a consistent record of righteousness, blessing, and prosperity. Rather it is a long and checkered account of sin and repentance, wars, both civil and foreign, and tragic interludes of invasion and destruction. Added to the folly of civil strife and the waste of other wars was the constant threat of epidemics, droughts, locusts, floods, and storms. Psalm 137 is an example of these laments. Carried away into exile, defeated, and enslaved, the people remembered the departed glory, and sang their sad song,

> *By the rivers of Babylon,*
> *There we sat down, yea, we wept,*
> *When we remembered Zion* (Ps. 137:1).

b. Nature Psalms. The psalms stand alone in the simplicity and directness with which they represent nature as the garb of God.[9] The glories of the natural order aroused in the Psalmist a sense of worship and spiritual insight. Here we find no artificial and self-conscious worship at the shrine of nature, nor any frustrated attempt to conduct life according to "the laws of nature." Rather the nature psalms speak of the divine back of the natural, God's supremacy over nature, and His power revealed in it.

The nature psalms illustrate the Psalmist's way of viewing the universe. Psalm 8 is one of the most familiar. It ranges from the splendors of the midnight sky to the multitude of creatures that inhabit the earth. It speaks of the fish in the path of the sea, and rings out with the dignity and nobility of man. But man enjoys such a lofty status because of his relationship to the God of creation, for the psalm ends:

> *O Lord our Lord,*
> *How excellent is thy name in all the earth!* (Ps. 8:9)

Psalm 19 is another psalm of nature. Rising above the narrow nationalism of his time, the Psalmist declares that God's glory is universally seen and all language gives vent to it. God's law, His precepts, His judgments, and even fear of the Lord have a beneficial effect on man. In the face of this

[9]*Ibid.,* p. 134.

revelation the singer petitions that his worship may be acceptable to the Lord.

> *Let the words of my mouth, and the meditation of my*
> *   heart,*
> *Be acceptable in thy sight,*
> *O Lord, my strength, and my redeemer* (v. 14).

The most complete of the nature psalms is Psalm 104, which has been called "an inspired oratorio of creation." The framework of the psalm is the account of creation in the first chapter of Genesis. The order of the days of creation is observed in the psalm with one exception (in the reference to life in the sea after that on the dry land).

The language is sublime in its figures of speech and vivid description:

> *Who coverest thyself with light as with a garment:*
> *Who stretchest out the heavens like a curtain:*
> *Who layeth the beams of his chambers in the waters:*
> *Who maketh the clouds his chariot:*
> *Who walketh upon the wings of the wind* (vv. 2-3).

But beyond the beauty of the words rises the majesty of Him who is the Creator and whose pristine glory pales the loftiest words and mightiest scenes.

c. Royal or Messianic Psalms. An important group of psalms is known as the royal or Messianic psalms. These are hymns that find their ultimate fulfillment in the person and ministry of Jesus. Foremost among these Messianic poems is Psalm 110. Christ used this psalm in argument with the Jews of His day. It contains one of the most striking references to the coming of a Messianic King:

> *The Lord said unto my Lord,*
> *Sit thou at my right hand,*
> *Until I make thine enemies thy footstool. . . .*
> *Rule thou in the midst of thine enemies* (vv. 1-2).

This can best be interpreted in a prophetic sense. The Messiah, the Anointed One, is to occupy a seat of honor at the right hand of God, sharing His glory, victorious over His enemies,

His people rejoicing at His triumph and voluntarily serving Him.

In o' er royal psalms many details of the life of Christ are foret(id with remarkable accuracy. His anointing by the Holy Spirit is envisioned in Ps. 45: 6-7:

Thy throne, O God, is for ever and ever:
The sceptre of thy kingdom is a right sceptre.
Thou lovest righteousness, and hatest wickedness:
Therefore God, thy God, hath anointed thee
With the oil of gladness above thy fellows.

An indirect reference to the prayer in the Garden is found in Ps. 40: 7-8:

Then said I, Lo, I come:
In the volume of the book it is written of me,
I delight to do thy will, O my God:
Yea, thy law is within my heart.

David's experience described in Ps. 22:16 foreshadows the piercing of Christ's hands and feet:

For dogs have compassed me:
The assembly of the wicked have inclosed me:
They pierced my hands and my feet.

The gambling of soldiers for His garments is predicted in Ps. 22:18:

They part my garments among them,
And cast lots upon my vesture.

The cry of distress that convulsed the soul of the Saviour is an echo of Ps. 22:1:

My God, my God, why hast thou forsaken me?

The hope of immortality in the heart of Israel's greatest king, expressed in Ps. 16:10, reached its verification in the King of Kings:

For thou wilt not leave my soul in hell;
Neither wilt thou suffer thine Holy One to see cor-
ruption.

Other Messianic psalms, in addition to those cited above, include Psalms 2, 18, 20, 21, 45, 73, 89, and 132.

d. *Penitential Psalms.* The singer of Israel, with his sensitive consciousness of God's presence, was keenly aware of evil in his own soul. It may be difficult for many moderns to understand the concern of the Psalmist about sin. For today drunkenness is called a disease, divorce is maladjustment, ill temper is frustration, immorality is self-expression, and other social sins are symbols of a neurotic personality. But in the Psalms sin is an affront to God; it is a malignant power which weakens and decays even the bones and flesh. Here we find a man who looks honestly into the depths of his soul, and humiliated by what he finds there, petitions God for forgiveness.

Three words are used to describe his condition. The word "transgression" denotes an overt act of stubborn revolt and willful defiance of a known law. "Iniquity" is an unnatural, distorted state due to the presence of a life-sapping, deadening, evil force which eventually will destroy all ethical qualities, leaving one in a state of helplessness. "Sin" indicates missing the mark, falling short of the goal.

As has been noted, three companion words are used in the appeal for pardon. "Blot out" means to erase or expunge, as words from a manuscript or data from a careful record, the misdeeds of the past. "Purge" and "wash" are strong terms used to describe the completeness of the purification needed. "Cleanse me" is a familiar phrase carried over from the ritual of the priests in the purification of lepers, and here given a wider application. The power of God alone could bring such deliverance.

Among the penitential psalms are Psalms 6, 32, 38, 51, 102, 130, and 143. In these pleas for forgiveness the entire gamut of religious experience is portrayed. Overwhelmed with a sense of lostness, the Psalmist cries:

> *Return, O Lord, deliver my soul:*
> *Oh save me for thy mercies' sake* (Ps. 6:4).

But he is not content merely to lament his fate. He is going to take action to deal with his sin:

> *For I will declare mine iniquity;*
> *I will be sorry for my sin* (Ps. 38:18).

Submissive and surrendered, he waits before God. The vessel is emptied, waiting to be filled:

> *I wait for the Lord, my soul doth wait,*
> *And in his word do I hope* (Ps. 130:5).

God extends mercy and forgiveness to the repentant petitioner, and with great joy the transformed man presents his testimony:

> *I waited patiently for the Lord;*
> *And he inclined unto me, and heard my cry.*
> *He brought me up also out of an horrible pit, out of the miry clay,*
> *And set my feet upon a rock, and established my goings.*
> *And he hath put a new song in my mouth,*
> *Even praise unto our God* (Ps. 40:1-3).

e. Miscellaneous Psalms. Many other aspects of life are reflected in the psalms. There are psalms of trust, of which the twenty-third is most universally loved. Its language is pertinent for our day:

> *I will fear no evil: for thou art with me;*
> *Thy rod and thy staff they comfort me* (v. 4).

Some psalms follow the didactic pattern of ancient wisdom literature and present the inevitable punishment of evil as well as the eventual blessing of righteousness. Psalm 1, as well as Psalms 14, 34, 94, 112, 119, 127, and 128, falls into this category. For example:

> *Blessed is the man that walketh not in the counsel of the ungodly,*
> *Nor standeth in the way of sinners,*
> *Nor sitteth in the seat of the scornful.*
> *But his delight is in the law of the Lord;*
> *And in his law doth he meditate day and night* (Ps. 1:1-2).

Out of his pilgrimage the Psalmist had learned to weave a note of thanksgiving into the frequently unhappy experiences of his days. Thus he sings:

> *Sing unto the Lord, O ye saints of his,*
> *And give thanks at the remembrance of his holiness* (Ps. 30:4).

Bless the Lord, O my soul:
And all that is within me, bless his holy name.
Bless the Lord, O my soul,
And forget not all his benefits (Ps. 103:1-2).

I will offer to thee the sacrifice of thanksgiving,
And will call upon the name of the Lord (Ps. 116:17).

3. The Teachings of the Psalms

The truths contained in the Psalms are truth of experience and life. No formal theology is presented, but the great doctrines of theology are here. Because these truths come from the crucible of life and not the library or quiet study, they appeal to the deepest life in man. Such basic ideas as the nature of God, the nature of man, the problem of sin, the social responsibility of man, and God's concern for the nations are all considered in this great hymnbook of the Old Testament.

a. The Nature of God. The existence of God, as elsewhere in the Bible, is not proved but taken for granted. As W. T. Davison states:

> David does not lay a metaphysical foundation for this fundamental article of his creed; he throws it down like a gage of defiance against the adversaries, chants it like a paean of battle, "Jehovah liveth, and is my rock."[10]

It is the fool who denies the ultimate truth of the universe, who disdains God in his thinking and ignores God in his conduct, who says "in his heart, There is no God" (Ps. 14:1). The Psalmist does not belabor the issue. If brutish people insist on arrogantly denying God and lowering themselves to the level of beasts, he will not waste his time in argument. With one lofty, sweeping comment he settles the matter:

He that planted the ear, shall he not hear?
He that formed the eye, shall he not see?
He that instructeth the nations, shall not he correct,
Even he that teacheth man knowledge? (Ps. 94:9-10,
    ASV, marg.)

[10]Davison, op. cit., p. 106.

The God of the Psalmist is a personal God. Jehovah, the one true God, is never lost in metaphysical speculations. He is a Person who thinks, knows, feels, loves, and is capable of anger, an interested God who speaks to man and to whom man can speak. W. T. Davison says, "It is the glory of the Psalms that they bring us simply, directly, impressively into the very presence of Him, who though God overall, deigns to be the great Companion and Friend of His creature man."[11]

The God of the Psalmist says to men: "I will counsel thee, with mine eye upon thee" (Ps. 32:8, ASV). He invites men to "seek ye Jehovah and his strength; seek his face evermore" (Ps. 105:4, ASV). The thoughts of God are graciously occupied with men, poor and needy though they be:

> *How precious also are thy thoughts unto me, O God!*
> *How great is the sum of them!*
> *If I should count them, they are more in number than*
> *   the sand:*
> *When I awake, I am still with thee* (Ps. 139:17-18,
>   ASV).

God is a Refuge, One who is a "very present help in trouble" (Ps. 46:1). Baffled by the riddle of life, the Psalmist can open his heart in prayer, for

> *The eyes of the Lord are upon the righteous,*
> *And his ears are open unto their cry* (Ps. 34:15).

Modern writers have made God an impersonal force, and speak of the naive writers of antiquity with their anthropomorphic idea of God. But this is the language of one who above all had knowledge of a living, interested, personal God.

b. *The Nature of Man.* The Hebrews were realistic in their thinking. This is indicated by the fact that nowhere is there any attempt made to hide or justify the sins and flaws in the characters of their national heroes. Abraham, Moses, and David are portrayed in a factual, realistic manner that is sometimes shocking but always true to life. The people of Israel were emotional, but not sentimental. Modern writers may sentimentalize about the natural goodness of man, but

[11]*Ibid.*, pp. 114-15.

not the Psalmist. He knew human nature, himself included, too well to prate about innate goodness. The Psalmist offers a frank presentation of man's condition and experience. For example, in Psalm 51 he begins with a candid acknowledgment of his depravity:

Behold, I was shapen in iniquity,
And in sin did my mother conceive me (Ps. 51:5).

This passage is not to be interpreted as meaning that the act of conception, or procreation, is an act of sin. Neither does it indicate that the process of birth is impure. It does recognize that he, and his parents, are part of the human race and as such they carry the taint or stain of sin on the race. As Samuel Terrien suggests, the writer might have said, "In a state of guilt was my mother when she conceived me, and thus I was born a sinner."[12]

In addition to inherent depravity, the Psalmist confesses to actual, deliberate, and willful sins:

For I acknowledge my transgressions:
And my sin is ever before me.
Against thee, thee only, have I sinned,
And done this evil in thy sight (Ps. 51:3-4).

But the inspired penman does not leave man groveling helplessly in the dust. While his condition is depraved, his possibilities of renewal are limitless. Thus he prays:

Wash me throughly from mine iniquity,
And cleanse me from my sin (Ps. 51:2).

Purge me with hyssop, and I shall be clean:
Wash me, and I shall be whiter than snow (Ps. 51:7).

Here the stain of depravity in the individual is cleansed and the seeker finds pardon and purity before God.

An exalted concept of human nature is compatible with a belief in depravity. For even though man is sinful, he is

[12]Samuel Terrien, *The Psalms and Their Meaning for Today,* p. 174.

still the crowning point of creation and the focal point of
God's interest:

> *What is man, that thou art mindful of him?*
> *And the son of man, that thou visitest him?*
> *For thou hast made him a little lower than the angels,*
> *And hast crowned him with glory and honour* (Ps. 8:
> 4-5).

c. *Love for God's Teachings*. Martin Luther's life was
full of danger and conflict. Perhaps his inner strength to
meet and overcome soul-shattering experiences came from
the words of Ps. 119:92, printed in the front of his Bible:

> *Unless thy law had seen my delights,*
> *I should then have perished in mine affliction.*

The Hebrews delighted in moral precepts and principles,
in contrast to the later Greeks, whose chief interests were
intellectual. Thus the law of God became a "lamp unto my
feet" and a "light unto my path." The "blessed" man was
that man who would meditate in the law of the Lord day
and night. The law of the Lord was perfect because it
renewed the soul, and the testimony of the Lord was accurate
because it gave wisdom to the erring. The statutes and decrees
of God were true and righteous, and more to be desired than
gold. In a day which has rebelled against almost all authority
the attitude of the Psalmist toward the law of God is worthy
of examination and emulation.

d. *Fellowship with God*. Everywhere the holiness and
spotless purity of Jehovah are recognized in the Psalms. He
"executeth judgment" and "loveth righteousness," but "the
wicked and him that loveth violence his soul hateth." The
saints of the Old Testament knew the joy of fellowship with
the Holy One of Israel.

Considering the meager revelation given them, and the
character of the Law, it is remarkable to find language expressing such intensity of personal devotion, such closeness
of spiritual communion, such confidence of access to God,
and such tenderness of personal relationship and fellowship.

This craving for fellowship with the Divine is repeated over and over:

As the hart panteth after the water brooks,
So panteth my soul after thee, O God (Ps. 42:1).

O send out thy light and thy truth: let them lead me;
Let them bring me unto thy holy hill,
And to thy tabernacles (Ps. 43:3).

O God, thou art my God; early will I seek thee:
My soul thirsteth for thee, my flesh longeth for thee
In a dry and thirsty land, where no water is (Ps. 63:1).

Psalm 84 has long stood as a standard expression of holy delight in public worship and fellowship. It is full of stately phrases describing the joy of spiritual worship and the strength which flows into the life of the devout worshiper.

   e. The Future Life. No very clear revelation of a future life was made to Israel. The accepted idea of Sheol, a mysterious, vast underworld, was that of a shadowy existence, not to be compared with the brightness and clarity of the Christian concept of heaven. The gloomy way in which death was viewed in other books of the Old Testament finds its echo in the Psalms:

For in death there is no remembrance of thee:
In Sheol who shall give thee thanks? (Ps. 6:5, ASV)

What profit is there in my blood, when I go down to
*   the pit?*
Shall the dust praise thee? shall it declare thy truth?
   (Ps. 30:9, ASV)

Perhaps the picture is thus painted because of the afflictions experienced at that time by the Psalmist, for later he gives voice to a great hope:

For thou wilt not leave my soul to Sheol;
Neither wilt thou suffer thy beloved to see the pit.
Thou wilt show me the path of life:
In thy presence is fulness of joy;
In thy right hand there are pleasures for evermore
   (Ps. 16:10-11 ASV, marg.).

> *As for me, I will behold thy face in righteousness:*
> *I shall be satisfied, when I awake, with thy likeness*
>   (Ps. 17:15).

The range of teachings in the Book of Psalms is much to broad to cover completely, for it is as full as life itself, God's providence, His ability to forgive, His watch care, and His concern for the individual are all found here. The Psalmist felt the pulse of humanity and describes the experiences common to life. He also had gifted insight into God's nature.

4. Use and Influence of the Psalms

The psalms are timeless in their appeal and universal in their influence. They sprang spontaneously from devout hearts in ancient Israel. Later they were sung by pilgrims on the way to the Holy City and chanted by the priests in the Temple worship. During the Exile homesick and heartsick dwellers in an alien land encouraged themselves with the inspiring words of sacred song. Associated with the name of David, Israel's greatest king, they were used extensively by Christ, the eternal King of Kings.

The New Testament is filled with the echo of psalms composed centuries before. The bleeding martyrs of the Early Church encouraged their hearts by singing the songs of the suffering saints of the Old Testament. Reformers of the Church have been quickened by the passionate hunger for righteousness poured out in the ancient hymns of the Psalter. Children have lisped the rhythmic lines of the psalms as they played, warriors have chanted the throbbing notes of psalms as they fought, and the aged have whispered their comforting strains as they died. The psalms offer a common ground for all men to raise an anthem of praise. No other portion of the Bible is so completely accepted and used by all faiths as the Book of Psalms.

a. Pilgrim Songs of Israel. Three times a year every male was expected to go to Jerusalem to attend the great annual festivals: the Passover, Pentecost, and the Feast of Tabernacles. Ordinarily the father was accompanied by his wife and family. These were times of great rejoicing and celebration—for all Jewish holy days were holidays, and all holidays were holy days. When the long-awaited day came, at a set time the official announcer called, "Arise ye, and let us go up to Zion unto the Lord our God" (Jer. 31:6).

The people responded to this announcement by coming from all directions, prepared for the exciting journey to Jerusalem. They were happy bands, marching to the rhythm of the pipes and frequently singing as they journeyed. Psalms 120—134 are a collection of such "pilgrim songs." They were not originally written for the travelers to Jerusalem, but were adopted by the pilgrims on their march. The songs are about a variety of subjects, but those dealing with the history of the nation were favorites.

One of the most appealing of these pilgrim songs is Psalm 126, expressing the indomitable spirit of exiles returning to their native land. On the journey they had envisioned the land in all its former beauty and prosperity. But they were forced to face the heartbreaking reality of a country desolate and poverty-stricken. Yet even here the pulse of song could not be muted, for they sang:

When the Lord turned again the captivity of Zion,
We were like them that dream.
Then was our mouth filled with laughter,
And our tongue with singing:

Then said they among the heathen,
The Lord hath done great things for them.
The Lord hath done great things for us;
Whereof we are glad.

Turn again our captivity, O Lord
As the streams in the south.
They that sow in tears shall reap in joy.
He that goeth forth and weepeth,
Bearing precious seed,
Shall doubtless come again with rejoicing,
Bringing his sheaves with him (Psalm 126).

b. *Temple Worship.* A second use of the psalms was in the worship of the Temple. To the average person today, with his idea of the omnipresence of God, it is difficult to understand the unique place the Temple occupied in the life of the Jew. The Temple was placed at the center of religious and national life. All life revolved about it, for here was the dwelling place of God. In this holy place God actually lived, and here He maintained His throne. With an anthropomorphic idea of God they believed that God's ear was bent to listen to their worship, and that as their praises echoed through the sacred shrine the heart of God was pleased.

The worship services usually began with processional hymns at the foot of Mount Moriah, upon which the Temple stood. As the worshiping pilgrims climbed the hill to the Temple the choir broke out in song:

> *Make a joyful noise unto the Lord, all ye lands.*
> *Serve the Lord with gladness:*
> *Come before his presence with singing.*
> *Know ye that the Lord he is God:*
> *It is he that hath made us, and not we ourselves;*
> *We are his people, and the sheep of his pasture.*
>
> *Enter into his gates with thanksgiving,*
> *And into his courts with praise:*
> *Be thankful unto him, and bless his name.*
> *For the Lord is good; his mercy is everlasting;*
> *And his truth endureth to all generations* (Psalm 100).

A significant insight into the genius of the Hebrew religion is given by another of these processional hymns. As the procession ascended the hill, the penetrating question challenged every person,

> *Who shall ascend into the hill of the Lord?*
> *Or who shall stand in his holy place?* (Ps. 24: 3.)

Here the prophetic element of moral purity is linked to the priestly ritual in an act of meaningful worship. This emphasis on the moral basis of worship is extremely valuable, especially when contrasted with the practices of other religions of the day. Only men with clean hands and a pure heart were eligible to stand in the dwelling place of God.

As the worshiping pilgrims reach the Temple gates they again burst into singing:

> *Lift up your heads, O ye gates;*
> *And be ye lifted up, ye everlasting doors:*
> *And the King of glory will come in* (Ps. 24: 7, ASV).

From within comes the ringing response:

> *Who is the King of glory?* (v. 8)

Immediately comes the joyous answer:

> *The Lord strong and mighty,*
> *The Lord mighty in battle* (v. 8).

Linked to this was the insistent request,

> *Lift up your heads, O ye gates;*
> *Even lift them up, ye everlasting doors;*
> *And the King of glory shall come in* (v. 9).

Once more came the challenging question:

> *Who is the King of glory?* (v. 10)

And again we hear the enthusiastic reply,

> *The Lord of hosts,*
> *He is the King of glory* (v. 10).

The gates are opened, the pilgrims sweep in, and the offerings begin.

c. *Private Worship in the Temple.* In addition to the great public festivals there were opportunities for the individual to worship in private. Every trespass and sin, every special vow and offering, and every defilement called the people to the Temple. Thus 40 days after the birth of a child the mother came to the Temple for the rite of purification. One who had been sick with a contagious disease, or who had committed some grievous sin, or one who was under accusation, went to the Temple to offer sacrifices and seek pardon and purity. Having received the assurance of forgiveness, the worshiper would sing:

> *Come and hear, all ye that fear God,*
> *And I will declare what he hath done for my soul.*
> *I cried unto him with my mouth,*
> *And he was extolled with my tongue.*
> *If I regard iniquity in my heart,*
> *The Lord will not hear me:*
> *But verily God hath heard me;*

He hath attended to the voice of my prayer.
Blessed be God,
Which hath not turned away my prayer,
Nor his mercy from me (Ps. 66:16-20).

d. In Personal Devotions. In the Psalms we find a revelation of souls deeply conscious of the presence of the Lord. There is also the confession of the soul deeply conscious of sin, seeking, in broken accents of shame and penitence and hope, to renew personal communion with God. The devotional psalms are a mirror in which each man sees the reflection of his own soul. They express in exquisite language the craving of every thoughtful human heart for communion with a supreme, unchanging, loving God, who will be to him a Protector, Guardian, and Friend.

A universal hunger is indelibly written in the words:
As the hart panteth after the water brooks,
So panteth my soul after thee, O God.
My soul thirsteth for God, the living God:
When shall I come and appear before God? (Ps. 42:1-2)

Sometimes the Psalmist was indignant at the injustices of life, and cried with prophetic fervor as he pictured God standing among the unjust judges of the earth, rebuking them:

God standeth in the congregation of the mighty;
He judgeth among the gods.
How long will ye deal unjustly,
And accept the persons of the wicked? Selah.
Defend the poor and fatherless:
Do justice to the afflicted and needy.
Deliver the poor and needy:
Rid them out of the hand of the wicked (Ps. 82:1-4)

e. Use of the Psalms by Christ. In the course of His ministry Christ on several occasions made reference to the psalms. The Beatitudes, given early in His Galilean ministry, contain several such references. All of these references throw light upon the relationship of the Old Covenant to the New. So it was with our Lord's reference to "the stone which the builders rejected" (Matt. 21:42; Ps. 118:22), in which He was followed often by His apostles (Acts 4:11; I Pet. 2:6).

Similarly the disciples, on the occasion of the cleansing of the Temple, "remembered that it was written, The zeal of thine house hath eaten me up" (John 2:17; Ps. 69:9). Matthew, in view of Christ's frequent use of parables, says He so spoke "that it might be fulfilled which was spoken by the prophet, saying, I will open my mouth in parables" (Matt. 13:35; Ps. 78:2). The Messiah closed His ministry with an echo from the heart cry of an ancient singer when He cried:

> *My God, my God,*
> *Why hast thou forsaken me?* (Ps. 22:1)

f. Use in the Early Church. The Psalter was the first book which the Early Church put into the hands of her young converts. It was the foundation of her religious teaching and no man could be admitted to the highest order of the clergy unless he knew the Psalter by heart. As late as the fifth century the Patriarch of Constantinople refused to ordain any cleric who could not repeat "David" by heart.[13] One scholar observes, "It was used for singing in the first assemblies for Christian worship, and it has ever continued to be used; sometimes it was the sole book of praise, and always it was the best and most enduring of all."[14]

Many of the Early Church leaders have described the use of the psalms in the worship of their day. Augustine writes:

> Oh, what accents did I utter unto Thee in those Psalms, and how was I kindled by them towards Thee, and on fire to rehearse them, if possible, through the world, against the pride of mankind.[15]

Athanasius, in his letter to Marcellinus, asks why the psalms are sung. It is not, he states, for enjoyment, but to glorify God by the sound of the singing of psalms and hymns, thereby obeying the precept to love God with all our strength. He adds:

> And secondly, this musical and vocal accompaniment of the Psalms serves the purpose of bringing all our faculties, boldily, rational, intellectual, and spiritual, into loving and harmonious sympathy and concert in the service of God, so that he who

[13]James Robertson, *Poetry and Religion of the Psalms*, p. 7.
[14]*Ibid.*, pp. 7-8.
[15]Augustine, *Confessions*, Book 9; par. 4.

244 ● *Exploring the Old Testament*

has the mind of Christ may become like a musical instrument, following the motions of the Holy Spirit . . ."[16]

g. Use by Christian Reformers. The forerunners of the Reformation gained much of their rugged faith and dauntless devotion from the fire and passion of the Psalms. As John Wycliffe lay dying, the friars, according to tradition, crowded round and urged him to confess the wrongs he had done to their order. But the doughty old warrior used the remains of his strength to challenge them with a paraphrase of a psalm:

> I shall not die, but live;
> And declare the evil deeds of the friars.

Like Wycliffe, both John Huss and Jerome of Prague died repeating the lines of a psalm. In 1415 Huss was sentenced to die by the Council of Constance. While the stake was made ready, he prayed, chanting Psalm 31. He died, suffocated by the flames, but repeated with a transformed countenance, "Into thy hand I commend my spirit" (Ps. 31:5, ASV). The brilliant, magnetic Jerome of Prague died a year later, at the same spot, for the same faith, repeating the same line: "Into thy hand I commend my spirit."

On Palm Sunday, 1498, Savonarola was thrown into prison at Florence, Italy, and brutally tortured. His torturers broke his left arm and pulled the shoulder bone out of its socket. The right arm was left unharmed, so that he could write a confession and a denial of his faith. Instead, he used his good right arm to write a meditation on Psalms 31 and 41.

Martin Luther began his career as a teacher at Wittenberg by lecturing on the psalm of psalms, the 118th. He said: " . . . it has saved me from many a pressing danger, from which nor emperor, nor kings, nor sages, nor saints could have saved me. It is my friend; dearer to me than all the powers and honors of earth."[17] When Luther had groped his way to spiritual light in the face of terrifying opposition, he found words in the psalms to express his spiritual freedom. With his life in danger he sang:

> *God is our refuge and strength,*
> *A very present help in trouble* (Ps. 46:1).

[16]Quoted in Davison, *op. cit.,* pp. 258-59.
[17]Prothero, *op. cit.,* p. 122.

And so "Eine feste Burg ist unser Gott" ("A Mighty Fortress Is Our God") became the marching song of the Protestant Reformation and Psalm 46 pointed the way to a new spiritual era.

Suffering from asthma and burdened with news of the persecutions which had befallen his associates, John Calvin revealed a submissive spirit as he quoted the words of Ps. 39:9: "I became dumb and opened not my mouth; for it was thy doing." Later in his writings he said: "I may truly call the Book of Psalms an anatomy of all the parts of the soul, for no one can feel a movement of the Spirit which is not reflected in this mirror."[18]

In England, Sir Thomas More was led to the scaffold in 1535 because of his opposition to the divorce of Henry VIII from Catherine of Aragon. Kneeling on the scaffold, he repeated his favorite prayer: "Have mercy upon me, O God" (Psalm 51). Then he calmly placed his head on the block and received the deadly stroke.

h. Miscellaneous Use. David Livingstone used a text from a psalm as the springboard of his amazing career. Threatened with death by savages, heartsick over the inhumanity of the slave trade, often weakened by fever or hunger, pestered by the ever-present insects, and frequently moving through such bodily pain that he felt that he was dying on his feet, he found his strength for each day in the words:

Commit thy way unto the Lord;
Trust also in him; and he shall bring it to pass (Ps. 37:5).

Many spiritual leaders of the evangelical faith owe much to the psalms. Most Christians are acquainted with John Wesley's famous Aldersgate experience. Earlier in the afternoon of May 24, 1738, Wesley listened to a psalm sung in St. Paul's Cathedral. The anthem sung was taken from Psalm 130:

Out of the depths have I cried unto thee, O Lord.
Lord, hear my voice . . .
For with the Lord there is mercy,
And with him is plenteous redemption (vv. 1-2, 7).

---

[18]John Calvin, *Preface to the Commentary on the Psalms.*

According to Wesley's testimony, he found it "full of comfort."[19] That same evening he had his famous "heartwarming" experience. As he died on March 21, 1791, the last words of Wesley were:

> *The Lord of hosts is with us;*
> *The God of Jacob is our refuge* (Ps. 46:7).

In addition to individuals, groups of Christians have encouraged each other by the singing of psalms. Psalm 51 became a favorite of the Huguenots during the dark days of the eighteenth century in France. One contemporary commentator, Florimond de Remond, observed: "It was the books of Psalms which fostered the austere morals of the Huguenots and cultivated those masculine virtues that made them the pick of the nation."[20]

To the Puritans of the seventeenth century the Psalter was the book of books. Soldiers sang psalms on the march, by the campfire, and in the heat of battle. The pious plowman droned them over his furrow; the peddler hummed them by the side of his wagon. Under Cromwell and the Commonwealth the strains of psalms floated from windows in every street of the Puritan strongholds. As the good ship "Speedwell" sailed from Delft Haven, Holland, for the New World, the Puritans and their friends on the pier sang psalms and prayed. To the singing of psalms the sails of the "Mayflower" unfurled to catch the wind that sped them to a new world. The words "in Salem also is his tabernacle" (Ps. 76:2) suggested to John Endicott's company the name for their first settlement. The *Bay Psalm Book* was the third book to be printed in America.

This universal and beloved hymnbook has been used for centuries by Christians and people of God with deep spiritual aspirations. Its notes have echoed to the beat of time and its messages have reverberated to the throb of the endless march of earthly pilgrims. Perchance its language will be heard eternally when pilgrims find their home with God.

[19]*Journal*, I, 103.
[20]Prothero, *op. cit.*, p. 228.

SUMMARY

The religious genius of the Hebrews was expressed in poetry and songs. From the earliest expression by Lamech in Genesis to the lament of the captives in Babylon, this poetry is rich in spiritual meaning and in verbal beauty. Marked by a stately rhythm of thought and parallelism of structure, it still lives as great literature and noble utterance. Added to the lyric poem and song was the didactic or teaching type of poetry found in the Book of Proverbs. Dramatic poetry, as illustrated in Job, reveals another kind of literary vehicle used to present great religious truth.

The Book of Psalms is the classic example of Hebrew poetry. While the Davidic authorship of a large portion of the psalms is certain, the authorship and date of others is indefinite. Whatever the source and time of these sacred hymns, they have been used for centuries by all faiths and are the common heritage of spiritual men everywhere. Some psalms are intensely nationalistic, while others are passionately personal. There are psalms hushed with the reality of sin in man. Brokenhearted repentance and joyous forgiveness ring out constantly. Throughout is the recognition of the sovereignty, the majesty, the mercy, and the holiness of God. This is the hymnbook of the ages.

RECOMMENDED READINGS

Julius A. Bewer, *The Literature of the Old Testament*, pp. 340-94.

W. T. Davison, *Praises of Israel*, pp. 31-144.

Frederick G. Eiselen, *The Psalms and Other Sacred Writings*.

Alex R. Gordon, *The Poets of the Old Testament*, pp. 1-141.

Elmer A. Leslie, *The Psalms*.

Rowland E. Prothero, *The Psalms in Human Life*, pp. 7-136.

A. S. Rappoport, *The Psalms*.

Theodore Robinson, *The Poetry of the Old Testament*, pp. 11-46, 163-216.

Samuel Terrien, *The Psalms and Their Meaning for Today*, pp. 19-92, 191-238.

Kyle M. Yates, *Preaching from the Psalms*, pp. 134-200.

Kyle M. Yates, *Studies in the Psalms*, pp. 1-48.

FOR FURTHER STUDY

1. Give several examples of early Hebrew poetry.

2. Compare the structure of Hebrew poetry with present-day poetry.

3. List several types of parallelism in Hebrew poetry. Find examples of each, other than those given in the text.

4. Of what value is didactic poetry? Can you cite any examples of this type of poetry today?

5. What is the secret of the universal appeal of the Psalms? Which psalm appeals to you most? Why?

6. Why is the question of the authorship of the Psalms so difficult to determine?

7. Select and examine one of the "national psalms." Do we have any hymns today of a national character?

8. The Psalmist was a lover of nature. Where in nature does the Psalmist find God? Do you agree with his ideas of God in nature?

9. What messages do the psalms contain relative to the coming of Christ as the Messiah?

10. How clear is the thought of sin and forgiveness in the Psalms?

11. It is often said that men of David's time had an inadequate idea of God. Do the psalms do justice to a Christian concept of God?

12. According to the Psalmist, is man born innately good, or depraved in nature?

13. Check as many references as possible dealing with cleansing and purification in the psalms.

14. How does the Psalmist regard the laws of God?

15. What do the psalms say about the future life? Why do we have a clearer teaching today regarding immortality?

16. Do people today have the same desire for fellowship with God that is revealed in the words of the psalms?

17. Describe the use of psalms by men of the Old Testament.

18. In what way did Christ and the writers of the New Testament use the psalms?

19. Discuss the influence of the psalms upon the reformers and leaders of the Church.

20. What is the primary use of psalms today? Why don't we sing psalms more frequently?

CHAPTER X

The Wisdom Literature

Hear the words of the wise (Prov. 22:17).

Sources: Job; Proverbs; Ecclesiastes; Song of Solomon

To Be Read: Job 1—2; 23; 28; 31; 42; Proverbs 1; 10; 16; 29; 31; Ecclesiastes 11—12; Song of Solomon 2; 8

Period: Approximately 950-350 B.C.

From the study of the Psalms we turn to another popular expression of Hebrew religion—the Wisdom Literature. Included are the Books of Job, Proverbs, Ecclesiastes, and Song of Solomon. The appeal of these books rests in the fact that they deal with the great issues of life, such as the problem of suffering, practical ethics and morality, and the meaning of life and love.

I. WISDOM AND THE WISE MEN

The Wisdom Literature of the Old Testament contains the carefully presented thoughts and teachings of the wise men of Israel. While originally directed to the Hebrews, these writings have a universal application which makes a valuable contribution to the whole scope of the inspired writings.

1. *Wisdom Among the Hebrews*

In ancient times when books were rare and readers scarce, the traditional wisdom of the race was passed on from one to another in brief maxims and aphorisms that were easy to memorize. Depending almost entirely upon oral instruction, the wise men or sages of Israel put their teachings into compact molds which could easily be treasured in the memory.

a. The Meaning of Wisdom. The early idea of wisdom was practical knowledge or sagacity. The word wisdom comes from a Semitic root which means in the Assyrian "to know" and in the Arabic "to be firm," "fixed," "free from defect." In the teaching of the wise men of Israel it represents not so much knowledge as the ability to use knowledge effectively.

249

In Gen. 41:33, 39 and II Sam. 14:20 the word "wise" describes a man skilled in administering public affairs. Throughout the Book of Proverbs it is applied to a person who in all his public and private acts is governed by the highest religious and ethical principles. With the wise men the mere acquisition of knowledge was never an end in itself. They aimed to make men rather than human encyclopedias.[1]

b. The Use of Wisdom. The wise men attempted to present a composite picture of the ideal man. It is not a sentimental, apologetic saint they portray, but a man of red blood and practical ability. He is a devoted husband, a true friend, a wise counselor, a charitable neighbor. He is industrious, honorable, and righteous. His insight into life is simple, yet profound. Above all he is sane, normal, and motivated by a sound faith in God and a desire to evidence his loyalty to God by living according to the divine precepts. He is happy and contented.

The wise men taught that God was the Supreme Teacher:

My son, despise not the instruction of Jehovah
Neither be weary of his reproof:
For whom Jehovah loveth he reproveth,
Even as a father the son in whom he delighteth (Prov. 3:11-12, ASV, marg.).

In addition the sages taught that religion is the source and foundation of all wisdom:

The fear of Jehovah is the beginning of knowledge;
But the foolish despise wisdom and instruction (Prov. 1:7, ASV).

2. The Wise Men

In King Solomon's day and later a class of writers lived who were called "the wise men." They were quite distinct from the priests and prophets and had no part in the Temple service. They gathered together the choice proverbs and epigrams and taught and passed them on to others.

The message of the wise men was primarily to the individual. They seem for the most part to have been older men who had stood the test of life in contact with stern

[1]Charles Foster Kent and Millar Burrows, *Proverbs and Didactic Poems*, p. 11.

reality.[2] They conducted no formal schools, but stopped where they found disciples. They were buttonhole philosophers, eager for responsive souls willing to listen to their teaching. They were "reprovers in the gate." It is thought that they may have served as a sort of ways and means committee of large influence in the gates of the town where government was administered.[3] From these men and those they influenced there grew the treasury of truth known as "wisdom literature."

Wisdom in Hebrew thought stands in striking contrast to the philosophy of the Greeks and of the Western world. The wise man was concerned with imparting a revealed truth. The philosopher deals with human reason. Thus the "Jews had no philosophers, and the Greeks had no prophets." Metaphysics, or theories about the nature of reality, is the predominant feature of Western or Greek thought. Ethics, with its intense concern for the moral life, was the first concern of the Hebrew. Epistemology, or theories of human knowledge, occupied the Greek mind, while revelation, or the divine impartation of truth, held the interest of the Hebrew. Logic was the foundation of the Greek system, while intuition and insight were the bases of the Jewish. One was materialistic, the other spiritual. One of the authors of this volume has summed it up in these words:

> While reason was the method of Greek philosophy and argumentation its form, intuition or insight was the method of Hebrew wisdom and the epigrammatic proverb its form. The Jewish wise man had no argument to sustain, no chain of reasoning to follow. He presents his truth with the simple assurance of one who has seen.[4]

II. Job—The Problem of Human Suffering

The Book of Job is the first of the wisdom books we shall study. This book has been called by Tennyson "the greatest poem of ancient or modern times." To Carlyle it was "one of the grandest things ever written with the pen . . . There is nothing written, I think, in the Bible or out of it of equal literary merit." As an epic poem it is sometimes com-

[2]John M. Rice, *The Old Testament in the Life of Today,* p. 192.
[3]*Ibid.,* p. 193.
[4]W. T. Purkiser, *Know Your Old Testament,* p. 141.

pared with Lucretius' "On Nature," Dante's "Divine Comedy," Milton's "Paradise Lost," and Goethe's "Faust." But as Robert Pfeiffer remarks:

> Job is so unique a literary work that its resemblances to these masterpieces are only superficial; what they have in common is chiefly grandiose conceptions, superb style, intense emotion, profound thought, feeling for nature, and noble ideals.[5]

This poet ranks with the greatest writers of mankind. His creative genius did not rely on earlier models for the general structure of his work and the filling out of its details. It is one of the most original works in the poetry of mankind.[6]

1. Authorship and Date

Julius Bewer says that Job was written by a man who had felt in his spirit the suffering of righteous souls, who had tasted the bitterness of death, and whose heart had despaired and protested. Every word that he wrote had been "fiercely furnaced in the blast of a soul that had struggled in earnest," for he wrote the history of one who had suffered and battled, despaired and hoped until he finally gained peace.[7]

The question of authorship and time of composition is an open one. The book itself is silent concerning the identity of its author. Some say the writer was Job himself; others ascribe the book to Moses; others, to an unknown writer in the time of Solomon; still others, to a writer in the Exile period. A few claim postexilic authorship because of an inference they draw from Ezek. 14:14-20.[8]

2. Toward Understanding Job

In order to understand the Book of Job it is necessary to recall the doctrine of suffering prevailing in Israel before this time. It was believed that suffering was not the work of some super-human power hostile to God, but was the result of man's disobedience. It was in the world with God's permission and was made use of by Him in His dealings with

---

[5]Robert H. Pfeiffer, *Introduction to the Old Testament,* p. 683.

[6]*Ibid.,* p. 684.

[7]Julius A. Bewer, *The Literature of the Old Testament,* p. 317.

[8]O. S. Stearns, *Introduction to the Books of the Old Testament,* pp. 103-4.

nations and individuals. It was a kind of cosmic club with which He punished wickedness and evil. But why did the righteous suffer? This was the problem with which the great minds of ancient days were concerned.

Also, in order to understand the Book of Job it is necessary to visualize the dramatic scenes so uniquely described. A person cannot "think" his way through Job, for this soul-probing masterpiece is not directed to the mind and thought of man. Rather it is aimed at the feelings and the imagination.

To understand this dramatic picture of the battle in a man's soul, one must enjoy the pastoral prosperity and perfection of this wealthy farmer named Job. He must shudder with Job as calamity after calamity bursts upon him. Sitting beside Job at the gate of the city, the reader must plumb the depths of agonizing despair. He must endure the fumbling attempts of the three friends to console. Rising to a crescendo of frustration, the reader must sit breathlessly while Job denounces his comforters and comes close to defying God. His ear must hear the voice of God and his heart must bow with Job in surrender and submission. Finally he must envision the restoration of Job to happiness and prosperity.

3. *Scene One—God's Perfect Man* (1: 1-5)

The author opens the book by describing a beautiful country scene in which Job, honored and respected, was enjoying the fruits of his labors. Job was a wealthy Oriental sheik, or prince, who was honorable, upright, and God-fearing. Among his possessions was a flock of 7,000 sheep, 3,000 camels, 500 yoke of oxen, and 500 mares.

Indicating the unity and affection within this large household, family reunions were held at frequent intervals, the families alternating in entertaining the relatives. Job's seven sons and three daughters were ideal children, a credit to any man. Their pious father regularly directed the offering of sacrifices for each of his children, to assure the continued blessing of God upon the household.

4. *Scene Two—a Cosmic Convention* (1: 6-12)

A dark shadow falls over the scene. A cosmic convention was held in which the sons of God came to present themselves before the Lord. Satan came as a self-appointed delegate and cynically challenged the goodness of Job, whom God referred to as a perfect man. Denying that Job was truly spiritual, Satan stated that Job was in reality a materialist, that he was serving God and living righteously because it paid handsome dividends. Furthermore, declared Satan, if Job's possessions were suddenly lost, he would curse God to His face. Accepting the challenge, God granted Satan permission to destroy Job's possessions, but withheld permission to harm the perfect man's person.

5. *Scene Three—Disaster Strikes* (1:13—2:10)

Losing no time, Satan began a systematic and soul-shattering attack on Job. In dramatic succession, Sabean and Chaldean bandits rustled the herds of oxen and camels and killed the hired help. Then a tornado demolished the home of the oldest brother, killing all 10 of Job's children instantly. Hearing of all this, Job arose, tore his robe in anguish, shaved his head, and fell upon the ground. In spite of calamities heaped upon him, he asserted his faith by saying, "Naked came I out of my mother's womb, and naked shall I return thither: the Lord gave, and the Lord hath taken away; blessed be the name of the Lord" (1:21). In all this Job did not sin or criticize God.

A second time the sons of God convened and Satan again was among them. He declared that Job had retained his integrity because his own person had not been touched. If Job's health were suddenly destroyed, then he would revolt. That this charge might be refuted, Job was given into Satan's hands, with the one provision that his life be spared. Job became a victim of running sores over his entire body, and like a leper was banished to the garbage heap outside the city gates. To climax his misery his wife advised him to "curse God, and die." The fiber of Job's character was revealed in his reply, "Shall we receive good at the hand of the Lord, and shall we not receive evil?" (2:10)

6. *Scene Four—Job's Comforters* (2:11—37:24)

Days and weeks passed while Job courageously bore his affliction. Reports of the terrible tragedy spread. Three close friends agreed to meet and visit their tortured friend. At first sight they did not recognize Job. When the shock of seeing him in such a condition had passed, in token of their mourning they wept, tore their clothes, and sprinkled ashes on their heads. Tearfully and silently they sat before him for seven days, the period of mourning. Finally Job spoke. His lament in chapter three is a pathetic attempt to find an answer to the overwhelming "why" of his situation.

Rev. John Rice suggests that the three friends, Eliphaz, Bildad, and Zophar, represent three sources of authority in religion. Eliphaz, the oldest, is intellectual, calm, dignified, godly; a man of strong religious prejudices, something of a Puritan and a mystic. Though kind of heart, he is rather cold in his approach, being more of a lecturer than a comforter. He gives experiences and warnings like a prophet, and claims that what he says has been received by revelation. The second comforter, Bildad, stands for tradition, the wisdom of the past. His outlook has crystallized. He has the answer to everything in neat formulas. Zophar, the third friend, represents practical common sense. He has deep convictions and wants to get things done in the light of his convictions. Job is an independent thinker, attempting to grope his way out of a faith-shattering experience.[9]

a. *First Cycle of Speeches: The Innocent Stands Accused* (cc. 4—14). Job's lament, in which he rues the day of his birth, seems to his friends to contain insinuations against the justice of God. They proceed to attempt to correct his thinking.

(1) Eliphaz' speech and Job's reply (4:1—7:31). Eliphaz is surprised that Job, who in the past comforted others, is now bowing and giving way to sorrow. If he is innocent his confidence should be unshaken, for the just never are destroyed. Only the evil perish. In vivid language he describes a vision in which he saw the majestic purity of God as compared with the sinfulness of all created things. These imperfections in man result in sin and bring punishment. The way out is not bitter complaint, but a turning to God, whose ways are wonderful, whose power is supreme, whose purpose is to benefit mankind, and whose chastenings are fruitful in blessings.

Job is offended because his complaint is magnified and

[9]Rice, *op. cit.,* p. 204.

his condition is minimized. After all, life has collapsed for him without cause. Seizing the suggestion of Eliphaz about perishing, he invites and desires death as the end of his problem. Why should he live? Even his friends have sided against him. He demands to know what sins they are hinting at. His calamities are simply part and parcel of the lot of helpless mankind. Finally Job seems almost to despair of God's mercy and forgiveness.

(2) Bildad's speech and Job's reply (8:1—10:23). Bildad denies Job's statement that the race is in the grip of a cruel force. He argues for the exacting justice of God, shown both in the punishing of sin and in the rewarding of righteousness. The experience of the past proves that the evil soon withers, and that God cannot and will not cast away a just man.

Job is still puzzled. How can a man be perfect before God? All human virtues and attainments become insignificant in comparison with the divine majesty. In a sublime passage (9:32-33), Job expresses the deep need of man for a "daysman" or mediator who might stand between God and man with a hand upon both divine and human. Job pleads for God's vindication while expressing his sense of impending death.

(3) Zophar's speech and Job's reply (11:1—14:22). Zophar now presses the charge of hypocrisy and sin even more vigorously. Actually, he avers, Job is being punished less than his self-justification deserves. God's perfect wisdom detects men's hidden sins, which cause sudden calamities. Job should, if he wants peace and restoration, put away evil.

The three comforters are using poor counseling techniques, but Job is realizing some of the therapeutic value of talking out his problem. His courage is now rising, for he has convinced himself of his innocence. He asks to be shown what his inquities are. Will God harass a driven leaf? From the depths of his despair he gains a flash of insight that perhaps he will live again. Perhaps somewhere he will once again regain fellowship with God. "If a man die, shall he live again? all the days of my appointed time will I wait, till my change come" (14:14).

The first cycle of speeches ends. Each of the friends appeals to Job's intellect in an effort to bring him back to right thinking about God: the first pleading God's purity and universal goodness; the second, His exacting justice; and the third, His perfect knowledge. Each ends with an exhortation to return to God and all will be well. Job's answer is that their arguments do not fit his case. He has presented his cause and in his mind stands vindicated.

b. *The Second Cycle of Speeches* (cc. 15—21). The three friends now attempt to arouse Job's conscience. Each speaks again, and each time Job replies.

(1) The second speech of Eliphaz and Job's response (15:1—17:16). Eliphaz now claims that Job's very words condemn him and certify his guilt, that Job's speech would destroy all godliness. Furthermore, Job is not the first man to live and suffer. Neither does Job have greater knowledge than others. Then why does he insist on contradicting the combined knowledge of his friends? Also, how can a man born of woman be righteous? All men are sinful in the eyes of God, and punishment comes as the result of sin. Job ought to confess.

Job realizes that man as well as God appears to have deserted him. If he were in the place of his "wearisome comforters" he could easily wag his head and make talk. His sufferings have made him desolate. All ability and desire to defend himself seem to have disappeared. He resigns himself to descending to the dust.

(2) Bildad's second speech and Job's response (18:1— 19:29). Bildad uses severe words, criticizing Job for his treatment of his friends. He proceeds to show that not only God but nature is against the sinner. Job's misfortunes are reviewed as proof that the universe is actively opposed to wrongdoing.

Job now feels that God has deserted him utterly. Even little children mock him and the elders spit on him. Sinking to the depths of despair and disillusionment, he suddenly comes to the assurance that God will yet appear to vindicate him:

But as for me I know that my Redeemer liveth,
And at last he will stand up upon the earth:
And after my skin, even this body, is destroyed,
Then without my flesh shall I see God;

Whom I, even I, shall see, on my side,
And mine eyes shall behold, and not as a stranger
(19:25-27, ASV).

(3) Zophar's second speech and Job's response (20:1—
21:34). Stirred to fiery indignation by Job's words, Zophar
quickly condemns Job's attack on his three friends. Job had
accused God of wronging him, and yet God was to be his
Vindicator. Zophar emphasizes the brevity of Job's prosperity
and the awful punishment which could come only from sin.

Job, however, points out how often the wicked are prosperous. Their heirs benefit from many good things. How then
can it be said that the wicked do not prosper? Character does
not always determine fortune. Why attribute to God what
He does not do? History denies the validity of their arguments.

Having failed to change Job's thinking or to arouse his
conscience, the three comforters now make point-blank ac-
cusations of specific sins.

c. *The Third Cycle of Speeches* (cc. 22:31). Eliphaz
opens with the assertion that suffering could not possibly be
due to piety, so it of necessity must be due to sin. He then
lists such sins as a powerful, rich, godless prince of the day
would be expected to commit. Job has done these because
he had a faulty idea of God, thinking God would not know.
Again he exhorts Job to be reconciled to God, with the promise
of peace and prosperity.

In reply Job wishes he knew where he might find God.
Then he would go to plead his cause before Him. But God
cannot be located:

Behold, I go forward, but he is not there;
And backward, but I cannot perceive him;
On the left hand, when he doth work, but I cannot
behold him.
He hideth himself on the right hand, that I cannot see
him.
But he knoweth the way that I take;
When he hath tried me, I shall come forth as gold
(23:8-10, ASV).

Bildad is unable to deny the facts of experience presented by Job. So he presents a final argument, hoping to penetrate the depth of Job's mind and conscience. He calls for a proper attitude of respect and reverence to God. No matter what the facts of history may be, such impertinence and arrogance on Job's part are to be condemned. In the final analysis, the purity of God must take precedence over the life of man. Job replies by agreeing on the greatness of God. But it is justice, not greatness, that is at the base of Job's difficulty. Zophar makes no further comment. A stalemate has resulted, for Job maintained to the end his innocence of known wrongdoing.

d. The Elihu Speeches (cc. 32—37). A bystander at the gates had taken a keen interest in these conversations. Now he interrupts. Apologizing for his youth, he feels impelled to speak. With the impulsiveness of youth he attacks both Job and his friends in an exhortation revolving around four thoughts. In the first he criticizes Job for complaining that God will not answer him. Secondly, Job's charge that God has wronged him is not true. Job has spoken foolishly, without wisdom. Thirdly, Job's complaint that righteousness does not profit more than sin is not true. All exceptions can be explained. Fourthly, Elihu explains the disciplinary value of afflictions, and closes with a description of the greatness, wisdom, and majesty of God.

7. *Scene Five—a Soul Finds Peace* (cc. 38—42)

A threatening storm is gathering. Darkness is settling down upon the earth. Job bows before the storm, but he is unafraid. Suddenly God answers out of a whirlwind. He overawes Job with His majestic presence and hurls question after question at him until he is completely subdued. Man had spoken his piece. Now God speaks: What does Job know concerning the mighty works of creation and the mysteries and wonders of the world of nature? What does Job know about the hollowing out of the seas and the fastening of the sun in its orbit? Is the mystery of death open to him, and is he acquainted with or does he control the forces of the sky or regulate the planets? Does he issue commands for clouds of rain and billows of snow?

Job begins to feel small and insignificant. If he cannot answer questions about nature, how can he answer the greater questions related to man, God's crowning but most complex creation? Now Job "lays his hand on his mouth and refuses to talk." He has said too much already. God has not answered Job's question about human suffering. But somehow it does not seem as important as before. When man understands that he is not the center of the universe, all his problems shrink. Job realizes this, and with this simple knowledge peace has come. He humbly confesses:

> *Therefore have I uttered that which I understood not,*
> *Things too wonderful for me, which I knew not.*
> *I had heard of thee by the hearing of the ear;*
> *But now mine eye seeth thee:*
> *Wherefore I abhor myself,*
> *And repent in dust and ashes* (42:3, 5-6, ASV).

Job ends his spiritual pilgrimage triumphantly. He plunged to the depths and was unconquered. Now he is restored. The book ends with Job once more prosperous and successful, with a happy family around him.

Some lessons of great import are learned from the Book of Job. Since the problem of human suffering is always with us, these lessons are of lasting interest. A few of the lessons are:

1. The purpose of human suffering is not always evident to the sufferer, or to those who look on.

2. Suffering may benefit the sufferer. It may refine his character, and ennoble his personality.

3. The problem of suffering is insoluble within the limits of this life. It must be considered in the light of the rewards and adjustments of eternity.

4. Perfection of moral character is compatible with misunderstanding, suspicion, ill health, poverty, and partial light. Job was perfect before God, and yet was misunderstood and suspected by men, suffered ill health and poverty, and had but a partial revelation of God's will.

5. The suffering of His saints proves the sustaining grace of God.

III. PROVERBS

As the Book of Psalms is a collection of Hebrew hymns, so Proverbs is a collection of Hebrew wisdom. As David is the author of many of the psalms, and is for that reason often popularly credited with the whole, so Solomon is the author of much of the Book of Proverbs and hence is popularly supposed to have written the entire book. Since one section bears the title "proverbs of Solomon, which the men of Hezekiah king of Judah copied out," it is apparent that the book did not receive its final form until at least the reign of Hezekiah in the eighth century. However, not all of the proverbs of Solomon have been preserved, for I Kings 4:32 speaks of 3,000 proverbs and more than 1,000 songs penned by Solomon.

1. *The Meaning of "Proverb"*

The word proverb in our day denotes a "short pithy saying in general use," such as "A stitch in time saves nine" or "Birds of a feather flock together." But to the Hebrews the proverb, or *mashal*, had a much broader meaning. It meant a likeness, comparison, or symbolic saying such as the popular remark in the time of Jeremiah (31:29), and Ezekiel (18:2), "The fathers have eaten sour grapes, and the children's teeth are set on edge." It is also applied to any brief saying such as, "Is Saul also among the prophets?" (I Sam. 10:12) Sometimes it refers to a longer statement, such as Ezekiel's allegory of the eagle carrying off the top of a cedar tree to plant it elsewhere, representing the capture of Jehoiachin by Nebuchadnezzar (Ezek. 17:2-6).

2. *Divisions and Authorship*

Proverbs is essentially a collection of collections, like the Book of Psalms. This is shown by the subtitles and by the differences of content in the sections marked off by these titles. If we outline the book according to these titles, we find seven main divisions:

a. "The Proverbs of Solomon the Son of David, King of Israel" (1:1). This heading covers the first nine chapters, which illustrate the longer type of discussion of moral and religious truth as applied to life. It serves as an introduction to the book. It is a fairly logical discussion of wisdom as contrasted with folly, explaining the purpose of the book and giving exhortations to a young man, a disciple of the sage, outlining the dangers confronting youth, and suggesting wisdom as a guide.

b. *"The Proverbs of Solomon"* (10:1). The second section of the book begins with Prov. 10:1 and extends through 22:16. These 12½ chapters form the central part of the book. The chapters consist of individual proverbs in a brief couplet form, generally based on a contrast, as:

> *The plans of the heart belong to man;*
> *But the answer of the tongue is from Jehovah* (16:1, ASV).

This corresponds to our own "Man proposes, but God disposes." This section is thought to be the oldest part of the book, its proverbs coming from the golden days of the monarchy. The tone is the brightest and happiest of the entire book. The subjects deal with man in his ordinary pursuits, the rewards of virtue, and the formula for success and riches.

c. *"The Words of the Wise"* (22:17). The third section is brief and has a still briefer appendix. Some authors list the appendix as a separate division. In Prov. 22:17 we read: "Bow down thine ear, and hear the words of the wise." The Septuagint shows that "The Words of the Wise" was the original heading of this section. Then in Prov. 24:23 another title is found: "These also are of the wise," heading a supplementary section which extends to the end of chapter 24. This entire section, including the supplement or appendix, is an exhortation, like the first section, made up of practical maxims instead of individual proverbs. Advice is given on many topics. The king and Jehovah are to be feared, and rebellion is a calamity. The parallelism here is synthetic, presenting one idea but extending to as many as six or more lines, as illustrated by the following passage describing the effects of intoxicating liquor:

> *Who hath woe? who hath sorrow? who hath contentions?*
> *Who hath complaining? who hath wounds without cause?*
> *Who hath redness of eyes?*

They that tarry long at the wine;
They that go to seek out mixed wine.
Look not thou upon the wine when it is red,
When it sparkleth in the cup,
When it goeth down smoothly:
At the last it biteth like a serpent,
And stingeth like an adder.
Thine eyes shall behold strange things,
And thy heart shall utter perverse things.
Yea, thou shalt be as he that lieth down in the midst
of the sea,
Or as he that lieth upon the top of a mast.
They have stricken me, shalt thou say, and I was not
hurt;
They have beaten me, and I felt it not:
When shall I awake? I will seek it yet again (23:29-
35, ASV).

The first part of this collection (22:17—24:22) is of
special interest in view of the discovery of a book of Egyptian
wisdom known as "The Teaching of Amenophis," which was
probably written about 600 B.C., and which shows many striking similarities to this section of Proverbs.[10] For example,
in Proverbs we read:

Make no friendship with a man that is given to anger;
And with a wrathful man thou shalt not go (22:24,
ASV).

To this Amenophis has a close parallel:

Do not associate to thyself the passionate man
Nor approach him for conversation.

d. *The fourth section* of the Book of Proverbs includes
chapters 25—29, and is named: "These Are Also Proverbs of
Solomon, Which the Men of Hezekiah King of Judah Copied
Out" (25:1). This third "Solomonic" collection is somewhat
different in character from the first two. The form is not
limited to the couplet, but extends in some cases to nine or
10 verses. There seems to be more of an attempt to group

[10]H. Wheeler Robinson, *The Old Testament, Its Meaning and Its
Making,* p. 152.

264 • *Exploring the Old Testament*

the sayings by subject. For example, the first seven verses of chapter 25 deal with kings, another section (vv. 26:13-16) with sluggards, and a little further on there is a series of condemnations and criticisms of the deceitful flatterer (vv. 18-28). The utilitarian or practical aim appears to exceed the religious and moral purpose in this section; as, for example:

> He that tilleth his land shall have plenty of bread;
> But he that followeth after vain persons shall have poverty enough (28:19, ASV).

e. *The fifth section,* chapter 30, is headed, "The Words of Agur the Son of Jakeh; the Oracle" (30:1, ASV). The character and form of this section are peculiar. It begins with a skeptic's unbelief concerning God (vv. 1-4), which is followed by a sound rebuke of his attitude in the light of revelation, and a prayer to be saved from it (vv. 5-9). Most of what follows is arranged in what might be called "foursomes," that is, groups of four things which are alike, and which may be held to throw light on each other. There are four kinds of evil men (vv. 11-14); four greedy things (vv. 15-16); four mysterious things (vv. 18-19); four unbearable things (vv. 21-23); four wise little animals (vv. 24-28); four stately things (vv. 29-31). The following is an example:

> There are three things which are too wonderful for me,
> Yea, four which I know not:
> The way of an eagle in the air;
> The way of a serpent upon a rock;
> The way of a ship in the midst of the sea;
> And the way of a man with a maiden (30:18-19, ASV).

f. *The sixth section* consists of the first nine verses of chapter 31 and is entitled: "The Words of King Lemuel; the Oracle Which His Mother Taught Him" (31:1, ASV). In these verses there is strong warning against sensuality and wine drinking, and an admonition to champion the cause of the helpless.

> Give strong drink unto him that is ready to perish,
> And wine unto the bitter in soul (31:6, ASV).

> Open thy mouth, judge righteously,
> And minister justice to the poor and needy (31:9, ASV).

g. *The seventh and last section* has no title, but is clearly marked off from the rest. Its subject centers around the praise of a virtuous woman. It is written in the form of an acrostic poem, in which each of the 22 verses (vv. 10-31) begins with a successive letter of the Hebrew alphabet.

3. The Teachings of the Proverbs

The teachings of the Book of Proverbs deal with the whole range of life. They involve the nature of God and of man. They emphasize personal virtues such as good manners and good morals. Many passages are found dealing with family relationships, including those of parents, children, and servants. Also discussed are social relationships between friends and enemies, between the rich and the poor. Regarding its teachings, Bewer comments:

> There is a wealth of wisdom, of sober and realistic observation, of sharp epigrammatic characterization, of kindly humor and biting sarcasm, of warm personal exhortation and urgent appeal that makes the Book of Proverbs a veritable gold mine of good counsel for the art of right living.[11]

a. *Teachings About God.* Proverbs presents an exalted concept of God. Jehovah is cognizant of the ways of men. His is the power behind creation and the realm of nature. His rulership over mankind is supreme. His is an implacable hatred of evil, and He is the invincible Champion of the needy. These concepts are indicated in the following verses:

For the ways of man are before the eyes of Jehovah;
And he weigheth carefully all his paths (5:21, ASV, marg.).

Jehovah by wisdom founded the earth;
By understanding he established the heavens (3:19, (ASV).

The king's heart is in the hand of Jehovah as the watercourses:
He turneth it whithersoever he will (21:1, ASV).

Jehovah will root up the house of the proud;
But he will establish the border of the widow (15:25, ASV).

[11]Bewer, *op. cit.*, p. 312.

b. Teachings About Man. This book presents insights into the nature and personality of man which are amazingly up-to-date:

> *Every way of a man is right in his own eyes;*
> *But Jehovah weigheth the hearts* (21:2, ASV).

> *A cheerful heart is a good medicine;*
> *But a broken spirit drieth up the bones* (17:22, ASV).

c. Education and Religion. Education and spirituality are not mutually exclusive. The spiritual man seeks knowledge and understanding, while the foolish man refuses to consider it.

> *The wisdom of the prudent is to understand his way;*
> *But the folly of fools is deceit* (14:8, ASV).

To gain wisdom one must be properly motivated and have an appreciation for learning:

> *A scoffer seeketh wisdom, and findeth it not;*
> *But knowledge is easy unto him that hath understand-*
> *ing* (14:6, ASV).

Anticipating the emphasis of present-day educators on the importance of the early years, the wise man wrote:

> *Train up a child in the way he should go,*
> *And even when he is old he will not depart from it*
> (22:6, ASV).

Directly contradicting a modern attitude toward discipline, this ancient teacher advises:

> *The rod and reproof give wisdom;*
> *But a child left to himself causeth shame to his mother*
> (29:15, ASV).

The results of learning are satisfying and permanent.

> *Understanding is a wellspring of life unto him that*
> *hath it;*
> *But the correction of fools is their folly* (16:22, ASV).

d. Miscellaneous Teachings. The entire scope of life is considered in the pungent epigrams of this book. Domestic relations receive ample attention:

> *A worthy woman is the crown of her husband;*
> *But she that maketh ashamed is as rottenness in his*
>   *bones* (12:4, ASV).

> *Hearken unto thy father that begat thee,*
> *And despise not thy mother when she is old* (23:22,
> ASV).

Hard work is necessary and laziness is condemned in no uncertain terms:

> *Slothfulness casteth into a deep sleep;*
> *And the idle soul shall suffer hunger* (19:15, ASV).

Self-restraint and inner control are lauded as being of more value than physical strength and military prowess:

> *He that is slow to anger is better than the mighty;*
> *And he that ruleth his spirit, than he that taketh a city*
> (16:32, ASV).

Old age, if a person is righteous, is a time of honor and satisfaction:

> *The hoary head is a crown of glory;*
> *If it be found in the way of righteousness* (16:31,
> ASV, marg.).

The teachings of the Book of Proverbs sweep the whole horizon of practical, everyday interests, touching upon every facet of man's existence. Man is taught to be honest, industrious, self-reliant, a good neighbor, an ideal citizen, and a model husband and father. Above all else, the wise man is to walk uprightly before the Lord.

IV. ECCLESIASTES

The Book of Ecclesiastes is one of the most puzzling of the Old Testament books. The problems which haunted the writings of Omar Khayyam, the authors of Greek tragedy, Schopenhauer, and the Russian pessimists are presented for discussion. Wedged in among the writings of "resplendent priests, ecstatic psalmists and implacable prophets," this book has held a fascination for Bible scholars. Both the nature of its contents and the mystery of its origin add to its attraction.

1. The Meaning of "Ecclesiastes"

The author adopts the Hebrew name "Koheleth," which probably was derived from *kahal,* meaning "congregation" or "community," and which is thought to have been used in the sense of "One of the Wise" or "The Wise Man." "Ecclesiastes" is borrowed from the Septuagint. It is a rarely used Greek term which means "one who sits and speaks in an assembly or church." Later, *ecclesia* became the name applied to New Testament Church.

2. Authorship

Traditionally the authorship of Ecclesiastes is assigned to Solomon because of the reading of the opening line: "The words of Koheleth, the son of David, king in Jerusalem" (1:1, ASV, marg.). The language of chapter 1:16 and again of chapter 2, in which he speaks of his wisdom and his wealth as having surpassed those of all his predecessors, points to Solomon as the author.

The Solomonic authorship was accepted by both Jewish and Christian tradition down to a comparatively recent period. According to the tradition of the synagogue, the book is specifically attributed to Solomon, son of David. One rabbinic source declares that Solomon wrote the Song of Songs, with its accent on love, in his youth; Proverbs, with its emphasis on practical problems, in his maturity; and Ecclesiastes, with its melancholy reflections on the vanity of life, in old age.[12]

Yet the view that Solomon is the author has been abandoned by many today, even the Hebraists among the Jews. The dates commonly assigned to the book by these modern scholars vary from the Persian period, about 500 B.C., down to about 120 B.C.[13] Many see in it a philosophical treatise saturated with Greek thought, or a religious tract reflecting Greek and Egyptian thinking.

---

[12]Robert Gordis, *Koheleth, The Man and His World,* p. 39.
[13]*Ibid.,* p. 37.

By various authorities the book has been ascribed to David, Solomon, Isaiah, Hezekiah, Talmudic writers, to some unknown writer during or after the Babylonian captivity, and to some unknown writer in the time of Antiochus Epiphanes. Despite this uncertainty of authorship, Ecclesiastes is generally regarded as an interpretation of life as seen through the eyes of Solomon.

3. *A Literary Evaluation of Ecclesiastes*

C. A. Dinsmore points out the high literary value of the Book of Ecclesiastes. The Preacher may allege that all things are vanity, but the care he took in perfecting his diction shows that he at least had high regard for literary excellence. His sentences "are smooth and balanced, and the emotional element, although subordinated to the intellectual, is sufficient for sustained rhythmic beauty."[14] E. C. Stedman pays this tribute to the book:

> Whether prose or verse, I know nothing grander than Ecclesiastes in its impassioned survey of mortal pain and pleasure, its estimate of failure and success; none of more noble sadness; no poem working more indomitably for spiritual illumination.[15]

4. *The Message of "The Preacher"*

Many suggestions have been made of secondary titles for this book: "On the Meaning of Life,"[16] "The Disillusionment of Worldliness,"[17] "The Philosophy of Self-Quest,"[18] and "The Book of the Natural Man."[19] These titles suggest the scope of the book. Job was concerned with the problem of suffering. Proverbs deals with formulas for happiness and success. Ecclesiastes is an attempt to solve the riddle of existence. It grapples with the eternal question: "Is there any meaning to life?" The author is a man of intelligence who is thinking his way through life's experiences to its ultimate meaning. Although "touched with cynicism, he is not bitter, but disillusioned."

[14]C. A. Dinsmore, *The English Bible as Literature*, p. 249.

[15]E. C. Stedman, *Nature and Elements of Poetry*, pp. 211-12.

[16]Bewer, *op. cit.*, p. 330.

[17]Purkiser, *op. cit.*, p. 149.

[18]Rice, *op. cit.*, p. 247.

[19]W. J. Erdman, *Ecclesiastes*, p. 10.

At the very outset (1:2) the Preacher states his conviction that there is nothing permanent or lasting in life: "All is vanity." In his disillusionment life seemed a round of meaningless cycles. One generation of men passes, only to be replaced by another. He repeats this theme and arrives at the same conclusion, that all is a ceaseless cycle (1:2-9) both in nature and in human experience. Then he summarizes his search for meaning in life (1:12—3:15): knowledge merely increases sorrow; joy is not found in material things; sensual pleasures leave one dull and dissatisfied; playing the fool brings bitterness; all a man gains by work he must leave when he dies, and a fool may inherit it; it is, moreover, impossible for the natural man to know God; but since man is subject to a divinely appointed order, his duty is to enjoy himself and his task as best he may.

In rapid succession he surveys the various spheres of human endeavor. He compares man to the beasts of the field, in that all die, ending in the dust (3:16-20). He congratulates the dead more than the living—it were better in fact that a man should never have been born. Religion is full of sham and insincerity (5:1-7). The clash between rich and poor is described, with neither happy, since both are in the grip of an impersonal fate. But even the cynic must have a formula for improving life, so he presents a series of proverbs (cc. 7—10) by which a person can gain a measure of satisfaction from life.

The Preacher's final advice, however, is strangely deep and moving. It is in the form of a "golden gem which is one of the most exquisitely beautiful poems in the Bible, 'The House of Life,' an incomparable picture of old age."[20] No one else, in fact, has ever written on this subject quite so well as does the writer of Ecclesiastes:

> *Remember now thy Creator in the days of thy youth,*
> *While the evil days come not,*
> *Nor the years draw nigh, when thou shalt say,*
> *I have no pleasure in them;*
> *While the sun, or the light, or the moon,*
> *Or the stars, be not darkened,*
> *Nor the clouds return after the rain:*

[20]Elmer W. K. Mould, *Essentials of Bible History*, p. 406.

In the day when the keepers of the house shall tremble,
And the strong men shall bow themselves,
And the grinders cease because they are few,
And those that look out of the windows be darkened,
And the doors shall be shut in the streets,
When the sound of the grinding is low,
And he shall rise up at the voice of the bird,
And all the daughters of musick
Shall be brought low;
Also when they shall be afraid of that which is high,
And fears shall be in the way,
And the almond tree shall flourish,
And the grasshopper shall be a burden,
And desire shall fail:
Because man goeth to his long home,
And the mourners go about the streets:
Or ever the silver cord be loosed,
Or the golden bowl be broken,
Or the pitcher be broken at the fountain,
Or the wheel broken at the cistern.
Then shall the dust return to the earth as it was:
And the spirit shall return unto God who gave it.

(Eccles. 12:1-7, lines arranged)

V. THE SONG OF SOLOMON

"The Song of Songs" as the title appears in the original Hebrew, is clearly intended to be a superlative, like the holy of holies and the King of Kings.[21] The poem is thus declared to be the best of all songs. Older writers also call it "canticles" from its name in the Vulgate. It is one of the smallest books of the Old Testament. In the standard divisions in the English Bible it consists of eight chapters totaling 117 verses.

1. *Nature and Theme of the Book*

In Job the writer describes the life-and-death struggle of a man to retain his faith in a just God as he broods over the tragedies of life. In Ecclesiastes the "gentle cynic" attempts to solve the riddle of existence as he discusses life's paradoxes. In the "Song of Songs" the author departs from

[21]Leroy Waterman, *The Song of Songs*, p. 59.

somber thoughts and disillusioned ponderings. For here there "is room for only one thought—the joy of life—and one emotion—love as the supreme manifestation of that joy."[22]

The particular design of this book is a matter of much dispute. According to a common interpretation, the poem concerns the noble love of a young woman who encountered and conquered the greatest temptations. The loyalty of this shepherdess to her country lover, in spite of the allurements of the king's court, makes it a romantic story of the highest caliber.

According to this interpretation, there was a family living at Shunem, consisting of a widowed mother, several sons, and one daughter. The brothers of this farming family were particularly partial to their sister, and guarded her with special care. In the course of events the beautiful young woman met and fell in love with a handsome and graceful shepherd. Eventually they became engaged.

Meanwhile King Solomon, on a summer visit to the neighborhood, noticed the young woman and was struck with her beauty and grace. Seeking to add her to his court, the king was repulsed. Then he took her to his capital in great pomp, in the hope of dazzling her with his splendor. But this failed, as did all his attempts to win her affections by promises of jewels, prestige, and the highest position among his wives. In spite of the attentions of the king, the country lass steadfastly declared her love for her rustic sweetheart. Finally, recognizing the depth and nature of her noble affection, Solomon released the girl from his court. Accompanied by her beloved shepherd, she quit the court for her humble country residence.

This view regards the Song of Solomon as something of a lyrical drama. Against it has been urged the objection that the contents are completely lacking in dramatic directions, and the proposed scenes are too brief to be arranged for drama. In addition, it is pointed out that drama as such was unknown to Hebrew literature, the nearest example being the Book of Job. However, the poem does possess a certain dramatic quality, even though the plot is not clear.

[22]Morris Jastrow, *The Song of Songs*, p. 27.

2. *Other Interpretations*

The Song of Solomon has probably been the subject of more different interpretations than any other book of the Bible. We review briefly two other attempts to interpret the book.

a. Interpreted as Poetical Allegory. Due mainly to the influence of Josephus, early Jewish interpreters considered it an allegory of the love of Jehovah for Israel. Later Origen popularized it among the early Christians as the love of Christ for His Church. In some instances the commentators went so far as to read various spiritual meanings into all the details of the book. Others do not go far beyond the identification of the hero as Jehovah or Christ, and the heroine as Israel or the Church. In support of this interpretation is the fact that scripture elsewhere frequently uses the love of a husband for his wife as a symbol of the love of Jehovah for Israel and of Christ for His Church.

b. A Collection of Wedding Songs. In recent years it has been popular to interpret the book as a collection of wedding songs. There is evidence that the Syrians, even until modern times, consider a newly married couple a king and queen during the week of their wedding festival.[23] Some consider the book a more general collection of songs which have love as their common theme.

SUMMARY

The Wisdom Literature, made up of the Books of Job, Proverbs, Ecclesiastes, and the Song of Songs, forms a distinct and important class of writing among the Jews. Wisdom was the result of the attempt to solve the problems faced by every individual. The wise men were a distinct group of teachers who passed on the accumulated knowledge of the nation. As teachers they were considered of equal importance with the prophets and priests.

The writings of the wise men have had universal and lasting appeal. In Job the problem of why the righteous suffer is uppermost. In Proverbs the theme is the develop-

[23]Samuel A. Cartledge, *A Conservative Introduction to the Old Testament,* p. 198.

274 ● *Exploring the Old Testament*

ment of character and successful living by seeking, understanding, and practicing wisdom based on the law of God. In Ecclesiastes the primary aim is to solve the riddle of existence, to discover the meaning of life. In the Song of Solomon the thought centers around the love of human hearts, with its corresponding implication of God's love for His people.

RECOMMENDED READINGS

W. S. Bruce, *The Wisdom Literature of the Old Testament*, pp. 53-125.

W. T. Davison, *The Wisdom Literature of the Old Testament*, pp. 20-105.

John F. Genung, *The Epic of the Inner Life*, pp. 3-119.

Robert Gordis, *Koheleth, The Man and His World*, pp. 3-122.

Anthony and Miriam Hanson, *The Book of Job*, pp. 7-118.

Morris Jastrow, *The Song of Songs*, pp. 116-50.

Charles Foster Kent, *Proverbs and Didactic Poems*, pp. 3-21.

Albion R. King, *The Problem of Evil*, pp. 1-56.

John E. McFayden, *The Wisdom Books*, pp. 99-165.

A. D. Power, *Ecclesiastes, or The Preacher*, pp. 1-53.

A. D. Power, *The Proverbs of Solomon*, pp. 3-91.

William B. Stevenson, *The Poem of Job*, pp. 1-86.

FOR FURTHER STUDY

1. Discuss the meaning of "wisdom" as used by the Jews. Contrast this with the Greek concept of wisdom.

2. What place did the wise men hold in the life of Israel?

3. Concerning the authorship of the Book of Job there are various theories. List and discuss them.

4. Should the reader approach Job logically or otherwise? What elements are essential to an understanding of the book?

5. What is the main problem of the Book of Job? Why is this problem important? Does it have any meaning for today?

6. What was Job's condition at the opening of the book? Why did God permit Satan to bring such affliction upon Job?

7. What was Job's reaction to the speeches of his friends?

8. Did anyone, in addition to the three friends, attempt to deal with Job?

9. Describe God's method of bringing Job to a place of surrender and submission.

10. What lessons relative to human suffering can one learn from the Book of Job?

11. What is the meaning of "proverb" as the term is used in the Bible? Did Solomon write all of the Book of Proverbs?

12. Has our culture produced any proverbs? Compare them with the proverbs of the Bible.

13. Make a list of five topics or areas of teaching in Proverbs, giving scripture references for each.

14. Of what value is the Book of Proverbs today? Are there any conflicts between the teachings of Proverbs and concepts held today?

15. Discuss the meaning of the word "Ecclesiastes."

16. What is the main theme of the Book of Ecclesiastes? Suggest a title of your own for the book.

17. Chapter 12 of Ecclesiastes is a famous passage of literature. Analyze and discuss its style and meaning.

18. Of what value is the Book of Ecclesiastes to a young person, especially if Solomon as the author or central figure be kept in mind?

19. Discuss the plot or theme of the Song of Solomon. In what ways has this book been interpreted?

20. Compare the Wisdom Literature with the writings of the prophets; with the Psalms.

CHAPTER XI

The Northern Kingdom
and Its Prophets

Ephraim is joined to idols: let him alone (Hos. 4:17).

Sources: I Kings 12—22; II Kings 1—17; II Chronicles 10—31; Jonah; Amos; and Hosea

To Be Read: I Kings 12; 15:25-34; 16—19; 21; II Kings 2:1-15; 5; 9; 14:23-29; 17:1-24; Hosea 1; 4; 11; 14; Amos 1:1-2; 5; Jonah 1—4

Period: The death of Solomon, about 931 B.C., to the capture of Samaria by the Assyrians, 721 B.C.

In this chapter we shall consider the causes of the political division which occurred at Solomon's death, and the history of the Northern Kingdom from the time of its formation until its tragic end in the taking of Samaria by the Assyrians. It is essentially a story of religious apostasy and its dire consequences. However, the gloomy character of the narrative is somewhat relieved by the accounts of the prophets who faithfully championed the cause of God in spite of the evil forces that opposed them.

The story of this period as contained in I and II Kings deals alternately with the Northern Kingdom of Israel and the Southern Kingdom of Judah. The parallel account in II Chronicles 10—36 deals primarily with the Southern Kingdom but often describes events in which both kingdoms participated.

I. The Division of Solomon's Empire

Upon the death of King Solomon and the accession of his son Rehoboam the Israelitish kingdom was divided into two parts. As a result two separate kingdoms were formed, the kingdom of Judah in the south and the kingdom of Israel in the north. The Northern Kingdom is also known as "Ephraim" from the name of its leading tribe.

The causes of this division were numerous. *First,* there was a long-standing jealousy between the tribes, particularly the tribes of Judah and Ephraim. David and Solomon had lifted the tribe of Judah to a position of leadership, but Ephraim had long claimed the most honorable position among the tribes, since it was descended from the eldest son of Joseph. It is noteworthy that at the death of Saul, his son Ish-bosheth was recognized as king for seven years among the northern tribes after the crowning of David at Hebron.

Second, the geographical isolation of Judah and the mountainous character of northern Palestine made communication between the two parts of the kingdom difficult. The fact that Rehoboam found it necessary to go to Shechem to receive the homage of the northern tribes suggests that it was customary for them to meet separately in their own territory rather than to go to Jerusalem.

Third, the infiltration of pagan forms of worship during the reign of Solomon had weakened the greatest bond of union which had existed among the tribes, namely, the worship of Jehovah. With the new trend toward idolatry the urge to go to Jerusalem for worship was removed except for a minority of the people. Consequently the political bond was easily broken.

Fourth, the extravagance of Solomon and his ambitious building program had resulted in excessive taxation and a policy of forced labor. The resentment which this aroused was heightened among the northern tribes by the fact that most of the building was done at Jerusalem. They had no interest in paying for public works which brought them no personal profit.

Fifth, the foolish policy of Rehoboam presented an occasion for the impending rupture. At Shechem, where he was to be crowned by the northern tribes, the young king was presented with a request to ease the burden which Solomon had laid upon them. Rejecting the wise counsel of the older men in his company, he framed a belligerent reply dictated by his rash young comrades.

A *sixth* cause of the division is seen in the shrewd and ambitious leadership of Jeroboam, an Ephraimite who had been one of Solomon's administrative officers. Because of some offense against his sovereign he had fled to Egypt, but upon hearing of Solomon's death he returned to champion the cause of his fellow tribesmen. To Rehoboam's haughty reply Jeroboam now joins in an equally haughty response: "What portion have we in David? neither have we inheritance in the son of Jesse: to your tents, O Israel: now see to thine own house, David" (I Kings 12:16).

A probable *seventh* cause may be surmised in the fact that Jeroboam, during his exile, had sought the protection of the Egyptian king, Shishak or Sheshonk, whose invasion of Judah is described in II Chron. 12:1-12. From the time of Solomon on we note that Egypt was an important factor in the history of the kingdoms. It has been said that "Egypt virtually lured both Hebrew states to their doom by involving them in her political schemes against Assyria and Chaldea."[1]

II. THE TRAGIC STORY OF AN APOSTATE NATION

The Northern Kingdom of Israel, formed by this secession, had at the outset many material advantages over her sister nation in the south. Her territory was approximately three times that of Judah, and her population more than twice as large. The land of Israel was fertile and its position commercially advantageous, leading to the prosperity and luxury which formed the background of the prophecies of Amos and Hosea. In contrast Judah was hilly and barren and her people had to work much harder for a livelihood, a fact that doubtless contributed to her greater stability. Her greatest assets were the possession of Jerusalem, the Temple, and the uninterrupted Davidic dynasty.

1. *Jeroboam to Omri: Spiritual Declension* (I Kings 12: 25—16:22; II Chronicles 13).

The disruption of Solomon's kingdom and the establishment of the kingdom of Israel under Jeroboam had been predicted by the prophet Ahijah in a dramatic encounter with Jeroboam, as the latter set out in flight to Egypt (I Kings 11:29-39). We gather from the prophet's words on this occasion that Jeroboam's ascendancy to the throne was not an accident, nor without divine approval. The kingdom was being

[1]Blaikie and Matthews, *A Manual of Bible History*, p. 206.

rent asunder and the larger share taken from the house of David because of Solomon's sin, and Jeroboam was chosen of God as ruler of the newly established kingdom of Israel. Had he been true to God he might have been, it seems, the spiritual successor of David. But, like Saul, Jeroboam was unfaithful to God's commission, bringing disgrace not only upon himself but upon the entire nation under his rule.

a. *The Sin of Jeroboam.* One of the first acts of Jeroboam was the establishment of two shrines for worship, that the people might have no need to go to Jerusalem, where they might be won away from loyalty to his government. At these two shrines, Dan in the extreme north and Bethel in the south, he set up calves of gold, supposedly as symbols of Jehovah but in direct violation of the second commandment.[2] As priests he chose, not sons of Levi, but the commonest of the people, that there might be no bond of religious union with Judah. For these acts of impiety he was condemned by the same prophet who promised him the kingdom, and in later years he was often referred to as the king "who made Israel to sin," and from whose sin none of the kings after him departed (II Kings 3: 3; 10: 29; etc.).

b. *Warfare and Civil Discord.* During Jeroboam's reign of 22 years there was incessant warfare between the two kingdoms, and on one occasion Jeroboam suffered a serious defeat at the hands of Abijam, the son of Rehoboam (II Chron. 13: 2-20). At Jeroboam's death Nadab, his son, succeeded to the throne, but not for long. While besieging a town of the Philistines, he was murdered by Baasha, a man of the tribe of Issachar, who after slaying all of Jeroboam's family seized the kingdom for himself.

Baasha's reign of 24 years sounds like a repetition of that of Jeroboam. The calf worship at Dan and Bethel was continued and there was war continuously between Baasha and Asa, king of Judah. In the earlier phases of this war Baasha was apparently successful and threatened to cut off Judah's important trade route toward the north. Asa, however, finally defeated him with the assistance of Ben-hadad, king of Syria, whom he bribed to make an attack upon Baasha from the north.

²Cf. J. P. Free, *Archaeology and Bible History,* p. 180.

Almost the same pattern of destruction awaited the house of Baasha as he had dealt out to the house of Jeroboam. In the third year after Baasha's death his son Elah was killed by Zimri, one of his captains, and all the family of Baasha was put to death. But Zimri in turn was besieged in the palace by Omri, another aspirant to the throne, and after ruling only seven days perished in the flames that he himself had set.

2. *The House of Omri: Idolatry Rampant* (I Kings 16:23— II Kings 9:37; II Chronicles 18, 22).

With Omri begins a new period in the history of Israel, characterized by the introduction of Baalism and the growth of idolatry to such an extent as to bring the worship of Jehovah almost to an end. This new influx of idolatry came about through the marriage of Omri's son, Ahab, to Jezebel, a Sidonian princess, who was fanatically devoted to her native religion.

a. Political Leadership of Omri and Ahab. Omri (885-874 B.C.), as indicated by the numerous references to him in the archaeological remains of Assyria and Moab, appears to have been a strong ruler politically, much respected by the outlying nations.[3] The Bible credits him with having built the capital city of Samaria. This was probably his most notable achievement, and did much to strengthen and stabilize the kingdom from a purely political standpoint.[4] His conquest of Moab is described in the famous Moabite Stone, discovered by a Prussian missionary in 1868:

> Omri, king of Israel, oppressed Moab many days, because Chemosh, the god of Moab, was angry with his land . . . Omri took possession of Medeba, and dwelt there all his days, and half the days of his son, forty years.[5]

Omri and his son Ahab may be said to be the real founders of the Northern Kingdom. As a statesman and as a soldier,

[3] Elmer K. Mould, *Essentials of Bible History*, p. 229.

[4] For the archaeological excavations at the sight of Samaria see Free, *op. cit.*, pp. 181-83; and J. C. Muir, *His Truth Endureth*, pp. 161, 167.

[5] Mould, *loc. cit.*

Ahab (874-853 B.C.) stands out as one of the shrewdest and bravest of the Israelitish kings. When the Syrian king Ben-hadad besieged Samaria and required as the price of peace that the city be pillaged by his soldiers and that all women and children be surrendered, Ahab sent him this memorable message, "Let not him that girdeth on his armor boast himself as he that putteth it off" (I Kings 20:11, ASV). Moreover, Ahab made good his challenge. In the battle which followed he defeated the Syrian army and took Ben-hadad prisoner.

In foreign relations Ahab in general followed a policy of peace. Through his marriage with Jezebel he maintained a friendly relation with the Phoenicians. Upon defeating Ben-hadad he concluded a treaty of peace with Syria, intended no doubt to strengthen his defense against the threat of an Assyrian invasion. According to Assyrian records the two kings fought side by side in the Battle of Karkar (854 B.C.),[6] a battle which apparently resulted in holding off the Assyrians for many years. A third alliance of friendship was made with the kingdom of Judah, concluding a period of hostility which had lasted over 50 years (I Kings 22:44). In order to make this peace permanent Ahab's daughter, Athaliah, was married to Jehoram, son of Jehoshaphat, king of Judah.

b. Baalism Supreme. In spite of this administrative ability Ahab is described by the inspired historians as the most wicked of the kings to his day: "And Ahab did more to provoke the Lord God of Israel to anger than all the kings of Israel that were before him" (I Kings 16:33). Under the influence of Jezebel he introduced the licentious worship of Baal and gave it the sanction of the state. Altars and temples were built to this Phoenician deity, and we hear of 450 prophets of Baal and 400 prophets of Asherah, who were invited to eat at the royal table (I Kings 18:19).[7] Rivalry between Baalism and Jehovah worship became violent. The prophets of God were systematically sought out and killed. The few who survived were forced to hide in caves, where they were secretly fed by Obadiah, one of the king's servants who remained faithful to God.

[6]Muir, *op. cit.*, p. 164.
[7]For Asherah, the mother of Baal, see Mould, *op. cit.*, p. 77.

The effects of this upsurge of idolatry, although temporarily checked by the prophet Elijah and the later reforms of Jehu, were felt in both Israel and Judah for many years to come. Through intermarriage of the royal families Baalism was introduced into the Southern Kingdom, where it had a vogue of about 15 years and probably furnished the groundwork for the idolatrous reigns of Ahaz and Manasseh.

c. *Death of Ahab and Jezebel.* Ahab's punishment for the evil he had thus brought upon his kingdom was not delayed for long. The temporary alliance which he had formed with Ben-hadad of Syria was soon broken. Ahab, with the aid of Jehoshaphat, king of Judah, made an attack upon the Syrian army near Ramoth-gilead on the pretext of enforcing the terms of the treaty. Fearing the words of the prophet Micaiah, who had predicted his approaching death (I Kings 22:17-23), Ahab disguised himself before entering the battle; but "a certain man drew his bow at a venture, and struck the king of Israel between the scale armor and the breastplate" (I Kings 22:34, RSV). The next day, as "one washed the chariot in the pool of Samaria," the dogs licked up the blood of Ahab, thus dramatically fulfilling a prophecy of Elijah (I Kings 21:24; 22:38).

For some 13 years after the death of Ahab, the queen mother Jezebel continued to exert a baleful influence over the Northern Kingdom. Ahab's two sons, Ahaziah and Jehoram,[8] who reigned successively during this period, continued the idolatrous practices of their father. Ahaziah came to his end in the second year of his reign through an accidental fall from his palace window. Jehoram was wounded in battle with the Syrians at Ramoth-gilead, where in a similar situation his father, Ahab, had been mortally wounded.

Anointed as king by a young prophet whom Elisha had commissioned, Jehu, the valiant commander of the army of Israel, raced in his chariot from Ramoth-gilead to the imperial palace at Tirzah to take over the kingdom and to rid the nation of the idolatrous house of Ahab. On the way he slew Jehoram, the king of Israel, and his cousin, Ahaziah, king of Judah, who happened to be visiting him.

[8]These kings are not to be confused with the two kings of the same name who reigned during the same period in Judah.

Riding furiously on to Tirzah, he had Jezebel thrown out of the palace window, where she sat defying him. Her body was left for the dogs to devour in fulfillment of the prophecy of Elijah, and as a symbol of God's punishment for sin.

3. *The House of Jehu: a Last Opportunity* (II Kings 10:1— 15:12; II Chronicles 25; Amos; and Hosea)

Jehu's reign (853-841 b.c.) is notable for the ruthless destruction of the house of Ahab and the abolition of the worship of Baal. Under the pretext of celebrating a festival to Baal, Jehu issued a call for all the worshipers of Baal to assemble in the great temple which Ahab had built. When he had made sure that all were inside, he ordered his soldiers surrounding the temple to massacre the whole company. Thus Baalism was at least temporarily suppressed in Israel.

a. The Syrian Invasion. In this story of Jehu's reformation we see the correcting hand of God chastising the people for their unfaithfulness and for their acceptance of such gross evils in their midst. With the messages of Elijah and Elisha ringing in their ears they should have demanded that the pure worship of Jehovah be restored. But Jehu did not carry out his reformation perfectly. The idolatrous shrines at Bethel and Dan were continued, perhaps on an even grander scale. Other events proved that he was not intent on promoting the true worship of God. So God sent another punishment to warn both king and people of His displeasure: "In those days Jehovah began to cut off from Israel: and Hazael smote them in all the borders of Israel; from the Jordan eastward" (II Kings 10:32-33, ASV; cf. Amos 4:10).

Hazael, the Syrian despot who conducted these barbarous raids, had, like Jehu, been anointed king by the prophet Elisha, apparently as a rod of chastisement for Israel.[9] He proved to be one of the cruelest and most relentless of Israel's foes. For example, in the reign of Jehoahaz, son of Jehu, it is recorded concerning the continued invasions of Hazael and of Ben-hadad III, that they "left not to Jehoahaz of the people save fifty horsemen, and ten chariots, and ten thousand foot-

[9]For the interesting story of Hazael's anointing see I Kings 19: 15-17; II Kings 8:7-15; and Muir, *op. cit.*, pp. 166-68.

men; for the king of Syria destroyed them, and made them like the dust in threshing" (II Kings 13:7, ASV).

However, a change occurred in Israel's fortunes during the latter part of Jehoahaz' reign. The king in desperation over the Syrian oppression besought the Lord for help, and the Lord "gave Israel a saviour" (II Kings 13:5). The Assyrians led by Adad-nirari III, who came to the throne in 805 B.C., began a series of devastating raids on Syria from the north, and Israel was temporarily saved. In the reign of Jehu, according to the famous Black Obelisk of Shalmaneser III,[10] Israel had already begun a policy of paying tribute to the Assyrian king, and this fact may account in part for the comparative tranquillity which was enjoyed at this later time.

b. Prosperous Reigns of Jehoash and Jeroboam II. A gradual increase in prosperity is noted during the reigns of the next two kings. Jehoash, son of Jehoahaz, in three decisive battles won back all the cities that had been lost to Syria by his father (II Kings 13:25).[11] He also fought a successful battle with Amaziah of Judah, plundered Jerusalem, took royal hostages, and demolished a large section of the city's fortifications (II Kings 14:11-14).

Jeroboam II (793-753 B.C.), the fourth to reign in the house of Jehu, became by far the most prosperous king since the time of Solomon. While not much is told of him in the history of the kings because of the evil character of his reign, many glimpses of his times are given in the contemporary prophets, Amos and Hosea. During the 40 years of his reign no invasion by a foreign power occurred, and he is credited with extending the boundaries of Israel from the south end of the Dead Sea (the country of Moab) to "the entering of Hamath" (II Kings 14:25) (probably the pass between Lebanon and Hermon).[12] Wealth was greatly increased in both Israel and Judah, but with it came a moral decadence which was the occasion of scathing denunciations by the prophets (e.g., Amos 3:9-15 and Hos. 4:1-11).

In the momentary prosperity which the people enjoyed during this period and in the warnings and pleadings of such

[10]Muir, *op. cit.,* p. 170; Mould, *op. cit.,* p. 239.

[11]Mould, *op. cit.,* p. 241.

[12]*Ibid.,* p. 243.

prophets as Amos and Hosea, we see God giving a last opportunity of repentance to the apostate nation of Israel (Amos 4:11-12; 5:4-6; Hos. 6:1-6; 11:1-7). As so aptly expressed by Dr. Blaikie:

> It was now apparent that in the kingdom of the ten tribes, at least, the disease of idolatry could not be healed by any remedy acting inwardly. It was also apparent that the ordinary judgments or chastisements would not produce the desired effect. It was necessary to have a great catastrophe, an over-whelming judgment, that would all but consume the nation, yet would admit, at a distant period, of a resurrection of new life.[13]

4. *The Fall of the Northern Kingdom: Final Retribution* (II Kings 15:13—17:41)

The last 32 years of the kingdom of Israel may be characterized as a period of anarchy. During this short period the nation had six sovereigns, of which only one died a natural death. Zechariah, the son of Jeroboam, after a reign of only six months, was murdered by a certain Shallum, who became king in his stead. Shallum in turn met a violent death one month later at the hand of Menahem, another aspirant to the throne. The dynasty of Menahem lasted 12 years but was suddenly brought to a close when Pekahiah, his son, was slain by Pekah, one of his own officers. Pekah himself, after a checkered reign, was murdered by Hoshea, the last to become king of the Northern Kingdom.

Assyria, which had once been sent as a "saviour" to Israel (II Kings 13:5), now came as her destroyer. The doom prophesied by Amos (3:11—4:3; 5:27; etc.) and Hosea (1: 4-6; 3:4; 9:3; etc.) was about to strike. Tiglath-pileser III, otherwise called Pul, made two invasions into Palestine. In the first of these invasions, which occurred in the days of Menahem, the king bought off the invader by extorting a large sum of money from the wealthy men of the land (15: 19-20). In the second invasion during the reign of Pekah (*ca.* 734 B.C.) the Assyrians stripped from Israel all her territory east of the Jordan, and much of Galilee (15:29). A vivid description of this invasion is given in the Assyrian records. J. C. Muir writes:

[13]Blaikie and Matthews, *op. cit.,* pp. 227-28.

The Assyrian invaders swept over Syria, northern Israel, Edom and Moab in a deluge of death. Over five hundred cities perished or paid tribute. Captives by the thousands were carried away to Assyria. The Assyrian monarch knew no mercy: "His captains alive on stakes I hung them and exhibited them to his land." The treasures of many lands were taken to Assyria to decorate the palaces of the king of Assyria and the mighty temples of his gods.[14]

The kingdom of Israel was now reduced to that portion of central Palestine directly dominated by the city of Samaria. Hoshea, the king, was compelled to pay tribute to the Assyrians. When he withheld it, apparently with the hope of an alliance with Egypt (17:4), Shalmaneser V, who had become king of Assyria in 728 B.C., made an attack upon Samaria. After a three-year siege the city was finally taken in 721 B.C. by Shalmaneser's successor, Sargon II (722-705 B.C.). According to his own records, Sargon took 27,290 of the inhabitants captive and in their place transplanted peoples from other lands which he had conquered.[15] King Hoshea was bound and imprisoned and the people of Samaria were scattered among the cities of Media and Mesopotamia (17:4-6).[16] Thus the kingdom of Israel came to its end and all of Syria and Palestine, except a small area around Jerusalem, became part of the Assyrian Empire.

5. *The Causes Enumerated: a Retrospective View* (II Kings 17:7-23; Amos; and Hosea).

The prophetic writer, in relating the story of Israel's fall, gives considerable attention to the causes which led to this catastrophe. Principal among these causes were unfaithfulness to God; the almost universal practice of idolatry, often, as in the time of Ahab, in its grossest forms; and stubbornness in rejecting the pleadings and admonitions of the prophets whom God had sent among the people. In spite of the faithful ministries of Elijah, Elisha, Amos, and Hosea the kings had

---

[14]Muir, *op. cit.*, p. 182.

[15]See G. A. Barton, *Archaeology and the Bible*, p. 466. Compare II Kings 17:24. The Samaritans of the New Testament period were descended from the mixed race which resulted.

[16]For an explanation concerning the 10 "lost" tribes see W. T. Purkiser, *Know Your Old Testament*, pp. 105-6, and Loyal R. Ringenberg, *The Word of God in History*, p. 183.

never departed from the sin of Jeroboam, son of Nebat, who had substituted an idolatrous calf worship for the true worship of God and had thereby opened the way to grosser forms of idolatry and its associated evils. The people's chief source of morale lay in their faith in God, and when bereft of this they became an easy prey to their enemies.

Closely related to religious apostasy was the moral degeneracy of the people. The moral strength of the nation had been dissipated in drunken revelry and licentiousness. Saddest of all, this immorality was at its worst during the religious feasts. Priests and people alike were corrupt, and the nation was almost devoid of true statesmen or religious leaders of integrity. The poor were oppressed that the rich might carry on their reveling parties.

> The picture that Amos and Hosea paint of these conditions is appalling. The nation literally sat upon a volcano, unaware of the seething forces that threatened at any moment to blow it to pieces. And because of Israel's wrongdoing the nation was compelled to meet its God.[17]

The contention and strife which existed between Israel and Judah during much of their history contributed also to the weak position of both of these nations. This, combined with the fact that Israel had the unenviable position of a buffer state between Judah and the fierce nations to the north, helped to defeat her in the end. Had she cultivated Judah's friendship, an alliance might have been formed which, combined with faith in God, would have been strong enough to hold off the foe.

III. God's Messengers to the Northern Kingdom

It is important, in studying the prophets and their messages, to know something of the characteristics of these Old Testament prophets. The term prophet is derived from a Greek word *prophetes,* which means "one who speaks on behalf of another." It may also be interpreted as "one who speaks forth" or "makes a public declaration." The modern concept of a prophet as "one who predicts" or "forecasts the future" is based upon the fact that the ancient prophet did

---

[17]W. N. Nevius, *The Old Testament, Its Story and Religious Message,* pp. 128-29.

occasionally predict future events through divine inspiration. But this represented only one aspect of his ministry. *Forth*telling, rather than *fore*telling, was his primary function.

The prophets, like the priests, were religious leaders for the people of their time. Unlike the priests, they depended for their commission upon the definite call of God. The God-consciousness that this call involved tended to set the true prophet apart from all others of his time as a person uniquely possessed of a divine Spirit. He literally became the mouthpiece of God and was so recognized by the people. In keeping with this profession of a deeper spirituality the prophet was invariably a man of prayer and of pure moral character.

From the time of Samuel the prophets had banded together in "schools," or guilds, for common encouragement and instruction. The young men who were grouped about some older prophet were known as "sons of the prophet." The beginning of such an association is well illustrated by the story of Elisha's following after Elijah (II Kings 2). These "schools," together with the individual prophets, had much influence in shaping the history of the Jews, especially at Jerusalem. The accusation made against the Northern Kingdom was that although the Lord had faithfully warned the nation by the mouth of the prophets they had refused to listen, and had stubbornly pursued their wicked ways (II Kings 17: 13-15).

Six prophets of the Northern Kingdom may be mentioned: Elijah, Elisha, Micaiah, Jonah, Amos, and Hosea. These, except for Micaiah, whose story is found in I Kings 22, we shall consider briefly in the following pages.

1. *Elijah, a Champion of God's Cause* (I Kings 17: 1—II Kings 2: 12)

Elijah, "the Tishbite," was probably born in the little town of Tishbet in Galilee, but his home seems to have been in Gilead, a territory east of the Jordan (I Kings 17: 1). His ministry fell chiefly in the time of Ahab and Jezebel, and his most important work was to check the advance of Baalism in the Northern Kingdom. He is described as "an hairy man, and girt with a girdle of leather about his loins" (II Kings 1: 8). In the manner of his dress, as in other characteristics, he was the prototype of the New Testament prophet, John the Baptist (Mal. 4: 5; Matt. 11:14; etc.).

a. Elijah and Ahab. The account of Elijah, as recorded in the Kings, is one of the most dramatic stories of the Old Testament. His appearance before Ahab was sudden and unannounced and his message startling: "As Jehovah, the God of Israel, liveth, before whom I stand, there shall not be dew nor rain these years, but according to my word" (I Kings 17:1, ASV). A drought and famine were being sent by God as a penalty for the idolatry of the people.

The prophet's departure was as sudden as his coming. The Lord had commanded him to hide in the wilderness east of the Jordan while the famine was in progress. Taking refuge in a cave near the brook Cherith, Elijah was providentially fed by ravens. When the brook dried up he was sent to a town named Zarephath in far-off Phoenicia, where he was miraculously sustained at the house of a poor widow.

b. The Contest on Mount Carmel. Three years later, when the famine was at its worst, he appeared again to Ahab. Ahab was the first to speak this time: "Is it thou, thou troubler of Israel?" (18:17, ASV) But Elijah had a ready reply: "I have not troubled Israel; but thou, and thy father's house, in that ye have forsaken the commandments of the Lord, and thou hast followed Baalim" (18:18). Then he challenged the king to a contest between God and Baal on Mount Carmel. The 450 prophets of Baal and the 400 prophets of Asherah were to be assembled to a mountain in the northwest part of the kingdom, not far from the original home of Baal worship in Tyre and Sidon. Two sacrifices were to be offered, one by Elijah and one by the worshipers of Baal. The god which sent fire to consume his sacrifice was to be recognized as the true God.

The land was parched with drought and Ahab had little recourse but to comply with Elijah's challenge. The Baalites assembled at the appointed place and the people came to look on.

Elijah addressed himself first to the people: "How long halt ye between two opinions? if the Lord be God, follow him: but if Baal, then follow him" (18:21). Then he directed that two sacrifices be made ready and that they call in turn upon their gods: "The God that answereth by fire, let him be God."

The people conceded the contest to be fair, and when the sacrifice was ready the prophets of Baal prayed and danced before their gods from morning until noon, but with no result. At about noon Elijah began to mock them: "Cry aloud: for he is a god; either he is talking, or he is pursuing, or he is in a journey, or peradventure he sleepeth, and must be awakened" (18:27).

When evening came and there was still no reply to the frenzied prayers of the Baalites, Elijah took his turn. He first had the altar of the Lord repaired and the sacrifice made ready. He next commanded that water be poured again and again on the sacrifice, that there might be no accusation of fraud. Then he prayed for fire: "Hear me, O Lord, hear me, that this people may know that thou art the Lord God, and that thou hast turned their heart back again" (18:37). No sooner had he uttered these words than the fire of the Lord came down. It not only consumed the sacrifice, but dried up the water and melted the very stones of the altar.

c. *The Flight to Mount Sinai.* The prophet of the Lord had been victorious. The people fell on their faces and said, "The Lord, he is the God; the Lord, he is the God." The prophets of Baal were seized and put to death. In a season of prayer on the mountaintop the prophet received the assurance that the long drought was ended and that rain was on the way.

But Jezebel was not so easily conquered. When she received word that the prophets of Baal had been slain, she vowed to make Elijah pay with his life. The prophet fled toward the southland. Leaving his servant at Beersheba, he went on in the direction of Mount Sinai. At one place in utter discouragement he lay under a juniper tree and prayed that he might die, but he was refreshed with food and water by an angel and sent on his way.

At Mount Sinai, Elijah took refuge in a cave and complained to God that he alone was left to worship Him, and that his enemies were seeking to take his life. But in a "still small voice" God reassured him of His protecting presence and informed him that there were 7,000 in Israel who had not bowed the knee to Baal. He then commissioned him to anoint the young Elisha to be his companion and successor.

d. *The End of a Remarkable Career.* On a later occasion Elijah appeared again to Ahab, denouncing his murder of Naboth, whose vineyard he was about to possess. At this time he pronounced the prophecies that we have seen fulfilled in the deaths of Ahab and Jezebel and of their son Jehoram.

The last scene in Elijah's life is one of unusual interest. Having passed beyond the Jordan in company with Elisha, the companion of his later years, the great prophet was taken up suddenly to heaven in a whirlwind with a chariot and horses of fire. As he ascended, his mantle fell on Elisha, who had prayed for a double portion of Elijah's spirit.

Elijah has been looked upon by both Jews and Christians as one of the greatest of the prophets. He is often referred to in the New Testament, and at the transfiguration of Jesus he appears with Moses as a representative of the prophetic order (Matt. 17:3).

2. *Elisha, a Type of the Messiah* (I Kings 19:15-21; II Kings 2:1—9:10; 13:14-21)

Elisha (*ca.* 855-795 B.C.), the greatest miracle worker in the Old Testament, was the disciple and successor of Elijah. He was the son of Shaphat, a man of some means who lived in the Jordan valley. The numerous stories which have been handed down concerning him are full of human interest.

a. A Disciple of Elijah. The prophet Elijah had been commanded by the Lord at Sinai to anoint Elisha as his successor in the prophetic office (19:15-17). When he arrived at Elisha's home he found the young man plowing in his father's field with 12 yoke of oxen. As Elijah passed by he cast his mantle upon him, a sign which young Elisha very well understood. "Let me, I pray thee, kiss my father and my mother, and then I will follow thee," was his prompt reply. The matter was arranged, and after making an appropriate sacrifice to the Lord and a feast for his friends and neighbors, "he arose, and went after Elijah, and ministered unto him" (19:19-21).

It may be assumed that he was in his great teacher's company for several years, although the record of his life chiefly concerns a later time. From the account of Elijah's translation we see the manner of their association and the confidence which was placed in him by the "sons of the prophets," whose leader he was soon to become (II Kings 2:1-18).

b. *An Influential Prophet.* In order to understand the significance of the remaining stories as they concern Elisha's influence in national affairs it is necessary to consider the importance of the prophets and the prophetic schools in molding public opinion and in determining the policies of the kings. The story of Elijah illustrates this influence; but while Elisha may not have possessed the strength and originality of his master, he was destined to be more immediately successful in achieving the religious and political goals which he sought.

It is noteworthy that while Elijah received the commission to anoint Hazael as king of Syria, and Jehu as king of Israel, it was Elisha who actually carried it out (II Kings 8:7-15; 9:1-10). It would appear that the reform of Jehu and the prosperity which began to be felt under Jehu's grandson, Jehoash, and came to its climax in the time of Jeroboam II, were in part a direct result of the religious and political leadership of Elisha, whose ministry covered the entire period from Ahab to Jehoash (about 60 years). This view is upheld by good authorities[18] and gives a special significance to Elisha for students of the Old Testament.

c. *A Type of Christ.* The personality of Elisha must have been peculiarly attractive, and in this, as well as in many other respects, he stands out as one of the important types of Christ in the Old Testament. His knowledge of men and his skill in speaking the right word at the right time made him an influence for righteousness wherever he went. His ability as a teacher of young men reminds us of the Great Teacher and the training of His disciples.

Most of the miracles of Elisha, like those of Christ, were works of mercy, and some of them have a peculiar resemblance to those recorded in the Gospels. He sweetens a spring of brackish water, renders harmless a dish of poisonous pottage, multiplies a poor widow's cruse of oil, raises from the dead the son of the Shunammite, multiplies the loaves of bread for a hungry throng, and heals a Syrian official of his leprosy.

---

[18]I. M. Price, *The Dramatic Story of the Old Testament,* pp. 277-79; C. F. Kent, *The Kings and Prophets of Israel and Judah,* pp. 47-50; and Mould, *op. cit.,* pp. 236-37.

His generous treatment of the Syrian troops who were sent to capture him seems to be in striking accord with the golden rule (II Kings 6:8-23). There were sterner acts as well, which remind us of the sternness with which Christ met the scribes and Pharisees.

As we view the ministry of Elisha as a whole, we are impressed with the remarkable fulfillment of his desire for a double portion of his master's spirit (II Kings 2:9-15). He seems, in fact, to have attained to a spiritual stature far in advance of his times, and to foreshadow, like Moses (Deut. 18: 15, 18; 34:10), the coming of the Greatest of the Prophets.

3. *Jonah, a Prophet of God's Mercy to a Sinful Nation* (Jonah 1—4)

The prophet Jonah is sometimes regarded as the earliest of the literary prophets, that is, the prophets whose books have been preserved. But the Book of Jonah is biographical, relating a single episode in the prophet's life, and need not have been written by the prophet himself, nor in the prophet's time. The author of the book is nowhere mentioned and the third person is consistently used in referring to him. From the reference to Nineveh in the past tense (3:3) scholars have generally concluded that it was written after the destruction of the city in 612 B.C.

a. *Identity of the Prophet.* Jonah, the son of Amittai, was a citizen of Gath-hepher, a village near Nazareth in Galilee. According to II Kings 14:25 he was active during the early part of the eighth century B.C., and was credited with having predicted the successful conquests of Jeroboam II. From the effectiveness of his ministry at Nineveh we may assume that he was a powerful preacher and that the prosperity in Jeroboam's time may have been, in part, the result of a spiritual revival which he instigated.[19]

b. *The Mission to Nineveh.* The story told in the four short chapters of Jonah is an exceedingly interesting one. The prophet is directed to go and preach to the wicked city of Nineveh. He is unwilling because he fears that the Ninevites will repent and be forgiven. Thinking to escape his unwel-

---

[19]Mould, *op. cit.,* p. 243.

come task, he goes to Joppa and takes a ship for Tarshish on the coast of Spain. A great storm arises and all the people on the ship call on their various gods to save them. As the storm continues they throw overboard the cargo to lighten the vessel and then cast lots to determine who is responsible for the anger of the gods. The lot falls on Jonah, who now confesses his guilt and directs the mariners to cast him into the sea.

"Now the Lord had prepared a great fish to swallow" Jonah and to provide him a place of repentance. "And Jonah was in the belly of the fish three days and three nights." In the fish's belly he prays to God and in desperation promises to pay the vows he has made. At the end of three days the fish casts him out on dry land. When God repeats his commission to preach to Nineveh, Jonah obeys without a question. As a result of Jonah's preaching Nineveh repents and God withholds His punishment. The prophet is angry at this result and, taking refuge under a gourd vine, he prays that he may die.

Jonah's motive in fleeing from God is now made clear in his prayer: "Lord, is not this what I said when I was yet in my country? That is why I made haste to flee to Tarshish; for I knew that thou art a gracious God and merciful, slow to anger, and abounding in steadfast love, and repentest of evil" (Jonah 4:2, RSV).

c. Message of the Book. As Jonah is sulking beneath the gourd a worm attacks the vine and it is withered. The hot sun beats down on Jonah's head and a sultry wind adds to his discomfort. Jonah is angry because the gourd has been destroyed, and now the Lord appears to admonish him:

> *Doest thou well to be angry? . . . Thou hast had pity on the gourd, for the which thou hast not laboured, neither madest it grow; which came up in a night, and perished in a night: and should not I spare Nineveh, that great city, wherein are more than six-score thousand persons that cannot discern between their right hand and their left hand; and also much cattle?* (4:9-11)

In this superb passage is contained the message of the Book of Jonah: God's infinite compassion for humanity, regardless of race or color, and our duty under God to convey the news of His salvation to every land. The Jews of Jonah's day were intense patriots, narrow-minded, and interested only in Israel's welfare. The prophet, although he knew of God's mercy, shared the prejudices of his nation and was taught this lesson that he might instruct his people in the ways of God.

d. History or Allegory? That the book is historical and not an allegory, as some hold, appears evident from the following facts:

(1) The story is told as simple history and nowhere gives evidence of being a parable or allegory.

(2) The hero of the story is a historical person (II Kings 14:25) and all places referred to were known in Jonah's day.

(3) The Jews have always regarded the story as historical and placed the book at an early date among the books of the acknowledged prophets.

(4) Most important of all, Jesus refers to the facts of the books as historical events, as in Matt. 12:39-41 and Luke 11:29-30.

4. *Amos, a Prophet of God's Righteous Demands* (Amos 1—9)

As Jonah had accepted a call, however unwilling at first, to preach to far-off Nineveh, Amos, a native of Tekoa in Judah, obediently left his own homeland to prophesy against the wickedness of Samaria and Bethel, the important cities of the Northern Kingdom. In the seventh chapter of his book he describes the circumstances of his call: "I was no prophet, neither was I a prophet's son; but I was an herdman, and a gatherer of sycomore fruit. And the Lord took me as I followed the flock, and the Lord said unto me, Go, prophesy unto my people Israel" (7:14-15). In another passage he exclaims, "The Lord God hath spoken, who can but prophesy?" (3:8)

a. Character of Amos. In spite of his humble origin Amos was a keen observer of men and possessed a remarkable insight into the secrets of international politics. Deeply religious, he burned with righteous indignation at the immorality, injustice, and insincerity which he found in the cities of Israel. In his blunt, direct, and courageous manner he championed the cause of the poor, who were being mercilessly oppressed by the rich and the ruling classes.

b. Background of His Prophecy. The prophecy of Amos falls, like that of Jonah and Hosea, in the reign of Jeroboam II; 760 B.C. was perhaps the approximate date of the messages that are included in his book. From the writings of Amos and Hosea we get a vivid picture of the conditions which existed in the kingdom of Israel at this time.

Israel was living in the heyday of its prosperity. The wealthier classes had given themselves over to luxury and extravagance. We hear of palaces furnished with ivory and houses of hewn stone, winter homes and summer homes, luxuriant dining couches of carved ivory with damask coverlets and cushions. The rich "chant to the sound of the viol, and invent to themselves instruments of musick"; they drank costly wines and anointed themselves with precious oils (3:12, 15; 4:1; 5:11; 6:4-7).

The people were outwardly religious. The shrines at Bethel and Gilgal were crowded with worshipers and the religious festivals were occasions of elaborate ceremonies. The psalms were sung piously and there was much mention of the coming "day of the Lord." But the insincerity of their religion was proved by the immorality of their lives. There were dishonesty, drunkenness, and lewdness on every hand. The rich were oppressing the poor, there was bribery in the courts, and the righteous were hated and opposed. Highway robbery, adultery, and murder were condoned, and practiced even by the priests. Idolatry was everywhere in evidence (2:6-8; 3:9-10; etc.).

c. The Book of Amos. There are four main sections in the Book of Amos:

(1) Chapters 1 and 2 form an introduction to the book. Beginning with the prophecy of an earthquake, which he interprets as the voice of the Lord (1:1-2; Zech. 14:5), Amos declares that God's judgment is about to fall on the nations. In superb rhetorical language he pronounces doom on Syria, Philistia, Phoenicia, Edom, Ammon, and Moab. Judah and Israel are tactfully placed at the end of the list, and their sin

is made to appear more terrible as they have had greater opportunity to know the will of God.

(2) Chapters 3—6, which form the core of the book, consist of three sermons on Israel's wickedness, each beginning with the phrase, "Hear this word." In spite of the favor which God had shown them, they were guilty of greater transgression than the Gentile nations around them (3:2, 9-10). They had been repeatedly warned by visitations of wrath: famine, drought, blasting and mildew, pestilence, sword, and earthquake. In spite of all these judgments they had not returned to the Lord: "Therefore thus will I do unto thee, O Israel: and because I will do this unto thee, prepare to meet thy God, O Israel" (4:6-12). Their pretentious worship was unacceptable to God, when their lives were full of immorality:

> *I hate, I despise your feast days, and I will not smell in your solemn assemblies. Though ye offer me burnt offerings and your meat offerings, I will not accept them: neither will I regard the peace offerings of your fat beasts. Take thou away from me the noise of thy songs; for I will not hear the melody of thy viols. But let judgment run down as waters, and righteousness as a mighty stream* (5:21-24).

The captivity of Israel is specifically predicted in this section, as in 3:11-15; 5:27; and other references.

(3) Chapters 7—9 (omitting 9:7-15) contain a series of five visions of judgment, all forecasting the doom of Israel. A scourge of locusts and a devouring fire are withheld at the strong intercession of the prophet. He then sees a plumb line in God's hand and the nation is warned that they cannot escape the judgment of God for their sin. A basket of summer fruit ready to spoil in the blazing sun suggests that Israel is ripe for destruction. Finally, in the last vision, the prophet is commanded to smite the idolatrous shrine, and the people are pictured as buried beneath the ruins of their false religion.

(4) Chapter 9 ends with a promise of salvation and restoration to the remnant of Israel (vv. 7-15). "In that day I will raise up the tabernacle of David that is fallen, and close up the breaches thereof; and I will raise up his ruins, and I will build it as in the days of old" (9:11).

5. *Hosea, a Prophet of God's Love for His People* (Hosea 1—14)

Amos, though prophesying to the Northern Kingdom, was actually a citizen of Judah, and the harshness of his message may reflect a certain lack of sympathy for a people who had long been in revolt against Jerusalem and had often been at war with the people of his own land. Hosea (*ca.* 750 B.C.), on the other hand, was a native of the Northern Kingdom and shows throughout his book a tender feeling of compassion for the people of his own land. Being of a naturally sensitive nature, he was able to understand the love of God for His people and to convey it to them in unforgettable terms.

a. The Prophet's Call. The call of Hosea was unique. The prophet relates how, at the divine command, he married a woman of questionable character, and how, after bearing him three children, she deserted him for her other lovers and eventually fell into slavery. But Hosea continued to love her and, impelled by his love, bought her back from slavery and sought by every means to induce her to be faithful to him (1:2—3:3).

We do not hear the end of the story but by this tragic experience in his own life the prophet was given a new revelation of God. Hosea's domestic sorrow became an object lesson for himself and for his people. His love for an unfaithful wife is taken as typical of the love of Jehovah for His idolatrous people.

b. The Prophet's Message. The major part of Hosea (cc. 4—14) is composed of a more or less continuous series of messages in which he alternately warns the people concerning their sins and pleads with them to give up their wicked ways and return to the God who loves them.

> *There is no truth, nor mercy, nor knowledge of God in the land. By swearing, and lying, and killing, and stealing, and committing adultery, they break out, and blood toucheth blood* (4:1-2).

> *Come, and let us return unto the Lord: for he hath torn, and he will heal us; he hath smitten, and he will bind us up. Then shall we know, if we follow on to know the Lord . . . and he shall come unto us*

as the rain, as the latter and former rain unto the earth (6:1, 3).

> *Sow to yourselves in righteousness, reap in mercy; break up your fallow ground: for it is time to seek the Lord, till he come and rain righteousness upon you* (10:12).

In chapter 11, God is pictured as a Father who taught His child to walk and when he became weary took him in His arms and carried him. Thus he impressed upon the people their dependence upon God and their obligation to be faithful to Him as He had been to them.

The last chapter contains another beautiful appeal for repentance, combined with a promise of forgiveness and final restoration, conditioned upon their yielding to the claims of God (14:1-8). The book ends with an admonition to make wise use of the light which they have received:

> *Whoever is wise, let him understand these things; whoever is discerning, let him know them; for the ways of the Lord are right, and the upright walk in them, but the transgressors stumble in them.* (14:9, RSV).

SUMMARY

We have followed the history of the Northern Kingdom from its formation at the death of Solomon under the leadership of Jeroboam to its fall in the time of Isaiah, when Samaria, after a three-year siege, was taken by the Assyrians. In the course of about 210 years 19 kings had reigned, representing nine ruling dynasties, while in comparison the Southern Kingdom of Judah, in the nearly 350 years of her history, had 20 rulers, all of them, except the usurper Athaliah, belonging to the line of David. In spite of the repeated warnings of the prophets and the chastening hand of God, seen in the many blood scourges which the land endured, the kings of the Northern Kingdom persisted in the "sin of Jeroboam," and the people failed to turn their hearts toward God. Finally, the blow struck and the people were taken into a cruel bondage, from which few, if any, ever returned. The whole of Palestine, meanwhile, except that which was occupied by the little kingdom of Judah, was given over to a mixed population, who were in part the ancestors of the later Samaritans, so often referred to in the Gospels.

RECOMMENDED READINGS

Blaikie and Matthews, *A Manual of Bible History*, pp. 204-33.

Joseph P. Free, *Archaeology and Bible History*, pp. 175-201.

Dorothy Ruth Miller, *A Handbook of Ancient History in Bible Light*, pp. 86-108.

James C. Muir, *His Truth Endureth*, pp. 153-96.

Ira M. Price, *The Dramatic Story of Old Testament History*, pp. 252-306.

Loyal R. Ringenberg, *The Word of God in History*, pp. 175-97.

G, L. Robinson, *The Twelve Minor Prophets*, pp. 15-29, 47-59, 70-93.

Kyle M. Yates, *Preaching from the Prophets*, pp. 23-82, 186-90.

FOR FURTHER STUDY

1. Which of the seven causes listed do you consider to have been the determining cause, or real occasion, of the political division after Solomon's death? Why?

2. By what various names did the Hebrews refer to the Northern Kingdom?

3. What reasons can you give for the comparative strength and prosperity of the Northern Kingdom? Which kingdom was the more stable and why?

4. Is there any evidence to show that Jeroboam in the beginning of his career was acting under divine guidance?

5. Divide the history of the Northern Kingdom into four logical periods. Give the approximate length of each period.

6. Upon what is the statement based that Omri and Ahab were the real founders of the Northern Kingdom? Mention some of the archaeological sources which refer to Omri.

7. Describe the conflict between Baalism and Jehovah worship in the time of Ahab. To what are we to attribute this great increase in idolatry?

8. What effect did the influence of Ahab and Jezebel have upon the Southern Kingdom of Judah? Explain.

9. What two great characters were largely responsible for the defeat of Baalism?

10. Describe the reformation under Jehu. Why is he not considered a good king?

11. What two nations invaded Israel during the last century of her history? Give some particulars regarding these invasions.

12. Can you give any reasons for the prosperity which the Northern Kingdom enjoyed during the reign of Jeroboam II? What were its principal results in the life of the people?

13. Which of the prophets ministered during the reign of this king?

14. Describe the fall of Samaria. From what important source outside the Bible do we have information concerning this event?

15. What were the principal causes, according to the prophetic historian, for Israel's fall?

16. Mention some of the ways in which God sought to restore Israel to faithfulness. (Compare Amos 4:6-12.)

17. What is the meaning of the term prophet in the Bible? How does it differ from the term as used in a modern setting?

18. Characterize the typical Hebrew prophet. Of what importance were the schools of the prophets?

19. Characterize briefly each of the Northern Kingdom prophets: Elijah, Elisha, Jonah, Amos, and Hosea. Can you show a progression in their ministry and message?

20. Give brief outlines of the books of Amos and Hosea and point out a key verse for each.

CHAPTER XII

The Beginning of Judah's Decline

O Judah, what shall I do unto thee? for your goodness is as a morning cloud, and as the early dew of morning it goeth away (Hos. 6:4).

Sources: I Kings 12:1—II Kings 16:20 (the history of Judah and Israel interwoven), and II Chronicles 10:1—28:27 (the history of Judah alone)

To Be Read: II Chronicles 10—28

Period: Approximately 931 B.C. to 726 B.C., from the beginning of Rehoboam's reign to the death of Ahaz

In this chapter we are to consider the history of the Southern Kingdom during the two centuries following the death of Solomon. The period considered is therefore the same as that of the preceding chapter. For Judah this was a period of general spiritual decline, checked only by occasional attempts at revival. Politically, it witnesses the growth of Syria and later Assyria as the greatest threats to Judah's peace; and views the impending overthrow of the 10 tribes of Israel to the north, under the heel of Nineveh's might.

I. PARALLEL ACCOUNTS IN KINGS AND CHRONICLES

The Old Testament sources are to be found in I and II Kings and II Chronicles. The account in Kings differs from that of Chronicles in that it describes the destinies of both halves of the divided kingdom, with major emphasis upon the northern 10 tribes and the prophetic movement which flowered there. It lays great weight upon the close relationship between the religious life of the nations and their political fate, a relationship continually stressed by the prophets.

Chronicles, on the other hand, stresses the priestly point of view, and confines itself during the period covered by this chapter to the affairs of Judah, where the priesthood and Temple worship were still maintained. As the Kings, so the Chronicles directly relates the civil fortunes of the nation to its moral and spiritual state. The Books of Kings form a historical unit with Joshua, Judges, and Samuel, to recount the history of the nation from the death of Moses to the Exile. The Books of Chronicles form a historical unit with Ezra and Nehemiah to describe the history of the nation from the beginning of David's reign to the Restoration. It will be noted that the close of II Chronicles and the beginning of Ezra are practically identical, indicating the continuity of the two works.

Both Kings and Chronicles quote frequently from sources which, being outside the inspired canon, have not come down to us. The writer of the Kings refers to "the book of the acts of Solomon" (I Kings 11:41) for additional material on King Solomon's reign; to "the book of the chronicles of the kings of Israel" (I Kings 14:19) for details concerning the northern tribes; and to "the book of the chronicles of the kings of Judah" (I Kings 14:29) for other facts about the Southern Kingdom.

The writer of the Chronicles, thought by many Bible scholars to be Ezra, the great priestly scribe of the Restoration, cites 15 different sources of supplementary material, including "the book of the kings of Judah and Israel" (II Chron. 16:11; 25:26; 27:7; etc.); accounts written by the prophets Samuel, Nathan, Gad (I Chron. 29:29), Ahijah, Iddo (II Chron. 9:29), and Jehu the son of Hanani (II Chron. 20:34); a book about Uzziah written by the prophet Isaiah (II Chron. 26:22); and a funeral lamentation at the death of Josiah, written by Jeremiah the prophet (II Chron. 35:25).

Collateral sources for the history of the period have been discovered by archaeologists, not only in Palestine, but also in Egypt and Assyria. These findings confirm the record of the Old Testament as it describes Judah's relations with her neighbors. One of the most remarkable is the accurate transcription of the names of foreign kings mentioned in the Old Testament, names which have been found on the monuments and in the inscriptions of Babylonia, Assyria, Egypt, and Persia.[1] It cannot be said that each point of Bible history can be confirmed from archaeology, for archaeological records are by their very nature fragmentary and incomplete. It can

[1]Cf. Floyd E. Hamilton, *The Basis of Christian Faith*, pp. 183-86.

be said, however, that wherever the Bible and archaeology intersect, the accuracy of biblical history is substantiated.

II. REHOBOAM TO JEHOSHAPHAT: A CYCLE OF DECLINE AND REVIVAL

The first 80 years of Judah's history was marked by a cycle of spiritual decline and religious revival. The four kings who guided the nation's destinies during this time, although all descendants of David and Solomon, were as unlike as one can well imagine. The early warfare between Judah and Israel gave way to a firm alliance, and Judah twice sustained attacks from Egypt during this period.

1. *Rehoboam* (I Kings 12:1-24; 14:21-31; II Chronicles 10—12)

After Solomon's death in about 931 b.c., his son Rehoboam became king without any apparent opposition from other contenders for the throne of David. The mother of Rehoboam was Naamah, an Ammonitess, one of the foreign wives whom Solomon had married. Strangely enough, nothing is said about any other sons of Solomon, although two daughters are mentioned in I Kings 4:11, 15.

a. The Revolt of the Ten Tribes. The attitude of Rehoboam at his coronation was in marked contrast to the early humility of Solomon. Solomon's education had been entrusted by David to the saintly prophet Nathan. Rehoboam had grown up in an atmosphere of luxury and worldliness. The concept of a benevolent monarch ruling his people wisely with an eye to their moral and spiritual welfare had given way to the typical oriental notion of an absolute monarchy in which the whim of the sovereign was law and the people possessed no natural rights.

When representatives of the tribes gathered at Shechem to make Rehoboam king, they came with an important reservation. With Jeroboam as their spokesman, they demanded as a condition of their allegiance relief from heavy burdens of taxation and despotism. In the three days taken to consider this demand, the young king turned first to his father's trusted counselors, then to the young men who had grown up with him. Rejecting the counsel of the older men that he should act with moderation, Rehoboam decided on a blustering show of force. His reply, "My father chastised you with whips, but I will chastise you with scorpions," seems to mean, "My father treated you as slaves, I will treat you as common criminals," who were beaten with whips to which were attached metal hooks to tear the flesh.[2]

Rehoboam seems barely to have escaped with his life in the revolution which followed. Adoram, who was sent to seek further arbitration, was stoned to death, and the king fled in terror back to Jerusalem. Here, his first act was to marshal an army to compel the revolting tribes to submit. This project he wisely abandoned when warned by Shemaiah the prophet that God's hand was in the uprising.

b. *Judah's Initial Advantage.* In some respects, Judah was in a stronger position from the beginning than Jeroboam's Northern Kingdom. Although having only half the population and one-third the territory of Israel, Judah was less exposed and easier to defend. Rehoboam's first three years seem to have been spent in fortifying his border towns, and preparing against any attack from without. Dr. Frederick J. Bliss has discovered a strong inner citadel fortified by eight large towers at Azekah, one of the cities mentioned in II Chron. 11:9 as having been built by Rehoboam.[3]

Judah also possessed the advantage of a well-defended capital city, Jerusalem, with its deep-rooted religious traditions and magnificent Temple worship. While Judah's loyalty to God frequently wavered, it was over three centuries before her apostasy brought about her national destruction. Many strong leaders arose at intervals to lead the Southern Kingdom back to God. Although these revivals were not lasting, they did delay the final overthrow of Judah for more than a century after Israel's destruction.

c. *The Egyptian Invasion.* Rehoboam's 17-year rule was marked by increasing idolatry and wickedness among the people. In spite of the fact that the bulk of the Levites and many other God-fearing families from the north moved down into Judah, where they might take part in the Temple worship, the tide toward apostasy was too strong to stop. A nation

---

[2]Alfred Edersheim, *The Bible History: Old Testament,* V, 127-28.
[3]Jack Finegan, *Light from the Ancient Past,* p. 161.

whose greatest strength had been loyalty to God thus became weak and an easy prey to foreign aggression.

Five years after Rehoboam's coronation, Shishak, the king of Egypt, invaded Judah's territory and plundered the Temple treasures. Known in the Egyptian records of Sheshonk I (reigned 954-924 B.C.), this Pharaoh left a highly embellished account of his campaign inscribed on the south wall of the great temple at Karnak in Egypt. Sheshonk is pictured leading Hebrew captives by cords fastened about their necks, and the names of many Palestinian towns can still be read on the time-battered inscription.[4]

From Sheshonk's point of view, there is little doubt but that his expedition was aimed at strengthening the new kingdom of Israel against the potentially more powerful Judah. It will be remembered that Jeroboam, while a refugee from Solomon's court, had found refuge with Sheshonk in Egypt. Sheshonk headed a new dynasty (the twenty-second) and thus was not bound by the marriage alliance Solomon had made with his predecessor. Besides, it was to Egypt's advantage to have Solomon's empire divided into two relatively equal halves, which would tend to cancel each other out as a potential threat to Egyptian security. However, the scepter of world leadership had already passed from Egypt into Assyrian and Babylonian hands, and soon the once mighty Pharaohs were in their turn to feel the yoke of the oppressor.

2. *Abijah* (I Kings 15:1-8; II Chronicles 13)

Abijah was the son of Maacah, a daughter (or descendant, as in II Chron. 13:2) of Absalom. Maacah was Rehoboam's favorite wife, and before his death in 914 B.C., the king seems to have been grooming Abijah (also known as Abijam) to be his successor (II Chron. 11:21-22).

Two significant facts are told concerning Abijah's three-year reign. First, he continued the idolatry and wickedness of his father. Here we find the influence of Maacah, who is said to have set up a wooden image representing Asherah, a Canaanite goddess of fertility frequently mentioned in the Tell el-Amarna and Ras Shamra tablets.[5] The worship of Asherah

[4]George A. Barton, *Archaeology and the Bible*, pp. 28, 456-57.
[5]Cf. J. McKee Adams, *Ancient Records and the Bible*, pp. 91-93.

was accompanied by indescribable immorality, and was particularly offensive to the God of purity. Only God's promise to David saved the family of Abijah from the same destruction which came to Jeroboam's wicked descendants (I Kings 15: 4-5).

The second fact mentioned was the outbreak of full-scale war between Judah and Israel, a war which Abijah seems to have provoked. Smoldering guerrilla action had marked the 18 years since the division of the empire (I Kings 15: 6). Then Abijah marshaled an army of 400,000, still only half the size of Jeroboam's Israelitish army. Although himself an idolater, Abijah did not hesitate to appeal to Judah's old-time religion, ignoring his own and his people's unfaithfulness to God (II Chron. 13: 4-12). The prospect of defeat drove the Judeans to a desperate cry for divine help, and God gave them the victory—a triumph they used to inflict a horrible massacre upon the northern army. History records many other instances of soldierly "piety," which is all too quickly forgotten when the dangers of war are passed. However, it could well be that this victory helped prepare the way for a revival of Judah's historic religion which came during the reign of Abijah's son.

3. Asa (I Kings 15: 9-24; II Chronicles 14—16)

Asa must have been very young at the time of his accession in 911 B.C., for his grandfather had died at the age of 58, just three years before. This may help to explain his better character, since during his youth he would govern under the influence of the high priest, and would be spared the example and influence of a godless father.

a. Early Years of Peace. During the first 10 years of Asa's 41-year reign, the land is said to have enjoyed a period of peace. Several factors contributed to this respite from war. Israel had not recovered from the disastrous defeat Abijah had inflicted, and was torn by the revolution in which Jeroboam's dynasty was destroyed. Egypt was weakened also by a change in dynasties, and only later recovered sufficiently to make another invasion of Palestine. Abijah seems to have had an alliance with Syria (II Chron. 16: 3), which lasted into Asa's time and protected Judah temporarily against attacks from the north.

These quiet years were well spent by the young king. First, a thorough religious reformation was begun. His grandmother, Maacah, was removed from the office of *Gevirah,* or queen mother, and the idol she had set up was destroyed. Wherever they could be found, idol shrines were burned, and the people were urged to serve the Lord and keep His commandments. The vicious sex perverts whose unholy activity was so prominent a part of the worship of Asherah and Baal were driven out of the land. "Asa's heart was perfect with the Lord all his days," is the comment of the inspired penman, who notes, however, that some of the people persisted in keeping their altars on "the high places" (I Kings 15:14).

b. The Invasion of Zerah. The decade of peace came to an abrupt end with another invasion from the southwest. This time the enemy was led by Zerah the Ethiopian, whose vast army was composed of Ethiopians and Lybians (II Chron. 16:8) as well as Egyptians. Zerah is commonly identified with Osorkon I (924-895 B.C.), the successor of Shishak, Pharaoh of Egypt, although this identification has been disputed.[6] Egyptian inscriptions are silent as to this particular campaign; but it was the universal practice of the day to record only victories, and to pass defeats in silence.

Asa's army was outnumbered more than two to one. While the place of the battle, the valley of Zephathah near Mareshah, was doubtless difficult for the larger, unwieldy invading force, the victory was unquestionably the result of divine intervention. Asa's great prayer before the battle (II Chron. 14:11) is one of the clearest expressions of faith in God to be found in the Old Testament.

Such an outstanding victory was a favorable occasion for completing the religious reforms which had been begun earlier. The prophet Azariah, son of Oded, met the returning army, and exhorted the king to continued obedience to God. Upon his return to Jerusalem, Asa gathered the people together and renewed the ancient covenant with God, destroying idol worship and decreeing death for those who would introduce idolatry into the land.

---

[6]Edersheim, *op. cit.,* p. 162. For the contrary view see William F. Albright, *From the Stone Age to Christianity,* p. 18.

c. Asa's Lapse of Faith. It is indeed a pity that the story of King Asa could not end on the same high plane on which it had begun. Prosperity and peace seem to have wrought subtle changes in the character of Asa. When Baasha, warlike usurper of the throne of Israel, made alliance with Syria and invaded Judah, Asa forgot his faith in God. Instead of seeking help from the Lord, the king sought relief in political measures. Taking the Temple treasures and gold and silver from his own palace, he bribed Ben-hadad, king of Syria, to break his league with Basha. This, Ben-hadad was all too ready to do. He quickly invaded northern Israel, and Baasha, caught between two fires, was forced to retreat from the outpost he had captured within the borders of Judah.

When Asa, trusting in the Lord, had defeated the Ethiopian-Egyptian army, he had been met by God's prophet with tidings of peace and a promise of prosperity. But when by political maneuvering Asa won a temporary victory over Baasha, he was met by God's prophet with a message of rebuke. Hanani the seer fearlessly denounced the folly of worldly alliances in place of the trust in God which had brought the earlier victories (II Chron. 16:7-9). One sin led to another, and Asa had Hanani thrown into prison. Many of the people evidently supported the prophet, and Asa was forced to enter on a policy of persecution against those who would have been his strongest supporters (II Chron. 16:10).

Unbelief did not stop even here. When two years before his death, Asa was stricken with disease, "he sought not to the Lord, but to the physicians" (II Chron. 16:12). Even in death, the suggestion of faithlessness follows. Asa was buried in a mausoleum of his own building, with semipagan rites of incense-burning and embalming. Here, as very often in Judah's history, we see that a good start does not guarantee a victorious finish. Loyalty to God must be maintained to be meaningful.

4. *Jehoshaphat* (I Kings 22:1-50; II Kings 3:7-20; II Chron. 17—21:1)

The quarter-century reign of Jehoshaphat, son of Asa, is one of the rare bright spots in Judah's checkered history. Thirty-five years old at the time of his accession in 872 B.C.,

Jehoshaphat seems to have served as co-regent with his father for the first two years of his reign, very likely during the period of Asa's final severe illness. In the later years of his reign, in spite of his personal piety, Jehoshaphat made some decisions which had serious consequences for the nation after his death.

a. Religious Revival. The new king's first task was to complete what his father had begun, the restoration of pure religion to Judah and the suppression of remaining idolatry. In the third year of his reign he sent princes and priests throughout Judah to teach the people obedience to the Law. There seems little doubt that the Pentateuch was the book here used.[7]

b. Alliance with Ahab. Then follows the one most serious blot on Jehoshaphat's record. Perhaps made overconfident by the victories God had given and the prosperity the nation enjoyed, Jehoshaphat ended the long war with Israel, and, in the words of the sacred writer, "joined affinity with Ahab" (II Chron. 18:1). He may have hoped by this to bring about a reunion of the Northern and Southern kingdoms. His first act was to take Athaliah, daughter of Ahab and his wicked queen Jezebel, as the wife of his son Jehoram. The consequences of this ill-fated union imperiled Judah for years, destroying most of the good Jehoshaphat had striven to do during his lifetime.

Next, Jehoshaphat went to visit Ahab and at that time was persuaded to join in an attempt to recapture Ramothgilead from the Syrians. In deference to the piety of Jehoshaphat, Ahab gathered 400 alleged prophets of the Lord together, who unanimously predicted success for the venture. Not satisfied, Jehoshaphat asked if there were not any other prophet. Ahab told him then of Micaiah ben Imla, but said, "He never prophesied good unto me, but always evil" (II Chron. 18:7). At Jehoshaphat's insistence Micaiah was brought, probably from prison. Dramatically, Micaiah spoke the word of the Lord, foretelling Ahab's forthcoming death. His noble reply to the officer who attempted to tone down his message will always be the motto of every true spokesman of God, "As the Lord liveth, even what my God saith, that will I speak" (II Chron. 18:13).

While Ahab went into the battle disguised as a common soldier, Jehoshaphat wore his royal robes, a gesture which almost cost him his life. After the battle in which the combined Jewish armies were defeated and Ahab killed, Jehoshaphat returned to Judah. Here he was met by Jehu, son of Hanani, the prophet, who fearlessly condemned his alliance with Ahab. Jehoshaphat seems to have been much more receptive of criticism than his father, Asa, had been; for Asa had imprisoned Hanani, when the father of Jehu had reproved him under similar circumstances. It must be noted, however, that Jehu's rebuke did not prevent two more attempts at active alliance with the more wicked Northern Kingdom.

Jehoshaphat continued his work of religious reformation, even to taking part personally in the instruction of the people. His reforms included the appointment of judges throughout the cities of the nation, with a sort of supreme court or court of appeals in Jerusalem composed of Levites, priests, and leading laymen—the possible forerunner of the Sanhedrin of Christ's time.[8]

c. *War with the Moabites and Ammonites.* The peace of the nation was soon interrupted by a great confederacy of Moabites and Ammonites, coming from east of the Jordan River. In desperation Jehoshaphat led his people in seeking help from God. Jahaziel, son of Zechariah, predicted victory with the assurance, "The battle is not yours, but God's" (II Chron. 20:15). With this confidence, Jehoshaphat encouraged his people. When they went out to battle, they found that their enemies had quarreled and attacked each other, and nothing remained for the Judean army but to claim the spoils of war.

d. *Further Alliances with Israel.* Once again Jehoshaphat sought alliance with Israel, this time in a commercial venture. Joining with Ahaziah, who had succeeded Ahab, the king of Judah built a merchant fleet to carry on commerce with Tarshish. Again one of God's prophets rebuked his alliance with a wicked monarch. The venture was a failure and the

[8]James Hastings, *A Dictionary of the Bible,* article "Sanhedrin," p. 398.

sacred writer remarks that the ships were broken before they could leave port at Ezion-geber, perhaps by a sudden storm for which they were not prepared. Apparently, Ahaziah wished to try again but Jehoshaphat had learned a lesson, at least temporarily, and refused (I Kings 22:49).

One further act of alliance with the Northern Kingdom marred Jehoshaphat's story. When the Moabites revolted from the control of Israel, Jehoram, Ahaziah's successor, sought help from Jehoshaphat in subduing the rebels. The scripture account receives interesting confirmation from the Moabite stone, discovered in 1868 and now reconstructed in the Louvre in Paris. It is an inscription by Mesha, the king of Moab mentioned in II Kings 3:4. Characteristically, Mesha describes his victories but says nothing of his defeats.[9]

Jehoram had shown some signs of better character than his predecessors, and Jehoshaphat was persuaded to join him. The expedition was threatened with disaster, but the prophet Elisha gave directions for relief, indicating that it was Jehoshaphat's presence which moved God to be merciful. The Moabites were defeated and much of their country ravaged by the victorious armies of Israel and Judah.

Jehoshaphat died at the age of 60. He is said to have "walked in the way of Asa his father, and departed not from it, doing that which was right in the sight of the Lord" (II Chron. 20:32). But the evil fruit of his policy of alliance with the Northern Kingdom is seen very clearly in the life of his son. Whatever he may have hoped to accomplish in the way of reuniting the kingdom, Jehoshaphat succeeded only in destroying the good which he himself had worked so hard to accomplish.

III. Jehoram to Joash: the Fruit of an Evil Alliance

The second period in Judah's history as a separate nation very clearly reveals the results of apostasy from faith in the one true God. It extends from approximately 848 B.C. to 796 B.C., and displays the bitter fruit of Jehoshaphat's unholy alliance with the house of Ahab. Three kings and a wicked queen sat on the throne during this half-century.

[9]James C. Muir, *His Truth Endureth*, pp. 159-60.

1. *Jehoram* (II Kings 8:16-24; II Chronicles 21)

Jehoram was the unhappy son of Jehoshaphat who had been married to Athaliah, the wicked daughter of Ahab and Jezebel. His character is tersely described by the sacred writer, "He walked in the way of the kings of Israel, as did the house of Ahab: for the daughter of Ahab was his wife: and he did evil in the sight of the Lord" (II Kings 8:18). He is also known as Joram, the forms being interchangeable in Hebrew. His reign extended from about 848 B.C. to 841 B.C., and is counted as eight years. Jehoram's first official act was to cause the murder of his six brothers, together with some of the princes of the realm who might have been a threat to his supremacy.

a. The Influence of Athaliah. Although the queen is not mentioned by name in connection with the reintroduction of idolatry, there is no doubt but that Athaliah was the real power behind the throne. No sooner had Jehoram secured his position by murdering the other sons of Jehoshaphat than he deliberately set about to turn the nation from the worship of the true God to the worship of Baal and Ashtoreth, pagan gods of nearby nations. The shrines his father and grandfather had destroyed were rebuilt. The language of the inspired writer would indicate that Jehoram used political pressures and actual persecution to compel the people to worship at these idolatrous shrines (II Chron. 21:11).

About this time a letter from Elijah was delivered to Jehoram, denouncing his idolatry and predicting both personal and national calamities as a result. It would appear that this letter had been written at the time of Jehoram's marriage to Ahab's daughter. The language of the Scriptures at this point would indicate that Elijah's letter had been intended for delivery at the time when its reception might do the most good (II Chron. 21:12-15). However, so strong was the influence of a vicious queen and so fixed were Jehoram's own idolatrous tendencies, Elijah's missive apparently went quite unheeded by the king.

b. The Results of Idolatry. Idolatry was soon followed by national weakness, and political disaster struck twice in quick succession. First, in the southwest, the people of Edom who had been subject to Judah for 150 years revolted against

Jehoram's authority. From the account in Kings, we learn that Jehoram's army was surrounded, and that, although the king and his captains fought their way out during the night, the rest of the people fled home, and Edom remained free (8:21-22).

Next, from the south and west, the Philistines and Arabians invaded Judea, captured and carried off the king's household and wealth, and left him only his youngest son, Ahaziah, and the source of most of his trouble, his pagan wife, Athaliah. Almost immediately the personal disaster predicted by Elijah fell upon Jehoram. He contracted dysentery, which became chronic, and after two years of suffering he succumbed to the disease.

The attitude of the people may be read in the comment of the sacred writer, that "his people made no burning for him, like the burning of his fathers. Thirty and two years old was he when he began to reign, and he reigned in Jerusalem eight years, and departed without being desired" (II Chron. 21:19-20). Not only Jehoram's attempt to turn his people from God, but the political disasters which filled his reign, must have contributed to his unpopularity with his people. Although buried in the city of Jerusalem, he was not thought worthy of interment with the kings who had preceded him. He lived a stormy, sinful life, died a lonely death, and even in his burial was cut off from his more worthy predecessors.

2. *Ahaziah* (II Kings 8:25-29; 9:15-29; and II Chron. 22:1-9)

Jehoram's son Ahaziah reigned but one year, about 841 B.C. He bears the same name as his uncle, Ahab's wretched son, who had been king of Israel some 12 years before. He is also known as Jehoahaz and Azariah.

There is no doubt but that Ahaziah's short reign was completely under the domination of his strong-minded and unscrupulous mother. II Chron. 22:3 says, "He also walked in the ways of the house of Ahab: for his mother was his counsellor to do wickedly."

Continuing the policy of collaboration with the Northern Kingdom, which had been begun by Jehoshaphat, Ahaziah joined his uncle Jehoram,[10] king of Israel, in an expedition

---

[10] Athaliah, Ahaziah's mother, was Jehoram's sister.

against Ramoth-gilead. This stronghold was at the time held by the Syrians, with whom Israel had had intermittent warfare for many years. That Jehoram should have been bold enough to make this attack upon a warlike and powerful neighbor is in part explained by the Assyrian inscriptions, which show that Syria was at that time being hard pressed on the north by the rising power of the Assyrian empire.[11]

While the attack seems to have been successful, Jehoram was wounded in the battle, and went to Jezreel to recover from his injuries. Ahab, his father, had maintained a summer palace at Jezreel, and Jezebel seems to have retained her home there after Ahab's death. While Jehoram was resting at Jezreel, Ahaziah came to visit him. It was at this time that the insurrection of Jehu, son of Nimshi, took place. Jehu felt himself to be divinely appointed to carry out God's judgment on the house of Ahab. Seeing his opportunity during the illness of the king, Jehu rode to Jezreel, assassinated Jehoram and his mother, Jezebel, and put to the sword all of the house of Ahab. Ahaziah fled for his life to Samaria, where he possibly hoped to find refuge among the adherents of his grandfather, Ahab. Here he was captured by Jehu's soldiers. He seems to have escaped briefly, but was mortally wounded in the attempt. Making his way to Megiddo, he died there. Respect for Ahaziah's paternal grandfather, Jehoshaphat, led Jehu to deliver his body to his servants to be brought to Jerusalem and buried.

3. *Athaliah* (II Kings 11; II Chron. 22:10—23:21)

Hearing of the death of her son, Athaliah, the queen mother, lost no time in seizing the throne. With the total disregard for life so characteristic of her mother and father, she caused the murder of all her grandsons, missing only Joash. The life of the infant Joash was saved by his aunt, Jehoshabeath, wife of Jehoiada, the high priest; and he was hidden within the sanctuary of the Temple. This sudden *coup* was doubtless made easier by the fact that Ahaziah had apparently left his mother in charge of the kingdom while he went on his ill-fated visit to the north.

---

[11]Finegan, *op. cit.*, p. 171-73.

Athaliah was probably moved by other reasons in addition to her own personal ambition. She knew well that, if the government passed into the hands of a regent for a minor son of Ahaziah, her own position and even her life would be imperiled. Although a few of the leaders of the Southern Kingdom seem to have fallen in with the anti-Jehovah tendencies introduced through Athaliah's influence during the reigns of Jehoram and Ahaziah, the great majority bitterly resented the influence of this foreign queen. The leader of the opposition party was the strong and capable high priest, Jehoiada, whose wife, Jehoshabeath, was a half sister to Ahaziah.

For six years Joash was secreted within the Temple, while his vicious grandmother occupied the throne she had usurped. During this time the lad probably passed as one of the sons or grandsons of the high priest. When Joash was seven, Jehoiada decided on a bold scheme for ridding the country of its unworthy ruler. Both the priests and the queen's bodyguard participated in the revolution. Jehoiada first called the five captains of the palace guard, and enlisted their help. Next, arrangements were made to have the leading people of the nation present, probably under the guise of a religious festival. The details were carefully worked out and, on the appointed Sabbath, Jehoiada brought out the child, anointed him, put the crown on his head, and proclaimed him king.

Hearing the jubilant shouts of the people, Athaliah rushed into the Temple. Here she was quickly seized, and before any of her possible adherents could rally she was carried out and executed near the palace which had been the scene of so much of her evildoing. Jehoiada's quick and well-planned stroke returned a descendant of David to the throne of Judah, with the loss only of the life of its usurper.

4. *Joash* (II Kings 12; II Chronicles 24)

Joash is also known as Jehoash, but the shorter form is preferred by the scripture writers, and used most frequently. He became king in 835 B.C., and reigned 40 years.

a. The Influence of Jehoiada. The life of Joash falls naturally into two parts. The first, and most illustrious, was the period of his early life when he was under the influence of the noble priest-patriot Jehoiada. Immediately after the coronation of the child-king, Jehoiada made a twofold covenant on his behalf. The young king and his people covenanted to be the Lord's people; and the king and people made a compact to maintain proper relations with each other.

Under Jehoiada's influence, an immediate religious reformation was undertaken. A temple of Baal which had been erected in Jerusalem was destroyed and its chief priest put to death. The Temple worship was reorganized along lines indicated in the law of Moses. But in spite of all the royal and priestly efforts, it is noted that many of the people still sacrificed at pagan shrines; and in the country districts idolatry still flourished (II Kings 12:3).

Probably the most notable achievement of Joash's early reign was the repairing of the Temple. The 15 years during which Athaliah had vigorously promoted paganism in the capital of Judah had seen the Temple building itself fall into disrepair. Having gathered the necessary funds through the willing gifts of the people, Joash and Jehoiada ordered the work carried through. As long as the high priest lived, the stated sacrifices of the Temple worship were carefully observed.

b. The Apostasy of Joash. The turning point in the life of Joash was the death of Jehoiada at the advanced age of 130 years. Almost at once the young king's lack of stable, personal religious convictions showed itself. Some of the princes of Judah persuaded the youthful monarch to recognize again the pernicious Baal worship and to allow its return to the kingdom.

Apparently the moral and spiritual breakdown of Joash was complete. Soon we find him instigating the shameful death of Zechariah, son (or in view of Matt. 23:35, grandson) of the great high priest Jehoiada, who had done so much for him. For the Spirit of God "clothed himself with" Zechariah (II Chron. 24:20, ASV, marg.) and vigorously protested the new swing to idolatry. The king's inexcusable crime was carried out in the very precincts of the Temple itself, and the death of Zechariah became a type of the martyrdom all too often visited upon faithful prophets of the Lord (Luke 11:51).

Judgment quickly followed, for before the year was out a small but highly successful army of Syrians invaded Judah and penetrated to the very gates of Jerusalem. The invaders destroyed the group of princes who had headed the movement toward paganism which resulted in the death of Zechariah. The inspired writer takes pains to point out that Joash' superior army was defeated by a small company because the king and his nobles had forsaken God. The king's life was temporarily spared, apparently because he was very sick, perhaps from battle wounds. The enemy took the Temple treasures in return for sparing the city of Jerusalem.

Very soon after the withdrawal of the plundering Syrians the servants of Joash assassinated him, taking vengeance for the death of Zechariah. That such a conspiracy could have succeeded testifies to the unpopularity attending the closing years of Joash' reign. The king's body was buried in Jerusalem, but not in the burial place of the kings who reigned before him.

The death of Joash brings to a close the second cycle in the decline of Judah. It is characterized largely by the influence of Jehoshaphat's misguided alliance with Israel, notably with Ahab and Jezebel. It revealed all too clearly the weakness and vacillation against which the prophets so vigorously protested.[12] The fatal combination of external pressure and internal weakness foreshadowed the national collapse so soon to come.

IV. AMAZIAH TO AHAZ: PROSPERITY AND PERIL

The third cycle in the decline of Judah covers about 70 years, and includes again the reigns of four kings. It begins with a period of external pressure, rises to a new height of prosperity, and ends with the renewed threat of conquest from the rising empires to the north.

1. *Amaziah* (II Kings 14: 1-20; II Chronicles 25)

The reign of Amaziah, son of Joash, extended from about 796 B.C. to around 767 B.C. During the latter part of this

---

[12]See the next chapter for the message of the prophets in relation to Judah's downfall.

period, Amaziah appears to have been in virtual exile in Lachish, while his son Uzziah governed in Jerusalem. The assassination of Joash caused so much unrest that it was some time before Amaziah felt secure in his position. As soon as he did he ordered the execution of the men who had killed his father. It is noted to his credit that he did not put to death the children of the assassins, a practice which was widespread at the time.[13]

Early in his reign Amaziah determined to subjugate again the country of Edom, southwest of Judah, which had revolted successfully during Jehoram's reign. He not only gathered a large army of Judeans, but hired 100,000 Israelitish mercenaries at great expense. As the force was moving into the field a prophet came to Amaziah and warned him against taking the northern army with him, assuring him that God would give victory without the help of the northern troops. Mourning only the waste of his money, Amaziah reluctantly complied and sent the mercenaries back. His own army was easily successful, and 10,000 of the enemy fell in battle. Another 10,000 were taken captive, and with vicious brutality were pushed from the top of the cliff near their capital city of Sela, or Petra, as it was later known.[14]

Enraged at their summary dismissal, and deprived of their share of the spoils of war, the Israelitish mercenaries vented their spite on their former employer by a campaign of plunder and destruction throughout Judah while returning home. Fickle Amaziah had brought back from his conquest of Edom many of the idols of that pagan nation. Warned by a faithful prophet that God had therefore given him over to destruction, he yet decided upon a campaign against Israel in retribution for the plunder taken by the returning mercenaries. After an exchange of insolent messages between the kings of Judah and Israel, the battle took place. Amaziah was defeated and captured, although he was later returned to his capital. Jehoash, king of Israel, destroyed a portion of the wall of Jerusalem itself, plundered the Temple of its re-

---

[13]Although forbidden in the Law (Deut. 24:16), it remained for Ezekiel (Ezek. 18:2, 4, 20) to enunciate this principle most forcefully. See Otto J. Baab, *The Theology of the Old Testament*, pp. 56-57, for a discussion of the Hebrew view of family solidarity.

[14]J. McKee Adams, *Biblical Backgrounds*, pp. 446-49.

maining treasures, took hostages to insure his continued control over Judah, and returned to his capital in Samaria.

Although the chronology is confused and difficult at this point, it would appear that Amaziah's defeat and disgrace at the hands of his northern neighbor provoked a popular uprising very soon after. Amaziah, we are told, fled for his life to Lachish. Here, apparently, he lived for some years until the relentless hatred of his enemies caught up with him, and he was assassinated. Meanwhile, the people are said to have made his son Uzziah king in his place in Jerusalem (II Kings 14: 19-22). Thus the reigns of Amaziah and Uzziah overlapped for a number of years, as did the reigns of Uzziah and Jotham later. This would seem to be implied in the statement that Uzziah was made king "in the place of his father," and that he built Eloth "after that the king slept with his fathers" (II Chron. 26: 2).

2. *Uzziah* (II Kings 14: 21-22; 15: 1-7; II Chronicles 26)

Uzziah is called Azariah in the account in Kings. He became co-regent with his father in approximately 791 B.C. and reigned a total of 52 years. His reign was the second longest recorded of any of the kings of Judah or Israel, and for the most part was a rare period of prosperity in the declining fortunes of the Southern Kingdom. "As long as he sought the Lord," we are told, "God made him to prosper" (II Chron. 26: 5). Much credit for this prosperity could be given to a priest or prophet named Zechariah, who, it is said, "had understanding in the visions of God," but who is not mentioned elsewhere.[15]

a. *Early Prosperity.* The fortunes of Judah were at an extremely low ebb when Uzziah became king at the age of 16 years. The Northern Kingdom had retained the degree of control it had gained when Amaziah was so decisively defeated. There is a note in II Kings 15:1 which suggests that it was about 12 years after the death of Amaziah that Judah under Uzziah regained full independence.

From that point on, Uzziah began a program of ad-

---

[15]There are a total of 31 men by the name of Zechariah mentioned in the Old Testament. This popular name meant "The Lord has remembered."

ministration and public works which brought his nation to one of the highest pinnacles of prosperity it ever attained. He took and rebuilt Eloth (or Elath), an important harbor city, thereby opening new channels for commerce. An expedition against the Philistines and the Arab communities in the southwest resulted in the capture and partial demilitarization of Gath, Jabneh, and Ashdod, all important enemy strongholds. The Ammonites are said to have paid tribute to Judah at this time, which would imply that Uzziah was successful in conquering a portion of Trans-Jordan which had formerly been under the control of Israel.

One of Uzziah's most important projects was the fortifying of the city of Jerusalem. Not only did he repair the damage done by Jehoash in the defeat of Amaziah, but he built important towers to further strengthen his capital. II Chron. 26:15 speaks of the installation of new and powerful devices to shoot arrows and stones against any besieging forces. The army was also reorganized and expanded.

Special attention was given to outlying districts also. Because of Uzziah's noteworthy interest in agriculture (II Chron. 26:10), he caused towers to be built in the deserts for observation and protection. Wells were dug and cattle raising encouraged in the lowlands, while vineyards covered the hillsides.

b. *Uzziah's Sacrilege.* It is unfortunate that this record of progress and prosperity cannot be continued without interruption. Hoever, we read that "when he was strong, his heart was lifted up to his destruction" (II Chron. 26:16). Pride did its deadly work, and Uzziah presumed to enter the sanctuary of the Temple to burn incense, usurping the work of the God-ordained Levitical priesthood. When the priests withstood him, he became enraged and seized the censer to forcibly carry out his rash and sacrilegious act. Instantly the king was smitten with leprosy. As the telltale plague spot appeared on his forehead, the priests as one man rushed their king from the sacred courtyard. Indeed, Uzziah himself hurried out in terror, recognizing the divine hand of judgment upon him.

How long before his death Uzziah's act of sacrilege and consequent leprosy occurred, there is no way to determine. We are told only that he was forced to relinquish actual authority to his son, Jotham, while he himself lived in an isolated dwelling outside the city until the day of his death. The prophet Isaiah is said to have written a chronicle of the acts of Uzziah (II Chron. 26:22), and it will be remembered that it was in the year that Uzziah died that Isaiah had his great vision of God (Isa. 6:1). The statement that Uzziah was buried in a field belonging to the kings (II Chron. 26: 23) seems to imply that his leprosy prevented his burial in the regular sepulcher of the kings in Jerusalem. It is tragic that one of such ability, who had been so markedly blessed and prospered by God, should have given in to the subtle sin of pride and self-sufficiency and should have come to such a miserable end.

3. *Jotham* (II Kings 15:32-38; II Chronicles 27)

This king is difficult to date exactly, since his reign overlapped that of his father before him for an undetermined length of time, possibly as much as 15 years. Jotham is said to have governed his people for 16 years, dying at the age of 41. The discovery of a signet ring bearing his name was reported in the *American Journal of Archaeology* in 1941. This find was made at Ezion-geber, close to the city of Eloth which his father had rebuilt. It was in the stratum dating from the eighth century B.C.[16]

Religiously, Jotham's reign was much like that of his father. He maintained the worship of the Lord in Jerusalem, but did not interfere with those of the people who worshiped false gods at their country shrines. The son did profit by his father's sin, however, for he carefully avoided any interference with the priestly office.

Jotham continued his father's vigorous building policy, adding to the wall of Jerusalem, and erecting towers and fortifications in outlying districts. A successful campaign against the Ammonites brought large tribute payments from these ancient enemies. The inspired chronicler attributes Jotham's victories to his loyalty to God: "So Jotham became mighty, because he prepared his ways before the Lord his God" (II Chron. 27:6).

---

[16]Finegan, *op. cit.*, p. 153.

4. Ahaz (II Kings 16; II Chronicles 28)

The last of this group of kings is Ahaz, Jotham's unworthy son. He reigned from about 740 B.C. to approximately 726 B.C. Ahaz is named in the lists of kings paying tribute to Tiglath-pileser of Assyria, as found among the Assyrian inscriptions.[17]

From the first, Ahaz was an idolater, and quickly undid all the good Jotham had accomplished. Twenty years old at his accession, he is said to have walked in the ways of the kings of Israel, and even to have caused the images of Baal to be cast (II Chron. 28:2). Not only did he sacrifice at idol shrines, but at least one of his own sons was offered as a human sacrifice.

The ministry of Isaiah the prophet comes into prominence during the reign of Ahaz. When threatened with attack by the Syrians, Isaiah came to Ahaz exhorting him to rely only on God and not to call for foreign aid. Instead, Ahaz sent the treasures of his palace and the Temple to Tiglath-pileser, the Assyrian emperor, who marched south with his armies forcing the Syrians to raise their siege of Jerusalem. When Ahaz went to Damascus personally to yield his allegiance to Tiglath-pileser, he saw there a heathen altar which so interested him that he had a pattern of it sent back to Jerusalem, and a copy made for the Temple there. His crowning sin against God was to cause the Damascus altar to be set up in the sanctuary in place of the brazen altar of Jehovah.

SUMMARY

The record of the two centuries we have just considered was a dismal one indeed. We have followed the fortunes of the Southern Kingdom through three cycles of decline and revival, closing with Ahaz and an epoch of deep apostasy. As we shall see, the reign of Hezekiah checked the progress of idolatry, but only for a season. Only these years of revival saved the kingdom of Judah from the early extinction which befell the Northern Kingdom of Israel.

[17]*Ibid.*, p. 174.

RECOMMENDED READINGS

Blaikie and Matthews, *A Manual of Bible History*, pp. 234-43.

Alfred Edersheim, *The Bible History: Old Testament*, Volume VI, pp. 9-34, 47-80, 84-109.

Joseph P. Free, *Archaeology and Bible History*, pp. 184-201.

Dorothy Ruth Miller, *A Handbook of Ancient History in Bible Light*, pp. 86-104.

James C. Muir, *His Truth Endureth*, pp. 153-77.

G. Frederick Owen, *Abraham to Allenby*, pp. 83-94.

Albertus Pieters, *Notes on Old Testament History*, Volume II, pp. 181-206.

Ira M. Price, *The Dramatic Story of Old Testament History*, Fourth Edition, pp. 252-303.

Loyal R. Ringenberg, *The Word of God in History*, pp. 200-215.

William Smith, *Old Testament History*, pp. 504-60.

Merrill F. Unger, *Archaeology and the Old Testament*, pp. 235-60.

FOR FURTHER STUDY

1. Why does the writer of Chronicles deal only with Judah, after the division of Solomon's empire, while the writer of Kings follows the destiny of both nations?

2. In what way are archaeological records "by their very nature fragmentary and incomplete"?

3. What, in the division of Solomon's empire, would lead one to expect greater fidelity to God on the part of Judah than of Israel?

4. Comment on the statement in I Kings 14:26-27, "And he [Shishak] took away all the shields of gold which Solomon had made. And king Rehoboam made in their stead brasen shields, and committed them unto the hands of the chief of the guard."

5. What examples of the enduring influence of women do you note in this chapter?

6. Do you believe Abijah was sincere in his declaration to the people before the great battle with the Israelites?

7. Note several incidents in the life of Asa which would cause one to classify him with the "good" kings of Judah. Wherein did he fail?

8. What can you learn from the fact that, although Jehoshaphat was a man of undoubted personal piety, he made some serious blunders in his foreign policy?

9. What does Micaiah ben Imlah stand for in the history of the prophetic movement?

10. List some of the consequences which followed from Jehoshaphat's attempts to make alliance with the northern tribes.

11. Summarize briefly the history of Judah from Jehoram to Joash.

12. Although Elijah had been taken to heaven some years before, Jehoram received a letter from him. Explain.

13. Why did Jehu cause Ahaziah to be killed during his extermination of the ruling house of Israel?

14. Describe the six years of Athaliah's reign in Judah.

15. How can you explain the change in Joash after the death of Jehoiada? What of his treatment of Zechariah?

16. For what reasons did Uzziah's reign overlap that of Amaziah and Jotham? Can you think of any reason why the prophet Isaiah might have had his momentous vision "in the year that king Uzziah died"? (See Isa. 6:1-8.)

17. Compare the reigns of Jotham and Ahaz.

18. Note the evidences in this chapter that the political destiny of a nation depends upon its spiritual and moral integrity.

19. Write sentence characterizations of each of the following:

Rehoboam	Jehoram	Amaziah
Abijah	Ahaziah	Uzziah
Asa	Athaliah	Jotham
Jehoshaphat	Joash	Ahaz

20. List the names of the prophets who are mentioned in this chapter together with the event for which each is noted.

CHAPTER XIII

The Golden Age of Prophecy

He spake by his servants the prophets (II Kings 24:2).

Sources: II Kings 15—20; II Chronicles 26—32; Isaiah; and Micah

To Be Read: II Kings 18—20; Isa. 1:1—2:4; 4—6; 7:1-20; 9:1-7; 11—12; 35; 40; 41:10-13; 53; 55; 62; 65:17-25; Mic. 1:1-9; 2:1-3; 3:1-12; 4:1-4; 5:2-4; 6:6-8; 7:18-19

Period: The death of Uzziah, about 740 b.c., to the end of Hezekiah's reign, ca. 697 b.c., or possibly later[1]

The age of Isaiah may well be called the Golden Age of Prophecy. Of all the prophets which had appeared since the day of Moses, and of all those that were to follow in the Old Testament period, Isaiah easily stands out as the greatest. As we view the influence of Isaiah, both on the people of his own day and on future generations, we see that his ministry represents the truest expression of the prophetic genius.

In the immediate background of Isaiah and his contemporary Micah were the ministries of the North Kingdom prophets Amos and Hosea, the fall of Samaria, and the reigns of Uzziah, Jotham, Ahaz, and Hezekiah, kings of Judah. All these except the last have been considered in the two previous chapters. To complete our study of Isaiah's background we turn now to the interesting story of Hezekiah's reign which is told in Isaiah, chapters 36—39, as well as in both II Kings and II Chronicles.

I. The Good King Hezekiah

Five or six years before the Northern Kingdom came to its end in the fall of Samaria, Hezekiah became king of

---

[1]There is a Jewish tradition t h a t Isaiah was martyred during Manasseh's reign. The prophet is said to have been placed inside a hollow tree, which was then sawed in half (cf. Heb. 11:37). That he may have lived on into the time of Manasseh can, in fact, be inferred from a reference in the historical section of his book (37:38) to the assassination of Sennacherib and the ascension of Esarhaddon to the throne of Assyria, events which occurred about 680 b.c.

Judah. In contrast to his father, Ahaz, Hezekiah proved to be the most faithful to God of all the kings since David's time.

> *He trusted in the Lord God of Israel so that after him was none like him among all the kings of Judah, nor any that were before him. For he clave to the Lord, and departed not from following him, but kept his commandments, which the Lord commanded Moses. And the Lord was with him; and he prospered whithersoever he went forth* (II Kings 18: 5-7).

1. *Religious Revival in Judah* (II Kings 18: 3-4; II Chronicles 29—31)

At the very beginning of his reign Hezekiah set in motion the most thoroughgoing religious revival that Judah had known. The prophet Isaiah, who was already active in the reign of Ahaz, was doubtless an important influence in this revival. The Temple was cleansed and repaired and the ceremonies were restored according to the law of Moses. A zealous attempt was made to stamp out idolatry in all its forms throughout the realm. The Passover, which had been neglected for many years, was observed again with great rejoicing on the part of the people, and worshipers from Israel as well as Judah were invited to participate.

2. *Invasion of Sennacherib* (I Kings 18: 13—19: 37; II Chron. 32: 1-26; Isaiah 36—37)

The outstanding event of Hezekiah's reign was the invasion of Judah by the powerful Assyrian king Sennacherib. The details of this invasion are elaborately recounted in three books of the Old Testament, as cited above, and are confirmed in many respects by Sennacherib's own chronicle, known as the "Taylor Cylinder," found in the Palace of Sennacherib at Nineveh.[2]

In 701 b.c., 20 years after the fall of Samaria, Sennacherib, who had become king of Assyria in 705 b.c., appeared with a great army in Judah and according to his own record forced the allegiance of 46 cities and strongholds of Judah, taking more than 200,000 people into captivity. King Hezekiah, who

[2]Cf. J. P. Free, *Archaeology and Bible History,* p. 209, and figure 18 facing p. 334.

had joined with other neighboring rulers in a revolt against Assyria, attempted to stave off the invader by an offer of tribute. Sending messengers to Sennacherib at Lachish, he said to him, "I have offended; return from me: that which thou puttest on me will I bear" (II Kings 18:14). To pay the enormous amount required by Sennacherib as the price of his withdrawal Hezekiah was compelled not only to empty the treasures of the Temple and the royal palace, but even to strip off the gold with which the doors and the pillars were plated.

But the paying of tribute did not satisfy the greedy Assyrian, who immediately broke his promise and prepared to lay siege to the city of Jerusalem. Through his general, Rabshakeh, he delivered a threatening and blasphemous message to Hezekiah in the hearing of the people, and upon receiving no reply he sent a personal letter to the king with a final ultimatum for surrender. This letter Hezekiah spread before the Lord in the Temple, praying earnestly that God would vindicate His great name and save His people from their foes. In the midst of his prayer he was comforted by a message from Isaiah, who assured him that God would defend Jerusalem and that the Assyrian would not come into the city nor shoot an arrow there. That very night "the angel of the Lord . . . smote in the camp of the Assyrians an hundred fourscore and five thousand" (II Kings 19:35).[3] Sennacherib withdrew to Nineveh, and in the remaining 20 years of his reign never returned to Palestine. Thus God protects those who put their trust in Him!

3. *Social Conditions in Judah in the Time of Hezekiah and Isaiah*

From the writings of Isaiah and Micah we get a fair picture of the social conditions in Judah during this period. In spite of the reforms of Hezekiah many abuses existed. G. L. Robinson describes them as follows:

> Grasping, avaricious landlords used their power to oppress, confiscating the property of the poor and even evicting widows from their houses. All sorts of economic crimes were perpetrated, the plutocrats devouring the humbler classes as "sheep

[3]James C. Muir, *His Truth Endureth*, pp. 188 f., and Price, *The Dramatic Story of the Old Testament History*, p. 324.

crop grass." Under Hezekiah, who attempted to reform the state, conditions became even more hopeless. Men ceased to trust one another; Jerusalem became a hotbed of factions and intrigue . . . The custodians of the law abused their powers, nobles fleecing the poor, judges accepting bribes, prophets flattering the rich, and priests teaching for hire. Lust of wealth ruled on all sides . . . Commercialism and materialism were supplanting almost the last vestige of everything ethical and spiritual.[4]

At such a crisis the prophets Isaiah and Micah appeared to call the nation back to God and to their moral obligations to their fellowmen.

II. ISAIAH, PRINCE OF OLD TESTAMENT PROPHETS

Isaiah, the son of Amoz, was born in Jerusalem, probably of noble parentage, about 765 B.C. There is a Jewish tradition that he was a cousin of King Hezekiah. He was a younger contemporary of the Northern Kingdom prophets Amos and Hosea, whom he must have known in his youth. He is said to have prophesied in the reigns of four kings of Judah: Uzziah, Jotham, Ahaz, and Hezekiah (1:1). But from the reference to Uzziah's death, which is mentioned in connection with the prophet's call (6:1), we may assume that his active ministry began about 740 B.C.[5] Perhaps soon after this date he was married to a "prophetess" (8:3), who bore him two sons. The very names given these sons embodied a message to Judah and Jerusalem (8:18).[6]

Having been brought up in Jerusalem, Isaiah doubtless received the best education the capital could afford. The style of his writing betrays a rhetorical training of the highest order, and his knowledge of world affairs was probably greater than that of any other man of his time. "He knew not only books but men; consequently he was well fitted to be the political and religious counselor of the nation."[7]

[4]G. L. Robinson, *The Twelve Minor Prophets*, pp. 95 f.

[5]Chapters 1—5 are probably placed at the beginning as a suitable introduction to the prophet's discourses. They are usually given a date somewhat later than chapter 6.

[6]Shear-jashub, "a remnant shall return" (7:3) and Maher-shalal-hash-baz, "he hasteneth to the prey" (8:3). The meaning seems to be that a fierce nation would take them into captivity, from which only a remnant would return.

[7]G. L. Robinson, *The Book of Isaiah*, p. 20.

Isaiah was without question the greatest of the writing prophets. We have from Yates a colorful and graphic description of the prophet as he is viewed by his critics:

> As a preacher of social righteousness, he had no equal among the prophets. He had deep convictions, kingly courage, clear vision, spiritual intuition, and unusual power in driving home the truth. . . . With his head in the clouds and his feet on the earth he spent his days trying to help sinful people to see God as he knew Him, hate sin as he hated it, and turn as devotedly to the work of blessing human hearts. . . . Dignified oratory poured forth from a pure heart with peculiar directness and uncanny effectiveness.
>
> As a spiritual giant Isaiah stands as the loftiest peak among the mountains . . . He walked with God, and that divine fellowship did something for him that is indescribable. From intimate touch with God he was able to make others sense something of His infinite loveliness and His precious nearness, as well as the transcendent qualities that set Him so far above men. The deep spirituality of the prophet gave his words added meaning as they came to human ears. With all his heart he hated uncleanness and loved holiness. He spent his life trying to get Israel to become acquainted with God and His word and to trust implicitly in His guidance.[8]

As a writer Isaiah is superb. For versatility of expression and brilliance of imagery he has no superior among Hebrew writers. His poetry is comparable to the best in ancient or modern times. He is a perfect artist in words. Jerome likens his oratory to that of Demosthenes. He was truly one who spoke as he was "moved by the Holy Ghost" (II Pet. 1:21).

1. *A Man with a Vision: the Call of Isaiah* (Isaiah 6)

The event which influenced Isaiah most was the vision he received of the majesty and holiness of God. He describes it for us in language which one never tires of reading:

> *In the year that king Uzziah died I saw also the Lord sitting upon a throne, high and lifted up, and his train filled the temple. Above it stood the seraphims: each one had six wings; with twain he covered his face, and with twain he covered his feet, and with twain he did fly. And one cried unto another, and said, Holy, holy, holy, is the Lord of hosts: the whole*

[8]Kyle M. Yates, *Preaching from the Prophets*, pp. 87-88.

*earth is full of his glory. And the posts of the door
moved at the voice of him that cried, and the house
was filled with smoke. Then said I, woe is me! for I
am undone; because I am a man of unclean lips, and I
dwell in the midst of a people of unclean lips: for
mine eyes have seen the King, the Lord of hosts.
Then flew one of the seraphims unto me, having a live
coal in his hand, which he had taken with the tongs
from off the altar: and he laid it upon my mouth, and
said, Lo, this hath touched thy lips; and thine iniquity
is taken away, and thy sin purged. Also I heard the
voice of the Lord, saying, Whom shall I send, and who
will go for us? Then said I, Here am I; send me* (6:
1-8).

Isaiah was not left uninstructed as to the difficulty of his
task. The more the prophet warned them, the more the
people's hearts would be hardened (vv. 9-10). How long
would this go on? Till the land was desolate and the people
carried into captivity (vv. 11-12). Nevertheless there would
be a faithful remnant who would be saved and would eventually be restored. From them would come "the holy seed," a
reference to the Messiah (v. 13).

2. *A Counselor of Kings: Isaiah, the Statesman Prophet*
(Isaiah 7—10; 30—31; 36—39)

To understand the part Isaiah played in the political
scene, one must review the events which were happening in
his day. At the beginning of Isaiah's ministry the outwardly
prosperous reigns of Jeroboam II in Israel and Uzziah in
Judah had come to an end. With Tiglath-pileser on the throne
of Assyria, not only Judah and Israel but other nations in the
Mediterranean area were trembling for fear of an invasion
from the east.

In the early part of Ahaz' reign in Judah (740-726 B.C.)
a coalition was effected between Syria and Israel for the purpose of warding off the Assyrian menace. Ahaz was invited
to join the league, and when he refused, the two kings of
Syria and Israel determined to dethrone him and place an
accomplice of theirs upon the throne of Judah. Isaiah pictures
for us the consternation in Jerusalem when the news came

that Syria and Israel were about to attack the city (7:1-2). The attack upon Judah by Israel and Syria represents the first phase in the so-called Syro-Ephraimitic War, which resulted in the final overthrow of Syria and the subjugation of large parts of the Northern Kingdom of Israel to the Assyrians in 734 B.C.

In this time of emergency Isaiah, inspired with a message from the Lord, counseled King Ahaz to trust in God and not fear the petty kings who were plotting against him, for God would soon bring an end to their evil machinations (7:3-9). But Ahaz ignored the word of the prophet and appealed to the king of Assyria for aid. Then in a second interview Isaiah predicted to Ahaz not only the fall of Syria and Israel but the near destruction of Judah in the wake of the devastating hordes of Assyria (7:10-20; 8:1-8; 9:8-21). This prediction came to pass in the invasion of Tiglath-pileser, 734 B.C., the taking of Samaria by Sargon in 721 B.C., and the later invasion by Sennacherib in 701 B.C.

Again, in the time of the good King Hezekiah when the fear of the Assyrians was greatly increased in Judah by the fall of Israel and Syria and the people looked to Egypt for aid, Isaiah with his usual farsighted vision predicted the end of the Assyrian nation (10:3-34) and warned against an unholy alliance with Egypt (30:1-7; 31:1-5). And when the armies of Sennacherib finally threatened the walls of Jerusalem, Isaiah came to the aid of the king with a message of assurance from the Lord. With spirited words the prophet met the defiant threats of Rabshakeh, the Assyrian general:

> *Thus saith the Lord concerning the king of Assyria, He shall not come into this city, nor shoot an arrow there, nor come before it with shields, nor cast a bank against it. By the way that he came, by the same shall he return, and shall not come into this city, saith the Lord* (37:33-34).

The prophecy literally came true. A sudden disaster overtook the Assyrian army and 185,000 soldiers perished in a single night. Sennacherib hurried homeward, without having accomplished his purpose in the taking of Jerusalem. A short while afterward he was slain at the hands of his own sons (37:36-38).

Not only the end of the Assyrian Empire but the Babylonian captivity (39:3-7) and the fall of Babylon (21:1-10) were predicted by Isaiah. His faith in God and the marvelous gift of prophecy which he possessed formed, of course, the basis of his wisdom; but his knowledge of world affairs and his keen, statesmanlike mind were certainly used to an advantage. "First and last, he was a statesman of the highest order, but a statesman whose counsels were the word of God himself."[9]

III. The Book of Isaiah, an Old Testament Gospel

By universal agreement the Book of Isaiah contains the most complete unfolding of the gospel to be found in the Old Testament. The portrayal of Christ is truly remarkable, considering that the prophecy was written more than 700 years before His coming. Specific mention is made of His birth (7:14), His family origin (11:1), His anointing with the Holy Spirit (11:2; 42:1), His ministry (42:7; 49:6; 61:1-3), His rejection by the Jews (53:3), His silence in the presence of His accusers (53:7), His atoning death (53:8), His burial in a rich man's tomb (53:9), and His eventual victory over death (53:10-12).

1. *Isaiah's Preview of Christ*

Many aspects of the character and ministry of Christ are presented in Isaiah: His wisdom and spiritual discernment (11:2-3), His righteous judgment (11:4), His gentleness and meekness (40:11; 42:2-3; 53:7), His patience or perseverance (42:4), His radiance, giving light to the world (9:2; 42:6), His compassion (53:4), His sinlessness (53:9), His intercession (53:12), and His message of good news for those who are bound in the fetters of sin (61:1-3). His titles are indicative of His divine character and the mission He came to perform: Immanuel ("God with us") (7:14); "Wonderful, Counsellor, The mighty God, The everlasting Father, the Prince of Peace" (9:6); Righteous King (32:1); Servant of God (42:1); Arm of the Lord (53:1); Mighty Saviour (63:1).

[9]W. N. Nevius, *The Old Testament: Its Story and Religious Message,* p. 142.

Many cardinal truths of the gospel are clearly taught in Isaiah; for example, human depravity or the need of a Saviour (53:6), the efficacy of Christ's sufferings in providing salvation (53:5, 10-12), the universality of the gospel (45:22; 55:1), the urgency of salvation (55:6), the willingness of God to pardon (55:7), the joy of salvation (cc. 12 and 35; 55:12-13), the mission of the Church in the spread of the gospel (52:7; 60:1-3; 62:1), the power of the Word (55:11).

The Messianic teachings of Isaiah show a remarkable progression as we follow through the book. In the earlier chapters we are looking forward to events in the distant future. In chapter 2:2-4 a golden age is envisioned in which Jerusalem (Zion) shall become the head of the nations and peace shall obtain throughout the world. In 4:2-6 the Messiah is represented as "the branch of the Lord," and His coming is declared to be a time of purging from sin and of comfort for those in distress. Chapter 7 (v. 14) announces that "a virgin shall conceive, and bear a son," whose name shall be Immanuel. In chapter 9 this Child is described as a Divine King who is to reign forever on the throne of David, bringing peace and justice to all the world. This King and His kingdom are further described in chapter 11 in terms which seem to apply both to the earthly ministry of Christ and to His heavenly kingdom. Chapter 12 is a psalm of praise and joy to be sung "in that day" by those who have partaken of the benefits of salvation. Chapter 35 brings to a climax the futuristic view presented in Isaiah's earlier prophecies. The Messianic Age is here portrayed in beautiful figurative language which is unparalleled in poetic excellence. "The desert shall rejoice, and blossom as the rose." The mountains about Galilee shall join in the general jubilation. The fearful shall be made strong in their faith in God. The blind shall see, the deaf shall hear, the dumb shall sing, and the lame man leap for joy.

> *An highway shall be there, and a way, and it shall be called The way of holiness; the unclean shall not pass over it; but it shall be for those: the wayfaring men, though fools, shall not err therein* (35:8).

In the later sermons of Isaiah (cc. 40—66) the standpoint seems to have been changed from Isaiah's own time to the time of the events themselves. In the prophet's vision the gospel age has already dawned. "Comfort ye, comfort ye my people," he cries, for their warfare is accomplished and their iniquity is pardoned (40:1-2). The voice of John the Baptist is heard crying, "Prepare ye the way of the Lord" (v. 3; cf. Matt. 3:3; John 1:23). And again the prophet answers with a command to announce the good tidings:

> *O Zion, that bringest good tidings, get thee up into the high mountain; O Jerusalem, that bringest good tidings, lift up thy voice with strength; lift it up, be not afraid; say unto the cities of Judah, Behold your God!* (40:9)

In chapter 42 we appear to be at the Baptism. The Lord is speaking, as when the Spirit descended as a dove:

> *Behold my servant, whom I uphold; mine elect, in whom my soul delighteth; I have put my spirit upon him: he shall bring forth judgment to the Gentiles* (42:1; cf. Matt. 3:16-17).

The ministry of Christ is described here in terms similar to those quoted by Christ himself from chapter 61:1-3:

> *I the Lord have called thee in righteousness . . . for a light of the Gentiles; to open the blind eyes, to bring out the prisoners from the prison, and them that sit in darkness out of the prison house* (42:6-7, cf. 60: 1-3; Luke 4:16-19).

In chapter 53 we are brought to the very foot of the Cross and are made to contemplate the meaning of Christ's death, which is envisioned by the prophet as a present reality. The passage is so well-known that we need not quote any part of it. The point we wish to emphasize is that in the progression of the Messianic vision the Crucifixion *has* taken place and the victory of Christ is predicted (vv. 10-12; cf. 25:8).

In chapter 55 we seem to have progressed to a time subsequent to the Day of Pentecost. Every provision is made for receiving the benefits of Christ's atonement. The message rings far and near:

> *Ho, every one that thirsteth, come ye to the waters, and he that hath no money; come ye, buy, and eat; yea, come, buy wine and milk without money and*

without price. Wherefore do ye spend money for that which is not bread? and your labour for that which satisfieth not? hearken diligently unto me, and eat ye that which is good, and let your soul delight itself in fatness. Seek ye the Lord while he may be found, call ye upon him while he is near: let the wicked forsake his way, and the unrighteous man his thoughts: and let him return unto the Lord, and he will have mercy upon him: and to our God, for he will abundantly pardon (55:1-2, 6-7).

The Church Age is in progress, and in chapter 60 the Church of Christ is commanded to go forth and witness concerning the truth of the gospel. The darkness of the world is to be dispersed by the glorious light of the Christ, and the little band of Christ's followers is to grow to a mighty nation (60:1-3, 22).

In the last chapters of the book the scene shifts again. We are now at the time of the end. The glorified Christ is seen in a vision, somewhat as in the Book of Revelation:

Who is this that cometh from Edom, with dyed garments from Bozrah? this that is glorious in his apparel, travelling in the greatness of his strength? I that speak in righteousness, mighty to save (63:1; cf. Rev. 1:10-18).

The blood on His garments signifies the conflict from which He has just emerged. The enemies of righteousness have been overcome and the kingdom of Christ is victorious. The former order passes away. A new heaven and a new earth are created and a universal peace is established (65:17-25; cf. 66:22; II Pet. 3:13; Rev. 21:1-5).

2. *A Miniature of the Bible: Outline of the Book*

The Book of Isaiah naturally falls into three parts. (1) Chapters 1—35 represent for us the earlier sermons of Isaiah, in which the judgments which are to be meted out for Judah's sins and for the sins of the other nations form the central theme, but in which we are given glimpses also of a coming Saviour and of a period in which the people of God will be brought into their true inheritance. (2) Chapters 36—39 narrate certain events which form the background of part of Isaiah's ministry and at the same time form a link with the third part through reference made to the time of the Captivity. (3) Chapters 40—66 are made up of the later sermons of Isaiah, which are detached, as it were, from contemporary events and anticipate the time of the Babylonian captivity. In these later chapters the general theme is Israel's future hope, a message of consolation given to the people represented as already in the period of captivity.

If we think of the two first parts as forming a single unit, the historical section being merely supplementary to the prophetical, we arrive at a twofold division of the book. An interesting point to notice in this connection is that the first of these two parts has 39 chapters, a number which corresponds to the books of the Old Testament. Likewise, the second part has 27 chapters, comparable in number to the 27 books of the New Testament. The analogy can be carried further. The first general section of Isaiah (1—39), like the whole of the Old Testament, contains history and prophecy and a good intersprinkling of poetry, while the theme is largely the application of law and judgment together with a foreshadowing of the Messiah and a period of grace to follow in the distant future. The second general section (40—66), like the New Testament, is made up largely of teachings on a lofty spiritual plane. The central theme is the grace and mercy of God in providing a plan of salvation; and the great events of the birth, ministry, and death of Christ, the preaching of the gospel, and the final victory of faith in the revelation of the "New Jerusalem" are presented as if they were occurring before the eyes of the prophet. This is not to say that the meaning is always evident to the reader. We are dealing here with prophecy and not with history. The events predicted, although presented sometimes with dramatic clarity, as in the fifty-third chapter, are often given a symbolic form and shrouded in mystery, so far as the context is concerned.

It will be well before studying the book in greater detail to consider the outline further. The following analysis will be useful for reference:

I. The earlier prophecies of Isaiah (1—35)

    1—12   Rebukes and promises directed to the people of Judah; glimpses of the Messiah (c. 6—The call of the prophet)

    13—23   Prophecies concerning foreign nations

    24—35   Prophecies of a general judgment combined with promises of a time of blessedness in store for the faithful remnant

II. The historical interlude, dealing with events in Hezekiah's reign (36—39)

III. The later prophecies of Isaiah (40—66)

    40—48   Comfort for the captives in exile (the birth of Christ announced)

    49—55   The Servant of Jehovah (the ministry and death of Christ portrayed; the gospel invitation)

    56—66   The final conflict and victory of the people of God

3. A Miracle of Prophecy: the Problem of Isaiah 40—66

It is agreed among scholars that Isaiah 40—66 was written from the standpoint of the Exile or Captivity, which occurred more than a century after the death of the prophet.[10] Cyrus, whose decree permitted the return of the captives (II Chron. 36:22-23; Ezra 1:1-3), is mentioned twice by name in this section of the book (44:28; 45:1; cf. 41:2, 25; 44:26). For these and other reasons many scholars, including some who are commonly recognized as conservatives, have attributed this part of the book to an unknown prophet of the exile period, whom they refer to as Deutero-Isaiah.

In answer to this view it may be said: (1) that for 25 centuries no one doubted that Isaiah was the author of all parts of the book that bears his name;[11] (2) that there is no evidence whatsoever that the two parts of the book ever existed separately; and (3) that the writers of the New Testament frequently refer to the latter part of the book as

---

[10]S. A. Cartledge, *A Conservative Introduction to the Old Testament*, pp. 125 f.; C. T. Francisco, *Introducing the Old Testament*, p. 116; and Yates, *op. cit.,* p. 88.

[11]See G. L. Robinson, *The Book of Isaiah*, p. 59.

Isaiah.[12] It is, indeed, improbable that a writer of the caliber of the author of Isaiah 40—66 could have remained anonymous at a time when prophets were so highly esteemed.

The question, after all, must eventually take this form: Are we willing to admit that Isaiah, living in the eighth century B.C., could, under divine inspiration, have prophesied so exactly the conditions of the Exile over 100 years later? Evangelical scholars have uniformly accepted this part of Isaiah's book as "a marvel of predictive prophecy."[13] The fifty-third chapter alone, with its remarkable description of the Crucifixion, written more than 700 years before its occurrence, should convince us of the unusual predictive power of the prophet with which we are dealing. It is no wonder then that he was able to speak as one who was in the Captivity or that he could mention Cyrus' name 120 years before he was born.

That the Book of Isaiah existed at least 100 years before the birth of Christ in substantially the same form we have it now has been definitely proved by the discovery in 1947 of a manuscript of Isaiah among the Dead Sea Rolls.[14]

4. *The Great Arraignment: Messages of Condemnation and Warning Mingled with Promises to the Faithful* (chapters 1—23)

Having scanned the Book of Isaiah as a whole and noted the general character of its contents, we now take a closer view of the several sections of this remarkable book. The first chapter of Isaiah has frequently received the title "The Great Arraignment."[15] but as it is representative of the whole first section of the book the title may well be used for all those prophecies that were directed specifically to Judah and to other nations of her time. Chapters 1—12 concern Judah and Jerusalem. Chapters 13—23 consist chiefly of warnings of doom against the Gentile nations.

---

[12]Matt. 3:3; 8:17; 12:17; Luke 3:4; 4:17; John 1:23; 12:38; Acts 8:28; Rom. 10:16-20.

[13]J. R. Sampey, *Syllabus for Old Testament Study*, p. 195.

[14]See Free, *op. cit.*, pp. 205 ff.

[15]Compare, for example, Sampey, *op. cit.*, p. 184.

340 • Exploring the Old Testament
The social and religious conditions in Judah as depicted
here do not differ radically from the conditions in the Northern Kingdom in the times of the prophets Amos and Hosea.
At a time when danger was threatening from without and
the ruling classes should have been making every preparation
to defend their country, they were spending their time instead of luxurious living and vice. The land was full of idols;
widows and orphans were the prey of the wealthy; bribes
were taken by administrators of justice; drunkenness was on
every hand. The rulers were worse than the people and the
priests as bad as the rulers. The women were no better than
their husbands. They "are haughty, and walk with stretched
forth necks and wanton eyes, walking and mincing as they
go, and making a tinkling with their feet" (3:16).

In the first chapter Jehovah is represented as entering
into a controversy with His people. He has chosen Israel and
exalted them above all nations, but they have rebelled against
their Lord and are even now suffering the consequences of
their folly (1:2-9). Their observance of the Mosaic ritual is
no substitute for right living. Formal and heartless worship
is an abomination to Jehovah, but repentance and obedience
will bring forgiveness and safety (1:10-20).

> *Wash you, make you clean; put away the evil of
> your doings from before mine eyes; cease to do evil;
> learn to do well; seek judgment, relieve the oppressed,
> judge the fatherless, plead for the widow. Come now,
> and let us reason together, saith the Lord: though
> your sins be as scarlet, they shall be as white as snow;
> though they be red like crimson, they shall be as wool.
> If ye be willing and obedient, ye shall eat the good of
> the land: but if ye refuse and rebel, ye shall be de-
> voured with the sword: for the mouth of the Lord
> hath spoken it* (1:16-20).

In chapters 2—4 three pictures are drawn of Zion (that
is, Judah and Jerusalem): (1) the ideal future to which God
had destined her, 2:2-4; (2) her present condition of sinfulness and idolatry, 2:5—4:1; and (3) her eventual purification
through the coming of the Messiah, 4:2-6.

In chapter 5 the prophet skillfully portrays under the

figure of a disappointing vineyard the ingratitude of Judah and their rejection of Jehovah. Then in a series of six woes he enumerates the sins of the nation for which they must suffer a speedy punishment.

The call of the prophet in chapter 6 forms an impressive background for his public appearance to plead God's cause before King Ahaz and the assembled people of Judah (chapters 7—10). The dark picture drawn in these chapters of the doom to which the unbelieving king was leading them is relieved by glimpses of the Messiah who should one day come to reign in righteousness over them (7:14; 9:2-7). In chapter 10 it is explained that when God has chastised His people, using the Assyrians as a rod of correction. He will in turn destroy the Assyrians for their cruelty and will bring back the faithful remnant of His people from the lands to which they have been carried in exile.

Chapters 11 and 12 carry us beyond the Exile to the time of the Messiah's reign. "Righteousness shall be the girdle of his loins, and faithfulness the girdle of his reins" (11:5). Peace and justice shall take the place of hatred and cruelty. "For the earth shall be full of the knowledge of the Lord, as the waters cover the sea" (11:9).

Isaiah's clear conception of God's universal dominion, and of the ultimate inclusion of the Gentile nations in His plan of redemption, is revealed in chapters 13—23. In the "burdens," or messages of warning and doom, directed toward the Gentile nations in these chapters the prophet teaches that "all men and all nations are morally . . . responsible to God, and God's moral judgment will not fail."[16] But in the spirit of a true missionary he shows a genuine compassion for the sufferings which the Gentiles must endure (15:5; 16:11; 21:3), and mingles with the judgments pronounced, promises of a brighter future to the few who fear Jehovah among those nations. For example, a remnant of the Moabites shall be saved (16:14); the Ethiopian and Egyptian nations shall ultimately come to know Jehovah (18:7; 19:22); and even Tyre shall one day be restored and serve the Lord in holiness (23:17-18).[17]

---

[16]B. A. Copass, *Isaiah, Prince of Old Testament Prophets,* p. 52.

[17]See Robinson, *op. cit.,* p. 95. For a different interpretation see Copass, *op. cit.,* p. 53.

5. *An Isaianic Apocalypse*[18]: *a Prophecy of the General Judgment and of the Glorious Inheritance of the Saints* (chapters 24—35)

Somewhat in the spirit of chapters 40—66, Isaiah in this section of his book, which forms a climax to his earlier prophecies, takes us beyond the period of his own times, or even the immediate future. He paints for us a vivid picture of a great world judgment and describes the manner in which the people of God will be protected from its terrors. There are parenthetical references to contemporary events, sometimes of considerable length as in chapters 28—33, but the controlling theme concerns the final consummation.[19]

A quotation from chapter 24 will illustrate the manner in which Isaiah treats this final world catastrophe:

> *Fear, and the pit, and the snare, are upon thee, O inhabitant of the earth. And it shall come to pass, that he who fleeth from the noise of the fear shall fall into the pit; and he that cometh up out of the midst of the pit shall be taken in the snare: for the windows from on high are open, and the foundations of the earth do shake. The earth is utterly broken down, the earth is clean dissolved, the earth is moved exceedingly. The earth shall reel to and fro like a drunkard, and shall be removed like a cottage; and the transgression thereof shall be heavy upon it; and it shall fall, and not rise again* (24:17-20).[20]

It is to be noted that sin is the cause of this great destruction on the day of the Lord's wrath, even as in the time of the Flood (Genesis 6—9), and that a gracious deliverance will be provided for the faithful servants of God, as

[18]The term apocalypse is used here of an eschatological prophecy directed toward events at the end of the world in contrast to those prophecies which relate either to contemporary events or to historical developments predicted in the future. Cf. Robinson, *op. cit.*, p. 99.

[19]A similar type of prophecy is found in Zephaniah and in Joel. See the discussion of these prophets in Chapters XIV and XV of this text, and in G. L. Robinson, *The Twelve Minor Prophets*, pp. 44-45 and 133-34.

[20]See also 24:21-23; 34:4, 9-12; and compare Joel 2:12a, 30-31; Zeph. 1:14-15; 3:8; II Pet. 3:10.

there was for Noah and his family. Some glimpses of God's providence over His people in the midst of these earth-shaking events are given in chapters 25—27 and 32:

> *For thou hast been a strength to the poor, a strength to the needy in his distress, a refuge from the storm, a shadow from the heat, when the blast of the terrible ones is as a storm against the wall* (25:4).

> *He will swallow up death in victory; and the Lord God will wipe away tears from off all faces; and the rebuke of his people shall he take away from off all the earth: for the Lord hath spoken it* (25:8).

> *In that day shall this song be sung . . . We have a strong city; salvation will God appoint for walls and bulwarks. Open ye the gates, that the righteous nation which keepeth the truth may enter in. Thou wilt keep him in perfect peace, whose mind is stayed on thee: because he trusteth in thee* (26:1-3).

> *Thy dead men shall live, together with my dead body shall they arise. Awake and sing, ye that dwell in the dust: for thy dew is as the dew of herbs, and the earth shall cast out the dead* (26:19).

> *Behold, a king shall reign in righteousness, and princes shall rule in judgment. And a man shall be as an hiding place from the wind, and a covert from the tempest; as rivers of water in a dry place, as the shadow of a great rock in a weary land* (32:1-2).

> *And the work of righteousness shall be peace; and the effect of righteousness quietness and assurance for ever. And my people shall dwell in a peaceable habitation, and in sure dwellings, and in quiet resting places* (32:17-18).

Two observations should be made on these passages: (1) that there is a clear reference to the last days, as shown by the emphasis upon the resurrection; and (2) that some of the passages seem to be capable of more than one interpretation. In fact, by using a "symbolic" method of interpretation all of the passages cited may be referred to the return from exile or to the dawn of the Christian era. Similarly, the culminating chapter in this section (c. 35) may be made to apply either (1) to the period of restoration in Judah, (2) to the ministry of Christ and the Christian age, or (3) to the second coming of Christ and the final victory of the saints.[21]

6. *The Book of Consolation: a Message to a Future Generation* (chapters 40—66)

In the first 39 chapters of his book Isaiah is concerned largely with the problems and needs of the people in his own time. Even the eschatological messages in chapters 24—35 were intended without doubt to stir the people to repentance and to inspire faith in God. The many references to the Messiah were intended to serve the same purpose. The announcement of Immanuel's birth (7:14), for example, was given as a sign to Ahaz to assure him of God's presence among His people and the glorious future He had in store for them if they would but trust implicitly to His providential care. But we come now to a portion of the book which apparently was written for an age to come. The standpoint of the writer is clearly that of the Exile, which began about 100 years after the time of Isaiah. Few references, if any, are made to events of the prophet's own time. The purpose from the very beginning is to furnish consolation to a people in distress.

Isaiah had specifically predicted the exile to Babylonia (39:6-7), and had often treated the theme which is prevalent in all the latter chapters of his book, namely, the return from captivity and the restoration of Jerusalem (e.g., 1:25-27; 6:11-13; 10:20-21; 14:1-4; 30:26; 35). Here the prophet takes his position, as it were, among the future captives, and assuming the role of a counselor he attempts to lighten their burdened hearts with promises of a return and of a glorious age to follow.

As in chapter 35 the predictions of the return or restoration are not always distinguishable from the prophecies of the coming Messianic Age. And it is not necessary that we always distinguish them. To the people in exile the immediate need

[21]On this whole section, see Copass, *op. cit.*, pp. 63-89.

was to be restored to their land and to be allowed to live a peaceful life in the service of Jehovah. But in the purpose of God there was a greater restoration in store for His people, a redemption from the guilt and power of sin and a restoration of His image on the heart.

Dr. Sampey characterizes "The Book of Comfort" and its value for Christians in the following terms:

> The saints of more than two thousand years have bound up their broken hearts with its comforting promises. It is full of descriptions of God's character and of His plans for His distressed people. We are in sight of God or the Suffering Servant or the Holy Spirit all the way through. God tells of the good things He means to do for His people. There is no better way of comforting the saints than to fill their minds and hearts with the sense of God's power and wisdom and goodness and free grace. A vision of the Servant of Jehovah suffering instead of the sinner also melts the heart to tears of gratitude. And when the Spirit draws the veil from the future and lets the believer see some of the glories that await him, this, too, strengthens the heart to bear present trials and afflictions.[22]

One needs merely to "browse," as it were, in this part of the book to find many precious promises which are as meaningful to us as to the people in exile for whom they were intended: for example, the promise of a tender shepherd's care (40:11), the promise of strength to those who wait upon the Lord (40:28-31), the promise of God's presence and assisting grace in times of trouble (41:10-13, the promise that the waters of affliction should not overflow His saints (43:1-2), the reassurance of sins forgiven (43:25; 44:22), the promise of hidden treasures of God's truth (45:3), and the promise of salvation to "all the ends of the earth" who will "look" to God by faith (45:22). These are but a few of the fine passages to be found in this beautiful portion of God's Word. The reader is bidden to hunt for himself and to let his soul "delight itself in fatness" (55:2).

a. The Suffering Servant of Jehovah. In chapters 40—55 there are numerous references to "my servant" or the "servant of Jehovah," who is referred at times to Israel as a personification of the nation which God had chosen to bring salvation to the world (41:8; 44:1-2, 21; 45:4; 49:3). In other con-

[22]John R. Sampey, *The Heart of the Old Testament*, p. 170.

nections it is clear that the name is made to refer specifically to the Messiah, who as the Representative of the chosen nation should somehow in obedience to God, His Father, accomplish the work of redemption.

There are four so-called "Servant Songs" in chapters 42—53 which describe the ministry and sufferings of this "servant of Jehovah." The first (42:1-9) describes the Servant's gentle manner and worldwide mission. The second (49:1-13) relates His call, the effectiveness of His ministry, His rejection by His own, and His exaltation through His saving mission to the Gentiles. The third poem (50:4-9) tells of the wisdom of the Servant, His perfection through obedience and suffering (cf. Phil. 2:7-8; Heb. 2:10), and His certainty of eventual triumph.

The fourth of the "Servant Poems" is one of the most notable passages in the entire Scriptures—the "Mount Everest of Messianic Prophecy."[23] "The profoundest thoughts in the Old Testament revelation are to be found in this passage . . . So far as fact and accuracy of description are concerned, it might well have been composed after the tragedy on Calvary."[24] Polycarp, one of the apostolic fathers (A.D. 125), calls it "the golden passional of the Old Testament."

The poem begins in chapter 52 (verses 13-15) and includes all of chapter 53. There are five stanzas of three verses each. The first (52:13-15) describes the Servant's destiny; the second (53:1-3), His career; the third (53:4-6), His sufferings; the fourth (53:7-9), His submission; and the fifth (53:10-12), His reward.

The most striking part of this remarkable passage is the description of the Servant's vicarious suffering for the sins of His people who had rejected Him as their Saviour and King:

> He is despised and rejected of men; a man of sorrows, and acquainted with grief: and we hid as it were our faces from him; he was despised, and we esteemed him not. Surely he hath borne our griefs, and carried our sorrows: yet we did esteem him stricken, smitten of God, and afflicted. But he was wounded for our

transgressions, he was bruised for our iniquities: the chastisement of our peace was upon him; and with his stripes we are healed. All we like sheep have gone astray; we have turned every one to his own way; and the Lord hath laid on him the iniquity of us all (53:3-6).

Dr. Sampey remarks that there is no greater verse in the Old Testament than Isa. 53:5—the Old Testament equivalent of John 3:16.[25]

In chapter 55, another of the great chapters in this book, we have the invitation to partake in the benefits of salvation, purchased through the meritorious suffering of Jehovah's Servant. The prophet speaks as a present-day evangelist: Why spend money for that which satisfieth not? The riches of God's grace are available to every man who will come to Him. But you must forsake your sins. You must seek Him with your whole heart, and do it now. The call is urgent; tomorrow may be too late. If you call upon Him, God is abundantly willing to pardon. He will make the way joyful. The very mountains and the hills will break out in singing before you, and the trees of the field will clap their hands.

b. A Vision of Zion Redeemed. Chapters 56 to 66 may be thought of as a unified vision of the final redemption of Zion, forming a fitting conclusion to this remarkable book. To comprehend the majesty and beauty of this vision one must have in mind the purpose of the entire book and the manner in which the author has already anticipated the grand ideas which are so dramatically presented in these final chapters.

The heart of Isaiah's message from beginning to end, as we have seen, is the salvation that God has in store for His people, the faithful remnant of Israel, and the mission that they are to perform in bringing the whole world under Jehovah's dominion. From Isa. 2:2-4 we learn that Zion shall one day become the head of the nations and shall instruct all peoples in the worship of Jehovah. In numerous passages throughout the book the plan by which Jehovah will accomplish this redemptive purpose is gradually unfolded, cli-

[25]Sampey, *op. cit.,* p. 173.

maxing in the fifty-third chapter, where the "servant of Jehovah" is represented as dying vicariously for the sins of the world.

In the final chapters of the book we have a vision of a purified Zion, filled with the glorious light and power of God, going forth with Christ to build the kingdom of God in the earth (cc. 56—62). The glorified Christ is then introduced (c. 63) and a scene of final judgment ensues. The righteous servants of God are justified in their prayer for deliverance (c. 64) and rewards are meted out to the just and to the unjust (cc. 65—66). "New heavens and a new earth" are created (65:17; 66:22) and, as in the Book of Revelation, the people of God are blessed with His literal presence among them (compare Isa. 65:17-25 with Rev. 21:1-4).

IV. The Prophet Micah, Champion of the Common People

The prophet Micah, a contemporary of Isaiah, was born in the obscure village of Moresheth-gath in southwestern Judah. His prophecies were directed to both Israel and Judah, indicating that they were written some years before the fall of Samaria in 721 B.C. Unlike his greater contemporary, whose major interests were in the city and in matters that concerned the nation, Micah's interests were with the common people and with the individual. For this reason he is often styled "prophet of the poor." With all the passion of his soul he cried out against the cruel measures with which the wealthy and ruling classes oppressed their poorer countrymen. "I truly am full of power by the Spirit of the Lord," he cried, "to declare unto Jacob his transgression, and to Israel his sin" (3:8, RSV).

The Book of Micah may be divided into three parts: chapters 1—3 concern the oppression of the poor by the ruling classes at Jerusalem; chapters 4 and 5 are Messianic, and resemble the Messianic prophecies of Isaiah; chapters 6 and 7 may be entitled "God's Controversy with His People" and contain a remarkable analysis of the demands of true religion.

1. *"Thou, Bethlehem":* a Prophecy of the Saviour's Birth (Mic. 5:2)

One of the most famous passages in the Old Testament is that in which Micah prophesied that the Messiah would be born in the Judean town of Bethlehem. It was this passage, apparently well-known to the Jews of Herod's time, that was pointed out to the wise men in their search for the newborn King. It is notable that, in conformance with the general character of Micah's prophecy, the Messiah is represented as one of the common people, born not in the great city of Jerusalem, as might have been expected, but in the country village of Bethlehem; and that it was He who should finally bring peace and contentment to those who were being oppressed:

> *They shall sit every man under his vine and under his fig tree; and none shall make them afraid: for the mouth of the Lord of hosts hath spoken it* (4:4).

> *He shall stand and shall feed his flock in the strength of the Lord;*
> *in the majesty of the name of the Lord his God;*
> *And they shall dwell secure, for now he shall be great to the ends of the earth* (5:4, RSV).

> *And this man shall be our peace* (5:5, ARV).

2. *"What Hath the Lord Required?" A Definition of True Religion* (6:6-8)

In chapters 6 and 7 the Lord is represented as holding a controversy with His people. The people are inclined to look upon their God as a cruel master, whose demands are hard to meet. In their attempt to appease Him they resort to mistaken methods.

> *Wherewith shall I come before the Lord, and bow myself before the high God? shall I come before him with burnt offerings, with calves of a year old? Will the Lord be pleased with thousands of rams, or with ten thousands of rivers of oil? shall I give my firstborn for my transgression, the fruit of my body for the sin of my soul?* (6:6-7)

To such queries God gives an answer by reminding them of the many things He has done for them through the years, and of the mercy and goodness He has showered upon them again and again. Then in an impressive passage, which ranks as one of the most important pronouncements of the Scriptures, the prophet summarizes the demands of God:

> *He hath shewed thee, O man, what is good; and what doth the Lord require of thee, but to do justly, and to love mercy, and to walk humbly with thy God?*
> (v. 8)

Dr. Merrill notes that in this one passage we see the messages of Amos, Hosea, and Isaiah epitomized:

> The keynote of Amos' teaching is *justice*. Hosea strikes the richer, deeper note of *love*. Isaiah calls for reverent, *humble fellowship* with the Holy One. These are their characteristic messages. The "Religion of the Spirit" has dawned. It is still a long way to the fulness of the noon; but the true light is shining, and shall shine more and more unto the perfect day in Christ Jesus.[26]

SUMMARY

In this chapter we have given careful consideration to three individuals who were wielding a strong influence for righteousness in the kingdom of Judah at the precise time when the apostate Northern Kingdom of Israel came to her tragic end. There can be no doubt that the spiritual contribution of these godly leaders had much to do with saving Jerusalem from a similar fate. Although each of these characters was important in his particular sphere, Isaiah, as judged by the remarkable book of his prophecies which has been preserved to us, is by far the greatest, as he is indeed one of the most outstanding personalities in the entire Old Testament. The fifty-third chapter of Isaiah is rightly judged "the Mount Everest of Old Testament prophecy," vividly portraying as it does, more than 700 years in advance, the atoning death of Christ on the cross of Calvary. It is to be regretted that the spiritual progress made during this Golden Age of Prophecy was so soon to be overcome in Judah by the evil influence of King Manasseh, son of Hezekiah.

[26]W. P. Merrill, *Prophets of the Dawn*, p. 156, as quoted in Yates, *op. cit.*, pp. 126 f.

RECOMMENDED READINGS

S. A. Cartledge, *A Conservative Introduction to the Old Testament,* pp. 121-34.

B. A. Copass, *Isaiah, Prince of Old Testament Prophets,* pp. 115-38.

James C. Muir, *His Truth Endureth,* pp. 184-93.

Ira M. Price, *The Dramatic Story of the Old Testament History,* pp. 307-27.

G. L. Robinson, *The Book of Isaiah,* pp. 19-24, 141-46.

———, *The Twelve Minor Prophets,* pp. 94-105.

John R. Sampey, *The Heart of the Old Testament,* pp. 159-75.

Kyle M. Yates, *Preaching from the Prophets,* pp. 83-127.

FOR FURTHER STUDY

1. What are some of the reasons for calling this period the Golden Age of Prophecy?

2. Outline the background of Isaiah under the following heads:
   a. Historical background
   b. Social conditions
   c. Contemporary prophets

3. What were the influences which may have contributed to the wholesome, godly character of King Hezekiah? Consider in this connection the evil character of his father, Ahaz, the godly influence of Isaiah, and the example of the Northern Kingdom.

4. Tell the story of Jerusalem's deliverance from the Assyrians in the days of Hezekiah.

5. Characterize in contrast the two prophets Isaiah and Micah. In what respects were they, or their prophecies, similar?

6. Describe the call of Isaiah and show how it could be made the basis of a holiness sermon.

7. Suggest the several occasions upon which Isaiah gave advice to the kings of Judah. What evidence was there in subsequent events to show that his advice was sound?

8. What problem has arisen concerning the Book of Isaiah? What arguments can you give for the unified authorship of the book?

9. What recent discovery has been made of an early manuscript of Isaiah? How does the date of this manuscript compare with those formerly known?

10. Give a brief outline of Isaiah, and show how the book might be compared structurally to the Bible as a whole.

11. What are some of the remarkable features of the Book of Isaiah that cause it to be called "An Old Testament Gospel"? Can you suggest the manner in which the truths concerning the Messiah and the plan of redemption are gradually unfolded throughout the book?

12. In what connections does Isaiah prophesy the inclusion of the Gentile nations in the plan of redemption?

13. Point out two or three important prophecies in Isaiah concerning the general judgment. How are these related to the prophecies concerning the restoration or return from captivity?

14. Explain the term apocalypse as applied to these passages. What two books of the Scriptures are recognized as apocalypses, and what is their principal subject matter?

15. Describe the content of chapter 35 and the possible applications which it may have.

16. To whom is the "Book of Consolation" (chapters 40—66) directed, and what is the comforting message that is conveyed?

17. Outline the prophecies concerning the "Servant of Jehovah" contained in the four so-called "Servant Songs." Describe especially the important fifty-third chapter.

18. Describe "The Great Invitation" contained in the fifty-fifth chapter, and show its relation to the passages concerning the Servant of Jehovah.

19. What is the general subject matter of chapters 56—66? Show how these chapters form an approriate conclusion to the book.

20. Outline the Book of Micah, giving appropriate titles to the following sections: chapters 1—3, chapters 4—5, and chapters 6—7.

21. Mention two outstanding verses in the book and show their relation to the principal message of the prophet.

CHAPTER XIV

The Fall of Judah

Hast thou utterly rejected Judah? (Jer. 14:19)

Sources: II Kings 21—25; II Chronicles 33—36; Jeremiah; Lamentations; Ezekiel; Obadiah; Nahum; Habakkuk; and Zephaniah; Dan. 1:1-7

To Be Read: II Kings 21—25; II Chronicles 33—36; Jeremiah 1—2; 4; 18:1-12; 25:8-13; 36; Lam. 1:1-12; 3:22-33; Nahum 3; Hab. 1:1—2:4; 3:17-19; Zephaniah 1; Obadiah

Period: The death of Hezekiah, about 697 B.C., to the destruction of Jerusalem, 586 B.C.

The story of this period is told in both II Kings and II Chronicles with slight variations. Many details are added in the prophecies of Jeremiah, Ezekiel, and Daniel, and a graphic picture is drawn of conditions following the fall of Jerusalem in the Book of Lamentations. In describing this period we shall deal first with the historical background, then with the sequence of events leading to the final fall of the kingdom, and lastly with the prophets associated with this period of Judah's history.

I. THE NATIONS IN THE BACKGROUND: WORLD-SHAKING EVENTS OF THE SEVENTH CENTURY B.C.

With the passing of Hezekiah (ca. 697 B.C.), the last vestige of political independence vanished from the little kingdom of Judah. During this final period of her history, which extended over slightly more than a century, she became a pawn in the hands of other nations, first claimed by Assyria, then by Egypt, and finally by Babylonia. The history of this period cannot be understood apart from the history of the nations which exerted this controlling influence over the one remaining Israelitish state.

1. *Height of Assyria's Power Under Esarhaddon*

Sennacherib, who had devastated the land of Judah and had nearly accomplished his objective in the occupation of

Jerusalem II Kings 18:13—19:37; Isaiah 36—37), died in 681 B.C. Esarhaddon, his son, became the ruler of Assyria. Under this shrewd monarch, with the subjugation of Phoenicia and Egypt, the Assyrian Empire became the master of the entire Fertile Crescent and of all the nations which counted in the politics of that day. Thus we see the reason for Judah's abject submission to Assyria during this period.

But Assyria's end was not far off. Ashurbanipal, who succeeded to the throne in 668 B.C., although one of the most enlightened rulers of ancient times,[1] was not a strong military leader.[2] During his reign Egypt was lost to Assyria and the seeds of unrest and open rebellion were sown in many parts of the empire.

2. *Fall of Assyria and Rise of the Babylonian Empire*

After the death of Ashurbanipal in 625 B.C., Assyria declined rapidly to her final overthrow, which came within a period of 20 years. In the western part of the empire hordes of barbarous Scythians were pouring down from the north. On the east the Babylonians were making ready to attack under their new king Nabopolassar, the father of the notorious Nebuchadnezzar. In 614 B.C. the Babylonians made an alliance with the Medes under Cyaxares, and with the help of the Scythians these two nations captured and destroyed the Assyrian capital city, Nineveh (612 B.C.). But the struggle dragged on for several years. Meanwhile, Pharaoh-necho of Egypt had entered the arena and had occupied considerable territory, including the little kingdom of Judah. In 606 B.C. Nebuchadnezzar, who was at this time the commander in chief of the armies of his father, Nabopolassar, administered a smashing blow to the combined forces of Assyria and Egypt at Carchemish, an important city on the upper Euphrates.

The mighty Assyrian Empire was a thing of the past. In its place arose a new world power, equally foreboding to the nations of that time, the Neo-Babylonian Empire. Under Nebuchadnezzar, who became emperor in 604 B.C., the Babylonians came into possession of all the nations from Chaldea

[1] J. P. Free, *Archaeology and Bible History*, pp. 217-18; Muir, *His Truth Endureth*, p. 193.

[2] Cf. Mould, *Essentials of Bible History*, pp. 260-61.

to Egypt, and the city of Babylon was beautified and made the mistress of the world. Such was the condition of affairs when the people of Judah were finally taken in captivity to Babylon, 606-536 B.C. We now return to the history of Judah.

II. THE LAMENTABLE STORY OF JUDAH'S FALL

The last 110 years of Judah's history is a pitiable story of religious disobedience and its dire results. Through the influence of wicked rulers the people were led into a state of apostasy and moral degeneration which made them an easy prey of foreign invaders. The city of Jerusalem was eventually destroyed and the people taken into exile.

1. *Manasseh's Evil Reign: Spiritual Degeneracy* (II Kings 21:1-18; II Chron. 33:1-20).

The death of the good king Hezekiah (*ca.* 697 B.C.) marks an important turning point in Judah's history. The long reign of his son, Manasseh (*ca.* 697-642 B.C.), was characterized by idolatry and wickedness such as had never been known in the history of Judah.

He built altars for all the host of heaven in the two courts of the house of the Lord. And he burned his sons as an offering in the valley of the son of Hinnom, and practiced soothsaying and augury and sorcery, and dealt with mediums and with wizards: he did much evil in the sight of the Lord, provoking him to anger . . . Manasseh seduced Judah and the inhabitants of Jerusalem, so that they did more evil than the nations whom the Lord destroyed before the people of Israel (II Chron. 33:5-6, 9, RSV).

This sudden apostasy of Judah after the commendable reforms of Hezekiah is explained in part by the youth of the king and by the presence of a pagan party which was waiting for an opportunity to assert itself. Manasseh ascended the throne at 12 years of age. During his father's reign the generation of idolaters who had grown up under the tutelage of Ahaz had been suppressed but not destroyed. Immediately upon the accession of Manasseh they took advantage of the king's youth and reestablished the altars to Baal and other pagan shrines which Hezekiah had torn down.[3]

Another factor which influenced the religious practices of Manasseh was his relation to Assyria. His grandfather, Ahaz, had begun the policy of buying Assyria's favor through the payment of tribute, thus making Judah, in effect, a vassal of Assyria (II Kings 16: 8-9). His father, Hezekiah, eventually broke relations with the Assyrians and successfully defended Jerusalem against their ravages. But Manasseh accepted without a struggle the Assyrian overlordship. This peaceful policy probably brought material benefits to Judah and saved her from an immediate doom, but it resulted also in the absorption of much Chaldean culture and the introduction of many pagan religious customs. "Religiously he was more Assyrian than Hebrew. Under his guidance the pagan practices of Assyria supplanted the worship of Jehovah throughout Judah."[4]

Manasseh has been described as "the arch idolater of Hebrew history."[5] He even named his son after the Egyptian god Amon. According to Josephus,[6] Manasseh persecuted and slew the prophets of the Lord. The Scriptures record that he "shed innocent blood very much, till he had filled Jerusalem from one end to another" (II Kings 21: 16). This passage doubtless refers to his persecution of the prophets and others who opposed his regime. Tradition has it that the prophet Isaiah was "sawn asunder" by this cruel monarch (Jer. 2: 30; Heb. 11: 37). Certain it is that one hears little concerning the prophets in the period of over half a century during which he ruled.

Manasseh's reign really decided the fate of Judah. After Manasseh's time it seemed impossible for a good king like Josiah or a great prophet like Jeremiah to wean the hearts of the people away from their idolatry and immorality. According to the prophet who has left us the account of Judah's captivity it was because of Manasseh that God found it necessary to remove Judah out of His sight (II Kings 24: 3-4). What a commentary on the power of evil influence.

---

[3]I. M. Price, *The Dramatic Story of Old Testament History*, p. 329; Mould, *op. cit.*, p. 331.

[4]J. C. Muir, *His Truth Endureth*, p. 193.

[5]Mould, *loc. cit.*

[6]Cf. Price, *op. cit.*, p. 331.

2. *The Reformation of Josiah: a Noble Example* (II Kings 21:19—23:30; II Chron. 33:10—35:27)

A story is told in II Chron. 33:10-17 of a brief captivity which Manasseh, the wicked king of Judah, suffered at the hands of the Assyrians. It would appear that through this bitter experience he was brought to repentance, and that having been restored to his kingdom he endeavored in the last years of his reign to undo the evil wrought in his wicked rule of a half century. The results are not described, but from the account of the attempted reforms of his grandson, the good king Josiah, we may conjecture that little real good was accomplished.

a. The Young King Josiah. After the brief and evil reign of Amon (642-640 B.C.) his eight-year-old son, Josiah, came to the throne. In his early years the young king was doubtless under the tutelage of a godly mother and of instructors who were devoted to the worship of Jehovah. The names of Hilkiah the priest, Shaphan the scribe, and Huldah the prophetess, which appear prominently in the story of his reign, may indicate some of the formative influences that made Josiah so different from his father, Amon, and his grandfather, Manasseh. At the age of 16 "he began to seek after the God of David his father" (II Chron. 34:3). Four years later he was engaged in a great religious reformation, endeavoring to rid the country of the idolatries fostered by the two previous kings.

When the young king had purged "Judah and Jerusalem from the high places, and the groves, and the carved images, and the molten images . . . the altars of Baalim . . . and the images, that were on high above them" (II Chron. 34:3-4), he determined to crown his reform by repairing the neglected Temple. The building was already 300 years old and had suffered not only from the ravages of time but from the hand of the despoiler. Time and again the treasures had been stripped from its holy walls to satisfy some foreign aggressor.

b. Finding of the Book of the Law. It was in the process of this work of repairing the Temple that a volume of the law of Moses was found (part or all of our Pentateuch). How so precious and important a volume was lost and why there were not other copies are not explained. We can only conjecture that it was due to the opposition which had been made to the worship of Jehovah in the reigns of Manasseh and Amon. At any rate the discovery of the book was an exciting occasion. The workmen who found it turned it over to Hilkiah, the priest; and he, after consulting Shaphan, the scribe, presented it immediately to the king.

When Josiah had read from the Book of the Law and realized how far the people came short of obeying its precepts, he rent his clothes and sent for the advice of the prophetess Huldah. The prophetess pronounced it the very Word of the Lord, and the king then called a great assembly of the people of Jerusalem and had the book read in their hearing.

> *And the king stood in his place, and made a covenant before the Lord, to walk after the Lord, and to keep his commandments, and his testimonies, and his statutes, with all his heart, and with all his soul, to perform the words of the covena t which are written in this book* (II Chron. 34:31).

This discovery of the Book of the Law doubtless had its effect in deepening the work of reformation which Josiah had undertaken, and which up to this time had been concerned chiefly with the destruction of the external symbols of idolatry. But the silence that follows this account and the ominous warnings of the prophetess (II Kings 22:15-20) lead one to believe that there was little true repentance on the part of the people. There may have been outward conformity to the Law and to the worship of Jehovah, but the hearts of the people were still set on idols, and they were only waiting for a change of kings to plunge again into their idolatrous practices.

c. *Death of Josiah.* The reign of Josiah ended in tragedy. As Pharaoh-necho of Egypt marched through Palestine on his way to Carchemish on the Euphrates, where he was to join forces with the Assyrians against the Babylonians and Medes, he was met by Josiah in battle near Megiddo. The reason for Josiah's attack is not clear, but he may have feared lest his people should somehow be endangered by the approach of the Egyptians. The outcome was costly for the kingdom of Judah. Mortally wounded in the battle, the king died as he was carried home in his chariot to Jerusalem, and was buried amid great lamentations on the part of his people.

The last great king of Judah had fallen. Now we turn to the sad story of the end of the kingdom and the final captivity of the people.

3. *The Captivity of Judah: the End of the Path of Disobedience* (II Kings 23:30—25:30; II Chron. 36:1-21; Jeremiah; Ezekiel; Dan. 1:1-7)

Upon the death of Josiah (609 B.C.), the people chose as king his son Jehoahaz. But Jehoahaz reigned only three months. The Egyptian king, Necho, having by this time established his headquarters at Riblah, in Syria, summoned the young king to appear before him. On grounds of disloyalty he bound him in fetters and sent him to Egypt, whence he never returned. Then Necho made a visit to Jerusalem and, assuming all authority in the name of Egypt, set Eliakim, another of Josiah's sons, on the throne of Judah, and changed his name to Jehoiakim.

a. *Reign of Jehoiakim.* Jehoiakim reigned in all 11 years, at first as a vassal to Egypt and then to Babylonia. Under his rule the religious abuses which had been abolished by his father, Josiah, seem to have returned in greater strength than ever. We have a fair picture of conditions which existed at this time in the prophecies of Jeremiah, whose ministry coincides with the last 40 years of the kingdom of Judah (626-586 B.C.). According to Jeremiah, polytheism and idolatry were rampant and many innocent persons were persecuted and slain for opposing the wicked and oppressive policies of the king (Jer. 2:8, 11, 13, 27-28, etc.).

On one occasion a prophet by the name of Uriah was condemned for prophesying against the wickedness of the king and people. Having fled for his life to Egypt he was pursued, brought back, and slain by Jehoiakim, and "his dead body [cast] into the graves of the common people" (Jer. 26:20-23).

b. *The First Captivity.* Politically, the fate of Judah was closely tied in with developments in the history of Assyria, Babylonia, and Egypt. Nineveh, as we have seen, had fallen in 612 B.C. to the Babylonians and Medes, and six years later the Babylonians, led by Nebuchadnezzar, overcame the Assyrians and Egyptians at Carchemish, on the Euphrates

River. The result was that Babylonia assumed control of the great empire that had been Assyria's.

From a comparison of II Kings 24:1 and Dan. 1:1-7 it appears that immediately after the Battle of Carchemish (*ca.* 606 B.C.) Nebuchadnezzar led a military mission to Jerusalem, forced the allegiance of Jehoiakim to Babylonia, and carried off part of the sacred vessels of the Temple to be used in the temples at Babylon. At this time, in order to insure the loyalty of Judah, he took Daniel and certain other favored young men of Jerusalem as hostages to Babylon. Thus we date the Captivity from 606 B.C.[7]

c. The Second Captivity. Three years later Jehoiakim rebelled against Babylonia, probably trusting in the help of Egypt, and refused to pay the required tribute. Nebuchadnezzar, busy in other parts of the empire, did not immediately attack Jerusalem but incited certain marauding bands of Chaldees, Syrians, Moabites, and Ammonites to harass the people of Judah. Finally, in 597 B.C., Jehoiakim died, leaving the throne to his young son, Jehoiachin. Within three months after the succession of the new king, Nebuchadnezzar captured and plundered the city of Jerusalem, carrying the young Jehoiachin, his mother, and 10,000 of the leading citizens as captives to Babylon. Among them was Ezekiel, as we learn from the beginning of his prophecy; and included in the number of those taken were 7,000 fighting men and 1,000 craftsmen and smiths (II Kings 24:14-16; Ezek. 1:1-2). None but the poorest of the people were left behind. This was the second captivity.

d. The Destruction of Jerusalem (Third Captivity). Meanwhile in Jerusalem, Zedekiah, another son of Josiah, was placed on the throne of Judah. The 11 years of his reign are in many ways a repetition of the reign of Jehoiakim. "He did that which was evil in the sight of the Lord his God, and humbled not himself before Jeremiah the prophet speaking from the mouth of the Lord" (II Chron. 36:12).

Encouraged by false prophets and by promises of help from Egypt, Zedekiah finally rebelled against Nebuchadnezzar, who promptly laid siege to the city again and slowly starved

---

[7]Cf. Free, *op. cit.*, pp. 224-25.

the people into submission. When supplies in the beleaguered capital were at length exhausted, Zedekiah and his army secretly escaped from the city, leaving the civilian population to their fate. But the Babylonians pursued and overtook them in the plain of Jericho. Zedekiah, the king, was bound and taken to Nebuchadnezzar's headquarters at Riblah, in Syria. There his two sons were slain before his eyes, and he was then blinded and sent to Babylon to spend the rest of his miserable life in prison.

Nebuchadnezzar was now determined to destroy the capital of the rebellious Jewish nation and to bring an end to the kingdom of Judah. Accordingly, the Temple was stripped of everything of value and burned. The royal palace and most of the houses of the city were destroyed and the walls broken down. The inhabitants except the very poorest, were carried into captivity, perhaps about 25,000 in all.[8] The city was destined to remain a rubble heap for the next half-century.

Jeremiah, the prophet who had faithfully delivered God's messages to the people during these fateful years, was allowed to choose whether to go with the people to Babylon or to be left in his own land. He chose the latter. Over the poor of the land who were left "to be vinedressers and husbandmen" (II Kings 25:12), Nebuchadnezzar appointed a governor, Gedaliah, one of their own countrymen, who set up a provincial capital at Mizpah, seven miles north of Jerusalem. Thus, in 586 B.C., the kingdom of Judah was abolished and the history of the nation shifts temporarily to the land of Babylon.

4. *Political Power Exchanged for Spiritual Understanding: God's Providence in the Fall of the Kingdom* (Jeremiah, Ezekiel, Habakkuk, and Zephaniah)

The end of the kingdom and the destruction of Jerusalem and the Temple was a fate very hard for the people of Judah to accept. Indeed from a material and secular viewpoint it was an extremely hard blow to the nation. But from the standpoint of their spiritual progress we may see God's prov-

[8]See Price, *op. cit.*, pp. 352, 359. Cf. L. A. Knott, *Student's History of the Hebrews*, p. 268.

idence at work in this, as in so many other events of Hebrew history. In the words of J. C. Muir:

> Hebrew nationalism was ending, but the great religious movement which originated among the Hebrews was but beginning. For fifteen hundred years the great spiritual idealism had been fettered by Hebrew formalism. Now it found freedom beyond all bounds of nationalism. Religion was denationalized, but was spiritualized and individualized. . . .
>
> With the fall of Jerusalem the Hebrews lost their place in the world of nations but found a broader place in the world of religion. Deprived of an earthly kingdom, Israel began to vision a Heavenly Kingdom. On the minds of the Chosen People dawned the deeper meanings of the spiritual idealism which Moses had expounded on Mt. Sinai. During the years of exile, the narrow, tradition-bound religion of Israel was broadened by a newer and nobler conception of the character of God. Great leaders of religious thought, exploring the realms of the spirit and mind with heaven-born inspiration, visioned a God who would redeem all mankind through the coming Messiah.[9]

Foremost among the religious leaders who were thus awakening the nation to a deeper understanding of God and of His redemptive purposes for mankind, were, of course, the prophets. Jeremiah and Ezekiel with their new teaching of individual responsibility for sin (Jer. 31:29-30; Ezek. 3:18, 33), and of the need of heart cleansing (Jer. 31:31-34; Ezek. 36: 25-27), Habakkuk with his deeper insight into the meaning and importance of faith (Hab. 1:1—2:4; 3:17-19), and Zephaniah with his broader view of God's judgments (Zeph. 2:3-15; 3:8-12), were making significant contributions to the spiritual understanding of the people. Ezekiel will be discussed in the following chapter. We now turn to Jeremiah and his contemporaries among the prophets at Jerusalem.

III. JEREMIAH, THE PROPHET OF JUDAH'S DARKEST HOUR

Jeremiah is one of the most colorful figures in Hebrew history. This is partly due to the fact that we know more about his personality and character than those of any other of the Old Testament prophets. His book abounds in biographical material. Unlike Amos, who tells us only of his occupation and of his call, or Hosea, of whom we know only the

---

[9] Muir, *op. cit.*, pp. 208, 225.

tragic story of his married life, and in even greater contrast to such men as Nahum and Zephaniah, who tell us nothing about themselves, Jeremiah literally pours out his mind and soul for us to see.

Called of God when but "a child" (Jer. 1:6), Jeremiah spent nearly a half-century endeavoring, by every means possible, to win his people back to repentance and faith in God, that they might, through heeding the inspired warnings of God's prophet, escape the doom that threatened them. Dr. Kyle Yates says:

> Tragically he stood in the main stream of rushing humanity warning the heedless throng of the certain destruction awaiting them. Madly they rushed on into death and exile over the struggling form of the faithful messenger of God. In all of these trying hours God sustained and strengthened His prophet.[10]

Like Isaiah, Jeremiah belonged to the upper class and was able to command the respect of kings and men of official rank. The fact that he was able to maintain the services of an amanuensis or scribe and to buy real estate (Jer. 32:6-15; 36:4-8; etc.) indicates that he was a man of some means. From the general tenor of his book it is clear also that he was a person of education and culture, thoroughly acquainted with the history of his nation, local and international politics, foreign cults and practices, and the deeper matters of divine revelation. Most important of all, he was a man who was filled with a sense of the urgency of his mission. When he was tempted to give up his ministry under the stress of fierce persecution, he found that the compulsion within himself more than outweighed the opposition which came from without.

> *If I say, "I will not mention him, or speak any more in His name," there is in my heart as it were a burning fire shut up in my bones, and I am weary with holding it in, and I cannot* (20:9, RSV).

The period of Jeremiah's ministry is clearly indicated by references to the kings Josiah, Jehoiakim, and Zedekiah, and to the fall of Jerusalem. The date of the prophet's call is given in Jer. 1:2 as the thirteenth year of Josiah's reign, or

[10]Kyle M. Yates, *Preaching from the Prophets*, p. 128.

626 B.C. Since he was still prophesying after the fall of Jerusalem in 586 B.C. (cc. 40—44), his ministry must have lasted more than 40 years. During the first 18 years of this period he was aiding the good king Josiah in his attempt to win the people back to the worship of Jehovah. The remainder of the 40 years was spent chiefly in the courts of the two wicked sons of Josiah who reigned during this time, Jehoiakim (608-597 B.C.) and Zedekiah (597-586 B.C.). It was during these reigns that the great opposition arose, which we shall describe in a later section.

The Book of Jeremiah is difficult to outline satisfactorily, since the messages recorded and the incidents narrated do not follow either a topical or a chronological order. In general the first 33 chapters, except chapter 1, which relates the call of the prophet, are composed of warnings and predictions concerning the approaching doom of the city. The next 12 chapters (34—45) are largely historical and biographical, recounting events which happened before and after the destruction of Jerusalem, and giving many graphic details of the persecutions suffered by Jeremiah. Chapters 46—51 contain predictions concerning the fate of foreign powers. The last chapter (52) is a historical appendix, virtually equivalent to II Kings 24:17—25:30, giving in review a brief account of the rebellion of Zedekiah, the destruction of the city, and the deportation of the people to Babylon.

1. *An Interesting Biography: the Personal Experiences of Jeremiah* (Jeremiah)

The biographical section of Jeremiah (cc. 34—45) follows the most important prophecies, but references are made to the experiences of the prophet throughout the book. Because of their human interest and the background they furnish for an understanding of the prophet's ministry, we shall consider the biographical portions first.

We learn in the earlier chapters of the book that Jeremiah was the son of a priest, Hilkiah by name, perhaps the same who is mentioned in the story of the finding of the Book of the Law (II Kings 22:8 ff.). In his earlier ministry he was doubtless a participant in the reformation sponsored by the good king Josiah. This may have won him enemies in the later period. Most of the prophecies that have been recorded seem to belong to the reigns of Jehoiakim and Zedekiah, Josiah's wicked sons, under whom Jeremiah suffered many persecutions.

In chapter 11:18-23 we learn that the men of Anathoth, Jeremiah's native village, were plotting against his life. Even his own kindred were in the plot (12:5-6). The false prophets, who courted the favor of the king, contradicted him continually (14:13-16; 28:10-11). In fact, it seemed to the sensitive prophet that everyone was cursing him (15:10, 15, 18).

Jeremiah was finally arrested, beaten, and put in stocks by a priest named Pashur, the chief officer of the Temple (20:1-2). On his release he made a prediction of exile for Pashur and for all the people who were collaborating with him. In the shadow of this experience the prophet in desperation curses the day when he was born (20:14-18).

In the fourth year of Jehoiakim's reign (c. 36) God commanded Jeremiah, who was at the time in prison, to write on a scroll all the words which He had given him against the people of Judah. So he called his constant friend, the scribe Baruch, and directed him to write at his dictation. Then at Jeremiah's command Baruch read the scroll in the Temple in the hearing of all the people. When the princes informed the king of the scroll, he sent for it. After hearing three or four leaves of it read, Jehoiakim seized it, cut it in shreds with his penknife, and threw it into the fire. He also sought to kill Jeremiah and Baruch, "but the Lord hid them" (v. 26).

On several occasions, in the reigns of both Jehoiakim and Zedekiah, the imprisonment of the prophet is mentioned (cc. 26, 32, 33, etc.). During the final siege of the city, on the accusation of collaborating with the Babylonians, he was arrested and cast into an inner dungeon, from which the king released him only when, the city having come into a desperate situation, he needed his counsel and prayers (37:11-21). That he might the more easily confer with him, Zedekiah changed his place of confinement to the "court of the prison," and at the king's command "a loaf of bread was given him daily from the baker's street, until all the bread in the city was gone" (37:21, RSV).

The enemies of Jeremiah were provoked at this apparently lenient treatment of the prophet, and on the pretension that he was destroying the morale of the city's defenders by predicting the destruction of the city, they demanded that he be put to death. "Then Zedekiah the king said, Behold, he is in your hand: for the king is not he that can do any thing against you" (38:5). So the prophet was lowered into a deep cistern under the prison. "And there was no water in the cistern, but only mire, and Jeremiah sank in the mire" (38:6, RSV).

From this predicament the prophet was rescued by a sympathetic Negro servant of the king. Thus we see God providing for Jeremiah's safety in all his trials, as He had promised at the time of his call: "For, behold, I have made thee this day a defenced city . . . they shall fight against thee; but they shall not prevail . . . for I am with thee . . . to deliver thee" (1:18-19).

In the final exile of the people Jeremiah was allowed to remain behind, under the protection of Gedaliah, the governor. After the treacherous murder of Gedaliah he was taken against his will to Egypt with a band of refugees led by Johanan (cc. 40—43). There, so far as the record goes, he may have lived the end of his life in peace.

2. *Weeping for Jerusalem: a Characterization of the Prophet and His Message* (Jeremiah 1—33 and Lamentations)

In the account of the prophet's call (chapter 1) we have an interesting characterization of Jeremiah. He appears as a timid, sensitive youth, anxious to perform the will of God, but conscious of the difficulty of his task: "Ah, Lord God! behold, I cannot speak: for I am a child" (v. 6). Reluctantly he accepted the call of God, but when he had once yielded, he carried out his commission with a holy zeal.

a. A Type of Christ. There are a tenderness and an emotional quality in the prophecies of Jeremiah that remind us strongly of Hosea,[11] and in the bitter tears that he shed for Jerusalem he becomes an outstanding type of Christ.[12] Like Hosea, however, and like Christ, he was able under the

[11]Cf. J. R. Dummelow, ed., *A Commentary on the Holy Bible,* p. 457.

[12]For a comparison of Jeremiah and Jesus see Yates, *op. cit.,* pp. 135-36.

influence of the Spirit of God to rebuke sternly and to speak fearlessly the message of God to the people.

b. *Pleading and Warning*. In his earlier sermons the call to repentance is predominant. Even the heathen are faithful to their gods; but Israel has exchanged the living God for worthless idols. "For my people have committed two evils; they have forsaken me the fountain of living waters, and hewed them out cisterns, broken cisterns, that can hold no water" (2:13). The reformation under Josiah was insincere: "Judah hath not turned unto me with her whole heart, but feignedly" (3:10). "O Jerusalem, wash thine heart from wickedness, that thou mayest be saved. How long shall thy vain thoughts lodge within thee?" (4:14)

Partial remedies will not suffice: "They have healed also the hurt of the daughter of my people slightly, saying, Peace, peace; when there is no peace" (6:14). The time of divine forbearance is slipping past rapidly; soon will be the cry, "The harvest is past, the summer is ended, and we are not saved" (8:20). The prophet utters a cry of distress as he sees in a vision the enemy approaching: "My anguish, my anguish! I am pained at my very heart; my heart is disquited in me; I cannot hold my peace; because thou hast heard, O my soul, the sound of the trumpet, the alarm of war" (4:19, ASV).

c. *Hope Amid Despair*. Jeremiah's grief becomes more intense as he discovers that Judah's sin is incurable. He longs for comfort against sorrow. He sometimes wishes that his eyes were a fountain of tears. He is tempted even to flee from his people and find a lodge in some wilderness (8:18— 9:16).

One of his greatest trials was the knowledge that God could not hear his prayers for the people, since their hearts were hardened and they would not repent. More than once the Lord forbade him to pray (7:16-18; 11:14; 14:11), but he could not refrain. The spirit of intercession seizes him and he pleads with the Lord not to abhor his people (14:19-22).

In the later chapters of this section (25—29) there is a settled conviction that the destruction of the city and the captivity of the people are inevitable, as they refuse to repent year after year. The prophet urges them to submit to the chastening of God; and desiring to make the lot of those already exiled as bearable as possible, he writes a letter to them urging them to settle down in their foreign homes and wait with patience for God's time of deliverance. Even yet there is hope, when through suffering they have learned to give their hearts wholly to God: "Ye shall seek me, and find me, when ye shall search for me with all your heart" (29:13).

d. *The Book of Lamentations.* The "Lamentations of Jeremiah," which follow the Book of Jeremiah in our English Bible, were anonymous in the Hebrew Scriptures and included with the Hagiographa. However a very strong tradition ascribes these laments to the weeping prophet himself, and they are very much in the spirit of Jeremiah's own sorrowful utterances and follow well upon the tragic description of the fall of Jerusalem given in Jeremiah 53.[13] For the theme of this little book is the capture and destruction of the Jewish capital with the terrible sufferings of its defenders, a catastrophe brought on by the sins and rebellion of the people. The first four chapters are acrostic poems composed, in the original, of 22 verses, each beginning with a successive letter of the Hebrew alphabet. In the English version chapter 3 has 66 verses, each verse of the original expanded to three in the translation. The last chapter, which also contains 22 verses but is not an acrostic, is a prayer of forgiveness and restoration. The book as a whole is a poem of great merit; and chapter 3:22-26 is a psalm the beauty and charm of which are seldom equaled in Sacred Writ, a true ray from the Cross, shining through unrelieved gloom of deep tragedy.

3. *Spiritual Discernment: the Prophet's Explanation of Judah's Fall* (Jeremiah 3—33)

We see in the message of Jeremiah a new interpretation of sin which explains, to the prophet's mind, the tragic events which it became his lot to witness. God was indeed their Source of salvation (3:23) and was able and willing to deliver them in their present evil plight if they would return to Hin with their whole hearts (4:1). They were exhorted to "ask for the old paths, where is the good way, and walk therein . . . But they said, We will not walk therein" (6:16). Here lay their trouble. It was apostasy of the heart that was

[13]Cf. Muir, *op. cit.,* p. 208.

keeping them from yielding to God's demands. "The heart is deceitful above all things, and desperately wicked: who can know it?" (17:9)

Jeremiah sees a distinction between sinning, the doing of acts which are wrong in God's eyes, and sin, a disposition of the heart to do wrong, which is something far worse, and harder to deal with. By this inner corruption of the nature the desires of the heart become so perverted that evil becomes the sinner's delight, and to choose the will of God becomes an impossibility for him: "Can the Ethiopian change his skin, or the leopard his spots? then may ye also do good, that are accustomed to do evil" (13:23). This has to do not only with original sin but with the formation of sinful habits which gradually tend to fix the character and make it impossible to seek God.[14]

With this new conception of sin as a condition of the heart came a new emphasis upon individual responsibility for sin, which we shall see amplified in the prophecies of Ezekiel. Jeremiah attacks the proverb by which the captives were excusing themselves: "In those days they shall say no more, The fathers have eaten a sour grape, and the children's teeth are set on edge. But every one shall die for his own iniquity: every man that eateth the sour grape, his teeth shall be set on edge" (31:29-30).

As sin is a matter of the heart, so is obedience to the law. In the New Covenant passage (31:31-34), Jeremiah predicts a time when God will put His law "in their inward parts, and write it in their hearts." This, according to Heb. 8:7-13, is the essence of New Testament religion.

4. *Hope for the Faithful: Prophecies of the Restoration and of the Coming of Christ* (Jer. 3:11-20; 23:1-8; cc. 30—33)

The prophecies of Jeremiah are so closely associated with the fall of Judah and the destruction of the Holy City that the pervading atmosphere is necessarily one of gloom. But against this dark background of threat and punishment there appear some of the most glorious Messianic prophecies of the entire Old Testament. These promises are not divorced

---

[14]Compare the treatment of apostasy in Heb. 6:4-6 and 10:26-27.

from the background of warning, but issue naturally from the prophet's pleadings with the nation to repent. For example, in the third chapter, after reasoning with His rebellious people, the Lord through the mouth of the prophet pleads with them thus: "Turn, O backsliding children, saith the Lord" (3:14). Then follows the promise:

> *And it shall come to pass, when ye be multiplied and increased in the land, in those days, saith the Lord, they shall say no more, The ark of the covenant of the Lord: neither shall it come to mind . . . At that time they shall call Jerusalem the throne of the Lord; and all the nations shall be gathered unto it . . . neither shall they walk any more after the imagination of their evil heart"* (3:16-17).[15]

In this passage, as commonly in the Old Testament prophets, we have a promise of the restoration of Israel combined with a prophecy of the gospel age in which Jew and Gentile will have equal share in the kingdom of God.[16]

A more distinctly Messianic passage is to be found in chapter 23:1-8, where in contrast to the false prophets who have scattered the flock, true shepherds are promised that will gather the flock and feed them until the coming of the Righteous Branch, the Son of David, to rule over them:

> *Behold, the days come, saith the Lord, that I will raise unto David a righteous Branch, and a King shall reign and prosper, and shall execute judgment and justice in the earth. In his days Judah shall be saved, and Israel shall dwell safely: and this is his name whereby he shall be called, THE LORD OUR RIGHTEOUSNESS* (23:5-6).

The principal prophecies, however, dealing with the restoration and the coming of the Gospel Age are to be found in chapters 30—33. These oracles were delivered during the darkest hour of the history of Judah. The city of Jerusalem was under siege and soon to be destroyed. Jeremiah himself was held in custody in the prison court. Under these cir-

---

[15]Compare Isa. 2:1-4.
[16]For a similar prophecy see Jer. 12:14-17.

cumstances he received the command of the Lord to write down words of comfort for the people.

If we may paraphrase the message in chapter 30, it runs somewhat like this: Fear now wrings every heart. Never have we known such calamities. But they shall not last forever. God will break the galling yoke of the conqueror and deliver His people from their painful servitude. They shall again be united in their own land and God will raise up a king of the house of David to rule over them (30:5-9). Fear not the hand of correction. Your many sins make it necessary for God to punish you; but when He has chastened you and you have learned to follow Him, He will raise up for you again the ruined city of Jerusalem and there shall be joy within her walls as in the olden time. Then you will again be God's people and He will be your God (30:10-22).

The heart of Jeremiah's message of hope is in chapter 31, where in a beautiful poetic passage he describes the New Covenant which God will make with His people, a covenant which will be written, not on stone, but on fleshly tables of the heart.

> *Behold, the days come, saith the Lord, that I will make a new covenant with the house of Israel, and with the house of Judah: not according to the covenant that I made with their fathers in the day that I took them by the hand to bring them out of the land of Egypt . . . After those days, saith the Lord, I will put my law in their inward parts, and write it in their hearts; and will be their God, and they shall be my people . . . for I will forgive their iniquity, and I will remember their sin no more (31:31-34).*

If we understand the implications of this passage, we realize that Jeremiah has given here the gist of the gospel message which Jesus came to reveal in its fullness, and which was based upon the atonement that He should make, as explained in the Book of Hebrews (8:6-13; 9:13-15; 10:14-22).

In chapter 32 the prophet tells us how God directed him to give tangible proof of his faith in the restoration of Jerusalem by purchasing an ancestral inheritance at Anathoth. He had the deed made out in full legal fashion and deposited it for safekeeping in a strong vessel of pottery, as was the custom in those days. For he was assured that, although the city would certainly fall, according to the word he had received from the Lord, it was as certain to be restored, and houses and fields and vineyards possessed again in the land of Judah (32:15).

In the final chapter of this section Jeremiah makes it clear that, while the restoration of Judah at the end of the 70 years (25:12) was the immediate event in prospect, there was to be a more complete fulfillment in the setting up of Christ's kingdom in the more distant future.

> *Call unto me, and I will answer thee, and shew thee great and mighty things, which thou knowest not. In those days, and at that time, will I cause the Branch of righteousness to grow up unto David . . . For thus saith the Lord; David shall never want a man to sit upon the throne of the house of Israel* (33: 3, 15, 17).

IV. The Contemporaries of Jeremiah

Of the four prophets who are commonly regarded as contemporaries of Jeremiah only Zephaniah and Habakkuk can be dated with reasonable certainty. Both of these prophets, like Jeremiah, were concerned with the approaching fall of Jerusalem. Nahum and Obadiah directed their prophecies against foreign nations.

1. *Nahum: a Graphic Prophecy of Nineveh's Fall* (Nahum 1-3)

The prophecy of Nahum, who prophesied at Jerusalem during, or just before, the reign of Josiah (638-608 B.C.), is a doom song predicting the fall of Nineveh. It is, in fact, one of the finest and most dramatic poems in the Old Testament, filled with graphic pictures of the warfare of that day, as the following passage illustrates:

> *Woe to the bloody city,*
> *all full of lies and booty—*
> *no end to the plunder!*
> *The crack of whip and rumble of wheel,*
> *galloping horse and bounding chariot!*

Horsemen charging,
    flashing sword and glittering spear,
hosts of slain,
    heaps of corpses,
dead bodies without end—
    they stumble over the bodies! (3:1-3, RSV)

The three chapters of Nahum's book fall naturally into two sections. The first, chapter 1, is an alphabetical psalm, setting forth the majesty and power of the Lord of Judah. God has His way everywhere: "The Lord hath his way in the whirlwind and in the storm, and the clouds are the dust of his feet" (1:3). At the heart of the universe are goodness and love: "The Lord is good, a strong hold in the day of trouble; and he knoweth them that trust in him" (1:7). But the justice of God demands that He bring judgment to bear upon His enemies (1:8-10). He is now about to break the Assyrian rod with which He has afflicted His people (1:11-15).[17]

The second section, chapters 2 and 3, is devoted to an account, in prophecy, of the destruction of the Assyrian capital and the reasons for the dire punishment meted out. The cruel city, represented in one passage under the figure of a den of lions (2:10-13), is to be utterly annihilated for her outrageous treatment of her sister nations; and in the day of her calamity none shall pity her (3:18-19).

Thus, by example, Judah was taught that, although "the Lord is slow to anger," He "will by no means clear the guilty" (1:3, RSV). The fulfillment of the prophecy in the destruction of Nineveh, 612 B.C., coming as it did in the midst of the reforms of Josiah and the preaching of Jeremiah, should have been an object lesson to the people of Judah to deter them from their evil course.

2. Zephaniah: a Foreboding Picture of the Day of Jehovah (Zephaniah 1—3)

The application to Judah of the lesson on divine judgment taught in Nahum's prophecy is made in forceful terms in the

[17]Compare Isa. 10:5-12. The reference is of course to the Assyrians, who took the Northern Kingdom into captivity and engaged in several cruel invasions of Judah.

sermons of the prophet Zephaniah, a descendant of the good king Hezekiah. Taking occasion perhaps from the threat of an invasion by savage hordes of Scythians from the north,[18] Zephaniah preached of the coming of a great day of judgment for Judah and Jerusalem:

> *The great day of the Lord is near, it is near, and hasteth greatly, even the voice of the day of the Lord: the mighty man shall cry there bitterly. That day is a day of wrath, a day of trouble and distress, a day of wasteness and desolation, a day of darkness and gloominess, a day of clouds and thick darkness, a day of the trumpet and alarm against the fenced cities, and against the high towers. Neither their silver nor their gold shall be able to deliver them in the day of the Lord's wrath* (1:14-16, 18).

The conditions that called forth this kind of preaching on the part of Zephaniah were largely the same as occasioned the reform of Josiah and the earlier prophecies of Jeremiah, for Zephaniah was a contemporary of these two great men (*ca.* 625 B.C.), and doubtless had a share in their work of reformation.

The prophecy of Zephaniah concerning the day of the Lord was the basis of the famous medieval Latin hymn, "Dies Irae,"[19] and has been considered by all authorities as the classic Old Testament treatment on the Judgment. According to this prophet God will bring judgment, not on Nineveh alone (2:13-15), nor on Judah only, but on all the nations of earth: "For my determination is to gather the nations, that I may assemble the kingdoms, to pour upon them mine indignation, even all my fierce anger: for all the earth shall be devoured with the fire of my jealousy" (3:8).

Combined with this warning of judgment there is also in the prophecy of Zephaniah a gracious invitation: "Seek ye the Lord, all ye meek of the earth . . . it may be ye shall

---

[18]Cf. C. T. Francisco, *Introducing the Old Testament*, p. 134.

[19]Composed by Thomas of Celano, a Franciscan friar of the thirteenth century, an associate of St. Francis of Assisi, the "Day of Wrath" is the acknowledged masterpiece of Latin hymnology and unexcelled among Christian hymns on the Judgment. See any English hymnal for a translation of this remarkable hymn.

be hid in the day of the Lord's anger" (2:3). And a promise of deliverance is given to the remnant who are faithful to God:

> Sing, O daughter of Zion;
> Shout, O Israel;
> Be glad and rejoice with all the heart,
> O daughter of Jerusalem.
> The Lord hath taken away thy judgments,
> He hath cast out thine enemy:
> The king of Israel, even the Lord, is in the midst of thee:
> Thou shalt not see evil any more (3:14-15).[20]

3. *Habakkuk: a Prophet's Questions and God's Answers* (Habakkuk 1—3)

Habakkuk is sometimes known as the philosopher-prophet, since his prophecy is largely in the form of an inquiry made by the prophet concerning the reasons for the distressing conditions which prevailed at Jerusalem during the reign of Jehoiakim (608-597).[21] The book opens with a dialogue between the prophet and Jehovah (1:1—2:4), then records certain woes pronounced against the Babylonians for their cruelty and oppression (2:5-20), and closes with a beautiful poem of confidence that God will deliver His people (chapter 3).

a. The Dialogue. In the opening dialogue Habakkuk makes two complaints to the Lord, and God makes an answer to each complaint. In the first complaint (1:1-4) the prophet laments the increasing iniquity of his people. In reply (1:5-11) God promises to punish their sin by raising up the Chaldeans (that is, the Babylonians) against them. In the second complaint (1:12-17) Habakkuk questions the use of a more wicked people to discipline those who have transgressed less flagrantly. The reply to this (2:1-4) is that the justification of God's action will be seen as events develop. All wickedness shall be judged and punished. Although divine wrath may seem to tarry, yet at the appointed time it will come.

---

[20]For the arrangement of these lines compare *Westminster Study Edition of the Holy Bible*, p. 1348.

[21]For the date of the prophecy see G. L. Robinson, *The Twelve Minor Prophets*, pp. 120 f.

b. The Conclusion. The five woes, directed perhaps primarily against the Babylonians, but made applicable to the people of Judah, are "to him that increaseth that which is not his" (2:6), "to him that coveteth" (2:9), "to him that buildeth a town with blood, and stablisheth a city by iniquity" (2:12), to "him that giveth his neighbour drink" to overcome him (2:15), and to all idolaters (2:19). In contrast we have the principle of righteous conduct enunciated in verse 5: "The just shall live by his faith."

c. The Psalm of Faith. Chapter 3 is an apocalyptic psalm, portraying the coming of God in judgment, and prefaced by a prayer for a revival of righteousness in the midst of the years of worldliness and sin (3:2). The final verses of the prophecy are among the finest expressions of faith to be found in the Bible:

> *Although the fig tree shall not blossom, neither shall fruit be in the vines; the labour of the olive shall fail, and the fields shall yield no meat; the flock shall be cut off from the fold, and there shall be no herd in the stalls: yet I will rejoice in the Lord, I will joy in the God of my salvation. The Lord God is my strength, and he will make my feet like hinds' feet, and he will make me to walk upon mine high places* (3:17-19).

4. *Obadiah: a Doom Pronounced on a Treacherous Nation* (The Book of Obadiah)

The little prophecy of Obadiah is the shortest book in the Old Testament. It has sometimes been considered the earliest of the prophetic books, but recent scholars are quite unanimous in the opinion that it was written shortly after the destruction of Jerusalem, that is, about 585 B.C.

The prophet chides the people of Edom for their rejoicing over the downfall of Judah, and points out that, although the Edomites feel secure in their mountain strongholds, they will share the common fate of the nations that have transgressed God's law. "The pride of thine heart hath deceived thee" (v. 3), he says; "As thou hast done, it shall be done unto thee: thy reward shall return upon thine own head" (v. 15). "The day of the Lord is near upon all the nations" (v. 15,

RSV). Only Zion shall be restored, that all nations shall know that "the kingdom shall be the Lord's" (v. 21).

SUMMARY

In this chapter we have traced the influences which led to the downfall of Judah, and have considered the efforts which were made by the prophets of Judah to save the nation from the catastrophe which finally engulfed her. We have observed the forces in the background which formed the natural cause of Judah's fall, but with the help of the prophets we have seen that the determining cause was her disobedience to God and her willingness to yield to her evil monarchs rather than to those who would have directed her in the ways of righteousness. God was punishing her for her sin, and at the same time bringing to bear upon her spiritual truths which were to be guides in the destiny of future generations. For the first time, in the teachings of the prophets, it had been made clear to the people that their worst enemy was the evil in their own hearts and that God's appointed way of deliverance lay through personal forgiveness, cleansing, and a life of faith and obedience to His will (Jer. 17:9; 29:13; 31:29-34; Hab. 2:4; cf. Heb. 12:11).

RECOMMENDED READINGS

Blaikie and Matthews, *A Manual of Bible History*, pp. 249-61.
Joseph P. Free, *Archaeology and Bible History*, pp. 213-23.
Dorothy Ruth Miller, *A Handbook of Ancient History in Bible Light*, pp. 102-19.
J. C. Muir, *His Truth Endureth*, pp. 193-208.
Ira M. Price, *Dramatic Story of Old Testament History*, pp. 329-53.
Loyal R. Ringenberg, *The Word of God in History*, pp. 198-99, 211-23.
G. L. Robinson, *The Twelve Minor Prophets*, pp. 61-69; 107-36.
Kyle M. Yates, *Preaching from the Prophets*, pp. 128-74.

FOR FURTHER STUDY

1. What were some of the reasons for Judah's abject submission to Assyria after the death of Hezekiah?

2. What providence may be seen in the fall of Assyria and the rise of the Babylonian Empire?

3. Characterize the reign of Manasseh and appraise its effect upon the destiny of Judah.

4. What seems to have been the principal occasion of the attempted reformation under Josiah? What prophets may be presumed to have aided in this movement? With what results?

5. Describe the events which led to the subjugation of Judah to Egypt, then to Babylonia, finally ending in the destruction of Jerusalem under Nebuchadnezzar.

6. Give dates for the three captivities of Judah and mention an important person or event associated with each.

7. As we view the developments of this period in relation to the teachings of the prophets and the future of the Jewish nation, can we see the providence of God at work in the fall of the kingdom and in the suffering of the people? What were to be the spiritual results of this experience?

8. Characterize the prophet Jeremiah in comparison to Isaiah. Which may be said to be a type of Christ? Explain.

9. Give an account of Jeremiah's call. How may we date his ministry?

10. Mention some of the experiences of Jeremiah which are related in his book. What was the fate of the prophet after the destruction of the city?

11. What new teachings may be found in Jeremiah relating to sin and redemption? In the writings of what later prophet are these teachings further amplified?

12. Point out some of the Messianic prophecies of Jeremiah.

13. Construct an eight-to-ten-point outline of Jeremiah, and relate each section of the prophecy to its specific historical background.

14. To what extent was Baruch, the scribe, used by the prophet in the construction and delivery of his messages? What inferences may be made from this fact?

15. Characterize the Book of Lamentations. What is its probable relation to the prophet Jeremiah?

16. What great event is depicted in the prophecy of Nahum? Describe the style and literary qualities of the book.

17. What lesson should Judah have learned from this prophecy and its fulfillment?

18. What is the great message of Zephaniah, and what application is commonly made to Christian theology?

19. Explain the title "philosopher-prophet" often applied to Habakkuk? What use was made, in the period of the Reformation, of a passage quoted from his prophecy? Cite the passage and explain its meaning.

20. On what basis is the short prophecy of Obadiah dated in this period? What other possible date is suggested?

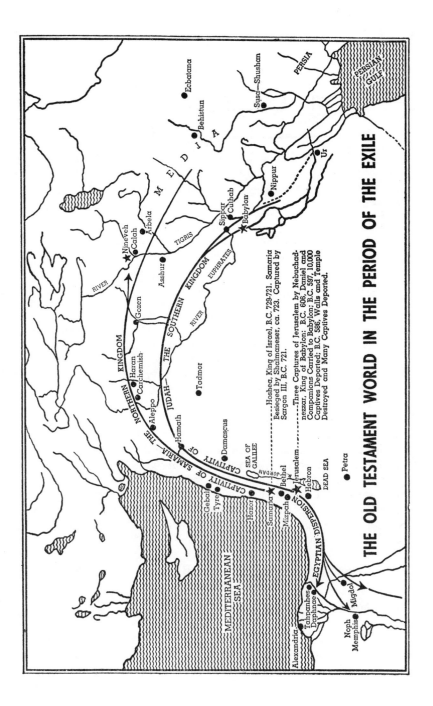

THE OLD TESTAMENT WORLD IN THE PERIOD OF THE EXILE

----Hoshea, King of Israel, B.C. 729-721. Samaria Besieged by Shalmaneser, ca. 723. Captured by Sargon III, B.C. 721.

......Three Captures of Jerusalem by Nebuchad-nezzar, King of Babylon: B.C. 606, Daniel and Companions Carried to Babylon: B.C. 597, 10,000 Captives Deported; B.C. 586, Walls and Temple Destroyed and Many Captives Deported.

PERSIA

PERSIAN GULF

Ecbatana

Susa—Shushan

Behistun

M E D I A

Ur

Nippur

Nineveh
Calah
Arbela

Sippar
Cuthah
Babylon

TIGRIS

Asshur

RIVER

THE SOUTHERN KINGDOM

EUPHRATES

RIVER

NORTHERN KINGDOM

Gozen

Haran
Carchemish

Tadmor

JUDAH

Aleppo

THE CAPTIVITY OF SAMARIA

Hamath

Damascus

SEA OF GALILEE

CAPTIVITY OF

JORDAN

Gebal
Tyre

Hazor

Samaria

Bethel

Jerusalem

Hebron

Petra

DEAD SEA

Mizpah

DIVISION

EGYPTIAN DISPERSION

MEDITERRANEAN SEA

Alexandria
Tahpanhes
Daphnae

Migdol

Noph
Memphis

CHAPTER XV

The Exile and Restoration

The Lord turned again the captivity of Zion (126: 1).

Sources: II Kings 25:27-30; II Chron. 36:22-23; Ezra; Nehemiah; Esther; Psalms 85; 102; 118; 126; 137; 146—50; Isaiah 39; Jeremiah 25; 29; Ezekiel; Daniel; Joel; Haggai; Zechariah; Malachi

To Be Read: Ezekiel 1—3; 18; 36:25-27; 37:1-14; Daniel 1—2; 5—6; 12; Ezra 1; 5:1-2; 7:6-10; Nehemiah 1—2; 4; 6:1-16; 8; Haggai 1; Zech. 1:1-17; 14:20-21; Malachi 3

Period: The destruction of Jerusalem, 586 B.C., to the end of the Old Testament period, about 400 B.C.

We come now to the last two periods of Old Testament history. We shall treat them together since they form one continuous story of a nation struggling, against great odds, to maintain some vestige of its national life. At best the details of the story as it has come down to us are very meager.

The facts of the Exile must be gleaned largely from the books of the exile prophets, Ezekiel and Daniel, and from archaeological and other extra-biblical sources. The books of Ezra and Nehemiah, on the other hand, together with the prophets Haggai, Zechariah, and Malachi, give us a fairly complete picture of the return from captivity and of the restoration under Zerubbabel, Ezra, and Nehemiah. The Book of Esther, which belongs to the restoration period, relates a single episode in the experience of the Jews who remained in Babylonia and other parts of the Persian Empire after the initial return in 536 B.C.

I. Historical Background: the Babylonian and Persian Empires

During the periods of exile and restoration the people of Judah were subject first to the Babylonians and then to the Persians. The history of these two great powers which ruled the Middle East during nearly 300 years (606-331 B.C.) needs

380

to be known in its broad outlines, that we may better understand what happened to the Jews during this time.

1. The Babylonian Empire

As previously explained, the power of the Assyrian Empire was finally broken at the Battle of Carchemish (606 B.C.), and Nebuchadnezzar at the death of his father, Nabopolassar, king of Babylon, in 605 B.C., became the ruler of the entire Fertile Crescent.[1] His rule of 43 years was one of the most illustrious in history. Cornill, an authority on Babylonia and Assyria, pronounces Nebuchadnezzar "the most towering personality in the whole history of the ancient Orient." He continues:

> He rebuilt destroyed cities, restored ruined temples, laid out canals and ponds, regulated the course of rivers, and established harbors, so as to open safeways and new roads for commerce and traffic. Forty-three years were allotted to him in which he reigned to the welfare of humanity.[2]

This is probably too high an estimate of the man, but will serve to underline his importance in the ancient world and his contribution to the civilization of his times.

a. The City of Babylon Under Nebuchadnezzar. Daniel, who lived in Babylon for nearly three-quarters of a century, gives us a little glimpse of the grandeur of the city of Babylon in the time of Nebuchadnezzar. He relates that one day Nebuchadnezzar, while walking on the roof of his royal palace and looking out over the city, remarked, "Is not this great Babylon that I have built by my mighty power as a royal residence and for the glory of my majesty?" (Dan. 4:30, RSV) The archaeological excavations which were carried on at Babylon by the German Oriental Society from 1899 to about 1915 have furnished striking confirmation of the boast of Nebuchadnezzar. Six columns of Babylonian writing were discovered telling of the stupendous building operations which the king carried on in enlarging and beautifying the city. In addition to the discovery of the huge double walls and imperial palace,

---

[1] Egypt was not reconquered, however, until the time of Cambyses, son of Cyrus, about 525 B.C. See *Elmer K. Mould, Essentials of Bible History*, p. 351.

[2] Cornill, *A History of the Babylonians and Assyrians*, p. 327.

the German excavators found a vast system of fortifications, buildings, canals, palaces, and temples.[3]

b. The Fall of Babylon. After the death of Nebuchadnazzar in 562 B.C. the Babylonian Empire declined rapidly to its end in the final capture of Babylon by Cyrus in 538 B.C. The son of Nebuchadnezzar, the Evil-Merodach of II Kings 25:27 who released Jehoiachin from prison, was assassinated after a three years' reign, by his brother-in-law Neriglissar, who succeeded him on the throne. Five years later the power passed to the young son of Neriglissar, but he in turn was soon deposed by the priestly party, who made one of their own number, Nabonidus, the ruler.

This Nabonidus has been proved by archaeological discovery to be the father of Belshazzar (Daniel 5), with whom he shared the rule of Babylon.[4] This fact identifies for us a character who was for a long period the object of much controversy between conservative and liberal critics of the Bible. Moreover the wife of Nabonidus and mother of Belshazzar seems to have been a daughter of Nebuchadnezzar. Hence Daniel could speak of Belshazzar as the son (grandson) of Nebuchadnezzar (Dan. 5:22).

The general circumstances of the fall of Babylon as described in the fifth chapter of Daniel are well substantiated in other historical sources. The "Nabonidus Chronicle," discovered in the excavations at Babylon, describes the suddenness of the attack and the taking of the city "without a battle."[5] Belshazzar was killed on the very night of a banquet which he was holding, quite oblivious of the city's peril.[6] His father, Nabonidus, was captured by the invading Persians.[7] Thus the Persians, who had united with the Medes about 550 B.C., and who meanwhile, under the leadership of Cyrus, had subdued all of Asia Minor, became the masters of the empire ruled by the Babylonians.

---

[3]J. P. Free, *Archaeology and Bible History*, pp. 228 f. C. J. Finegan, *Light from the Ancient Past*, p. 185.

[4]Free, *op. cit.*, pp. 233-35; J. C. Muir, *His Truth Endureth*, p. 217.

[5]Muir, *op. cit.*, p. 221; G. A. Barton, *Archaeology and the Bible*, pp. 482 f.

[6]Dan. 5:31; cf. Barton, *op. cit.*, p. 483.

[7]Muir, *loc. cit.*

2. The Persian Empire

With the advent of Cyrus a new policy was inaugurated with regard to the treatment of conquered nations. Instead of tyrannizing over them and holding them in subjection by brute force, Cyrus chose to treat his subjects with consideration and to win them as his friends. By his famous decree, issued in the second year of his reign, Cyrus permitted the return of all exiled peoples to their homelands, thus reversing the policies of the Assyrians and the Babylonians. Judging by the account in Ezra he seems to have specially favored the return of the Jews and to have granted them generous aid. Muir notes that this liberal policy of the Persians marks "a distinct step forward in the rise of civilization. Individual and religious freedom for subject peoples was a new note in national administrative policies."[8]

Cyrus reigned for 10 years after his capture of Babylon, and on his death in 529 B.C. Cambyses, his son, became king. But Cambyses, unfortunately, lacked his father's gift for government, and upon his death seven years later the empire was taken over by one of the Persian nobles, who became known in history as Darius the Great,[9] and who extended the empire from India to the Danube, and east to Greece itself. It was Darius who gave express command to his governors to aid in the rebuilding of the Temple at Jerusalem (Ezra 6: 1-12).

Darius is also famous for his attempt to subjugate the Greek peninsula to the Persian Empire. A huge army and fleet were dispatched against Greece in 492 B.C. but met with disaster. Another greater army was defeated at Marathon in 490 B.C. In the midst of preparations for a third expedition Darius died, but his son, Xerxes (486-465 B.C.), known as Ahasuerus in the Book of Esther, continued the campaign against Greece. He raised an enormous army and fleet which he accompanied in person, that he might witness their prowess. But at the Battle of Salamis, in 480 B.C., the huge fleet was routed by that of Athens, and the Persian army was subsequently scattered and compelled to flee.

[8]*Ibid.*, p. 227.

[9]This is not the Darius who is an important character in the Book of Daniel (5:1).

The last Persian emperor mentioned in the Old Testament is Artaxerxes Longimanus (465-424 B.C.), who allowed Ezra to lead a large number of Jews back to Palestine, and who is renowned for his friendship with Nehemiah, which resulted in the rebuilding of the walls of Jerusalem. We return now to the story of the Exile.

II. BY THE RIVERS OF BABYLON: THE NATION IN EXILE

A striking picture of the Jewish exiles in Babylon is found in Psalms 137:

> *By the rivers of Babylon,*
> *There we sat down, yea, we wept,*
> *When we remembered Zion.*
> *Upon the willows in the midst thereof*
> *We hanged our harps.*
> *For there they that led us captive required of us songs,*
> *And they that wasted us required of us mirth, saying,*
> *Sing us one of the songs of Zion.*
> *How shall we sing Jehovah's song*
> *In a foreign land?*
> *If I forget thee, O Jerusalem,*
> *Let my right hand forget her skill.*
> *Let my tongue cleave to the roof of my mouth,*
> *If I remember thee not;*
> *If I prefer not Jerusalem*
> *Above my chief joy* (Ps. 137:1-6, ASV).

Such was the feeling of homesickness and discouragement which was doubtless often prevalent among the Israelites in Babylonia. However, it does not characterize too well their situation as a whole. Nor should we take too much for granted from the term "captivity." The Babylonian monarchs were much milder in their treatment of subject peoples than were the Assyrians. It seems to have been in the providence of God that the power had been taken over by the Babylonians. Thus the people of Judah might be chastised for their disobedience and waywardness without receiving the cruel treatment which had been the fate of exiles from the apostate Northern Kingdom.

1. *Jewish Life in Babylonia* (Jeremiah 25, 29; Ezekiel; Daniel)

A letter sent by Jeremiah to the Jewish people in Babylonia before the fall of Jerusalem suggests the relatively peaceful life which the exiles were permitted to live:

> *Build ye houses, and dwell in them; and plant gardens, and eat the fruit of them; take ye wives, and beget sons and daughters; and take wives for your sons, and give your daughters to husbands, that they may bear sons and daughters; that ye may be increased there, and not diminished. And seek the peace of the city whither I have caused you to be carried away captives, and pray unto the Lord for it: for in the peace thereof shall ye have peace* (Jer. 29:5-9).

At first there seems to have been the impression that the Exile was to last only a short time, and that the many predictions concerning a return, which had been voiced by Isaiah, Jeremiah, and others of the prophets, would soon be realized. But the letter of Jeremiah and the exhortations of the prophet Ezekiel soon convinced the people that their stay was to be a long one. They bought property, engaged in commerce, established their religious communities, built synagogues, and carried on a normal existence. Many of their number were elevated to positions of prominence in the state. Examples are Daniel and his three friends, Hananiah, Mishael, and Azariah; and Mordecai, Ezra, and Nehemiah. Indeed so pleasant was their lot that at the end of the 70 years only a small percentage of the people were willing to risk the hazardous homeward journey and face the problems of reconstruction and rehabilitation that would inevitably be their lot at Jerusalem.

2. *Results of the Exile*

Certain changes in Jewish life and thought may be noted as resulting from their experience in Babylonia. First, the spoken language of the people underwent a change. To a great degree they adopted the Aramaic dialect. It is notable that in the restoration period, when Ezra read the law in Hebrew, he had to give the sense in the spoken dialect (Neh. 8:8).

In fact, parts of the books of Ezra and Daniel are written in the Aramaic ("Chaldaic") tongue.

Second, there was a marked increase in literary production among the Jews in exile. In addition to the prophecies of Ezekiel and Daniel, the Books of I and II Kings may be presumed to have been completed in this period and many psalms were added. For example, Psalms 85; 102; 118; 126; 137; 146—50, and probably 74 and 79, belong to the exile period.[10] It is a common assumption among scholars that the movement for a definite collection of Sacred Writings began in this period.

Third, and most important, were the changes which took place in the religious life of the people, including the final break with idolatry, the universalization of their concept of the kingdom of God, and the setting up of the synagogue as a place of worship. A great factor in this change, we shall see, was the influence of the prophet Ezekiel. There was also the fact that in the absence of the Temple ceremonies new forms of religious expression were necessarily adopted. As James C. Muir observes,

> Without a temple in which religious life could be centralized, current soul-needs called for its closer human application. Revealed religion took a long step forward. Jehovah was no longer the exclusive Lord God of the Hebrews administering through His Holy Temple in Jerusalem. He, the Holy One, was the Divine Ruler of all mankind, Jew and Gentile alike, and the universe the Kingdom of God.[11]

3. The Book of Esther

A significant example of God's continued providence over His people in exile is related in the Book of Esther. The setting is actually later than the return under Zerubbabel, and probably to be referred to the reign of Xerxes (486-465 B.C.). Esther, a beautiful Jewish maiden, having been introduced into the Persian court with high honor as queen of the realm, effects through the help of her uncle, Mordecai, a prominent Jew, a great deliverance of her persecuted kinsmen. Haman,

[10]Cf. J. R. Sampel, *The Heart of the Old Testament*, pp. 200-201, 219.

[11]Muir, *op. cit.*, p. 211.

a powerful and ambitious Persian courtier, who by subtle means has induced the king to issue a ban of extermination against the Jews, is proven a traitor and eventually hanged on the very gallows he has prepared for Mordecai. The Jews are delivered, and in grateful remembrance of God's providence they institute the Feast of Purim, which has become one of the important Jewish festivals.

III. JERUSALEM REBUILT: THE RESTORATION OF JUDAH

As the Captivity had occurred in three stages (606, 597, and 586 B.C.), so the return was threefold: under Zerubbabel in 536 B.C., under Ezra in 458 B.C., and under Nehemiah in 444 B.C. Under Zerubbabel the Temple was restored, under Ezra a great religious reform was carried out, and under Nehemiah the walls were rebuilt and the city rehabilitated. The story of the first two returns is told in Ezra; the story of the third is found in Nehemiah.

1. *Zerubbabel's Return and the Rebuilding of the Temple* (Ezra 1—6)

On two different occasions Jeremiah had prophesied that the length of the Exile would be 70 years (Jer. 25:12 and 29:10). Cyrus' famous decree, allowing exiled peoples to return to their homelands, was made in 537 B.C., and a few months later, just 70 years after the first captives had been taken to Babylon, a party of Jews began their homeward journey under the leadership of Zerubbabel (also called Sheshbazzar), a prince of the house of David, and Jeshua (or Joshua), the high priest. According to the figures given in Ezra (2:64-65), about 50,000 people were included in the group who returned on this first occasion.[12] Most of these were of the tribes of Judah, Benjamin, and Levi, but there were a few belonging to the 10 tribes also.[13] Tradition has it that this immense caravan was accompanied by a bodyguard of 1,000 cavalry and that they were four months on the way.[14]

---

[12]See L. A. Knott, *Student's History of the Hebrews*, p. 288; and cf. Elmer K. Mould, *Essentials of Bible History*, p. 350.

[13]Cf. Blaikie and Matthews, *A Manual of Bible History*, p. 282.

[14]Cf. I. M. Price, *The Dramatic Story of Old Testament History*, pp. 377 f.

Ezra indicates that they were materially aided in their preparations for the journey by gifts from their brethren who remained behind and by grants from the king (Ezra 1:6-11).

Upon their arrival at Jerusalem an altar was immediately erected under the supervision of the high priest and the worship of God was restored. After the temporary housing was taken care of, the first project of the returned exiles was to clear the site and lay the foundation for a reconstructed Temple.

But the work of rebuilding the Temple was soon rudely interfered with by neighboring peoples who were not sympathetic with the restoration of Jerusalem. The Samaritans, under a guise of friendship, asked permission to join in the work of reconstruction, and when their pretended offer was rejected, they began to give annoyance and to make opposition. They reported to the Persians that the Jews were building fortifications and planning a revolt. Consequently, the work of rebuilding the Temple was stopped by an order from the king and not revived until after the accession of Darius in 521 B.C.

The resumption of the work of rebuilding was due in large part to the exhortations of the two prophets Haggai and Zechariah. When the work was again challenged, the king was persuaded to examine the records to determine whether the reconstruction had been authorized. Upon his discovery of Cyrus' decree, authorizing in specific terms the rebuilding of the Temple, he commanded his governors in the neighboring provinces to aid in the work by supplying the needed materials and to see that no further hindrance was offered to the project. Thus it was that in 516 B.C., just 20 years after the work had been begun, the Temple was completed and rededicated amidst great rejoicing on the part of the people.[15]

The new Temple was not comparable in many respects to the elaborate structure which Solomon had built,[16] but it was this Temple which, in its modified form under Herod, was to be the scene of the inauguration of a glorious new

[15]Cf. Blaikie and Matthews, *op. cit.*, p. 284.

[16]Compare the lament of the older Jews who had seen the former Temple (Ezra 3:10-13).

epoch in the history of redemption. The prophecy of Haggai (2:1-9) concerning the future glory of "this latter house" was to be fulfilled, and, in the words of Malachi (3:1), the Lord whom they sought would "suddenly come to his temple."

2. Ezra and Nehemiah: the Restoration Completed (Ezra 7— 10, Nehemiah)

The second and third returns of the exiled Jews to Jerusalem were similar in that they originated in a desire to help the newly organized colony at Jerusalem to complete their work of restoration.

a. The Second Return Under Ezra. Ezra, a man of priestly lineage and a ready scribe in the law of Moses,[17] was informed in Babylonia of the need of a religious reform and of instruction in the Law on the part of his kinsmen at Jerusalem. Consequently he sought and received permission from Artaxerxes, the emperor, to lead another group of Jews to Palestine, that he might investigate the moral and religious conditions prevailing there. Authority was given him to requisition from Persian governors of nearby provinces the supplies and funds needed.

On this expedition, which was undertaken in 458 B.C., over 1,700 men accompanied Ezra, taking with them the Temple vessels which had not as yet been returned from Babylonia. On his arrival at Jerusalem, Ezra learned that in direct violation of the law of Moses the Jews had freely intermarried with the Canaanites and other foreign peoples. Even the rulers and priests were involved in committing this sin. Ezra was so shocked at this defection that he rent his garments, plucked off the hair of his head and beard, and sat confounded until the hour of evening sacrifice. Then he gave himself to prayer, confessing the sins of the people. At this time he succeeded in persuading most of the priests to divorce their pagan wives, but further steps were necessary to be taken in this matter at a later time.

Ezra's more significant ministry in connection with the

[17]Ezra 7:6. The function of a "scribe" was principally that of a teacher or authority in the Scriptures. Writing was only incidental to the work of this class of religious leaders.

instruction of the people in the law of God is related in the Book of Nehemiah, to which we turn now for the story of the third return and the final events of the restoration period.

b. The Rebuilding of the Walls Under Nehemiah (Third Return). Nehemiah is described as a person of prominence in the court of Artaxerxes at Susa (Shushan). Hearing of the wretched plight of his countrymen at Jerusalem and of the ruined condition of the city walls, which were still a mass of debris as they had been left by Nebuchadnezzar, Nehemiah prevailed upon the king to allow him to go to Jerusalem, that he might in some way help his countrymen. The king appointed him as governor of Judah, gave him letters of commendation to the provincial governors along the way, and provided a military escort to accompany him and his small party on the 1,000-mile journey from Susa to Jerusalem.

In 444 B.C., soon after his arrival at Jerusalem, Nehemiah went on an inspection tour by night about the walls of the city. Then he called upon the people to aid him in rebuilding the ruined fortifications. The help was given loyally and the walls were rebuilt within a period of two months, despite the fierce resistance and insidious opposition of Sanballat, the Samaritan, and other hostile neighbors, who were evidently jealous of the aid which was being given the Jews. At times it became necessary for the artisans to work with a trowel in one hand and a sword in the other, to guard against a surprise assault.

c. Reforms Under Ezra and Nehemiah. In the months that followed, Ezra and Nehemiah worked together to improve the social and religious condition of the people. In this they were aided also by the prophet Malachi.

On one occasion, described in the eighth chapter of Nehemiah, the law of God was read to the people as they were assembled at the Feast of Tabernacles.

> *Ezra the scribe stood upon a pulpit of wood, which they had made for the purpose . . . And Ezra opened the book in the sight of all the people; for he was above all the people;) and when he opened it, all the people stood up: and Ezra blessed the Lord, the*

*great God. And all the people answered, Amen,
Amen, with lifting up their hands: and they bowed
their heads, and worshipped the Lord . . . So they
read in the book in the law of God distinctly, and
gave the sense, and caused them to understand the
reading* (Neh. 8: 4-6, 8).

With one accord the people agreed to a renewal of their
covenant with God, especially with respect to their separate-
ness from their worldly neighbors.[18]

After remaining in the city as governor for 12 years
Nehemiah went back for a brief visit to Babylonia. His
second return to Jerusalem in 432 B.C. is the last datable
event in Old Testament history. We now turn to the prophets
of the Exile and Restoration.

IV. PREACHING TO THE CAPTIVES IN BABYLONIA: THE PROPHECY OF EZEKIEL

The prophet Ezekiel was carried captive to Babylonia in
597 B.C. among the 10,000 who were exiled with the young
king Jehoiachin. He settled with a group of exiles at Tel-abib,
a town in the interior of Babylonia on the river Chebar,
probably the great ship canal connecting the Euphrates with
the Tigris. In 592 B.C., five years after the arrival of the exiles
in Babylonia, when Ezekiel was probably 30 years old (Ezek.
1: 1), he received a call from the Lord to prophesy to the people of the Captivity.

1. *A Pastor Appointed: the Call of the Prophet* (Ezekiel 1—3)

In dramatic fashion Ezekiel tells us of a vision which
appeared to him: a whirlwind from the north, a great cloud,
a fire and dazzling brightness, four living creatures, and wheels
with their rims full of eyes, a wheel within a wheel. By such
fantastic images—strange to us, but perhaps not so strange
in the environment of Babylonia—the prophet paints for us
the revelation he received of the glory of God.[19]

---

[18]Nehemiah instituted drastic marriage reforms (13:25), and broke
up Sabbath desecration (13:21).

[19]Compare Isaiah's vision (Isaiah 6) and John's vision (Rev. 1:10-
18).

Out of the midst of this glory God appeared to Ezekiel in "the likeness . . . of a man" and presented to him a scroll bearing the words of the Lord, with the command that he should eat it. And when the prophet obeyed, it was in his mouth "as honey for sweetness" (3:3).[20] Then God commanded him to go to the people of the Captivity and preach to them the words of the Lord. So he went, he tells us, and "sat where they sat, and remained there astonished among them seven days" (3:15). He had gone there with anger and bitterness in his spirit because of the rebelliousness of the people, but during these seven days his anger passed away and he was moved with compassion for them.

Ezekiel, in the years that followed, became a guiding light to the people in the dark days of the Captivity. Charged with the responsibility of a watchman over them (3:17), he gave himself to the task of warning, exhorting, consoling, allaying their fears, and building up their hopes for the future. His method was unique. It has been well said that he thought in images. But as a preacher, a writer, a pastor, and a prophet of God, Ezekiel takes his place among the greatest men of the Old Testament.

2. *An Old Testament Evangelist: Ezekiel's Message of Personal Salvation* (Ezekiel 18—36)

The highly symbolical language in which much of Ezekiel's prophecy is couched is in striking contrast to his clear and forceful preaching on other occasions. No modern evangelist could present the subject of personal responsibility before God more clearly than Ezekiel in the eighteenth and thirty-third chapters.

> *The soul that sins shall die. The son shall not suffer for the iniquity of the father, nor the father suffer for the iniquity of the son; the righteousness of the righteous shall be upon himself, and the wickedness of the wicked shall be upon himself. But if a wicked man turns away from all his sins which he has committed and keeps all my statutes and does what is lawful and right, he shall surely live; he shall not die.*

[20]Cf. Ps. 19:10.

*None of the transgressions which he has committed
shall be remembered against him . . . Repent and
turn away from all your transgressions, lest iniquity
be your ruin . . . Get yourselves a new heart and a
new spirit! Why will you die, O house of Israel? For
I have no pleasure in the death of anyone, says the
Lord God: so turn, and live* (18: 20-22, 30-32, RSV).[21]

Likewise the responsibility of the "watchman" as the ambassador of God is made perfectly clear:

*When I say unto the wicked, O wicked man,
thou shalt surely die; if thou dost not speak to warn
the wicked from his way, that wicked man shall die
in his iniquity; but his blood will I require at thine
hand. Nevertheless, if thou warn the wicked of his
way to turn from it; if he do not turn from his way,
he shall die in his iniquity; but thou hast delivered
thy soul* (33: 8-9).[22]

It is clear from these passages that the teaching on
personal responsibility for sin, which had been touched upon
by the earlier prophets and partially elaborated in Jeremiah,[23] has become in Ezekiel one of the cardinal teachings
and is given a prominent emphasis.

One more significant aspect of Ezekiel's teaching concerning salvation is his emphasis on heart cleansing, which,
of course, is in the form of a prophecy of the dispensation
of the Holy Spirit. Here, too, his teaching should be compared
with Jeremiah's, as in his famous New Covenant passage
(Jer. 31: 31-34). What modern holiness preacher could make
the cleansing of the heart clearer to the understanding than
Ezekiel in the following?

*Then will I sprinkle clean water upon you, and
ye shall be clean: from all your filthiness, and from
all your idols, will I cleanse you. A new heart also
will I give you, and a new spirit will I put within*

[21]Cf. Ezek. 33: 11-20.

[22]Cf. Ezek. 3: 17-21 and the account of the shepherd's responsibility
(34: 1-16)

[23]Cf. Kyle M. Yates, *Preaching from the Prophets*, pp. 134 f., 180.

you: and I will take away the stony heart out of your flesh, and I will give you an heart of flesh. And I will put my spirit within you, and cause you to walk in my statutes, and ye shall keep my judgments, and do them (36:25-27).

3. *A Mystic with a Message of Hope: the Visions of Ezekiel Concerning the Future of Israel* (Ezekiel 37—48)

The Book of Ezekiel falls naturally into three parts. (1) Chapters 1—24 contain the earlier sermons, which preceded the fall of Jerusalem, consisting largely of a continued call for repentance and reformation and predictions of divine judgment to result from failure to hear God's voice. (2) Chapters 25—32 contain a series of dooms pronounced against neighboring nations. (3) Chapters 33—48 are composed of Ezekiel's later sermons, delivered after the news had reached the captives of the final overthrow and destruction of their beloved capital.

These later chapters, which may be compared with Isaiah 40—66, are devoted largely to a message of consolation and hope. The constant theme is the future glory of Israel. We have dealt with one phase of this theme which occurs in chapter 36, namely, the promise of the Holy Spirit, who should purify the hearts of the people and render them once more acceptable to God. In chapters 37—48 the prophet in his characteristically symbolic manner portrays through a series of visions the glorious future which was in store for the faithful remnant.

In the well-known vision of dry bones (37:1-14) he teaches that God is able by His Spirit to revitalize His people, and in His own good time to restore them to their own land and make of them again a nation that shall bring honor to His name.

The last nine chapters are devoted to a vision of a spiritual temple to be set up in Israel. This is not the Temple of the restoration, as some suppose, but a purely idealistic vision, by which the prophet foreshadowed the coming Messianic Age. Paul uses the same imagery in describing the true Church of Christ (Eph. 2:19-22).

One of the most hopeful passages in the whole Bible is

the description in chapter 47:1-12 of the life-giving stream which flows from the altar of God bringing life and salvation wherever it goes. The water of life is a favorite figure in both the Old and New Testaments and is used by our Lord in describing the influence of a godly life through the power of the Spirit which they that believe on Him should receive (John 7:37-39).[24]

V. PROPHESYING THE KINGDOM OF HEAVEN: THE PROPHET DANIEL

Daniel was taken into captivity among the first to be exiled, in 605 B.C. With him were taken three other youths, Hananiah, Mishael, and Azariah, whom the Babylonians renamed Shadrach Meshach, and Abed-nego. The experiences of these four are recounted in the first six chapters of the Book of Daniel.

1. *Patterns of Godliness: the Experiences of Daniel and His Companions* (Daniel 1—6)

Since they were all of noble birth, Daniel and his companions were chosen by King Nebuchadnezzar for special training in statecraft. But when placed among other youths in the Babylonian school they soon evidenced their superior moral caliber in refusing to eat food ceremonially unclean for the Jews. They resolved to live according to the law of God in Babylon, just as they had always done in Judah. It was not easy to gain their request for a change of food, but after a test had been made the four young Jews were found to be in a better physical condition than those that partook of the king's dainties. Moreover, they made such progress in their learning that they soon surpassed all their fellows in wisdom, and so came into great favor with the king.

Daniel, like Joseph in the story of Genesis, possessed a rare gift of interpreting dreams. This brought him rapidly to a position of high honor in the king's court. Other remarkable experiences told in these interesting chapters include the deliverance of Daniel's three companions from the fiery furnace (chapter 3), the handwriting on the wall which Daniel

[24]Cf. Joel 3:18; Zech. 14:8; John 4:10-15; Rev. 22:1-2.

interpreted at the feast of Belshazzar (chapter 5), and Daniel's deliverance from the lions' den (chapter 6), an event which happened under the rule of the Persians, perhaps soon after the first return of the Jews under Zerubbabel. The teaching which seems to be common to all these stories is that God never fails those who remain steadfast and true to Him. "The angel of the Lord encampeth round about them that fear him, and delivereth them" (Ps. 34: 7).

2. *The Giant Image: Nebuchadnezzar's Dream of the Four Kingdoms* (Daniel 2)

It is noteworthy in studying the prophecies of Daniel that we are using the word prophecy here in its usual modern signification. Daniel was not a prophet in the sense that he preached to the Jewish people of his day, as was the case with all other Old Testament prophets. He was trained as a statesman, as we have seen, and yet was so devoted to God that he had received from God a special gift of predicting the future through the interpretation of dreams and visions. We see in his book a veritable history of the ages to come, extending not only to the coming of Christ, but to the very end of the world. As a prophecy of the last days it is referred to as an apocalypse and is to be classed with the Revelation (or Apocalypse) of St. John.[25]

In Nebuchadnezzar's dream and its interpretation in chapter 2 we have Daniel's first great prophecy of the future. The proper understanding of this chapter is important for the interpretation of the visions of Daniel in the last six chapters of the book.

Nebuchadnezzar had seen in his dream a gigantic image— a man with a head of gold, breast and arms of silver, belly and thighs of brass, legs of iron, and feet and toes of iron mixed with clay. As the king looked at the image, ". . . a stone was cut out without hands, which smote the image upon his feet . . . and brake them to pieces"; and when the wind had blown all the pieces away like chaff, the stone "became a great mountain, and filled the whole earth" (2: 31-35). In his interpretation of the dream to the king, Daniel identified the head

[25]Cf. C. A. Cartledge, *A Conservative Introduction to the Old Testament*, pp. 218-25.

of gold as the empire of the Babylonians, of which Nebuchadnezzar himself was the head. The other three parts of silver, brass, and iron respectively were to be three successive empires, comparable to the Babylonian and increasing in strength although diminishing in royal splendor. The careful student can scarcely fail to recognize in these three successive powers the Medo-Persian, Greek, and Roman empires, which followed the Babylonian. The stone is described as the kingdom of God, which was to be set up in the last days of these empires (2:44)—certainly then in the Roman times, and clearly to be identified with the kingdom of Christ, "which shall never be destroyed," but shall one day fill the whole earth "as the waters cover the sea" (Isa. 11:9).

3. *The Visions of Daniel: the Times of the Gentiles and the Kingdom of Christ* (Daniel 7—12)

We pass now rapidly to the seventh chapter of Daniel to note the similarity of interpretation between the dream of Nebuchadnezzar and the first of Daniel's visions.

In the first year of Belshazzar (553 b.c.), when Daniel was nearly 70 years of age, he had a vision of four beasts which came up from the sea: the first like a lion, the second like a bear, the third like a leopard, and the fourth a dreadful and terrible beast with great iron teeth and ten horns. Note that a progression is seen here similar to that in the image of chapter 2. What the successive beasts lose in grandeur they gain in savagery.

In this vision we seem to be carried forward to the very time of the Judgment:

> *I beheld till the thrones were cast down, and the Ancient of days did sit, whose garment was white as snow . . . thousand thousands ministered unto him, and ten thousand times ten thousand stood before him: the judgment was set, and the books were opened. . . . and, behold, one like the Son of man came with clouds of heaven, and came to the Ancient of days, and they brought him near before him. And there was given him dominion, and glory, and a kingdom, that all people, nations, and languages, should serve him: his dominion is an everlasting dominion,*

which shall not pass away, and his kingdom that
which shall not be destroyed (7: 9-10, 13-14).

Another vision of Daniel which we should note is related
in the ninth chapter. It is commonly referred to as the Vision
of the Seventy Weeks. In the first year of the Persian rule,
when Daniel was now nearly 85 years old, he remembered
the prophecy of Jeremiah that after 70 years the Captivity
would come to an end and the Jews would be allowed to
return to their homeland. So he set himself to fast and pray
and to confess the sins of his people in hope that the restoration would take place as promised. In answer to his prayer
the angel Gabriel was sent to him with the vision of the 70
weeks. It is interesting to note that the decree of Cyrus
permitting the return of the Jews was issued the very year
of Daniel's prayer.

The angel, however, reveals to Daniel that the 70 years
in reality stand for 70 weeks (of years), or a period of 70
times seven years. Of these 70 weeks, 69 ("seven weeks, and
threescore and two weeks") represent the time "from the going
forth of the commandment to restore and to build Jerusalem"
to the coming of the Messiah (9: 25). The remaining week
seems to refer to the reign of the Antichrist and to be delayed
until the time of the end (9: 27). The command referred to is
commonly thought to be the commission given to Ezra by
Axtaxerxes, king of Persia, in 458 or 457 B.C. (Ezra 7: 11-28).
If the latter date is used, we note that the time from Ezra's
commission until the beginning of Christ's ministry in A.D. 26
was exactly 483 years (69 times seven years)—a remarkable
fulfillment of prophecy!

Not even Daniel understood fully the visions which he
describes. Time has made clear the meaning of some of them,
but others remain to be interpreted. In the last chapter we
are given another glimpse of the times of the end.

There shall be a time of trouble, such as never
was since there was a nation even to that same time:
and at that time thy people shall be delivered, every
one that shall be found written in the book. And
many of them that sleep in the dust of the earth shall
awake, some to everlasting life, and some to shame
and everlasting contempt. And they that be wise shall

shine as the brightness of the firmament; and they that turn many to righteousness as the stars for ever and ever (12:1-3).

VI. The Prophets of the Restoration Period

The prophets of the restoration period are usually listed as Haggai, Zechariah, and Malachi, whose books appear at the end of the minor prophets. To these we have added Joel, whose date is not known, but who has often been referred to this period.

1. *Haggai, the Temple-building Prophet* (Haggai 1—2)

The first prophet of the restoration period at Jerusalem was Haggai, of whom nothing is known except the brief references to him in Ezra (Ezra 5:1-2; 6:14), and the sermons which constitute the two chapters of his book. It is sometimes inferred from chapter 2:3-9 that he was a very old man who had seen the glory of Solomon's Temple before it was destroyed by the Babylonians.

When the people returned to Jerusalem in 536 B.C. it was their first thought to rebuild the Temple. However, because of the difficulty of the task and because of opposition from hostile neighbors they had ceased entirely from their efforts to restore the Temple and had devoted themselves more and more to their own affairs, building great houses for themselves, enlarging their herds, and expanding their businesses. At the time of the first dated message of Haggai, 520 B.C., 15 years had passed since the work of Temple building was begun. Haggai chides the people for dwelling complacently in their fine homes while the house of the Lord lies in ruins. He tells them that the reason for their lack of prosperity is their negligence concerning the Lord's house: "Ye have sown much, and bring in little; ye eat, but ye have not enough . . . and he that earneth wages earneth wages to put it into a bag with holes" (1:6).

As a result of Haggai's urgent preaching the work of rebuilding was resumed and Haggai and Zechariah, "the prophets of God," worked side by side with Zerubbabel and the people.

About a month later Haggai brought a further message to the people, this time a message of encouragement. When the older men lamented because the Temple they were building was so small and inglorious in comparison with the one they remembered, he answered with one of the most significant announcements in the prophetic writings.

> *Thus saith the Lord of hosts; Yet once, it is a little while, and I will shake the heavens, and the earth, and the sea, and the dry land . . . and the desire of all nations shall come: and I will fill this house with glory . . . The glory of this latter house shall be greater than of the former, . . . and in this place will I give peace, saith the Lord of hosts* (2: 6-9).

2. *Zechariah, the Prophet of the Triumphal Entry* (Zechariah 1—14)

Within two months after Haggai began to preach to the people concerning the rebuilding of the Temple, the prophet Zechariah began his ministry of encouragement to the builders.

In striking contrast to the practical-minded Haggai, Zechariah was a person endowed with a vivid imagination and a sensitive soul, and his inspirational messages, pointing forward as they do to the time of the Messiah, continue to glow with meaning for the world today.

> *Thus saith the Lord; I am returned to Jerusalem with mercies: my house shall be built in it, saith the Lord of hosts . . . the Lord shall yet comfort Zion, and shall yet choose Jerusalem. For I, saith the Lord, will be unto her a wall of fire round about, and will be the glory in the midst of her. . . . for he that touchest you toucheth the apple of his eye* (1: 16-17 2: 5, 8).

Zechariah represents the work of building God's house as a spiritual work, which is to be accomplished, "not by might, nor by power, but by my spirit, saith the Lord" (4: 6). The true Builder is the Branch (or Messiah). "He shall grow up out of his place, and he shall build the temple of the Lord" (6: 12). In His person are to be combined the offices of king and prophet, and His rule shall be without an end.

Like Ezekiel and Daniel, Zechariah, perhaps under the influence of the environment of Babylonia under which he grew up, speaks often in visions and symbols. In the first six chapters the prophet describes eight visions which he had in the night, all intended to encourage the people to believe that God was aiding them in their task. These visions are climaxed with a symbolic coronation of Zerubbabel, the scion of David, and Joshua, the high priest, who together represent the royal and priestly character of the coming Messiah (6: 1-15).

The last six chapters of the book (9—14) are thought to have been written much later than chapters 1—8, probably in the old age of the prophet. The symbolic method is still present, showing a similarity to chapters 1—8. But the outstanding characteristic of this section of the book is the abundance of references to the Messiah. In fact, next to Isaiah, Zechariah is considered the most important Messianic prophet in the Old Testament. The betrayal of Christ for 30 pieces of silver is prophesied in 11:12-13; the piercing of His side and the mourning at the Cross in 12:10; the shedding of His blood for the sins of the world in 13:1; the prints of the nails in His hands in 13:6; the scattering of His disciples in 13:7; the destruction of Jerusalem in the New Testament age in 14:2; and the second coming of Christ in 14:4.

Perhaps the most striking Messianic passage of all is to be found in 9:9-10, where the language of the prophet portrays before the eye a picture of the Triumphal Entry as vivid as any artist could paint:

> *Rejoice greatly, O daughter of Zion; shout, O daughter of Jerusalem: behold, thy king cometh unto thee: he is just, and having salvation; lowly, and riding upon an ass, and upon a colt the foal of an ass. . . . he shall speak peace unto the heathen: and his dominion shall be from sea even to sea, and from the river even to the ends of the earth.*

3. *Malachi, an Old Testament Holiness Preacher* (Malachi 1—4)

Malachi, the last in the group of 12 m i n o r prophets, was probably a contemporary of Ezra and Nehemiah. Nothing is known of him actually except his name, which means "my messenger." Some have even conjectured that his real name was concealed by this title.[26]

The background of the prophet as reflected in his book corresponds closely to the times of Ezra and Nehemiah. The fair promises of Ezekiel and Zechariah, which were interpreted as of immediate fulfillment, had not been realized. The people had become increasingly indifferent to spiritual matters. Religion had lost its glow, and many had become cynical, skeptical, and unscrupulous. The priests were corrupt and immoral, and the people refused to pay their tithes and offerings. Worship had degenerated into empty formalism. Blind and lame animals were being offered on the altar of Jehovah. Marriage alliances were made with their heathen neighbors contrary to the Law, and divorce was common.

The prophet's method in dealing with these evils is unique. He does not present independent sermons as do the other prophets, but he enters into an argument with his contemporaries. We can, as it were, hear the audience respond to his open-air preaching with comments, questions, objections, and excuses. The prophet takes each objection and answers it before going on to another pronouncement. Two examples will suffice to illustrate this method:

> A son honoureth his father, and a servant his master: if then I be a father, where is mine honour? and if I be a master, where is my fear? saith the Lord of hosts unto you, O priests, that despise my name. And ye say, Wherein have we despised thy name? Ye offer polluted bread upon mine altar; and ye say, Wherein have we polluted thee? In that ye say, The table of the Lord is contemptible. And if ye offer the blind for sacrifice, is it not evil? and if ye offer the lame and the sick, is it not evil? . . . I have no pleasure in you, saith the Lord of hosts, neither will I accept an offering at your hand (1: 6-8, 10).

> Will a man rob God? Yet ye have robbed me. But ye say, Wherein have we robbed thee? In tithes and offerings. Bring ye all the tithes into the store-

---

[26]Cf. G. L. Robinson, *The Twelve Minor Prophets*, pp. 157 f.

*house, that there may be meat in mine house, and
prove me now herewith, if I will not open you the
windows of heaven, and pour you out a blessing, that
there shall not be room enough to receive it* (3:8, 10).

The standard Malachi raises is a standard of holiness in
the daily walk and in the heart attitude toward God. Also
the Messiah's coming, according to this prophet, will be chiefly characterized by a cleansing of the people's sin. He will
refine and purify the sons of Levi, and purge them as gold
and silver, "that they may offer unto the Lord an offering
in righteousness" (3:1-3).

4. *Joel, the Prophet of Pentecost* (Joel 1—3)

The date of Joel's prophecy is unknown. From internal
evidence Cartledge concludes that it was written either at
about 400 B.C., or, with less probability, at a much earlier
date, namely, about 800 B.C.[27] For convenience in comparing
his message with that of the prophets of the Exile and restoration we place him at the end of the group of restoration
prophets.

The occasion for the prophecy of Joel was a terrible
plague of locusts which, in combination with a devastating
drought, was causing great suffering among the Jews. The
prophet sees in the terrible scourge that was sweeping across
the land a symbol of the great and deadful day of the Lord,
which he describes in similar language to that of Zephaniah.[28]
Like Zephaniah, too, he makes the announcement of the
coming day of the Lord an occasion for calling the people to
repentance:

*Rend your heart, and not your garments, and
turn unto the Lord your God: for he is gracious
and merciful, slow to anger, and of great kindness,
and repenteth him of the evil* (2:13).[29]

Joel, however, in 2:18-32, goes beyond Zephaniah in
suggesting not only a restoration of the good times in Judah,
but the coming of an age in which the Spirit of God would be

[27]Cartledge, *op. cit.*, pp. 170-71. Xf. Yates, *op. cit.*, pp. 191 f.
[28]Compare Joel 2:2 and 11 with Zeph. 1:14-15.
[29]Compare with Zeph. 2:1-3.

poured out upon His people and they would be delivered from their bondage to sin. In this he is to be compared with Jeremiah (31: 31-34), Ezekiel (36: 25-27), Zechariah (13: 1), and Malachi (3: 1-3). Joel, in fact, carries us beyond all the other prophets in portraying to us the very manner in which the Spirit would be given at Pentecost, and some of the manifestations that would be evident at His coming; so that Peter in his sermon on the Day of Pentecost was constrained to say:

> *This is that which was spoken by the prophet Joel; And it shall come to pass in the last days, saith God, I will pour out of my Spirit upon all flesh: and your sons and your daughters shall prophesy, and your young men shall see visions, and your old men shall dream dreams: and on my servants and on my hand-maidens I will pour out in those days of my Spirit; and they shall prophesy: and it shall come to pass that whosoever shall call on the name of the Lord shall be saved* (Acts 2: 16-18, 21).

Summary

In approximately 200 years, from 600 to 400 B.C., we have seen the Jewish nation carried into captivity, and the Temple and the city of Jerusalem destroyed. Then, after a 70-year captivity, a remnant of the people were brought back to their homeland and reinstated in their former habitations, the Temple and walls were restored, and the law of Moses was established again as the law of the land. But there was no semblance of the pomp of former days in the subject state of Judah. The Old Testament closes in a somber atmosphere of peace through political subjection. Through the restoration at Jerusalem, as well as through the dispersion of segments of the Jewish community among the Gentile nations, the stage was being set for the coming of Christ and the spread of Christianity. The teachings of the prophets, as we have seen, had prepared the minds of the people in many ways for the reception of the gospel. In God's good time the gloom, which was fast spreading over all the ancient world, would give place to joy in the hearts of the faithful, at the coming of the Son of God and of the Christian revelation.

RECOMMENDED READINGS

Blaikie and Matthews, *A Manual of Bible History,* pp. 266-302.

Joseph P. Free, *Archaeology and Bible History,* pp. 224-54.

Dorothy Ruth Miller, *A Handbook of Ancient History in Bible Light,* pp. 110-37.

J. C. Muir, *His Truth Endureth,* pp. 209-43.

Ira M. Price, *Dramatic Story of Old Testament History,* pp. 354-98.

Loyal R. Ringenberg, *The Word of God in History,* pp. 227-63.

G. L. Robinson, *The Twelve Minor Prophets,* pp. 30-45, 137-69.

Kyle M. Yates, *Preaching from the Prophets,* pp. 175-85, 191-219.

FOR FURTHER STUDY

1. Describe the city of Babylon in Nebuchadnezzar's time. To what extent was Nebuchadnezzar responsible for the grandeur of the city? Where do we get information in regard to these matters?

2. Give dates for the beginning and end of the exile of Judah. How do we understand that the 70 years prophesied by Jeremiah (25:12) was fulfilled?

3. Describe the conditions under which the Jews lived in exile. In what books of the Bible do we have information about this period?

4. What were some of the permanent results of the Babylonian exile on Jewish life and thought?

5. Give an account of the call and mission of Ezekiel.

6. Compare Ezekiel's view of personal responsibility and heart cleansing with that of Jeremiah.

7. From chapters 10 and 11 describe the departure of the Shekinah glory from the Temple as represented by Ezekiel. On what occasion is it represented as returning? (c. 43)

8. How is the vision of dry bones in chapter 37 to be interpreted?

9. What is the significance of Ezekiel's vision of the restored Temple in chapters 40—48?

10. Explain the circumstances of Daniel's being taken into captivity. What was his position at Babylon and under what monarchs did he serve?

11. Explain the meaning of "apocalypse" as applied to Daniel's prophecy. How do Daniel's prophecies differ from those of the other prophets?

12. What difficulty is presented to scholars in identifying Belshazzar, mentioned in the sixth chapter of Daniel? How has archaeology aided in solving this difficulty?

13. Suggest the interpretation of the visions in Daniel 2, 7, and 9. What is the one event in which all of these visions find their climactic fulfillment according to the common Christian interpretation?

14. What event opened the way for a return to Palestine? Explain the circumstances involved.

15. Give a brief account of the three returns under Zerubbabel, Ezra, and Nehemiah. What contribution did each of these leaders make to the restoration at Jerusalem? Where is their story told?

16. What does the story in the Book of Esther concern? Who was Esther, and how is the setting of the book related to the returns of Zerubbabel, Ezra, and Nehemiah?

17. How many years were occupied in the rebuilding of the Temple? What difficulties were encountered in the completion of this task? Explain.

18. What two prophets aided in the rebuilding of the Temple? Characterize the books which they have left to us.

19. In what respects may Malachi be compared to a modern holiness preacher? Point out some of the notable passages in his book, and show how it is an appropriate transition from the Old Testament to the New.

20. What dates are suggested for the prophet Joel? What was the occasion for his prophecy? In what respect may he be said to have transcended the other prophets in his view of the gospel age?

CHAPTER XVI

The Message and Meaning
of the Old Testament

God ... spake in time past unto the fathers by the prophets
(Heb. 1:1).

We turn now to consider the enduring message of the Old Testament and its abiding values for us today. It is an admitted fact that the Old Testament serves a preparatory purpose. It looks ahead to the great event which divides the centuries into "B.C." and "A.D." It lays the groundwork for an understanding of the New Testament. It is in a sense incomplete, the half of a larger whole. As G. Ernest Wright has said:

> It is, therefore, quite obvious that a t r u e understanding of the Old Testament is indispensable for a proper realization of the full meaning of the New. It was the Scripture of Jesus and the Apostles. At a very early time the Christian church put it together with the new Christian writings because the two belonged together and were held together by an inner unity. And to those in Christian history who have known their Bibles well there is such a thing as *biblical* religion, the *biblical* mind, the *biblical* attitude, the *biblical* conception of God—implying a basic relatedness which renders the separation into Old and New, while, to be sure, legitimate, of secondary concern. In addition, there is in the Old Testament much material of great value to the Christian life which is not duplicated in the New. The Psalms, Isaiah, Genesis, Job, etc., have always been a great treasury of Christian devotional literature.[1]

At the same time, it should be seen that the Old Testament has a message and meaning of its own. This message is not opposed to or different from the message of the New Testament. It is, however, developed and stressed in a way which gives this portion of God's Word its own unique place and eternal value. No study of the Old Testament scriptures would be complete which did not review and highlight these great and abiding contributions.

[1]G. E. Wright, *The Challenge of Israel's Faith*, p. 99.

We shall consider five areas in which the Old Testament offers its unique and undying contribution to the sum total of biblical truth.

I. THE OLD TESTAMENT DOCTRINE OF GOD

The idea of God is the central truth of the Old Testament. Otto J. Baab says, "In the Old Testament itself the single concept which is overwhelmingly emphasized is the concept of God."[2] There are many ways in which this idea is expressed, but underlying all this variety is a vision of the Lord God which never varied from Genesis to Malachi—and, for that matter, on to Revelation. As Dr. Snaith has put it, the aim of Greek thought was, "Know thyself," but the goal of the Hebrew religion was the knowledge of God.[3] The Old Testament is therefore an invaluable source book of theology.

Different scholars have sketched the outlines of the Old Testament vision of God in different terms.[4] We shall attempt to classify the knowledge of God given in the Hebrew scriptures under seven heads. Obviously one cannot hope for a complete treatment, but may at least point out some of the most important items in a subject which would require volumes to treat properly.

1. God as Creator

The creative purpose and power of God is the first feature which confronts us in the Old Testament. "In the beginning God created the heavens and the earth" (Gen. 1:1). The entire finite universe owes its existence to the creative will of God. These opening words of the Bible are echoed many times throughout the pages which follow:

The heavens declare the glory of God;
And the firmament showeth his handiwork (Ps. 19:1,
    ASV).
Of old didst thou lay the foundation of the earth;

[2]O. J. Baab, *The Theology of the Old Testament*, p. 23.
[3]N. H. Snaith, *The Distinctive Ideas of the Old Testament*, p. 9.
[4]Cf. Baab, *op. cit.*, Ch. 2; A. C. Knudson, *The Religious Teaching of the Old Testament*, pp. 49-191; H. W. Robinson, *The Religious Ideas of the Old Testament*, pp. 51-76; Snaith, *op. cit.*

And the heavens are the work of thy hands.
They shall perish, but thou shalt endure;
Yea, all of them shall wax old like a garment;
As a vesture shalt thou change them, and they shall
*   be changed:*
But thou art the same,
And thy years shall have no end (Ps. 102: 25-27, ASV).

The creative work of God is often the theme of the prophets, and one of the bases of their unceasing opposition to and occasional ridicule of idolatry, the worship of gods made by human hands (cf. Isa. 40:18-24; 46:5-7; Jer. 10:3-6; etc.).

Thus saith God the Lord, he that created the
heavens, and stretched them out; he that spread forth
the earth, and that which cometh out of it; he that
giveth breath unto the people upon it, and spirit to
them that walk therein (Isa. 42:5).

That God has power to create assures His people that His promises will not fail:

Hast thou not known? hast thou not heard, that
the everlasting God, the Lord, the Creator of the
ends of the earth, fainteth not, neither is weary? there
is no searching of his understanding. He giveth
power to the faint; and to them that have no might
he increaseth strength. Even the youths shall faint
and be weary, and the young men shall utterly fall:
but they that wait upon the Lord shall renew their
strength; they shall mount up with wings as eagles;
they shall run, and not be weary; and they shall walk,
and not faint (Isa. 40:28-31).

The Creator is likewise in control of the processes of nature, which He may use to bring judgment upon a disobedient people (Jer. 3:2-3; Amos 4:6-11). The day of the Lord, about which the prophets had much to say, will witness great changes in the realm of nature (Zech. 14:4-7; Joel 3: 14-16). The contemplation of God's great power in creating and controlling nature should make us realize how weak and dependent we are as human beings (Job 38:1—42:6). The Old Testament view of the Creator-God who controls and sustains His creation is a theism of the purest kind. God is not an absentee Landlord, a First Cause existing in splendid unconcern for what happens in His world. He not only creates; He controls and upholds His world.

2. God as Personal, the Living God

God is not only a creative Power; He is supreme Personality. He plans, speaks, loves, chooses, jealously guards His people, and enters into a covenant with men. The God of the Old Testament is not a philosophical abstraction or a logical principle. He is the living God, an infinite Person. His highest creative act was the creation of finite persons in His own image, whose love and loyalty He desires.

We saw in Chapter III how quickly the God of creation (*Elohim,* translated "God" in Gen. 1:1—2:3) was recognized as the Lord God of redemption (*Yahweh,* or Jehovah, translated "Lord God" in Gen. 2:4 ff.). "The Lord God called unto Adam" (Gen. 3:9); "The Lord God said" (3:13); "The Lord God sent him forth" (3:23). It is impossible to read the Hebrew Scriptures without coming to the conviction that God is a divine Person, with the distinguishing personal marks of intelligence, self-direction, and self-awareness.

This is also indicated in the use of the term "the living God." Otto Babb observes:

> Perhaps the most typical word for identifying the God of the Old Testament is the word "living." The living God is the peculiar God of these writings. This signifies the God who acts in history, who performs mighty deeds of deliverance, and who manifests his power among men.[5]

It is true that in speaking of the living God the contrast most often drawn is with the baals who were represented by idols of wood and stone.[6] However, it also indicates the nature of God as One with whom personal relationships may be cherished. The living God, dwelling in the midst of His people, would drive out their enemies (Josh. 3:10). The devout soul yearns for communion with the living God:

> *As the hart panteth after the water brooks,*
> *So panteth my soul after thee, O God.*

[5]Baab, *op. cit.,* p. 24.
[6]*Ibid.,* pp. 26-29.

My soul thirsteth for God, for the living God:
When shall I come and appear before God? (Ps. 42:
1-2, ASV)

Hezekiah's hope when besieged by Sennacherib's army
was stated in his urgent message to Isaiah (II Kings 19:2-5).
It was in the fact that the Assyrians had dared to pit their
might against the living God: "It may be that the Lord thy
God will hear all the words of Rab-shakeh, whom the king of
Assyria his master hath sent to reproach the living God"
(19:4). Israel's great sin was not in forgetting an impersonal
Force, or a Power for righteousness. Jeremiah's charge was,
"Ye have perverted the words of the living God, of the Lord
of hosts our God" (Jer. 23:36). God who preserves His own
when no human hand can help is indeed worthy of reverent
awe. When Darius, pagan though he was, witnessed Daniel
unharmed in the den of lions, he said, "I make a decree, That
in every dominion of my kingdom men tremble and fear
before the God of Daniel: for he is the living God, and sted-
fast for ever, and his kingdom that which shall not be destroyed, and his dominion shall be even unto the end" (Dan.
6:26).

3. God as Self-revealing

The God of the Old Testament is not inscrutable Mystery,
before whom only a sentimental agnosticism is possible. He
is a God who reveals himself through nature, through angels,
through dreams and visions, through the prophetic consciousness, and through the great events of history. The vision of
the Creator-God contradicts naturalism in all its forms. The
concept of the personal, living God rules out an impersonal
pantheism. The idea of the self-revealing God does away
with agnosticism, the theory that the knowledge of God is
beyond the reach of human minds. Man may not know all
there is to the nature of an infinite God, but God can find
ways to communicate to finite minds such truth about himself
as is necessary for their well-being.

"Thus saith the Lord" comes very close to being a keynote to the entire Old Testament. It was not thought strange
that God would thus speak to men. To the writers of the Old
Testament the belief that God would reveal himself follows as

naturally from His creativity and personality as day follows the rising of the sun. From the Garden of Eden to the plains of Babylon, God made His will known to His chosen people.

Much of the self-revelation of God in the Old Testament is very simply but eloquently stated: "The Lord God said unto the woman" (Gen. 3:13); "The Lord said unto Cain" (4:6); "And God said unto Noah" (6:13); "Now the Lord had said unto Abram" (12:1); "And the Lord said unto Jacob" (31:3); etc. Concerning the form and manner of this speaking we are not told. That it was very real and personal we can have no doubt, for there are recorded instances of men arguing a point with the Lord, as when Abraham bargained for Lot's life (Gen. 18:17-33), or Moses protested his call to leadership (Exod. 3:4—4:17), or Jeremiah replied to God's prophetic call by reference to his youth and his difficulties as a public speaker (Jer. 1:4-9).

A common agent of divine revelation was the "angel of the Lord" (Gen. 16:7; Num. 22:35; Judg. 2:4; etc.), who in some instances is identified with God himself (Gen. 16:7, 13; 22:15-16; 48:15-16; etc.). Some have believed that these references refer to pre-incarnation appearances of the Logos, the Second Person of the Trinity. Others have seen in them a self-presentation of God, manifesting himself visibly to His creatures under a space-time form.[7]

Dreams and visions form still another mode of revelation in the Old Testament. Notable examples are Jacob's dream on his flight to Haran (Gen. 28:12-16); Joseph's dreams relating to his coming authority over his family (37:5-10); Pharaoh's dream as interpreted by Joseph (Genesis 41); and Nebuchadnezzar's dream and Daniel's interpretation (Daniel 2). Also prominent is the apocalyptic vision, examples of which are found in Daniel 7 and 8, and 10—12; Ezekiel; Jeremiah; and frequently throughout the minor prophets. Here the purposes of God, present and future, are made known by symbolic figures and events.

God's handiwork in nature, His supernaturally given law, His working in miracles and signs, His providential control

---

[7]Cf. the discussion in G. F. Oehler, *Theology of the Old Testament*, pp. 129-34.

of history, and the awakening of the prophetic consciousness are all additional ways in which He made himself known in the experiences of men.

4. The Holiness of God

From the very beginning the holiness of God is presented as the most wonderful aspect of His nature. The prophets, particularly Isaiah, knew the Lord as "the Holy One of Israel," a term they use no less than 30 times. The song of Moses after the deliverance from the land of Egypt contains the first reference to God's holiness, although the idea underlies all His dealings with men:

Who is like unto thee, O Jehovah, among the gods?
Who is like thee, glorious in holiness,
Fearful in praises, doing wonders? (Exod. 15:11, ASV)

When the ark of the covenant was brought to Jerusalem, King David commemorated the event with a psalm in which he exhorted: "Give unto the Lord the glory due unto his name: bring an offering, and come before him: worship the Lord in the beauty of holiness" (I Chron. 16:29; Ps. 16:8-9). Isaiah's sense of personal defilement came through his vision of God's holiness in the Temple: "Holy, holy, holy, is the Lord of hosts: the whole earth is full of his glory" (Isa. 6:3). "Holiness to the Lord" (Exod. 28:36; etc.) marked the vestment of the high priest; and that "holiness becometh thine house, O Lord, for ever" is declared by the Psalmist (Ps. 93:5).

The holiness of God stands for His supreme moral excellence, His total separation from all defilement and sin. It is not remoteness from human need and suffering, but describes a Being who is "uniquely and distinctively sacred and removed in kind from the secular aspects of life."[8] Borden Parker Bowne defines the divine holiness as ethical perfection. He says:

> Negatively, holiness implies the absence of all tendencies to evil and of all delight in evil. Positively, it involves delight in and devotion to goodness. The knowledge of evil must exist in the divine thought, but perfect holiness implies that it finds

[8]Baab, *op. cit.*, p. 34.

414 • *Exploring the Old Testament*

no echo in the divine sensibility and no realization in the divine
will. It further implies, positively, that in God the ideal of
moral perfection is realized; and this ideal involves love as one
of its chief factors.[9]

Because God is holy He cannot be pleased with unrigh-
teousness and rebellion in men. The entire Book of Leviticus
is a great object lesson teaching the holiness of God, and the
necessity for an atonement to satisfy the requirements of
God's holiness. The holiness of God is made the great in-
centive for the holiness of His people: "Speak unto all the
congregation of the children of Israel, and say unto them, Ye
shall be holy: for I the Lord your God am holy" (Lev. 19:2;
cf. 11:44-45; 20:26; and I Pet. 1:15-16).

5. *The Justice of God*

The Old Testament vision of God includes a strong sense
of the divine justice. It is never seen as a question of the
justice or righteousness of God versus His love and forgiveness. Justice, love, righteousness, and mercy are blended in
perfect symmetry in God's holiness.[10] "He is the Rock, his
work is perfect: for all his ways are judgment: a God of
truth and without iniquity, just and right is he" (Deut. 32:4).
"There is no God else beside me; a just God and a Saviour;
there is none beside me" (Isa. 45:21). "The just Lord is in
the midst thereof; he will not do iniquity: every morning doth
he bring his judgment to light, he faileth not" (Zeph. 3:5).
"Rejoice greatly, O daughter of Zion; shout, O daughter of
Jerusalem: behold, thy King cometh unto thee: he is just,
and having salvation; lowly, and riding upon an ass, and upon
a colt the foal of an ass" (Zech. 9:9). "Justice and judgment
are the habitation of thy throne: mercy and truth shall go
before thy face" (Ps. 89:14).

By virtue of His infinite justice, God is above all the unfailing Judge of human actions and attitudes. "Shall not
the Judge of all the earth do right?" (Gen. 18:25) "God is
a righteous judge, and God is angry with the wicked every
day" (Ps. 7:11, marg.). "For promotion cometh neither from
the east, nor from the west, nor from the south. But God is

---

[9]B. P. Bowne, *Theism*, p. 286, quoted by Knudson, *op. cit.*, p. 137.
[10]Robinson, *op. cit.*, p. 70.

the judge: he putteth down one, and setteth up another" (Ps. 75:6-7). Frequently we read of His righteous judgment: "And he shall judge the world in righteousness, he shall minister judgment to the people in uprightness" (Ps. 9:8); "He shall judge the people righteously" (96:10); and, "He shall judge the world with righteousness, and the people with his truth" (96:13).

The Old Testament is faithful to the twofold meaning of justice and judgment. It means to vindicate and reward those who are upright. "Judge me, O Lord, according to my righteousness, and according to mine integrity that is in me. Oh let the wickedness of the wicked come to an end; but establish the just: for the righteous God trieth the hearts and reins. My defence is of God, which saveth the upright in heart" (Ps. 7:8-10).

Justice also means the condemnation and punishment of the wicked. "Now is the end come upon thee, and I will send mine anger upon thee, and will judge thee according to thy ways, and will recompense upon thee all thine abominations" (Ezek. 7:3). "All the heathen shall see my judgment that I have executed, and my hand that I have laid upon them" (39:21).

6. God as a Merciful Redeemer

Many have pictured the God of the Old Testament as a God of justice and righteousness, inexorably executing judgment upon men as nations and individuals. By so doing they have all but obscured the equally prominent truth that God early revealed His redemptive purpose, and is a long-suffering and merciful Redeemer. Dr. G. E. Wright points out:

> There are three main themes running through the Old Testament, or for that matter, throughout the whole Bible: *God, human sin, and redemption.* For this reason the Cross has stood through the centuries and still stands today as the one symbol which adequately summarizes biblical religion. On the one hand, it illustrates the nature of human sin, sin which can crucify the Savior of this world. On the other, it represents the purpose and the power of God to redeem man from that sin—not necessarily to deliver him from the consequences of it but to lift him above the tragedy of it.[11]

[11]Wright, *op. cit.*, p. 19. Italics in the original.

The unfolding of God's purpose in salvation began with the very dawn of biblical history in the promise that the Seed of the Woman should bruise the serpent's head (Gen. 3:15), and in the receiving with favor of Abel's sacrificial lamb. The institution of the sacrifices and ceremonies of the priestly code, the care manifested by God in protecting His often-erring people, and particularly the message of the prophets, all add their evidence to support this view of the nature of God.

It is in the concept of the covenant that the vision of God's mercy and forgiveness finds its highest expression. "The book of the covenant" and "the blood of the covenant" (Exod. 24:7-8) testified to the special relationship which was to exist between God and His people. Because of His covenant promises, the Lord's mercy was made known. In the "Covenant Psalms" (Psalms 105—7) we read, "O give thanks unto the Lord, for he is good: for his mercy endureth for ever. Let the redeemed of the Lord say so, whom he hath redeemed from the hand of the enemy" (Ps. 107:1-2).

God is the Saviour of His people, redeeming, preserving, and protecting His own:

> But now thus saith the Lord that created thee, O Jacob, and he that formed thee, O Israel, Fear not: for I have redeemed thee, I have called thee by thy name; thou art mine. When thou passest through the waters, I will be with thee; and through the rivers, they shall not overflow thee: when thou walkest through the fire, thou shalt not be burned; neither shall the flame kindle upon thee. For I am the Lord thy God, the Holy One of Israel, thy Saviour: I gave Egypt for thy ransom, Ethiopia and Seba for thee. Since thou wast precious in my sight, thou hast been honourable, and I have loved thee: therefore will I give men for thee, and people for thy life (Isa. 43:1-4).

God's loving-kindness is extolled: "Shew thy marvellous lovingkindness, O thou that savest by thy right hand them that put their trust in thee from those that rise up against them" (Ps. 17:7). He is a God of compassion: "But thou, O Lord, art a God full of compassion, and gracious, longsuffering, and plenteous in mercy and truth" (Ps. 86:15). "His mercy endureth for ever" (I Chron. 16:34; etc.). The prophecy of Hosea is the lament of unrequited love, God's heart yearning after a wayward nation (Hos. 11:1-4). It is this divine faithfulness to an unfaithful people which brings the glorious promise of a New Covenant in Jer. 31:31-34.

7. God as Father

God as a divine Father is part of the Old Testament concept of God, though not as clear as it is in the New. Moses exhorts the Israelites to obedience and loyalty to God because He is the Father who has redeemed them: "Do ye thus requite the Lord, O foolish people and unwise? is not he thy father that hath bought thee? hath he not made thee, and established thee?" (Deut. 32:6) In a psalm credited to David at the moving of the ark we read:

Sing unto God, sing praises to his name:
Cast up a highway for him that rideth through the
  deserts;
His name is Jehovah; and exult ye before him.
A father of the fatherless, and a judge of the widows,
Is God in his holy habitation (Ps. 68:4-5, ASV).

In the Book of Consolation, Isaiah addresses the Lord in prayer, "Doubtless thou art our father, though Abraham be ignorant of us, and Israel acknowledge us not: thou, O Lord, art our father, our redeemer; thy name is from everlasting" (Isa. 63:16); "But now, O Lord, thou art our father; we are the clay, and thou our potter; and we all are the work of thy hand" (Isa. 64:8). Jeremiah says, "They shall come with weeping, and with supplications will I lead them: I will cause them to walk by the rivers of waters in a straight way, wherein they shall not stumble: for I am a father to Israel, and Ephraim is my firstborn" (Jer. 31:9; cf. 3:4, 19). Hosea gives God's promise, "Yet the number of the children of Israel shall be as the sand of the sea, which cannot be measured nor numbered; and it shall come to pass, that in the place where it was said unto them, Ye are not my people, there it shall be said unto them, Ye are the sons of the living God" (Hos. 1:10). Malachi urges God's fatherhood as a basis for honesty and integrity in the dealings of the people one with another: "Have we not all one father? hath not one God created us? why do we deal treacherously every man against his brother, by profaning the covenant of our fathers?" (Mal. 2:10)

II. A PHILOSOPHY OF HISTORY

Second only to the concept of God in the Old Testament, and in fact growing out of it, is the philosophy of history we find throughout its pages. In a most real sense of the word, history for the writers of the Hebrew scriptures was "History." Bernhard W. Anderson says, "Men remembered stories, treasured traditions, and wrote in various forms of literature because of one inescapable conviction: they had been confronted by God in events which had taken place in their history."[12] Professor Wright points out the God-centered view of history held by these men of old:

> It is thus evident that in the Old Testament there is little history for history's sake, but a religious interpretation of history in which there is a continuing encounter between men and God, an encounter which compels decision . . . They [the Old Testament writers] approached their task with a basic assumption. History is important because God *is;* he is its Ruler, the Determiner of its final issue, the One who gives it significance. He is to be found behind all the events of life, controlling them, revealing his will through them, and determined that he shall reign supreme in the hearts of men.[13]

Some of the leading ideas in the Old Testament philosophy of history are briefly summarized below.

1. *History Is Important*

Nowhere in the Old Testament do we find the skeptical view of history expressed by Hegel, "The only thing we can learn from history is that no one ever learns anything from history." History, for the people of the Old Testament, was worth recording. They were a commemorative people. They erected monuments to remind them of great events, as at the crossing of the Jordan (Josh. 4:9) and at the time of Samuel's great victory over the Philistines (I Sam. 7:12). They used

---

[12]B. W. Anderson, *Rediscovering the Bible,* p. 9.

[13]Wright, *op. cit.,* pp. 30-31.

commemorative names, as Jacob at Bethel (Gen. 28:17-19); and wrote commemorative poetry, as Moses at the Red Sea (Exodus 15) and Deborah and Barak when they won their notable victory over the Canaanites (Judges 5). They wrote genealogies as in Genesis, and chronicles such as "the book of the wars of the Lord" (Num. 21:14) and "the book of Jasher" (Josh. 10:13).

The actual writing of the history embodied in the Old Testament begins with Moses. God commanded Moses to write (Exod. 34:27), a command he faithfully obeyed. In their turn, prophets, priests, and kings took up the pen and recorded the events through which they lived or with which they were familiar.

The importance of the history recorded by men of the Old Testament lies, not in the recital of events, but in the meaning seen in those events. History is event plus meaning. As C. H. Dodd states, "According to the unanimous view of the biblical writers, the meaning of the events resides in a meeting of men with God." [14] For this reason, what we call "historical books" were classified by the Jews as "The Former Prophets," and large sections of the books of prophecy are recitals of historical events.

2. The Chosen Nation

God works in history through a chosen nation. From Genesis to Malachi the fact that Israel was God's chosen people is the guiding principle by which the events of history are interpreted. In the age of the patriarchs, Abraham was chosen and called to a special place of privilege and responsibility (Neh. 9:7-8). Isaac and not Ishmael, Jacob and not Esau, the nation Israel and not some other more powerful nation were chosen of God.

This divine choice was the basis for the separation of Israel from the idolatrous and wicked ways of other peoples:

> *For you are a people holy to the Lord your God;*
> *the Lord your God has chosen you to be a people for*
> *his own possession, out of all the peoples that are on*
> *the face of the earth. It was not because you were*

[14] C. H. Dodd, *The Bible Today*, p. 99.

> *more in number than any other people that the Lord*
> *set his love upon you and chose you, for you were*
> *the fewest of all peoples: but it is because the Lord*
> *loves you, and is keeping the oath which he swore to*
> *your fathers, that the Lord has brought you out with*
> *a mighty hand, and redeemed you from the house of*
> *bondage, from the hand of Pharaoh king of Egypt.*
> *Know therefore that the Lord your God is God, the*
> *faithful God who keeps covenant and stedfast love*
> *with those that love him and keep his command-*
> *ments, to a thousand generations* (Deut. 7:6-9, RSV).

Israel had need to be reminded that this great choice
on the part of God was an election to special responsibility,
not privilege alone. "You only have I known of all the
families of the earth: therefore I will punish you for all your
iniquities" (Amos 3:2). Much light means much responsibility, and special privilege always implies special obligation.

The faith of the prophets in the restoration of the people
after captivity had purged idolatry from their midst was
based upon the fact of the divine choice:

> *But thou, Israel, art my servant, Jacob whom I*
> *have chosen, the seed of Abraham my friend. Thou*
> *whom I have taken from the ends of the earth, and*
> *called thee from the chief men thereof, and said unto*
> *thee, Thou art my servant; I have chosen thee, and*
> *not cast thee away. Fear thou not; for I am with*
> *thee: be not dismayed; for I am thy God: I will*
> *strengthen thee; yea, I will help thee; yea, I will up-*
> *hold thee with the right hand of my righteousness*
> (Isa. 41:8-10).

3. The Anointed Leader

An important part of the Old Testament philosophy of
history is the place taken by the anointed of the Lord. Great
leaders, directed and inspired by God, are the key figures
in shaping the destiny of the chosen nation. Joseph, Moses,
Joshua, the judges, Samuel, Saul for a time, David, Solomon,
and many of the later kings loom large as particularly influential in making the nation what it became.

On occasion, one outside the nation might be specially directed in his choices and decisions. Cyrus, whose decree paved the way of Israel's return after the Captivity, was spoken of as the Lord's anointed (Isa. 45:1). Even after Saul had forfeited his right to the throne, David steadfastly refused to harm him on the ground that he was the Lord's anointed (I Sam. 24:10).

After the return from the Babylonian exile Zerubbabel and Joshua the high priest were spoken of as "the two anointed ones, that stand by the Lord of the whole earth" (Zech. 4:14). Preeminently, however, the term "the anointed" came to be used of the divine Deliverer on whom the hopes of the oppressed Jews began to rest. "Messiah" is the Hebrew term for "anointed," just as "Christ" is the Greek term for the same concept.

4. The Sovereign Providence of God

Already hinted in what has been said earlier is the great core concept in the Old Testament view of history: that its controlling forces come from a Source outside the stream of human actions and purposes. This is the belief that God is exercising sovereign control over the affairs of men, that "man proposes but God disposes." "The wrath of man shall praise thee," declares the Psalmist (Ps. 76:10). Joseph reminded his brothers, "But as for you, ye thought evil against me; but God meant it unto good, to bring to pass, as it is this day, to save much people alive" (Gen. 50:20). The rebellious rage of the Pharaoh of the Exodus was made to carry out the ultimate purpose of the Lord God of Israel (Exod. 9:16).

One of the cardinal ideas of the prophets was God's use of historical processes to punish and correct His people. The pagan peoples thus used were, of course, unaware that they were instruments in the hand of God:

> *O Assyrian, the rod of mine anger, and the staff in their hand is mine indignation. I will send him against an hypocritical nation, and against the people of my wrath will I give him a charge, to take the spoil, and to take the prey, and to tread them down like the mire of the streets. Howbeit he meaneth not*

so, neither doth his heart think so; but it is in his heart to destroy and cut off nations not a few. Wherefore it shall come to pass, that when the Lord hath performed his whole work upon mount Zion and on Jerusalem, I will punish the fruit of the stout heart of the king of Assyria, and the glory of his high looks. Shall the axe boast itself against him that heweth therewith? or shall the saw magnify itself against him that shaketh it? as if the rod should shake itself against them that lift it up, or as if the staff should lift up itself, as if it were no wood (Isa. 10: 5-7, 12, 15).

5. *Moral Responsibility*

The fact of God's providence and sovereign control of history must not blind us to the equally important fact of man's moral freedom. God's sovereignty establishes the limits of choice and the consequences of choice, but the choosing is the act of human self-determination, with which capacity God has endowed the human kind. The exercise of man's freedom does not limit the sovereignty of God but rather expresses it. C. H. Dodd has found three principles in the biblical philosophy of history which may aid us in understanding our own present situation in history:

1. God is sovereign over history, which serves His will and works out His purpose. This is presupposed all through.
2. On the other hand, the Bible lends no support to any theory which demands that the course of history should be fixed beforehand. . . .
3. The Bible contemplates man as morally responsible within the framework of the divine purpose. "See, I have set before thee this day life and good, and death and evil . . . Therefore choose!" (Deut. 30:15, 19). That the choice is real, and has real consequences in history, is a biblical postulate.[15]

The prophets were very sure of God's unfailing righteousness and justice. This is a universal principle which never changes. They were also very sure that sin and rebellion would lead only to death and destruction. Man does not "break" God's law; he only breaks himself upon it. Whether or not man shall defy God's righteous rule is within his power

[15]*Ibid.*, pp. 130-32.

to choose. What happens as the consequence of that choice is quite beyond the power of man to change. Thus the Old Testament prophets arrived at a true understanding of pre-destination and election. God has elected to salvation and eternal life those who will believe and obey Him. "Blessed is the nation whose God is the Lord" (Ps. 33:12). But, "The wicked shall be turned into hell, and all the nations that forget God" (Ps. 9:17).

III. A View of Human Nature and Need

The Old Testament gives us a priceless understanding of human nature and its need of redemption. Without delving into the technical details of Hebrew psychology, we may profit by a brief resumé of the teaching of the Old Testament scriptures concerning human nature.

1. *The Image of God*

The earliest statements concerning man are found in Gen. 1:26-28:

> *And God said, Let us make man in our image, after our likeness: and let them have dominion over the fish of the sea, and over the fowl of the air, and over the cattle, and over all the earth, and over every creeping thing that creepeth upon the earth. So God created man in his own image, in the image of God created he him; male and female created he them. And God blessed them, and God said unto them, Be fruitful, and multiply, and replenish the earth, and subdue it: and have dominion over the fish of the sea, and over the fowl of the air, and over every living thing that moveth upon the earth.*

Here the emphasis is upon the image of God. By virtue of this image, man is to have a place of authority in the world of nature (v. 27). His life is to be held inviolate by the same reason, for "whoso sheddeth man's blood, by man shall his blood be shed: for in the image of God made he man" (Gen. 9:6).

In Genesis 2 we learn that man in the image of God is "a living soul" (v. 7). The human body is "formed . . . of the dust of the ground" and inbreathed with the breath of life.

Here is found one of the greatest insights into human nature ever given. Man is a creature of two worlds. He is related to the realm of nature through his physical body, a creature of earth and time and space. Yet he is also a citizen of a moral and spiritual order, inbreathed by God, a living soul with capacities which transcend the realm of the earthly and the natural. Like lower forms of life, he breathes, eats, suffers, enjoys, bleeds, and dies. Yet in the image of God he reasons, imagines, hopes, aspires, purposes, is aware of his higher destiny even though but vaguely at times—and above all makes moral choices between good and evil, between God and the adversary. Little wonder, the awe of the Psalmist, "I am fearfully and wonderfully made" (Ps. 139:14), and:

> *When I consider thy heavens, the work of thy fingers,*
> *The moon and the stars, which thou hast ordained;*
> *What is man, that thou art mindful of him?*
> *And the son of man, that thou visitest him?*
> *For thou hast made him but little lower than the angels,*
> *And crownest him with glory and honor.*
> *Thou makest him to have dominion over the works of thy hands;*
> *Thou hast put all things under his feet:*
> *All sheep and oxen,*
> *Yea, and the beasts of the field,*
> *The birds of the heavens, and the fish of the sea,*
> *Whatsoever passeth through the paths of the seas.*
> *O Jehovah, our Lord,*
> *How excellent is thy name in all the earth!* (Ps. 8:3-9, ASV, marg.)

Thus man is body or flesh (Heb., *basar*), he is spirit or life (Heb., *ruach*), and these are together the psychophysical unity of a living soul (Heb., *nephesh*). The body or flesh, most closely related to the realm of matter, is not thought to be the seat or source of sin and evil as it was by many of the Greek philosophers. Evil does not arise from man's material nature, but from the misuse or misdirection of its drives and needs. That "the Word became flesh, and dwelt among us" (John 1:14) is the clearest possible proof that biblical writers do not regard the physical life of man as the necessary source of his moral evil.

2. *Freedom of Choice*

Growing out of the divine image is the recognition of moral freedom. Old Testament writers assumed both the sovereignty of God and the moral freedom of man. They found no contradiction between these great ideas, as indeed there is none when they are properly understood. As Albert C. Knudson has said:

> So far as human freedom is concerned, it is everywhere assumed in the Old Testament. It is not said that man is free; the more concrete expression is used, that man "chooses." But the idea is the same. Man is everywhere treated as morally responsible. His free will does not lie beyond the influence of the divine will, but it is a fact nevertheless quite as much as the divine influence itself. Had the Hebrew felt it necessary to choose between human freedom, on the one hand, and the divine sovereignty, on the other, it is possible that his choice might have fallen on the latter. But no such necessity presented itself to his mind. The freedom and responsibility of man stood as a fixed fact in his thought, and in so far as this was the case the ethical interests of religion were adequately safeguarded.[16]

Freedom and responsibility cannot be separated. From the account of the Fall in the Garden of Eden to the return of the exiles from their sojourn in Babylonia, it is assumed that human beings are responsible for the choices they make, and therefore free to choose without compulsion from without. This freedom, as we have seen, is not without its limits. Adam and Eve could choose between God's commandment and Satan's suggestion, but having chosen Satan's suggestion they were not free to choose to remain in the garden. Choices have consequences which follow inescapably.

The divine challenge to man always involves the fact of choice. Moses faced Israel with the words, "I call heaven and earth to record this day against you, that I have set before you life and death, blessing and cursing: therefore choose life, that both thou and thy seed may live" (Deut. 30:19). Joshua, Israel's second great leader, also said, "Choose you this day whom ye will serve; whether the gods which your fathers served that were on the other side of the flood, or the gods of the Amorites, in whose land ye dwell: but as

[16]Knudson, *op. cit.,* pp. 237-38.

for me and my house, we will serve the Lord" (Josh. 24:15). Heroic Elijah brought the same issue into focus when he asked, "How long halt ye between two opinions?" (I Kings 18: 21) The call of the prophets was summed up in Jeremiah's terse exhortation, "Therefore now amend your ways and your doings, and obey the voice of the Lord your God" (Jer. 26: 13). No subtle fatalism, be it the naturalistic behaviorism of Watson or the theological determinism of John Calvin, can set aside the clear teaching of the Old Testament that human beings are capable of real choice between alternatives, and are personally responsible for the consequences of their choices.

3. *The Sinful Nature of Man*

The Old Testament not only pictures human nature with freedom of choice and in the image of God; it also recognizes that the divine image in man is marred by sin. In the Garden, Adam and Eve forfeited what theologians call "the moral image of God" while retaining much of the "natural image of God." This means that sin robbed the race of the initial holiness with which it had been created, and left man's moral nature deprived of the presence of the Holy Spirit, estranged from God, and hence depraved and sinful. The tragic truth is that there was a double consequence of Adam's sin. First, he was no longer able to transmit a righteousness which he had so sadly lost; and second, because of his disobedience a nature deprived of the moral image of God, and hence depraved and inclined to sin, was passed on as the bitter heritage of every child born of the human race. Therefore we read that "Adam . . . begat a son in his own likeness, after his image" (Gen. 5:3).

Thereafter the universal extent of sin is recognized throughout the Old Testament. "God saw that the wickedness of man was great in the earth, and that every imagination of the thoughts of his heart was only evil continually" (Gen. 6:5). "There is no man that sinneth not" (I Kings 8:46).

The fool hath said in his heart, There is no God.
They are corrupt, they have done abominable works;
There is none that doeth good.

*Jehovah looked down from heaven upon the children
    of men,
To see if there were any that did understand,
That did seek after God.
They are all gone aside; they are together become
    filthy;
There is none that doeth good, no not one* (Ps. 14:
1-3, ASV; cf. also Ps. 53:1-3).

The problem is not only what man does. The deeper
problem lies in what he is. Consider Isaiah's vivid description
of human corruption:

*Hear, O heavens, and give ear, O earth: for the
Lord hath spoken, I have nourished and brought up
children, and they have rebelled against me. The ox
knoweth his owner, and the ass his master's crib: but
Israel doth not know, my people doth not consider.
Ah sinful nation, a people laden with iniquity, a seed
of evildoers, children that are corrupters: they have
forsaken the Lord, they have provoked the Holy One
of Israel unto anger, they are gone away backward.
Why should ye be stricken any more? ye will
revolt more and more: the whole head is sick, and the
whole heart faint. From the sole of the foot even
unto the head there is no soundness in it; but wounds,
and bruises, and putrifying sores: they have not been
closed, neither bound up, neither mollified with oint-
ment* (Isa. 1:2-6).

The prophet himself stands convicted of his own sin-
tainted nature when he sees God's holiness in all its glory:
"Woe is me! for I am undone; because I am a man of unclean
lips, and I dwell in the midst of a people of unclean lips"
(Isa. 6:5). He found a cure only in the symbolic act of the
seraph in touching his lips with a living coal from the altar,
saying, "Thine iniquity is taken away, and thy sin purged"
(v. 7).

This sinful nature, manifest in sinful acts, is not acquired
but is inherent in the natural man from birth. The Book of
Job provides us with a searching analysis of the nature of sin
as it is related to suffering. Job and his "comforters" are

often at odds. However they agree as to the inherited character of the carnal nature. Job says, "Man that is born of a woman is of few days, and full of trouble. Who can bring a clean thing out of an unclean? not one" (Job 14:1, 4). Eliphaz also states, "What is man, that he should be clean? and he which is born of a woman, that he should be righteous?" (Job 15:14) Bildad echoes the same thought, "How then can man be justified with God? or how can he be clean that is born of a woman? Behold even to the moon, and it shineth not; yea, the stars are not pure in his sight. How much less man, that is a worm? and the son of man, which is a worm?" (Job 25:4-6) David, in his great penitential psalm, says, "Behold, I was shapen in iniquity; and in sin did my mother conceive me" (Ps. 51:5).

So deep and so radical is this evil in human nature that man unaided cannot escape its power. This is the dilemma of the Old Testament. It sees clearly the justice of God's law, but it also feels keenly human inability to keep the law. "Can the Ethiopian change his skin, or the leopard his spots? then may ye also do good, that are accustomed to do evil" (Jer. 13:23). "The heart is deceitful above all things, and desperately wicked: who can know it?" (Jer. 17:9) As we noted in Chapter XIV, the hope of deliverance is from above, in promise of a New Covenant to be fulfilled in the gospel age with its assurance of forgiveness and a renewal of heart (Jer. 31:31-34). Both Ezekiel (36:25-28) and Malachi (3:1-3) definitely teach the complete cleansing provided in the sanctifying fullness of the Holy Spirit. A study of the scriptural texts used by John Wesley in support of the doctrine of entire sanctification shows his frequent use of Ezek. 36:25-26, 29 in this connection.

IV. A PROMISE OF REDEMPTION

Following the diagnosis of man's disease comes the assurance of a divine remedy. Thus, the great theme of the Old Testament is the promise of redemption, expressed in what is known as the Messianic hope—a vision which became increasingly important as the centuries went by.

Mention has previously been made of the fact that the Old Testament is an unfinished volume. It ends with a promise and a prediction. If we had no contact at all with Christianity and were handed a copy of the Hebrew Scriptures, we should feel that we had been given an account for which there must be a sequel. It could not end where it does. There must be something more to complete the history, to fulfill the prophecy, and to fill in the outlines of the theology. We should need to learn the outcome of the great transition from an earthly kingdom to a kingdom of God, at which transition point the Old Testament ends. Political sovereignty had been lost, and spiritual adequacy was yet to be gained. God had appeared to His people in historical events which were still moving to a grand climax beyond the horizon.

1. A Spiritual Kingdom

Liberal scholars have generally held the theory that the Messianic hope grew out of the patriotic longing of the Jewish people for a restoration of their earthly sovereignty. When such a restoration was seen to be impossible in any foreseeable future, it was then projected into a more distant time.

Such a theory, however, ignores the Old Testament vision of the nature of God's kingdom. It was to be ethical and spiritual, established over all the earth, blessing and permeating all nations.[17] In it lies the hope of man, for only God can break the deadly cycle of sin, judgment, redemption, and sin again. Here we are dealing with more than the extension of nationalistic dreams. Here is a grasp, however limited, of the true kingdom of God.

Scores of references could be given wherein God is shown to be the true King. The psalms are replete with them:

Hearken unto the voice of my cry, my King, and my God;
For unto thee do I pray (Ps. 5:2, ASV).

Jehovah is King for ever and ever:
The nations are perished out of his land (10:16, ASV).

Thou art my King, O God:
Command deliverance for Jacob (44:4, ASV).

[17]Cf. Baab, *op. cit.*, Ch. 6, "The Kingdom of God," especially pp. 162-65 and 180-86.

> *Sing praises to God, sing praises:*
> *Sing praises to our King, sing praises.*
> *For God is the King of all the earth:*
> *Sing ye praises with understanding.*
> *God reigneth over the nations:*
> *God sitteth upon his holy throne* (47: 6-8, ASV).

Isaiah viewed his God as King. In his vision in the Temple he says, "Mine eyes have seen the King, the Lord of hosts" (Isa. 6:5). Salvation comes from God the King: "For the Lord is our judge, the Lord is our lawgiver, the Lord is our king; he will save us" (33:22). God is the "King of Jacob" (41:21), "the creator of Israel, your King" (43:15). Jeremiah proclaims God as "the living God, and an everlasting king" (10:10), and "the King, whose name is the Lord of hosts" (46:18; 48:15; 51:57). In the Book of Daniel, King Nebuchadnezzar of Babylon is brought to "praise and extol and honour the King of heaven, all whose works are truth, and his ways judgment" (4:37). And Zechariah predicts, "The Lord shall be king over all the earth" (Zech. 14:9).

God's kingdom is an order based on perfect justice, an ideal not attainable by men. It is only the Branch out of the root of Jesse (Isa. 11:1) of whom it is said that He

> . . . *shall not judge after the sight of his eyes,*
> *neither reprove after the hearing of his ears: but*
> *with righteousness shall he judge the poor, and re-*
> *prove with equity for the meek of the earth: and he*
> *shall smite the earth with the rod of his mouth, and*
> *with the breath of his lips shall he slay the wicked.*
> *And righteousness shall be the girdle of his loins, and*
> *faithfulness the girdle of his reins* (Isa. 11: 3-5).

Nor is the Kingdom the exclusive thing some of the people of God made it to be, as witness the words of Micah:

> *But in the last days it shall come to pass, that the*
> *mountain of the house of the Lord shall be established*
> *in the top of the mountains, and it shall be exalted*
> *above the hills; and people shall flow unto it. And*
> *many nations shall come, and say, Come, and let us*
> *go up to the mountain of the Lord, and to the house*
> *of the God of Jacob; and he will teach us of his ways,*

and we will walk in his paths: for the law shall go forth of Zion, and the word of the Lord from Jerusalem. And he shall judge among many people, and rebuke strong nations afar off; and they shall beat their swords into plowshares, and their spears into pruninghooks: nation shall not lift up a sword against nation, neither shall they learn war any more (Mic. 4:1-3; cf. Isa. 2:4).

Many other proofs of the universal extent of God's true kingdom could be given. Psalms 22 is one of the great Messianic psalms. Here we read:

All the ends of the world shall remember and turn unto the Lord: and all the kindreds of the nations shall worship before thee. For the kingdom is the Lord's: and he is the governor among the nations (vv. 27-28).

God's way of salvation is to be known among all nations:

God be merciful unto us, and bless us,
And cause his face to shine upon us;
That thy way may be known upon earth,
Thy salvation among all nations (Ps. 67:1-2, ASV).

2. *"Messiah the Prince"* (Dan. 9:25)

The Kingdom awaits the coming of the King. Much has been written on the Messianic hope of the Old Testament, and need not be repeated here. We have already seen that the Hebrew term "Messiah" and the Greek term "Christ" are the same in meaning, and signify "the anointed one." This exalted title, earlier given to kings and prophets (I Sam. 12:3, 5; 24:6, 10; I Chron. 16:22; etc.), came to be used of Him who should come to deliver and redeem His people (Zech. 9:9; Mal. 3:1-4; etc.). A very early such use is found in the prayer of Hannah, Samuel's mother, many years before there was a king in Israel: "The adversaries of the Lord shall be broken to pieces; out of heaven shall he thunder upon them: the Lord shall judge the ends of the earth; and he shall give strength unto his king, and exalt the horn of his anointed [Heb., Messiah]" (I Sam. 2:10). In the Messiah are found the climax and destiny of all history. Interpreting Nebuchadnezzar's prophetic dream (Dan. 2:31-45), Daniel spoke of the kings of the last days:

> *And in the days of these kings shall the God of heaven set up a kingdom, which shall never be destroyed: and the kingdom shall not be left to other people, but it shall break in pieces and consume all these kingdoms, and it shall stand for ever. Forasmuch as thou sawest that the stone was cut out of the mountain without hands, and that it brake in pieces the iron, the brass, the clay, the silver, and the gold; the great God hath made known to the king what shall come to pass hereafter: and the dream is certain, and the interpretation thereof sure* (Dan. 2:44-45).

The coming Deliverer is described as a Prince (Dan. 9:25), a King (Zech. 9:9), a Ruler in Israel (Mic. 5:2), the Prince of Peace (Isa. 9:6), the suffering Servant (Isa. 52:13—53:12). He is to be of the line of David (Jer. 23:5), and at the same time He is to be called "The Lord our Righteousness" (v. 6) and "The mighty God, The everlasting Father" (Isa. 9:6; see also v. 7). His triumph, as noted in our study of Isaiah 53 in Chapter XIII, is through suffering and death (vv. 7-9), rejected by His own (vv. 2-3).[18]

The last book of the Old Testament brings to a climax this great redemptive hope:

> *Behold, I will send my messenger, and he shall prepare the way before me: and the Lord, whom ye seek, shall suddenly come to his temple, even the messenger of the covenant, whom ye delight in: behold, he shall come, saith the Lord of hosts. But who may abide the day of his coming? and who shall stand when he appeareth? for he is like a refiner's fire, and like fullers' soap: and he shall sit as a refiner and purifier of silver: and he shall purify the sons of Levi, and purge them as gold and silver, that they may offer unto the Lord an offering in righteousness* (Mal. 3:1-3).

[18]Cf. the complete review of Old Testament prophecies of Christ in John R. Sampey, *Syllabus for Old Testament Study*, pp. 276-91.

> *But unto you that fear my name shall the Sun of*
> *righteousness arise with healing in his wings; and ye*
> *shall go forth, and grow up as calves of the stall*
> *(4: 2).*

V. A SOURCE BOOK OF LIFE

Our last section deals with the use of the Old Testament in the teaching of the Bible. This great portion of God's Word affords a wealth of source materials of great value for the teacher who wishes to come to grips with the basic issues of life. No one can teach religion adequately who is not thoroughly familiar with these resources. To describe them fully would be to repeat much of what has filled the preceding chapters of this book. Our suggestions here will be directed toward the effective use of Old Testament materials in teaching the religion of the Bible.

1. *The Teacher's Knowledge of the Old Testament*

The proper use of Old Testament materials depends upon a thorough knowledge of the Book. A casual reading of its pages is not enough. He who would teach must first be a learner. Effective teaching demands the ability to relate each part to its larger whole. This means that the teacher's acquaintance with his subject matter must be larger than the single topic or lesson he may undertake to teach at any one time.

The value of such a survey of the Old Testament as has been attempted here is that it provides a framework within which each section may be located. The teacher of the Old Testament should possess an outline knowledge of the whole book. He should know the major periods of Old Testament history, and the leading figures and events of each. He should know the relationship of the books of the Old Testament to the historical outline. He should know the various types of literature found in the Old Testament, and the values to be discovered in each.

In addition to an outline knowledge of the whole book, the teacher needs a detailed knowledge of the particular portion or portions to be taught. General information can never take the place of a grasp of details. When events are being studied, a knowledge of background materials is important. The teacher should attempt to "feel himself" into the historical context, and into the attitudes, actions, and circumstances of the people involved. In portions of the Old Testament given to instruction, the teacher must seek to find the meanings and implications of each statement. There are no wasted words in the Bible.

Above all, the teacher must seek by every possible means to make the Old Testament live for his pupils. He must apply its teachings to the circumstances of those whom he teaches. He must retell its great message in language which falls within the range of experience of those he seeks to instruct. Herein lies the art of effective teaching.

An interesting example is found in Anne Lindbergh's account of a visit to an Eskimo church service conducted by a missionary in a little white frame church at Point Barrow:

> But nothing distracted the congregation. Men, women, and children leaned forward earnestly watching the minister. Many could not understand English. Even those who had learned it in school days were bewildered by psalms sung by a shepherd on a sun-parched hillside.
>
> " 'We have gone astray like sheep,' " began the reading. Sheep, what did that mean to them? I saw stony New England pastures and those gray backs moving among blueberry bushes and junipers.
>
> "Like the reindeer," explained the minister, "who have scattered on the tundras." The listening heads moved. They understood reindeer.
>
> " 'Your garners will be filled.' " Big red barns, I saw, and hay wagons rumbling uphill. But the Eskimos? "Your meat cellars," the minister answered my question, "will be full of reindeer meat."
>
> " 'Your oxen will be strong,' " read the next verse. "Your dogs for your dog teams will pull hard," continued the minister. " 'The power of God.' " How could he explain that abstract word *Power*?
>
> "Sometimes when the men are whaling," he started, "the boats get caught in the ice. We have to take dynamite and break up the ice to let them out. That is power—dynamite—"the dynamite of God."
>
> "For Thine is the Kingdom, 'the dynamite,' and the Glory forever and ever. Amen," I said over to myself.[19]

[19] Anne Lindbergh, *North to the Orient* (New York: Harcourt, Brace & Co., 1935), pp. 106-7. Part of this is quoted in Park Hays Miller, *How to Study and Use the Bible*, pp. 134-35.

All Scripture was written *to* a particular group; but all was written *for* our profit and understanding. To lift the great eternal truths from the passing and incidental circumstances of a far-off age and let their clear light shine upon the conditions of modern life is both the glory and the power of good teaching. Such teaching requires thoughtful preparation, but it is rewarding in both interest and effectiveness.

2. The Doctrinal Use of the Old Testament

The Christian teacher will not ignore the doctrinal values of the Old Testament. There is little in the New Testament which does not have its foundations in the teachings of the Old Testament. As has been said, the Sermon on the Mount is almost wholly drawn from Old Testament sources. The amazement of the people (Matt. 7:28-29) was not at the novelty of the teaching but the evident authority with which it was given. The scribes had said many of the same things, but Jesus spoke with the ring of divine authority and the old truths sounded new.

It will be recognized that the fruit and flower of Bible truth is found in the New Testament. Thus all Old Testament teaching must be related to its outcomes in the gospel. However the advantage of beginning with the Old Testament lies in the relative simplicity with which truth is there presented. Just as the individual human mind must be schooled in the simpler truths before it is capable of grasping abstract principles, so God revealed himself in more concrete terms in the Old Testament. Truth is acted out in ceremony, symbol, and event. It is presented in such ways that it grips the attention and stirs the imagination. It is, as Paul suggested, "our schoolmaster to bring us unto Christ" (Gal. 3:24).

3. The Illustrative Value of the Old Testament

It is in its wealth of illustrative material that the Old Testament excels as a source book for the Christian teacher. New Testament writers themselves made extensive use of its illustrative values. Jesus referred to the martyrdom of Zechariah as an example of the contempt in which God's messengers were held by the leaders of their own time (Luke 11:50-51). He used the record of Jonah's deliverance from the great fish to illustrate the length of His own burial and subsequent resurrection (Matt. 12:40). Paul illustrated the doctrine of justification by grace through faith with a reference to Sarah and Hagar and their sons, Isaac and Ishmael (Gal. 4:22-25). Peter drew a vivid analogy between the fate of the ancient world during Noah's time and the destruction of Sodom and Gomorrah, and the judgments which are to be visited upon people of wicked character in our own age (II Pet. 2:5-10). Many other examples may be listed.

The illustrative values of the Old Testament are found in a variety of kinds of subject matter. Biographies, historical events, ceremonies, typical persons and places, all provide materials for the teacher's use. Almost every theme of importance in the Christian life and faith may be illustrated from the pages of the Old Testament. As Dr. Scroggie has so well summarized:

> Here the foundations of religion are laid in the revelation of the one and only true God. Here the sin-blight with its origin and development is disclosed, the curse which separates men from God. Here is clearly taught the utter inability of the law to bring to man the salvation he needs. Here is anticipated the saving purpose and plan of God, in prophecies and types. Here the Savior Himself is promised, the Son, the Servant, the Prophet, the Priest, and the King. Here we find men at grips with great moral problems, such as of sin, and of suffering. Here is made evident the immanence of God in history, and the fact that a principle of righteousness underlies universal government. Here all the chords of the human heart are swept in immortal songs. And here we learn of the rise and progress of that People to whom God was pleased to reveal His purpose, and by whom He is fulfilling it through Jesus Christ.[20]

SUMMARY

In this closing chapter we have endeavored to survey the abiding message and meaning of the Old Testament. The Old Testament finds its fulfillment in the New, but it yet offers much of unending value. Its concept of God, its philosophy of history, its penetrating analysis of human nature, its redemptive hope, and its resources for the teaching of religion, all offer ample rewards to the careful student. What has been attempted in this book is only an introduction. The

[20]W. G. Scroggie, *Know Your Bible*, I, 13-14.

broad outlines have been sketched in. It should now be the ambition of every reader to cultivate an extensive acquaintance with this great portion of God's Word, filling in the limitless wealth of detail. Let yours be the wisdom and prayer of the ancient poet:

> *Wherewith shall a young man cleanse his way?*
> *By taking heed thereto according to thy word.*
> *With my whole heart have I sought thee:*
> *Oh let me not wander from thy commandments.*
> *Thy word have I laid up in my heart,*
> *That I might not sin against thee.*
> *Blessed art thou, O Jehovah:*
> *Teach me thy statutes.*
> *With my lips have I declared*
> *All the ordinances of thy mouth.*
> *I have rejoiced in the way of thy testimonies,*
> *As much as in all riches.*
> *I will meditate on thy precepts,*
> *And have respect unto thy ways.*
> *I will delight myself in thy statutes:*
> *I will not forget thy word* (Ps. 119: 9-16, ASV).

RECOMMENDED READINGS

Otto J. Baab, *The Theology of the Old Testament,* pp. 23-53.

C. H. Dodd, *The Bible Today,* pp. 122-43.

Albert C. Knudson, *The Religious Teaching of the Old Testament,* pp. 137-72.

Park Hays Miller, *How to Study and Use the Bible,* pp. 120-40.

G. F. Oehler, *Theology of the Old Testament,* pp. 437-536.

George L. Robinson, "The Abiding Value of the Old Testament," in Barbour, *The Bible in the World of Today,* pp. 127-48.

H. Wheeler Robinson, *The Religious Ideas of the Old Testament,* pp. 154-83.

John R. Sampey, *Syllabus for Old Testament Study,* pp. 260-91.

Norman H. Snaith, *The Distinctive Ideas of the Old Testament,* pp. 9-242.

G. Ernest Wright, *The Challenge of Israel's Faith.*

FOR FURTHER STUDY

1. In what sense is the Old Testament an incomplete book? To what event does it look ahead?

2. What is said to be the central concept of the Old Testament?

3. Comment on the teaching of the Old Testament regarding the origin of the world and its inhabitants. What is meant by calling this "theism"?

4. What do you understand by the designation "The living God"?

5. How did God reveal himself to men of old?

6. What is the first biblical reference to God's holiness? Show how the holiness of God is related to the holiness of God's people.

7. What is said concerning God's justice versus His love and mercy? Note the twofold meaning of judgment.

8. Comment on the statement, "The Cross . . . stands today as the one symbol which adequately summarizes biblical religion." What has the Old Testament to say about God as Redeemer?

9. How does the idea of the covenant between God and His people reveal God's nature and purpose?

10. Summarize the Hebrew attitude toward history. How would you say it compares with modern views?

11. How does the idea of the chosen nation play a part in Israel's concept of history? What is the part of "the anointed"?

12. Can you reconcile the providence of God with the freedom and responsibility of man?

13. Discuss the statement, "Man is a creature of two worlds."

14. Summarize the teaching of the Old Testament concerning the freedom of man, and the sinfulness of human nature. What does it have to say about deliverance from sin?

15. What evidence may be given to support the belief that the Old Testament doctrine of the kingdom of God included more than a restoration of David's kingdom?

16. What is the place of the Messiah in the kingdom of God? Is there anything to show that the Messiah must die an atoning death before His final victory?

17. What was Malachi's contribution to the redemptive promise of the Old Testament?

18. What may be said concerning a teacher's knowledge of the Bible? Wherein lies the art of effective teaching?

19. List the doctrinal and illustrative values of the Old Testament.

APPENDIX I

CHRONOLOGICAL TABLE OF OLD TESTAMENT HISTORY
With Collateral References to Contemporary Events

Period I. Primeval Age, to about 2100 B.C. (Genesis 1—11)
    (a) Antediluvian period, to about 3500 B.C.
    (b) Postdiluvian period, c. 3500—c. 2100 B.C.

DATE (B.C.)	EGYPT	O.T. NARRATIVE	BABYLONIA-ASSYRIA, ETC.
Before 5000		Creation of Man (If the Septuagint text is followed, which allows about 2,250 years for the antediluvian period, a date may be computed as	
5000-3400 (?)	Predynastic period (not much known of this period).	early as 5650 B.C., which is easily reconciled with the earliest discoveries in either Egypt or Babylonia. Estimates of conservative scholars vary between 8000 and 5000 B.C. See especially Free, "Archaeology and Bible History," pp. 16-18.)	Earliest evidences of civilization 5000 B.C. or earlier in the region of Shinar (south Babylonia).
4500 (?)			Earliest city kingdoms.
4000 (?)			Foundation of Babylon (?) Pre-Flood writing (?)
3500 (?)		The Great Flood (The period from the Flood to the call of Abraham is over 1,300 years according to the Septuagint. Adding this figure to the earlier date for Abraham, as given below, we get 3400 B.C. For estimate of archaeologists see column on the right.)	Clear evidences of a flood in two widely separated places in Babylonia, Ur in the south and Kish in the north, were found by different archaeologists at almost the same time (1929). Estimated date about 3500 B.C. (Woolley)

439

DATE (B.C.)	EGYPT	O.T. NARRATIVE	BABYLONIA-ASSYRIA, ETC.
3400-3000 (?)	Archaic period. First two dynasties (capital at Memphis).		Early writing (pictographic).
c. 3000-2160	Old Kingdom (Dynasties III-X). Great pyramids, especially at Gizeh, 3000-2500.		Nineveh founded by colonists from Babylonia, c. 3000.
c. 2900			First dynasty of kings at Ur c. 2900. Marks of an advanced civilization.
c. 2700			Sargon I, the Akkadian, first powerful king at Babylon, c. 2700.
c. 2500-2160	Dark period. Collapse of Memphis. Temporary capital at Heliopolis		Asshur founded by Babylonian colonists, c. 2500.
c. 2400	(On, in story of Joseph).	Tower of Babel (??). Cf. "ziggurats" in Babylonia at this period.	Ur rises to power over Babylonian cities for a short time about 2400 (civilization Sumerian, i.e., from Sumer or Shinar). Cuneiform invented.
c. 2300			Ziggurats or temple-towers common in Babylonia from this time, e.g., at Ur, built about 2300 B.C.
c. 2160	Beginning of the Middle Kingdom with capital at Thebes.		

Period II. Patriarchal Period, c. 2100—c. 1850 B.C.

(Genesis 12—50)

In the chronology of this period and of the following period much depends on the interpretation of the passages (Gen. 15:13; Exod. 12:40; Acts 7:6; and Gal. 3:17) in which 400 years or 430 years of bondage are mentioned. The earlier date for Abraham allows for 430 years from Jacob's going down to Egypt to the Exodus under Moses. The later date is based on Gal. 3:17, where it would seem that the 430 years was counted from the giving of the promise to Abraham. The dates given by archaeologists for Hammurabi (Amraphel, Genesis 14?), a contemporary of Abraham, vary from about 2550 to 1700 B.C., but there is some quite recent agreement on a date close to 2050 B.C., confirming the earlier date for Abraham.

DATE (B.C.)	EGYPT	O.T. NARRATIVE		BABYLONIA-ASSYRIA, ETC.
c. 2160-1788	Middle Kingdom (Dynasties XI-XII), with capital at Thebes (No Amon in O.T.).	Early date	Later date (see explanation above)	
c. 2100				Old Babylonian Empire under Hammurabi (Amraphel, Genesis 14?) including Elam (and lands to Mediterranean?). Hammurabi's Code, discovered in 1902, has many common elements with Hebrew laws and customs.
c. 2091	Hyksos kings perhaps already in power. Abraham visits Egypt in early part of this period and Jacob's family migrate to Egypt in the later part.	Call of Abraham 2091	1876	
c. 2066		Birth of Isaac 2066	1851	
c. 2006		Birth of Jacob 2006	1791	
c. 2000	Thebes gives way to new (Hyksos?) capitals.			Archaeological discoveries, especially at Mari and Nuzi, have proven the existence of patriarchal life and customs, as described in the Old Testament, throughout the period 2000 to 1700 B.C. See "Westminster Atlas" and recent archaeological manuals.
c. 1991		Death of Abraham 1991	1776	
c. 1915		Birth of Joseph 1915	1700	
c. 1876	Hebrews from Palestine settle in northern Egypt (Goshen, in the Delta of the Nile).	Migration of Jacob's family to Egypt. 1876	1661	
c. 1859		Death of Jacob		

441

DATE (B.C.)	EGYPT	O.T. NARRATIVE	BABYLONIA-ASSYRIA, ETC.
c. 1805		Death of Joseph	Assyrian kingdom arises with capital at Asshur, 1800 B.C. (?).
c. 1788-1580	Second dark period. Hyksos kings in power. Children of Israel in Land of Goshen. (D. XIII-XVII)		
c. 1580	Hyksos kings driven out. Empire established by Ahmosis I (Dynasty XVIII). The new native Egyptian rulers were unsympathetic with the Semites who had come in under the Hyksos (Semitic) rulers.	"There arose up a new king . . . which knew not Joseph. And he . . . set over them taskmasters to · afflict them."	
c. 1525		Birth of Moses, who was rescued as an infant by Pharaoh's daughter.	
c. 1500			Height of early Cretan civilization as revealed at Cnossos.
1501-1447	Thothmes III, "Pharaoh of the Oppression" according to most conservative critics. Conquest of Syria and Palestine. Queen Hatshetsup, "Pharaoh's daughter" (?).	Moses as a youth brought into the court of Pharaoh.	
c. 1485		Flees into the desert after killing an Egyptian.	

Period IV. Exodus and Wilderness Wanderings, c. 1450—1400 B.C.

(Exodus 12—40; Leviticus; Numbers; Deuteronomy)

The date of the Exodus is computed on the basis of I Kings 6:1, where 480 (i.e., 479) years is given as the time from the Exodus to the building of Solomon's Temple, of which the probable date is 967 B.C. Archaelogical discoveries at Jericho have satisfactorily substantiated the date of the taking of Jericho according to this computation (about 1400 B.C.). Many otherwise conservative scholars of a generation ago, and some of recent years, have felt compelled to abandon biblical figures and on archaeological grounds to set a date for the Exodus somewhere in the thirteenth century, reducing the period of the Judges to less than 200 years. This procedure, in view of the most recent evidence, seems no longer tc be necessary and we may affirm with confidence the historicitv of the Bible, insofar as the original text can be established.

DATE (B.C.)	EGYPT	O.T. NARRATIVE	BABYLONIA-ASSYRIA, ETC.
c. 1447-1423	Amenhotep II, "Pharaoh of the Exodus" (?).	Moses returns to champion the cause of his oppressed people.	
c. 1446		Exodus under Moses.	
c. 1445		Giving of the Law at Mount Sinai. Building of the Tabernacle.	
c. 1445-1407		Thirty-eight years of wandering in the Wilderness of Paran, with Kadesh-barnea as their principal base.	
1423-1377	Period of weak rule in Egypt under Thothmes IV and Amenhotep		
c. 1407		The Israelites arrive in Moab. Campaigns against the Amorites and Midianites. Death of Moses.	

Period V. Conquest and Settlement, c. 1400—1350 B.C. (Joshua)

c. 1400-1360	Tel el-Amarna Tablets: "Habiri" enter Palestine. Conditions de-	Crossing of the Jordan. Destruction of Jericho (about 1400 B.C. ac-	

DATE (B.C.)	EGYPT	O.T. NARRATIVE	BABYLONIA-ASSYRIA, ETC.
	scribed tally with those recorded in the Bible.	cording to Garstang's excavations at Jericho. Cf. "Westminster Atlas," pp. 15 and 39.)	
c. 1400-1375		Conquest of Canaan under Joshua. (See Josephus, "Antiquities," V. 1, 29.)	Hittites win powerful empire in region of Asia Minor.
c. 1375-1350	Period of greatest splendor of the empire under Ikhnaton (Akhenaton) and Tutankhamen.	Death of Joshua, c. 1375.	
c. 1370		"And Israel served the Lord all the days of Joshua, and all the days of the elders that overlived Joshua."	Hittites conquer Mitannians and take over northern Mesopotamia and Syria, c. 1370.

Period VI. Period of Judges, c. 1350—c. 1050 B.C.
(Judges; Ruth; I Samuel 1—7)

The exact duration of the Period of Judges is not known. The years assigned in the Book of Judges to the oppressions and to the judges with the periods of rest total 410. But it is likely that there was considerable overlapping, since the land was not united and the jurisdiction of the judges referred to was therefore local. Toward the end of the period Jephthah (c. 1100) mentions a period of 300 years (Judg. 11:26) since the conquest of the Amorites under Sihon (c. 1400). This seems to correspond well enough to the 480 years mentioned in I Kings 6:1 as the length of the period from the Exodus to the building of the Temple (c. 1446—c. 967 B.C.).

DATE (B.C.)	EGYPT	O.T. NARRATIVE	BABYLONIA-ASSYRIA, ETC.
c. 1350-1150	Second period of the Empire (XIXth and XXth dynasties).	Othniel: first of the "judges," delivers the people from the oppression of the Mesopotamians.	
c. 1300			Shalmaneser I, first powerful king of Assyria.
c. 1295-1229	Rameses II supposed by some scholars to be the "Pharaoh of the Oppression." Pithom and Raamses said to have been built by him with Israelite labor.		

444

DATE (B.C.)	EGYPT	O.T. NARRATIVE	BABYLONIA-ASSYRIA, ETC.
c. 1290			Babylon conquered and held by the Assyrians for a short time only.
c. 1250		Deborah and Barak become judges in Israel after defeating the Canaanites.	
c. 1200	Asiatic empire regained.	Gideon defeats the Amalekites and Midianites.	
c. 1225-1215	Merneptah, supposed by some to be "Pharaoh of the Exodus."		
c. 1184			Traditional date for the fall of Troy.
c. 1150-950	Period of weak monarchs (Dynasty XXI).		
c. 1100		Jephthah delivers Israel from the Ammonites, and Samson from the Philistines. Samuel as a youth ministers at Shiloh.	Tiglath-pileser I, first great conqueror in Assyria. Beginning of Assyrian Empire.

Period VII. Period of the United Kingdom, c. 1050—c. 931 B.C.

(I Samuel 8—31; II Samuel; I Kings 1—11; I Chronicles; II Chronicles 1—9; Poetical Books in part, especially certain of the Psalms and of the Proverbs)

c. 1050		SAMUEL, judge and prophet in Israel, yields to the people and establishes a monarchy. Saul is anointed as their first king.	Decline of Assyrian power.
c. 1010-970		Reign of David, at Hebron 7½ years, at Je-	

445

DATE (B.C.)	EGYPT	O.T. NARRATIVE	BABYLONIA-ASSYRIA, ETC.
		rusalem the remainder of 40 years. Israel made the dominant power of that time. Preparations made for building the Temple.	
c. 970-931		Reign of **S o l o m o n**. Wins fame far and wide as the wisest and most glorious of rulers.	
c. 967-960		Temple built at Jerusalem. Power extended from the Red Sea nearly to the Euphrates River.	
c. 950 on	Foreign domination of Egypt.		
c. 950-750	Lybian rule (Dynasties XXII-XXIV).		
c. 931		Division of the Kingdom of Solomon into Kingdoms of Judah (Judah and Benjamin) and Israel (ten tribes).	

Period VIII. Divided Kingdom, c. 931—586 B.C. (I Kings 12—22; II Kings; II Chronicles 10—36; prophets Isaiah, Jeremiah, and Hosea to Zephaniah except perhaps Joel and Obadiah)

(a) Period of Two Kingdoms, 931-721 B.C.

(b) Period of Judah's Decline, 721-586 B.C.

DATE (BC)	KINGDOM OF JUDAH	(NORTH) KINGDOM OF ISRAEL	ASSYRIA, ETC.
c. 931*	Rehoboam (reigns 17 years).	Jeroboam (reigns 22 years). Establishes idolatrous shrines at Bethel and Dan.	
c. 926	Shishak (Sheshonk I) of Egypt invades Judah. Takes many cities.		Inscription of Sheshonk tells of several cities captured in the North Kingdom.
c. 914	Abijam, or Abijah (reigns 3 years).		
c. 911	Asa (reigns 41 years). Inaugurates religious reforms. Carries on a war against Israel.		
c. 910		Nadab, son of Jeroboam (reigns 2 years).	Ben-hadad I becomes king of Syria about 910 B.C.
c. 909		Baasha (reigns 24 years).	
c. 901		Ben-hadad invades Israel.	
c. 900-800			Age of Homer in Greece.
c. 886		Elah (reigns 2 years).	
c. 885		Zimri (reigns 7 days). Omri (reigns 12 years). Builds Samaria as capital of Israel. Encourages idolatrous worship.	

*For the period of the Divided Kingdom we have followed, with some modification, the chronology set up by E. R. Thiele in "The Chronology of the Kings of Judah and Israel," *Journal of Near Eastern Studies* (Univ. of Chicago), July, 1944, p. 184. Cf. J. P. Free, *Archaeology and Bible History*, p. 178 f.

DATE (B.C.)	KINGDOM OF JUDAH	(NORTH) KINGDOM OF ISRAEL	ASSYRIA, ETC.
c. 884			Ashurnasirpal II of Assyria (c. 884-860) first to extend Assyrian power to Mediterranean Sea.
c. 874		Ahab, son of Omri (reigns 22 years). Falls under baleful influence	
c. 872	Jehoshaphat (reigns 25 years, at first as co-regent with Asa). Political and religious reforms.	of his Sidonian wife, Jezebel. Baal worship becomes state religion. Ministry of ELIJAH during this reign.	
854	Peaceful relations with the North Kingdom.		Battle of Karkar in Syria, where Ahab and Ben-hadad II of Syria were defeated by Shalmaneser III of Assyria. Earliest date known with accuracy.
c. 853		Ahaziah (reigns 2 years).	
c. 852		Jehoram (reigns 12 years).	
c. 850-795		Ministry of ELISHA.	
c. 848	Jehoram, or Joram (reigns 8 years).		
c. 845	(Prophecy of OBADIAH according to some authorities.)	Invasion of Israel by Ben-hadad II.	
c. 841	Ahaziah (reigns 1 year). Athaliah, daughter of Jezebel, usurps the throne of Judah, slays all the seed royal except Joash, and reigns 6 years.	Jehu (reigns 28 years). Destroys house of Ahab and uproots Baal worship. Pays tribute to Assyria.	Hazael becomes king of Syria.
c. 835	Joash (Jehoash) becomes king at seven years of age. Reigns 40 years.	Hazael of Syria invades Israel. Takes possession of the country east of the Jordan.	

DATE (B.C.)	KINGDOM OF JUDAH	(NORTH) KINGDOM OF ISRAEL	ASSYRIA, ETC.
c. 835	Religious reforms under Jehoiada as regent.		
c. 830-800	(Prophecy of JOEL according to some authorities.)		Babylonia under Assyrian control.
c. 814		Jehoahaz (reigns 17 years).	
c. 798		Jehoash, or Joash (reigns 16 years).	
c. 796	Amaziah (reigns 29 years).		
c. 793		Jeroboam II (reigns 41 years, at first as co-regent with Jehoash). Boundaries of Israel greatly enlarged. Period of greatest prosperity. Earliest books of prophecy. JONAH, AMOS, and HOSEA prophesied during this reign.	
c. 791	Uzziah, or Azariah (reigns 52 years, at first as co-regent with Amaziah). Period of prosperity in Judah.		
c. 753		Zachariah (reigns 6 months).	Founding of Rome.
c. 752		Shallum (reigns 1 month). Menahem (reigns 10 years).	
c. 750	Jotham (reigns 16 years, at first as co-regent with Uzziah).		

449

DATE (B.C.)	KINGDOM OF JUDAH	(NORTH) KINGDOM OF ISRAEL	ASSYRIA, ETC.
745-727			Tiglath-pileser III (Pul) reigns in Assyria. Extends power of Assyria into Syria and Palestine.
c. 742		Pekahiah (reigns 2 years).	
c. 740-700	Prophecies of ISAIAH and MICAH.	Pekah (reigns "20 years," apparently at first as co-regent with Menahem and Pekahiah).	
c. 740	Ahaz (reigns 16 years, at first as co-regent with Jotham). Encourages idolatry. Invites Pul (Tiglath-pileser III) to aid him against Syria and Israel.		
c. 734		Invasion of Israel by Tiglath-pileser, who subjugates the district of Galilee and the land east of the Jordan. Carries many captives to Assyria.	Fall of Damascus.
c. 729		Hoshea, last king of Israel (reigns 9 years). Is required to pay a yearly tribute to Assyria.	
c. 728			Shalmaneser V (728-722) lays siege to Samarai about 723 B.C.
c. 726	Hezekiah (reigns 29 years). Many reforms introduced. Temple services restored.		
722			Sargon III (known formerly as Sargon II)* reigns 17 years at Nineveh. Conquers Israel in the first year of his reign.
721		Capture of Samaria and FALL OF THE KINGDOM OF ISRAEL. Most of the inhabitants of Samaria taken captive to Assyria and exchanged for a foreign population according to the Assyrian policy.	
705-681			Sennacherib, king of Assyria. Continues the aggressive policy of his predecessors.

*See Free, *Archaeology and Bible History*, p. 195, n. 7.

DATE (B.C.)	KINGDOM OF JUDAH	CONTEMPORARY EVENTS
701	Invasion of Judah by Sennacherib. Many cities taken and a large number of the inhabitants taken captive to Assyria. Attempted siege of Jerusalem. Miraculous destruction of the Assyrian army.	
697-642	Evil reign of **Manasseh**, who indulges in gross idolatry, superstition, and cruelty.	
670		Egypt conquered by Esar-haddon. Culmination of Assyrian power.
650-625 (?)	Prophecy of NAHUM.	
642	**Amon** (reigns 2 years). Continues evil policy of Manasseh.	
640-609	Reign of **Josiah,** who inaugurates a great religious reform.	
633		Cyaxeres founds the Median Empire.
626-c. 580	Prophecy of JEREMIAH.	
c. 625	Prophecy of ZEPHANIAH.	Scythian invasion (?)
625-604		Nabopolassar (father of Nebuchadnezzar), king of Babylon. Throws off the yoke of Assyria and establishes the independence of Babylon. Makes an alliance with Cyaxeres the Mede.
621	Finding of the "book of the law" in the Temple gives great impetus to Josiah's reforms.	
612		Nineveh destroyed by Babylonians and Medes, with perhaps the help of Scythians.
609	Death of Josiah in battle with Necho, king of Egypt. **Jehoahaz** (reigns 3 months). Deposed by Necho, who annexes Judah temporarily to Egypt. End of Judah's independence.	

DATE (B.C.)	KINGDOM OF JUDAH	CONTEMPORARY EVENTS
608-597	Jehoiakim reigns in Judah, first as a vassal of Necho, then of Nebuchadnezzar.	
c. 606	Nebuchadnezzar, perhaps as a general, visits Jerusalem and assumes authority in the name of the new Babylonian Empire. Daniel and certain other noble youths taken to Babylon as hostages (First Captivity).	Nebuchadnezzar defeats Necho and the remnant of the Assyrian army at Carchemish on the Euphrates. Beginning of Neo-Babylonian or Chaldean Empire.
604-561		Reign of Nebuchadnezzar at Babylon.
c. 603	Jehoiakim rebels against Babylon. Prophecy of HABAKKUK.	
597	Jehoiachin (reigns 3 months). Nebuchadnezzar invades Jerusalem with an army. Carries 10,000 into captivity, including Jehoiachin and the prophet Ezekiel (Second Captivity). Zedekiah last king of Judah, reigns 11 years).	
592-570	Ministry of the prophet EZEKIEL to the exiles in Babylonia.	
588	Zedekiah, in alliance with other petty Kings, rebels against Babylon.	
586	Jerusalem and the Temple destroyed in second invasion by Nebuchadnezzar. FINAL END OF THE KINGDOM OF JUDAH. Many captives taken to Babylon (Third Captivity).	

Period IX. The Babylonian Captivity (Exile), 586-536 B.C.*

(II Kings 24—25; II Chronicles 36; Lamentations; Ezekiel; Daniel; Obadiah;
and certain of the Psalms)

DATE (B.C.)	KINGDOM OF JUDAH	CONTEMPORARY EVENTS
585	Probable date of the prophecy of OBADIAH and the Book of Lamentations.	
555	Gedaliah, governor of Judah, slain. Jeremiah and others carried away by force into exile in Egypt.	Nabonidas, last king of Babylon. Shares his kingdom with his son, Belshazzar.
c. 550-535	Visions of DANIEL (Daniel 7-12). Date of the book unknown.	
549		Cyrus of Persia conquers Media.
545		Cyrus conquers Croesus of Lydia.
538		Cyrus, with the combined armies of the Medes and Persians, takes the city of Babylon and adds the Babylonian Empire to the Medo-Persian. Darius, the Mede, made ruler in Babylon for brief period (Daniel 6).

Period X. Period of the Restoration, 536—c. 400 B.C. (Ezra; Nehemiah;
Esther; Haggai; Zechariah; Malachi; Joel (?); and Poetical Books in Part)

537		Decree of Cyrus, permitting the Jews to return to Palestine.
536	First Return to Jerusalem under the leadership of Zerubbabel. A beginning is made of rebuilding the Temple, but the work is interrupted by opposition of neighboring peoples, especially the Samaritans.	

*The seventy years of exile prophesied by Jeremiah (25:11) and mentioned by Daniel (9:2) are usually referred to the entire period from 606 B.C. (First Captivity) to 536 B.C. (First Return).

DATE (B.C.)	KINGDOM OF JUDAH	CONTEMPORAR. EVENTS
529-521		Reign of Cambyses, son of Cyrus.
525		The Persians conquer Egypt.
521-485		Reign of Darius the Great.
520	Prophey of HAGGAI and ZECHA-RIAH, who incite their country-men to continue the rebuilding of the Temple.	
516	The "Temple of Zerubabbel" is completed and dedicated.	
509		Founding of the Roman Republic.
c. 500		Final stages in the rise of democracy at Athens.
492-479		Persian attempt to conquer Greece (Graeco-Persian Wars).
490		Battle of Marathon.
485-465	Esther, a Jewish queen at the court of Ahasuerus, king of Persia, rescues her countrymen from a tragic fate.	Reign of Xerxes (Ahasuerus?) at Susa (Shushan).
480		Battle of Salamis.
465-424		Reign of Artaxerxes Longimanus.
458	Second Return under Ezra.	
c. 450		Laws of Twelve Tables at Rome.
c. 450-430	Prophecy of MALACHI.	Age of Pericles at Athens (Golden Age of Greek Art and of the Athenian Empire).

DATE (B.C.)	KINGDOM OF JUDAH	CONTEMPORARY EVENTS
444	Third Return to Jerusalem under Nehemiah, who is appointed governor of Judah. Rebuilding of the walls. Instruction of the people in the law of Moses. Social and religious reforms under the leadership of Ezra and Nehemiah.	
432	Nehemiah returns to Jerusalem after a brief visit to Susa, the Persian capital. Last datable event in O.T. history.	
431-404		Peloponnesian War in Greece.
404		Downfall of Athens, as a political power.
c. 400	Approximate date of JOEL'S prophecy, according to some conservative authorities.	

SUMMARY OUTLINE OF OLD TESTAMENT HISTORY

Period

I. Primeval Age, to about 2100 B.C. (Genesis 1—11)
  (a) Antediluvian period, to about 3500 B.C.
  (b) Postdiluvian period, c. 3500—c. 2100 B.C.
II. Patriarchal Period, c. 2100—c. 1850 B.C. (Genesis 12—50)
III. Egyptian Bondage, c. 1850—c. 1446 B.C. (Exodus 1—11)
IV. Exodus and Wilderness Wandering, c. 1446—c. 1400 B.C.
  (Exodus 12—Deuteronomy 34)
V. Conquest and Settlement, c. 1400—1350 B.C. (Joshua)
VI. Period of Judges, c. 1350—1050 B.C.
  (Judges; Ruth; I Samuel 1—7)
VII. Period of the United Kingdom, c. 1050—931 B.C.
  (I Samuel 8—I Kings 11)
VIII. Divided Kingdom, c. 931—586 B.C. (I Kings 12—II Kings 25)
  (a) Period of Two Kingdoms, 931—721 B.C.
  (b) Period of Judah's Decline, 721—586 B.C.
IX. The Babylonian Exile, 586—536 B.C.
  (II Kings 24—25; Ezekiel; Daniel)
X. Period of the Restoration, 536—c. 400 B.C.
  (Ezra and Nehemiah)

APPENDIX II

SUMMARIES OF THE BOOKS OF THE OLD TESTAMENT

I. THE FIVE BOOKS OF THE LAW

GENESIS: The story of creation; the temptation and fall of man; Cain and Abel; the Flood; God's covenant with Noah; the Tower of Babel; the stories of Abraham, Isaac, Jacob, and Joseph.

EXODUS: The bondage of the Israelites in Egypt; the birth, early life, and call of Moses; the plagues, the Exodus, and the crossing of the Red Sea; the journey to Mount Sinai; the giving of the Law and the making of the covenant; various laws, the preparation of the Tabernacle, and the priestly garments.

LEVITICUS: Laws of sacrifice, purification, and atonement; the law of holiness; the five annual feasts; the sabbatical year; the year of jubilee; vows and tithes.

NUMBERS: The camp at Sinai, and the numbering and organization of the tribes; the journey from Sinai and the failure at Kadesh-barnea; the 40 years of wilderness wanderings; the brazen serpent; Balaam; sundry laws; the cities of refuge appointed; around Edom to Moab.

DEUTERONOMY: Three addresses of Moses in the plains of Moab, restating the law of Sinai and exhorting the people to obedience; the vision and death of Moses.

II. THE TWELVE BOOKS OF HISTORY

JOSHUA: The crossing of the Jordan; the conquest of Canaan and division of the land; the cities of refuge established; the renewal of the covenant at Shechem; death of Joshua.

JUDGES: Stories of Israel's repeated apostasies, oppression by enemies, return to God, and deliverance by the judges.

RUTH: A story of famine in the land of Israel, emigration and return, village life and marriage in the time of the judges.

I SAMUEL: A period of transition; the lives of Samuel and Saul and the early life of David.

II SAMUEL: The reign of King David.

I KINGS: The last days of David; the reign of Solomon and the building of the Temple; the division of the kingdom, and the history of the kingdoms of Israel and Judah to the death of Ahab; the story of Elijah.

II KINGS: The story of Elisha and remaining history of the two kingdoms to the time of the Babylonian exile.

I CHRONICLES: A retelling of the history of Judah from the beginning, with special emphasis on the genealogies, to the death of David.

II CHRONICLES: A continuation of the history of Judah with special reference to the Temple and priestly organization, from Solomon to the Exile.

EZRA: The return of the first exiles from Babylon under Zerubbabel; the rebuilding of the Temple; the return of the second group under Ezra and his reforms at Jerusalem.

NEHEMIAH: The rebuilding of the walls of Jerusalem and the reforms carried out by Nehemiah as governor.

ESTHER: Esther's elevation to be queen; Mordecai and Haman; Esther's feast and the death of Haman; the institution of the Feast of Purim and the exaltation of Mordecai.

III. THE FIVE POETICAL AND WISDOM BOOKS

JOB: A dramatic poem, with prose introduction and conclusion, dealing with the problem of divine justice in view of the suffering of the righteous; Job's sufferings, the efforts of his friends to convince him that he is a sinner, his strong denials, and God's reply in the whirlwind, confirming Job's innocence but convicting him of ignorant presumption in questioning the justice of God; Job's repentance and prayers for his friends; his wealth restored.

PSALMS: The Hebrew hymnbook; five collections of 150 hymns or poems, expressing the spiritual experience and aspirations of God's people.

PROVERBS: The "words of the wise," a collection of moral and religious maxims presenting the wisdom of long experience in the affairs of life.

ECCLESIASTES: Reflections and observations of "the Preacher" in conflict with the problems of life, who finally finds the highest good in the fear of God.

SONG OF SOLOMON: A collection of love songs, allegorized to represent God and His people, and Christ and the Church.

IV. THE FIVE MAJOR PROPHETS

ISAIAH: Condemnation of the sins of Judah; predictions of judgment by and on the Assyrians, leading up to the captivity of Judah; visions of the ideal kingdom of the future; predictions, warnings, and promises referring to events beyond

457

the Captivity and reaching on down through the Christian dispensation.

JEREMIAH: Sermons and graphic stories of Jeremiah, the weeping prophet, in the last days of the kingdom of Judah; God's judgments on the nations; the broken covenant and the New Covenant.

LAMENTATIONS: A sequel to the Book of Jeremiah; five dirges in the form of an acrostic, expressing the mourning and repentance of the exiles in Babylon.

EZEKIEL: Messages of judgment on Israel and the nations, and visions of the restoration to Palestine and rebuilding of the Temple.

DANIEL: Stories of the wise and devout Hebrew captive Daniel at the Babylonian court; his visions of the world empires, and the ultimate kingdom of God.

V. THE TWELVE MINOR PROPHETS

HOSEA: Expressions of God's suffering love for His unfaithful bride, Israel, and predictions of her punishment and final redemption; a prophecy of love and mercy.

JOEL: Visions of a locust plague, a drought, and the invasion by enemies, the future outpourings of God's Spirit; and the judgment of the nations.

AMOS: A Judean shepherd proclaims God's justice, His demand for social justice among men, and the consequent condemnation and coming doom of Israel.

OBADIAH: A brief prophecy against Edom.

JONAH: A story about a prophet; Jonah's mission to Nineveh.

MICAH: Condemnation of corruption and social injustice in Judah; regeneration of the nation through suffering; a coming Davidic King, evangelization of the nations by Israel.

NAHUM: Prophecy on the destruction of Nineveh.

HABAKKUK: The problem of the punishment of God's people by the more wicked Chaldeans, and the response of faith.

ZEPHANIAH: The coming day of wrath and final redemption.

HAGGAI: Exhortations to the people to rebuild the Temple.

ZECHARIAH: A series of eight symbolic visions concerning the rebuilding of the Temple, and the restoration of Judah; later visions of the future redemption of the nation.

MALACHI: Condemnation of corrupt worship and life, and the promise of the messenger to precede the Lord's coming in judgment.

BIBLIOGRAPHY

ADAMS, J. MCKEE. *Ancient Records and the Bible.* Nashville: Broadman Press, 1946.

———. *Biblical Backgrounds* (rev.). Nashville: Broadman Press, 1938.

ALBRIGHT, W. F. *The Archaelogy of Palestine and the Bible.* New York: Fleming H. Revell Co., 1933.

———. *From the Stone Age to Christianity.* Baltimore: The Johns Hopkins Press, 1940.

ANDERSON, BERNHARD W. *Rediscovering the Bible.* New York: Association Press, 1951.

AUERBACH, JOSEPH. *The Bible and Modern Life.* New York: Harper and Brothers, 1914.

BAAB, OTTO J. *The Theology of the Old Testament.* New York: Abingdon-Cokesbury, 1949.

BAIKIE, JAMES. *The English Bible and Its Story.* London: Seeley, Service and Co., Ltd., 1928.

BANKS, EDGAR J. *The Bible and the Spade.* New York: Association Press, 1913.

BARBOUR, CLARENCE A. *The Bible in the World of Today.* New York: Association Press, 1911.

BARTON, GEORGE A. *Archaeology and the Bible* (7th ed.). Philadelphia: American Sunday School Union, 1937.

BEWER, JULIUS A. *The Literature of the Old Testament* (rev. ed.). New York: Columbia University Press, 1933.

BLAIKIE, WILLIAM G., and CHARLES D. MATTHEWS. *A Manual of Bible History* (rev.). New York: The Ronald Press Co., 1940.

BREASTED, JAMES H. *A History of Egypt.* (2nd ed. rev.) New York: Charles Scribner's Sons, 1945.

BROWN, FRANCIS, DRIVER, S. R., and BRIGGS, CHARLES A. *Hebrew and English Lexicon of the Old Testament.* New York: Houghton Mifflin Co., 1907.

BRUCE, W. S. *The Wisdom Literature of the Old Testament.* London: James Clark and Company, 1904.

BURROWS, MILLAR. *An Outline of Biblical Theology.* Philadelphia: The Westminster Press, 1946.

———. *What Mean These Stones?* New Haven, Conn.: American Schools of Oriental Research, 1941.

CAIGER, S. L. *Bible and Spade.* Oxford: Oxford University Press, 1936.

CARMICHAEL, P. H. *Understanding the Books of the Old Testament*. Richmond, Va.: John Knox Press, 1950.

CARTLEDGE, SAMUEL A. *A Conservative Introduction to the Old Testament* (2nd ed.). Athens, Ga.: University of Georgia Press, 1944.

CLARKE, ADAM. *Commentary on the Holy Bible* (new ed.). New York: Abingdon-Cokesbury Press, n.d.

COLLETT, SIDNEY. *All About the Bible* (3rd ed.). Chicago: Christian Witness Co., n.d.

COPASS, B. A. *Isaiah, Prince of Old Testament Prophets*. Nashville: Broadman Press, 1944.

CUNLIFFE-JONES, H. *The Authority of the Biblical Revelation*. Boston: The Pilgrim Press, 1948.

DAICHES, DAVID. *The King James Version of the English Bible*. Chicago: The University of Chicago Press, 1941.

DANIEL-ROPS, HENRY. *Sacred History*. New York: Longmans, Green and Co., 1949.

DAVISON, W. T. *The Praises of Israel*. London: Charles H. Kelly, 1902.

————. *The Wisdom Literature of the Old Testament*. London: Charles H. Kelly, 1894.

DEAN, B. S. *An Outline of Bible History*. Cincinnati: Standard Publishing Co., 1912.

DEANE, WILLIAM J. *David, His Life and Times*. "Men of the Bible" series. New York: Fleming H. Revell Co., n.d.

————, *Samuel and Saul: Their Lives and Times*. "Men of the Bible" series. New York: Fleming H. Revell Co., n.d.

DEARDEN, ROBERT R., JR. *the Guiding Light on the Great Highway*. Philadelphia: John C. Winston Co., 1929.

DINSMORE, C. A. *The English Bible as Literature*. New York: Houghton Mifflin Co., 1931.

DODD, C. H. *The Bible Today*. New York: Macmillan Co., 1947.

DRIVER, SAMUEL R. *Introduction to the Literature of the Old Testament*. New York: Charles Scribner's Sons, 1912.

DUMMELOW, J. R. (ed.). *A Commentary on the Holy Bible*. New York: The Macmillan Co., 1908.

EDERSHEIM, ALFRED. *The Bible History: Old Testament* (reprint). Grand Rapids: William B. Eerdmans Publishing Co., 1949.

EISELEN, FREDERICK C. *The Psalms and Other Sacred Writings*. New York: Methodist Book Concern, 1918.

ERDMAN, W. J. *Ecclesiastes*. Philadelphia: Publisher not known, 1895.

FARRAR, F. W. *Solomon, His Life and Times.* New York: Fleming H. Revell Co., 1895.

FINEGAN, JACK. *Light from the Ancient Past.* Princeton: Princeton University Press, 1947.

FINKELSTEIN, LOUIS (ed.). *The Jews, Their History, Culture, and Religion.* New York: Harper and Brothers, 1949.

FRANCISCO, CLYDE T. *Introducing the Old Testament.* Nashville: Broadman Press, 1950.

FREE, JOSEPH P. *Archaeology and Bible History.* Wheaton, Ill.: Van Kampen Press, 1950.

GAEBELEIN, FRANK. *Exploring the Bible* (reprint). Wheaton, Ill.: Van Kampen Press, 1950.

GARSTANG, JOHN. *Joshua, Judges.* London: Constable and Co., 1931.

GEIKIE, CUNNINGHAM. *Hours with the Bible.* New York: John B. Alden, n.d.

GENUNG, JOHN F. *The Epic of the Inner Life.* New York: Houghton Mifflin Co., 1891.

GORDIS, ROBERT. *Koheleth, The Man and His World.* New York: Jewish Theological Seminary of America, 1951.

GORDON, ALEX R. *Early Traditions of Genesis.* Edinburgh: Clark, 1907.

———. *Poets of the Old Testament.* New York: Hodder and Stoughton, 1912.

GRANT, ELIHU (ed.) *Haverford Symposium on Archaelogy and the Bible.* New Haven: American Schools of Oriental Research, 1938.

GREENWAY, LEONARD. *Basic Questions About the Bible.* Grand Rapids, Mich.: Zondervan Publishing House, 1948.

HAMILTON, FLOYD E. *The Basis of Christian Faith* (3rd rev. ed.). New York: Harper and Brothers, 1946.

HANSON, ANTHONY AND MIRIAM. *The Book of Job.* London: SCM Press, Ltd., 1953.

HARPER, ROBERT F. *The Code of Hammurabi.* Chicago: The University of Chicago Press, 1904.

HARPER, WILLIAM. *Hebrew Method and Manual.* Revised by M. POWIS SMITH. New York: Charles Scribner's Sons, 1922.

HASTINGS, JAMES. *A Dictionary of the Bible.* New York: Charles Scribner's Sons, 1902.

HUFFMAN, JASPER A. *Voices from Rocks and Dust Heaps of Bible Lands* (rev. and enlarged). Marion, Ind.: The Standard Press, 1943.

IRWIN, WILLIAM A. *The Old Testament: Keystone of Human Culture*. New York: Henry Schuman, 1952.

JASTROW, MORRIS. *The Song of Songs*. Philadelphia: J. B. Lippincott Co., 1921.

KELCHNER, JOHN WESLEY, *A Description of Solomon's Temple and the Tabernacle in the Wilderness*. New York: A. J. Holman, 1925.

KELLY, HOWARD A. *A Scientific Man and the Bible*. Philadelphia: The Sunday School Times Co., 1925.

KENT, CHARLES F., and MILLAR BURROWS. *Proverbs and Didactic Poems*. New York: Charles Scribner's Sons, 1927.

KENT, CHARLES F. *The Kings and Prophets of Israel and Judah*. New York: Charles Scribner's Sons, 1913.

KENYON, SIR FREDERIC. *Our Bible and the Ancient Manuscripts* (4th ed.). New York: Harper and Brothers, 1939.

KING, ALBION R. *The Problem of Evil*. New York: The Ronald Press, 1952.

KIRK, THOMAS. *Solomon: His Life and Works*. Edinburgh: Andrew Elliot, 1915.

KNOPF, CARL S. *The Old Testament Speaks*. New York: Thomas Nelson and Sons, 1934.

KNOTT, LAURA A. *Student's History of the Hebrews*. New York: Abingdon Press, 1922.

KNUDSON, ALBERT C. *The Religious Teaching of the Old Testament*. New York: Abingdon-Cokesbury Press, 1918.

LESLIE, ELMER A. *The Psalms*. New York: Abingdon-Cokesbury, 1949.

McFAYDEN, JOHN E. *The Wisdom Books*. London: James Clarke and Co., n.d.

MANLEY, G. T. *The New Bible Handbook*. Chicago: The Intervarsity Christian Fellowship, 1949.

MILLER, DOROTHY RUTH. *A Handbook of Ancient History in Bible Light*. New York: Fleming H. Revell, 1937.

MILLER, H. S. *General Biblical Introduction* (2nd ed.). Houghton, N.Y.: The Word-bearer Press, 1940.

MILLER, PARK HAYS. *How to Study and Use the Bible*. Boston: W. A. Wilde Co., 1949.

MORGAN, G. CAMPBELL. *Hosea, the Heart and Holiness of God*. New York: Fleming H. Revell Co., 1934.

——. *Living Messages of the Books of the Bible*. New York: Fleming H. Revell Co., 1912.

MOULD, ELMER K. *Essentials of Bible History* (rev. ed.). New York: The Ronald Press Co., 1951.

MUIR, JAMES C. *His Truth Endureth.* Philadelphia: National Publishing Co., 1937.

NELSON, LAWRENCE E. *Our Roving Bible.* New York: Abingdon-Cokesbury Press, 1945.

NEVIUS, WARREN N. *The Old Testament: Its Story and Religious Message.* Philadelphia: The Westminster Press, 1942.

OEHLER, GUSTAVE F. *Theology of the Old Testament.* translated by GEORGE E. DAY (reprint). Grand Rapids: Zondervan Publishing House. Original printing, 1889.

OTTLEY, R. L. *A Short History of the Hebrews to the Roman Period.* New York: Macmillan Co., 1940.

OWEN, G. FREDERICK. *Abraham to Allenby* (2nd ed.). Grand Rapids: William B. Eerdmans Pub. Co., 1941.

PEROWNE, J. J. S. *The Book of Psalms* (7th ed. revised). Boston: Bradley and Woodruff, n.d.

PFEIFER, ROBERT H. *Introduction to the Old Testament* (rev. ed.). New York: Harper and Bros., 1948.

PHELPS, WILLIAM LYON. *Human Nature in the Bible.* New York: Charles Scribner's Sons, 1923.

PIETERS, ALBERTUS. *Notes on Old Testament History* (reprint). Grand Rapids: William B. Eerdmans Pub. Co., 1950.

PIPER, DAVID R. *Youth Explores the Bible.* Boston: W. A. Wilde Co., 1953.

POWER, A. D. *Ecclesiastes, or the Preacher.* New York: Longmans, Green and Co., 1949.

———. *The Proverbs of Solomon.* New York: Longmans, Green and Co., 1949.

PRICE, IRA M. *The Ancestry of Our English Bible.* (2nd rev. ed.) New York: Harper and Brothers, 1949.

———. *The Dramatic Story of Old Testament History* (4th ed.). New York: Fleming H. Revell Co., 1945.

———. *The Monuments and the Old Testament* (17th ed.). Philadelphia: The Judson Press, 1946.

———. *A Syllabus of Old Testament History* (8th ed.). New York: Fleming H. Revell Co., 1912.

PROTHERO, ROWLAND E. *The Psalms in Human Life.* New York: E. P. Dutton and Co., 1905.

PURKISER, W. T. *Know Your Old Testament.* Kansas City, Mo.: Beacon Hill Press, 1947.

RAPPOPORT, A. S. *The Psalms.* London: The Centenary Press, 1935.

RAVEN, JOHN H. *Old Testament Introduction, General and Special.* New York: Fleming H. Revell Co., 1910.

RICE, JOHN M. *The Old Testament in the Life of Today.* New York: Macmillan Co., 1920.

RINGENBERG, LOYAL R. *The Word of God in History.* Butler, Ind.: The Higley Press, 1953.

ROBERTSON, JAMES. *Poetry and Religion of the Psalms.* London: William Blackwood and Sons, 1898.

ROBINSON, G. L. *The Book of Isaiah* (rev. ed.). Elgin, Ill.: David C. Cook Publishing Co., 1938.

――. *The Twelve Minor Prophets.* New York: George H. Doran Co., 1926.

ROBINSON, H. WHEELER. *the Old Testament, Its Making and Meaning.* Nashville: Cokesbury Press, 1932.

――. *The Religious Ideas of the Old Testament.* New York: Charles Scribner's Sons, 1913.

ROBINSON, THEODORE. *the Poetry of the Old Testament.* London: Duckworth, 1947.

ROWLEY, H. H. *The Rediscovery of the Old Testament.* Philadelphia: Westminster Press, 1946.

――. *The Zadokite Fragments and the Dead Sea Scrolls.* Oxford: Basil Blackwell, 1952.

SAMPEY, JOHN R. *The Heart of the Old Testament* (rev. ed.). Nashville: Broadman Press, 1922.

―― *Syllabus for Old Testament Study.* New York: George H. Doran Co., 1924.

SAYCE, A. H. *Babylonians and Assyrians, Life and Customs.* New York: Charles Scribner's Sons, 1909.

――. *Fresh Light from Ancient Monuments.* New York: Fleming H. Revell Co., 1895.

SCROGGIE, W. GRAHAM. *Know Your Bible.* London: Pickering and Inglis Ltd., 1940.

SMART, W. A. *Still the Bible Speaks.* New York: Abingdon-Cokesbury Press, 1948.

SMITH, HENRY P. *Old Testament History.* New York: Charles Scribner's Sons, 1915.

SMITH, WILBUR M. *Profitable Bible Study.* Boston: W. A. Wilde Co., 1939.

SMITH, WILLIAM. *Old Testament History.* New York: American Book Company, n.d.

SMYTH, J. PATTERSON. *How to Read the Bible.* New York: James Pott and Co., 1925.

SNAITH, NORMAN H. *The Distinctive Ideas of the Old Testament.* Philadelphia: The Westminster Press, 1946.

STEARNS, O. S. Introduction to the Books of the Old Testament. New York: Silver, Burdett and Co., 1892.

STEDMAN, E. C. *Nature and Elements of Poetry.* New York: Houghton Mifflin Co., 1904.

STEVENSON, WILLIAM B. *The Poem of Job.* London: Oxford University Press, 1947.

STINSON, ERNEST C. *The Temple of King Solomon.* No publisher given, 1934.

SYKES, PERCY H. *A Brief History of King Solomon's Reign.* Philadelphia: Hiram Abibb, 1929.

TERRIEN, SAMUEL. *The Psalms and Their Meaning for Today.* New York: Bobbs-Merrill Co., 1952.

TAYLOR, WILLIAM M. *David, King of Israel.* New York: Harper and Brothers, 1874.

UNGER, MERRILL F. *Archaeology and the Old Testament.* Grand Rapids: Zondervan Publishing House, 1954.

————. *Introductory Guide to the Old Testament.* Grand Rapids: Zondervan Publishing House, 1951.

WATERMAN, LEROY. *The Song of Songs.* Ann Arbor: University of Michigan Press, 1948.

Westminster Historical Atlas to the Bible. Philadelphia: The Westminster Press, 1945.

Westminster Study Edition of the Bible. Philadelphia: Westminster Press, 1948.

WHISTON, WILLIAM (trans.). *The Life and Works of Flavius Josephus* (standard ed.). Philadelphia: The John C. Winston Co., 1854.

WILEY, H. ORTON. *Christian Theology.* 3 vols. Kansas City, Mo.: Nazarene Publishing House, 1940.

WILLETT, HERBERT L. *Our Bible: Its Origin, Character, and Value.* Chicago: The Christian Century Press, 1917.

WRIGHT, G. ERNEST. *The Challenge of Israel's Faith.* Chicago; The University of Chicago Press, 1944.

YATES, KYLE M. *Preaching from the Prophets.* New York: Harper and Brothers, 1942.

————. *Preaching from the Psalms.* New York: Harper and brothers, 1948.

————. *Studies in Psalms.* Nashville: Broadman Press, 1953.

YOUNG, EDWARD J. *An Introduction to the Old Testament.* Grand Rapids: William B. Eerdmans Publishing Co., 1949.

INDEX

469

471